PRESIDENTIAL ADVISORY COMMISSION ON HOLOCAUST ASSETS IN THE UNITED STATES

PRESIDENTIAL
ADVISORY COMMISSION
ON HOLOCAUST ASSETS
IN THE UNITED STATES

Edgar M. Bronfman
Chairman

Kenneth L. Klothen
Executive Director

December 15, 2000

The President
The White House
Washington. D.C. 20500

Dear Mr. President:

I am honored to present to you the results of the work of the Presidential Advisory Commission on Holocaust Assets in the United States.

The Commission has approached its tasks with a seriousness born of the understanding of the critical importance of achieving justice for the victims of the immeasurable crimes of the Nazi era, and with the knowledge that its work has occurred in the context of many parallel efforts by other national commissions around the world.

The Commission has identified a number of policy initiatives that will maintain U.S. leadership in the effort to achieve justice for Holocaust victims. The Commission firmly believes that an organized Federal role in implementing these initiatives must be maintained, although it is equally of the belief that the Federal government should not, and cannot, accomplish these goals by itself. For this reason, the Commission recommends the creation of a Federally-sponsored public/private Foundation to serve as an institutional focal point and coordinator of efforts that will involve the private sector, the States, and individual citizens both in the United States and abroad.

The Commission Report, <u>Plunder and Restitution: the U.S. and Holocaust Victims' Assets,</u> includes the Commission's unanimously approved Findings and Recommendations and the historical report written by the Commission staff upon which these Findings and Recommendations are largely based. This report is the most comprehensive examination ever conducted of the Federal government's handling of the assets of Holocaust victims that came into its possession or control. The Commission has fully reviewed the staff's report, and unanimously incorporates it into its presentation to you.

Through its research, the Commission developed important information about Holocaust-era assets now held by Federal institutions; our Findings and Recommendations make several suggestions regarding policy initiatives that we believe are appropriate in light of this new

901 15th Street, NW • Suite 350 • Washington, DC 20005 • 202-371-6400 • Fax 202-371-5678

knowledge. As a result of its other activities, the Commission has also concluded ground-breaking agreements with both Federal and non-Federal institutions regarding best practices to be followed in the identification, recognition and restitution of Holocaust assets to their rightful owners.

The fundamental conclusion of the Commission is that our government performed in an unprecedented and exemplary manner in attempting to assure the restitution of the assets of victims of the Holocaust. However, even the best intentioned and most comprehensive policies were unable, given the unique circumstances of the times, to assure that all victims' assets were restituted.

In the case of assets recovered by our Armed Forces in Europe, a number of factors intervened to limit restitution, including: 1) the overwhelmingly chaotic situation in post-war Europe as the United States tried to bring our soldiers home and Europe grappled with the dislocation and destruction caused by years of war; 2) the international legal precedent of restituting recovered loot to governments and not individuals; 3) U.S. concerns about the cost of post-war involvement in Europe, coupled with the strategic desire to rebuild the economies and re-constitute the governments of Germany and Austria along democratic lines; and 4) developing Cold War concerns.

In the case of assets frozen by Federal government action in the United States, bureaucratic delays and complex procedures to release frozen assets to those who were victims and not perpetrators of Nazi persecution, and the desire to maximize the amount of seized assets available to cover war-related claims by U.S. citizens and companies, also limited restitution.

The restitution of Holocaust-era assets involves not only the material restitution of what was stolen, but also the moral restitution that is accomplished by confronting the past honestly and internalizing its lessons. While in theory closure can be obtained on material restitution, moral restitution is an open-ended process that ought not to be limited in time, as there can be no point at which we stop trying to confront the past honestly. Indeed, a commitment to telling the truth about the past has been, and must remain, a fundamental component of American democracy's pursuit of justice and human dignity.

Speaking for the Commission, I would like to express thanks for your leadership, as well as that of the Congress, on this commitment. It is my urgent request, and that of the Commission, that the support that has been offered to the Commission's work will be the beginning, and not the end, of our government's effort to achieve justice for Holocaust victims and their heirs.

Sincerely,

Edgar M. Bronfman
Chair

Commission Members

Edgar M. Bronfman, Chair
Joseph E. Seagram and Sons
New York, NY

Senator Barbara Boxer
United States Senate
California

Senator Christopher J. Dodd
United States Senate
Connecticut

Stuart E. Eizenstat
Deputy Secretary,
    Department of the Treasury
Washington, DC

Representative Benjamin A. Gilman
United States House of Representatives
New York

Rabbi Irving Greenberg
Chair, United States Holocaust
Memorial Council
Washington, DC
(from March 2000)

Patrick T. Henry
Assistant Secretary of the Army
Washington, DC

Roman R. Kent
Chair, American Gathering of
    Holocaust Survivors
New York, NY

Representative Rick A. Lazio
United States House of Representatives
New York

Ira H. Leesfield
Leesfield, Leighton, Rubio and
Mahfood, PA
Miami, FL

Miles Lerman
Chair, United States Holocaust
Memorial Council
Washington, DC
(until March 2000)

Representative James H. Maloney
United States House of Representatives
Connecticut

Dr. Jehuda Reinharz
President, Brandeis University
Waltham, MA

Margaret Milner Richardson
Ernst & Young, LLP
Washington, DC

James K. Robinson
Assistant Attorney General
Department of Justice
Washington, DC

Patricia S. Schroeder
Association of American Publishers
Washington, DC

William S. Singer
Kirkland & Ellis
Chicago, IL

Representative Brad Sherman
United States House of Representatives
California

Senator Gordon H. Smith
United States Senate
Oregon

Senator Arlen Specter
United States Senate
Pennsylvania

The Reverend Cecil Williams
Glide Memorial United Methodist Church
San Francisco, CA

Neal Wolin
General Counsel,
    Department of the Treasury
Washington, DC

For sale by the Superintendent of Documents, U.S. Government Printing Office
Internet: bookstore.gpo.gov   Phone: (202) 512-1800   Fax: (202) 512-2250
Mail: Stop SSOP, Washington, DC 20402-0001

ISBN 0-16-050615-8

Report to the President

of the Presidential Advisory Commission on Holocaust Assets in the United States

December 2000   Washington, DC

Findings and Recommendations
of the Presidential Advisory Commission on Holocaust Assets in the United States

Table of Contents:
Findings and Recommendations

Appendices

Findings and Recommendations

Introduction

The Creation of the Presidential Advisory Commission on Holocaust Assets in the United States

The Presidential Advisory Commission on Holocaust Assets in the United States was created by P.L. 105–186, which was passed with unanimous bipartisan support in the Congress and signed into law by President William Jefferson Clinton on June 23, 1998. The 21-member Commission, chaired by Edgar M. Bronfman, is charged by statute to:

- "conduct a thorough study and develop a historical record of the collection and disposition of the assets [of Holocaust victims] [1] if such assets came into the possession or control of the Federal government, including the Board of Governors of the Federal Reserve System and any Federal Reserve bank;"

- "review comprehensively any research" by others "into the collection and disposition" of assets of Holocaust victims "to the extent that such research focuses on assets that came into the possession or control of private individuals, private entities, or non-Federal government entities within the United States;" and

- "submit a final report to the President that shall contain any recommendation for such legislative, administrative, or other action as it deems necessary or appropriate." The President then "shall submit to the Congress any recommendations" that he "considers necessary or appropriate."[2]

---

[1] For purposes of the Commission's work, we have defined "victim" to mean an individual who was deprived of his or her civil or political rights on the basis of race, religion, ethnicity, disability, or sexual orientation. We have defined "Holocaust-era assets" to mean assets that were in existence between 1933 and 1945, whether or not they belonged to victims, as defined above. "Victims' assets" is a more limited category comprised of Holocaust-era assets that belonged to those victims.

[2] The U.S. Holocaust Assets Commission Act of 1998, 22 USC 1621 (note). For the full text of the statute, see Appendix A.

Research into the historical catastrophe known as the Holocaust serves several purposes. By documenting the actual events, it helps to create an irrefutable record that forever locates that period in world history. By revealing previously unknown details, it assists in extending some measure of justice to those scarred by the crimes against humanity committed by the Nazis and their collaborators. By promoting analysis and confronting the question "Why?," historical investigation helps all nations and societies decipher lessons for the future conduct of human affairs. For these reasons, the international community has found many ways to support and promote Holocaust-era research.

The Commission believes that a review of the American historical record is important because Americans should know how their government dealt with the assets looted from victims of the Nazis that came into its possession. Such an accounting is consistent with the moral imperative to remember, and learn from, the darkest period in modern times. This work may also ultimately assist some victims or their heirs to recover property stolen from them years ago. Thus, the Commission's very existence is significant, helping our country, in President Clinton's words, to "begin this new millennium standing on higher ground."[3]

This document sets forth the critical findings of the Commission regarding the collection and disposition by the United States of the assets of Holocaust victims, and the Commission's policy recommendations based on those findings.

The Commission's Work

The findings grow out of the Commission's consideration of extensive original historical research (contained in the Staff Report to the Presidential Advisory Commission on Holocaust Assets in the United States), as well as the Commission's hearings and participation in conferences and meetings, the professional expertise and personal experience of the Commissioners, and other information-gathering efforts.[4]

The Commission considered the Staff Report and deliberated over findings and policy recommendations over the course of eight meetings. At these meetings, the Commissioners sought to advance the understanding of the U.S. government's handling of the assets of victims of the Holocaust by planning and setting the parameters of the research effort. They met with experts on archival research, on tracking financial assets, and on how best to secure the release of classified documents. The Commission appreciates the extremely helpful presentations by Michael Kurtz, Assistant Archivist for Records Services at the National Archives and member of the Nazi War Criminal Records Interagency Working Group, and Irwin Nack, Investigative Counsel with the New York State Banking Department. The Commission consulted the Departments of State, Treasury and Justice, the New York State Holocaust Claims Processing Office, the Conference on Jewish Material Claims Against Germany, and the comptrollers of the State and City of New York, among others. The Commissioners also reviewed research papers prepared by the staff and grappled with a wide range of policy recommendations.

---

[3] Remarks by President Clinton to the World Jewish Congress's "Partners in History: A Tribute," The Grand Ballroom, The Pierre Hotel, New York, NY, September 11, 2000.

[4] For a list of the activities of the Commission, see Appendix B.

In addition to its regular working meetings, the Commission held a hearing on art and cultural property in New York City on April 12, 2000. The hearing brought together experts from the museum community, the art trade and organizations that assist victims in making their claims for cultural property looted from their families. It facilitated a dialogue on the responsibilities of the art world toward victims, their heirs and the public.[5]

The Commission benefited from the results of the London Conference on Nazi Gold (December 1997) and the Washington Conference on Holocaust-Era Assets (December 1998), and participated in the Stockholm International Forum on the Holocaust (January 2000) and the Vilnius International Forum on Holocaust Era Cultural Assets (October 2000). In addition, Commission staff held meetings abroad and in Washington with representatives and scholars from Argentina, Australia, Austria, Belgium, the Czech Republic, Estonia, France, Germany, Hungary, Israel, Latvia, Lithuania, Mexico, the Netherlands, Portugal, Spain, Sweden, Switzerland, and the United Kingdom.

The Commission staff also convened a panel of outside experts to comment on the draft report. In September 2000, Dr. Jeffrey Clarke of the Center of Military History, Professor Marion Deshmukh of George Mason University, Professor Gerald Feldman of the University of California, Berkeley, Professor Peter Hayes of Northwestern University, Dr. Martin Dean of the United States Holocaust Memorial Museum, author Lynn Nicholas, Professor Jonathan Steinberg of the University of Pennsylvania, and Dr. Elizabeth White of the Justice Department's Office of Special Investigations reviewed the staff draft and offered recommendations.

In addition to overseeing the preparation of the historical report, the Commission worked to develop suggested "best practices" for banks and corporations that should govern those entities' conduct of their own investigations. Because the overwhelming majority of foreign assets were originally on deposit in New York State, the Commission worked with the New York Bankers Association and several of its members to encourage them to develop best practices to assure the transparency of the research into various assets of those who may have become victims of the Holocaust. Those assets include: (1) dormant bank accounts; (2) interest and dividend payments that might have accrued to shareholders or bondholders; and (3) dormant safe deposit boxes. These discussions have resulted in a set of suggested best practices that can be endorsed by banking associations and followed by individual banks.

The Commission, the Association of Art Museum Directors (AAMD), and the American Association of Museums (AAM) agreed that the museum community would affirm its commitment to a series of standards to govern provenance research about art from the Holocaust era, including full disclosure and publication of that research on the Internet in a central and accessible registry. Commissioners and staff also held discussions with representatives of the art trade, including the Art Dealers Association of America and Christie's Auction House, and hope to conclude a similar agreement before the Commission's mandate expires.

The Commission has contributed to ongoing art provenance research in two ways: (1) through the posting on its website of two American intelligence reports on the Hermann Goering and Adolf Hitler collections; and (2) through the

---

[5] Presidential Advisory Commission on Holocaust Assets in the United States, Hearing on Art and Cultural Property, New York, NY, April 12, 2000.

development of a database for outstanding claims for certain items of art and cultural property collected between 1952–1956 by Ardelia Hall, the Arts and Monuments Advisor in the Department of State. Hall initially proposed that the claims be published in leading U.S. art magazines, but this plan was never implemented and only a few experts are aware of the information she collected. This information has not been widely consulted in the last 45 years.

Posting this database in a searchable form on the Internet will help museum officials to research the provenance of works in their collections and help claimants recover lost or stolen art works. The Commission's database could become the first step toward the realization of the more comprehensive claims database it recommends below.

Finally, the Commission wishes to acknowledge the extraordinary contribution of members of the staff.[6] Their dedication and hard work multiplied their talents as historians, policy analysts, diplomats and managers. Because of their unique work as a team, the Commission believes that the goal of expanding the world's knowledge and understanding of the role of the United States in its management of Holocaust-era assets has been well met. The Commission here thanks each of them for their efforts.

The Historical Context

There has been an increased focus on the Holocaust and its consequences in recent years. Many factors have contributed to this heightened awareness, including the intransigence of Swiss banks, the activities of European insurance companies, the recognition of the experiences of slave and forced laborers, the fall of communism and the commitment to democratic and open societies in formerly communist countries. There is also a general sense that the closing of the millennium demands that Western society seek to effect the maximum measure of justice possible for the victims of Nazi crimes. As a result, many governments, nongovernmental organizations, businesses, and individuals began or renewed efforts to grapple with aspects of their records regarding the collection and restitution of the assets of Holocaust victims.

Research has helped to shed light on this history. The United States carried out pioneering studies on the role of the neutral countries in supporting the German war effort and on the fate of gold looted by the Nazis from central banks and individuals.[7] Policymakers from countries as diverse as Argentina, France, Lithuania, and Sweden realized the importance of revisiting painful episodes from their pasts if history was to be properly served. Numerous other countries in Europe and Latin America convened commissions to examine the records of their governments, banks, and other institutions.[8] In 1997, many of these countries

---

[6] For a list of staff contributing to the Commission's work, see Appendix C.

[7] U.S. Department of State, *Preliminary Study on U.S. and Allied Efforts To Recover and Restore Gold and Other Assets Stolen or Hidden by Germany During World War II*, coordinated by Stuart E. Eizenstat and prepared by William Z. Slany (Washington, DC: U.S. Government Printing Office), May 1997; U.S. Department of State, *U.S. and Allied Wartime and Postwar Relations and Negotiations with Argentina, Portugal, Spain, Sweden, and Turkey of Looted Gold and German External Assets and U.S. Concerns About the Fate of the Wartime Ustasha Treasury*, coordinated by Stuart E. Eizenstat and prepared by William Z. Slany (Washington, DC: U.S. Government Printing Office), June 1998.

[8] For a list of countries and commissions addressing the issue of assets of Holocaust victims, see Appendix D.

gathered for the London Conference on Nazi Gold, and the following year the United States convened the Washington Conference on Holocaust-Era Assets, the first major international gathering to address the fate of the entire spectrum of looted assets, including art and cultural property.[9] The Stockholm International Forum on the Holocaust, held in January 2000, and the Vilnius International Forum on Holocaust-Era Looted Cultural Assets, held in October 2000, were the latest major meetings of concerned nations to reflect the continued commitment of the world to focus attention on the Holocaust and increase efforts to recognize the scope of its crimes.

The United States has been and remains a leader in these international efforts. The work of the Presidential Advisory Commission continues this country's quest for the truth, and demonstrates that the United States has asked of itself no less than it has asked of the international community.

The Commission's goal is to describe, as completely and as clearly as the documentary evidence permits, the record of the United States government in dealing with victims' assets during the Holocaust and subsequent years. The Commission is not a restitution commission charged with locating and returning assets. Rather, Congress directed it to write the history of the collection and disposition of assets that came into the possession and control of the Federal government of the United States. In so doing, the Commission is mindful of the point emphasized more than 40 years ago by the Conference on Jewish Material Claims Against Germany that "the compensation sought was for material losses suffered by Nazi victims and was not in reparation for moral wrongs inflicted. Those wrongs were irreparable in their totality...."[10]

While the Commission has focused its recommendations to the President on themes that directly address aspects of our government's record in handling the assets of Holocaust victims, it does not believe that the examination of the role of the United States during the Holocaust era should be limited to the topics addressed by the Commission. Fortunately, the work of research, remembrance and education—without limitation as to scope—is being conducted by other institutions both within and outside the Federal government. The work of the Congress, the National Archives and Records Administration, the Office of Holocaust Issues in the Department of State, the President's Special Envoy on Holocaust Issues, the Office of Special Investigations of the Department of Justice, the Interagency Working Group on the Declassification of Nazi Era Documents, the U.S. Holocaust Memorial Museum, and many private organizations, individual scholars and advocates all contribute to a broader understanding of the Holocaust and America's role during that period.

Overview of the Commission's Findings

The Commission has concluded that United States forces in Europe made extraordinary efforts to locate, safeguard, identify and restitute assets taken by the Nazis and their collaborators from victims of the Holocaust. Because of the

---

[9] *Nazi Gold: Transcript of the London Conference* (London: The Stationery Office), 1997; *Proceedings of the Washington Conference on Holocaust-Era Assets* (Washington, DC: U.S. Government Printing Office), 1999.

[10] *Five Years Later. Activities of the Conference on Jewish Material Claims Against Germany*, 1959.

enormity of Nazi crimes, the undertaking by U.S. agencies to preserve, protect and return looted assets was unparalleled in history and willingly carried out by a victorious power committed to righting the wrongs of a defeated enemy regime. U.S. military and civilian personnel encountered a myriad of obstacles under the very difficult circumstances prevailing in postwar Europe. Their achievements were nothing short of heroic.

Nevertheless, the restitution policy formulated in Washington, D.C. and implemented in the countries in Europe occupied by the United States could never fully address the unimaginable dimension and complexity of restituting assets to victims of the Holocaust. For the most part, the inadequacies in both policy and implementation reveal that U.S. authorities were driven by necessity. They were often unable to restitute all of the victims' assets under their control because of practical concerns that commingled with conflicting interests, priorities and political considerations. Restitution competed with, and was often subordinated to, the desire to bring American troops home, the need to rebuild devastated European economies and provide humanitarian assistance to millions of displaced persons, and the Cold War. These shortcomings can be partially explained as an unintended consequence of adherence to international legal principles, but the Commission's research has also revealed that, when it came to assigning scarce manpower and resources, the United States accorded a relatively low priority to restoring the looted assets and lost property rights of individual victims and their heirs.

With respect to many types of assets, the United States followed international legal tradition and undertook only to restore property to national governments, which it assumed would be responsible for satisfying the claims of their citizens. When the United States recognized that this arrangement excluded those who no longer had a nation to represent their interests, or who had fallen victim to the ruthless efficiency of Nazi genocide and whose property had been rendered heirless and unidentifiable, it designated certain "successor organizations" to sell heirless and unclaimed property and apply the proceeds to the care, resettlement and rehabilitation of victims. This innovation seemed to present an attractive alternative to the difficult and resource-intensive job of tracing individual ownership, but its adoption led many assets to be too hastily labeled as heirless or unidentifiable, with the result that they were assigned to the successor organizations, rather than returned to their rightful owners. This approach had a particularly negative impact on the ability to identify and restitute assets that had been taken from Roma and Sinti, homosexual, and disabled victims, who had no international organizations representing their interests.

Far more regrettable is the United States' failure to adequately assist victims, heirs and successor organizations to identify victims' assets, instead relying upon them to present their own claims, often within unrealistically short deadlines, with the result that much victim property was never recovered. Even when property was returned to individual owners or their heirs, it was often only after protracted, expensive and insensitive administrative proceedings that yielded settlements far less than the full value of the assets concerned.

While the overall record of the United States is one in which its citizens can legitimately take pride, even the most farsighted and best-intentioned policies intended to restitute stolen property to its country of origin failed to realize the goal of returning property to the victims who suffered the loss. Indeed, there remain today many survivors or heirs of survivors who have not had restored to them that which the Nazis looted. And, in large part, it will remain forever impossible to return the actual assets stolen from them over 50 years ago.

The uniqueness of the Holocaust does not negate its ability to offer lessons for the behavior of government in other contexts, and the Commission also believes that it is important that these findings lead our government to develop policies to promote the preservation and restitution of the assets of victims of persecution associated with future armed conflicts.

It is an enduring strength of American democracy that we can look honestly at the results of our actions, address their implications, and assess accountability and responsibility. In setting forth the following findings, the Commission does not imply that failures of policies to accomplish their goals are attributable to bad motives on the part of any official, agent or institution of the United States. Where combinations of policy and circumstance led to results that can be improved upon now, the Commission suggests ways to achieve these improvements. Where new facts have come to light that argue for changes in policy, the Commission proposes appropriate changes. The findings that are associated with particular policy recommendations are meant to locate those recommendations in the historical context and not to mechanistically quantify or assign dollar values to perceived historical shortcomings in U.S. policy making or implementation.

The Commission believes that this history, viewed as a whole, suggests that a series of actions to be taken now are appropriate to provide a modicum of justice to Holocaust victims and their heirs. It is the desire to do justice that animates American policy in this area, including this Commission's recommendations.

Findings

Implementation of Restitution Policy in Europe

Victims' assets were restituted to countries and organizations, not individuals.

United States authorities generally restituted those victims' assets that came under U.S. control to the national government of their country of origin or to international relief or successor organizations, rather than to the individual owner or heir. This was a pragmatic but flawed solution to the idealistic aim of returning stolen assets to individuals.

"External restitution," as it was known, refers to the process whereby U.S. authorities returned certain categories of assets—cultural property, securities, machinery, heavy agricultural and industrial equipment, locomotives, rolling stock, barges, transportation equipment, and communication and power equipment—found in Germany or Austria to the governments of the countries from which they were stolen. Assets were restituted once the country of origin could be identified, and missions sent by other governments helped to identify assets that were subject to restitution. In cases where assets were restituted in this manner, the recipient government bore the responsibility to locate the rightful owner and to restitute the property turned over to it by U.S. authorities. The Commission has found no evidence that the United States monitored the recipient countries' compliance with these responsibilities.

Currencies were returned to the government of issue. One anomaly in the external restitution process involved currencies. Currencies that appeared to have been seized by Germany in defeated countries were returned to the government of issue rather than to the country from which they were seized. In most cases it was impossible to establish whether currencies were looted or acquired legitimately from a country before or during the period of German occupation. This policy precluded the restitution of this type of asset to individual victims or successor organizations because, by definition, any currency could be restituted to the government of issue.

There were two exceptions to this broad policy: first, the Soviet Union received Hungarian, Romanian, Bulgarian, and Finnish currencies; and second, the currency held in the Melmer account of looted victims' assets recovered from the Merkers mine was turned over to the Inter-Governmental Committee on Refugees (IGCR).

Victims' assets were turned over to humanitarian organizations. In cases where assets were restituted or released to successor or relief organizations, individual concerns were not ignored; they were, however, subordinated to collective needs. Property that was identified as having been looted from Jews or Jewish communal institutions, but was heirless and unclaimed, was released to the Jewish Restitution Successor Organization (JRSO). The JRSO was the only successor organization designated by U.S. authorities to claim heirless Jewish property.

The United States, as a signatory to the Paris Reparations Agreement (January 1946), turned over all captured "non-monetary" gold in its possession to an agency known successively as the Inter-Governmental Committee on Refugees

(IGCR), the Preparatory Commission for the International Refugee Organization (PCIRO), and, finally, the International Refugee Organization (IRO). A general humanitarian impulse, intersecting with fiscal concerns noted by the Department of State, influenced the American decision to adopt a broad definition of "non-monetary" gold as valuable personal property (other than cultural property) that had been looted by the Nazis and was unidentifiable, so that the IGCR might amass the sums necessary to address the needs of refugees and displaced persons. These decisions channeled needed funds to the refugee organization and also had the effect of decreasing the financial burden on the United States of supporting the refugees.

German officials were entrusted with restitution responsibilities.

U.S. officials repeatedly emphasized that in Germany the administration of restitution to victims ("internal restitution") should be handled by Germans. This policy caused delays in restitution to individual claimants. Not surprisingly, many Germans who "owned" property that might have been looted hesitated before acceding to claims brought against "their" property. By the end of the war, victims' assets permeated the German economy. The first *Länder* (German state) representatives charged with drafting restitution legislation knew as early as 1946 that such laws would prove unpopular and refused to enact measures that reflected the U.S. Government's insistence on a presumption of duress (i.e., U.S. authorities presumed that any transfer of property from persecutees from September 15, 1935 to May 8, 1945 was done under duress). In 1949, German "owners" sought to delay proceedings evidently because they believed the severity of the law would soon be mitigated after the establishment of the Federal Republic of Germany in May of that year. Many German citizens affected by the laws believed that the U.S. Military Government would ultimately amend them, so they undertook efforts to delay any restitution. Some Germans in possession of Aryanized property waited until the last possible moment to respond to restitution notices and then requested postponements of hearings.

In addition, some German restitution officials formerly had served the defeated Reich; U.S. authorities relied on the problematic denazification process to identify them. American Property Division officers in Bavaria and Baden-Württemberg noted in 1949 that there was resistance to restitution laws. American officials were aware that cases involving influential people were being postponed and that the restitution program might follow along the lines of denazification—the more prolonged the procedure, the more favorable the decision for the person in possession of Aryanized property. Procedural obstacles and the dragging out of the restitution process forced some claimants to settle for less than they were due and discouraged others from seeking restitution at all.

Strict deadlines created a narrow window for claims and some victims' assets were therefore transferred to Germany and Austria.

United States Military Law 59, promulgated in November 1947, provided the legal basis for internal restitution. The law enabled persecutees to demand the return of property that had been transferred during the Nazi regime. It also defined the procedure for implementing the restitution of identifiable property in the U.S. Zone in Germany. Military Law 59 promised "full and speedy" recovery, but the regulations adopted by the Office of Property Control undercut both. Strict adherence to the December 31, 1948 deadline for filing petitions for restitution (extended to May 1, 1949 for incomplete submissions) together with the lengthy, cumbersome and expensive procedures prevented many rightful owners from asserting their rights. United States officials consistently endeavored to wrap up operations as quickly as they could—sometimes to the detriment of the restitution process. The U.S. Military Government placed the burden of initiating and proving claims on the victims and their heirs, who were struggling to survive and rebuild their shattered lives. The last of the collecting points was closed in 1952 and unrestituted assets, including identifiable cultural property of known national origin, were transferred to the governments of Germany and Austria. Some of these objects were later found to belong to victims.

Austrian officials were entrusted with restitution responsibilities.

Austria held a unique position in the postwar period. In signing the Moscow Declaration (November 1, 1943) the Allies stated their intention to regard Austria as the "first free country to fall victim to Hitlerite aggression," and to "see re-established a free and independent Austria." They declared, however, that Austria—despite its status as a "liberated" nation—still had "a responsibility, which she cannot evade, for participation in the war" at the side of Nazi Germany. Because of the Moscow Declaration, Austria held a very ambiguous postwar status as both a victim and a victimizer.

"Internal restitution" efforts in Austria differed from those in Germany. In Germany, American officials initially directed internal restitution, but in Austria a new democratically elected government was responsible for enacting and implementing internal restitution policy. The Austrian government began to pass legislation concerning internal restitution soon after the end of the war, but it was created piecemeal and took years to complete. Although the Allied powers maintained a supervisory role they entrusted Austrian bureaucrats, many of whom had served the German Reich, with the task of restituting victims' assets that had been Aryanized while Austria was a part of the Reich (1938–1945).

The Allies also sought to ensure that Austria fulfilled its obligation to return property looted from victims as the occupation ended. They could, by unanimous consent, annul legislation passed by the Austrian parliament. In the early 1950s, for example, when the Austrian parliament attempted to weaken certain aspects of the restitution legislation (allowing Aryanizers to reclaim enterprises already restituted, for instance), the Allied Commission objected. The Austrian parliament, therefore, never enacted this "Reacquisition Law," as it was known.

Austrian authorities were directed to return property to former owners, or grant compensation when restitution was "impossible." Austrian control over the slow and restrictive restitution process impeded the return of assets to victims.

Political considerations impeded the restitution process.

Cold War political considerations that first became paramount in the late 1940s sometimes resulted in inconsistent restitution policy. A great deal of cultural property was restituted to the Soviet Union, but there were cases where cultural property was not returned to Eastern bloc countries. The decisions to place artworks that clearly came from Hungary in trust with the Austrians and not to return library collections and cultural objects to the Baltic states are examples of this. The fact that Hungary, Romania and Bulgaria were former Axis countries and that treaties between them and the U.S. were not concluded for several years delayed restitution substantially.

Problems at central collecting points and government warehouses impeded identification of victims' assets.

Military and civilian guards were not always able to prevent the theft of victims' assets from temporary repositories and central collecting points. The U.S. armed forces had strict and sensible regulations against theft, but security at some facilities was lax or unavailable at times. Because property control officers did not always take detailed inventories, it was impossible for them to determine the extent of theft. Inventory and valuation of assets at central collecting points differed from facility to facility and were hindered by the lack of appointed experts to review asset collections. Troop redeployment, supply shortages, damaged facilities and lack of transportation also resulted in collections that were left unguarded and unprotected.

The huge amount of assets in Germany overwhelmed the skeletal staff charged with their protection. The Monuments, Fine Arts & Archives (MFA&A) section of the U.S. Army, charged with locating and preserving cultural property, was particularly understaffed. The Office of Military Government for Germany, United States (OMGUS) was forced to rely on German civilians to do much of the accounting and sorting of assets. More consistent and thorough inventories would have made restitution more practicable and would have facilitated more precise valuation of looted assets.

Better policy implementation in Germany and Austria would have prevented identifiable victims' assets from being stored in disorganized and poorly secured military warehouses and facilities where they were occasionally subject to theft and requisitioning by U.S. servicemen and civilian employees. The 1945 "Gold Train" episode—in which American troops captured a train loaded with assets taken largely from the Hungarian Jewish community—shows in concrete terms some of the effects of inadequate personnel, inadequate security and a lack of command sensitivity to the restitution of victims' assets.

Implementation of Restitution Policy in the United States

Claims procedures for restitution were flawed.

The Alien Property Custodian prolonged adjudications. Pursuant to a series of Executive Orders issued in 1941 and 1942, any property within the United States owned or controlled by a designated enemy country or national thereof could be transferred or vested in the Alien Property Custodian (operating within the Executive Office of the President), as the Custodian deemed necessary for the national interest. No exception was made for assets belonging to foreign nationals who were victims of the Holocaust. After the war, and until April 1955, a Holocaust victim could file a claim for the return of property taken by the Alien Property Custodian. Because of the expense and difficulty in filing, as well as for other reasons, many victims did not submit claims before the deadline and therefore did not recover their frozen assets. Others did not recover the full value of their assets.

In the treatment of a claimant as victim there appears to have been no noticeable relaxation of applicable rules or procedures. In some cases, the process was sufficiently prolonged that the initial claimant died while the claim was still pending. In those circumstances, the Alien Property Custodian conducted additional investigations of each heir and cases that might have been on the brink of conclusion were further delayed. In 1953, a Senate Judiciary Subcommittee delving into the activities of the Office of Alien Property (OAP) sharply criticized the agency for lack of good business practices in the way it conducted its own affairs and handled the assets under its control. The report particularly singled out the "inefficient and dilatory" manner in which claims were processed. Of approximately 15,000 title claims only about 6,000 had been processed. The average length for resolving a claim in 1952 was 46.6 months and the average over the entire period was 31.7 months.

Victims' assets may have been used to pay U.S. war claims. During the war assets of some Holocaust victims were caught up in the freezing mechanisms of the U.S. Treasury Department. Although clear distinctions were drawn between foreign nationals considered enemies and those considered non-enemies, among enemy assets no distinction could be drawn between victims and perpetrators until after the war. In 1946, special provisions were made for the return of vested property to those who had been persecuted during the war. After 1946, when German and Japanese assets were vested, a special effort was made not to vest the assets of those who had been persecuted. Nevertheless, compensation for U.S. assets lost in Europe took precedence over compensation for foreign-owned assets frozen in the United States. Congress regarded frozen German assets as a source from which to pay U.S. war claims for damages suffered by American businesses and individuals. The U.S. War Claims Commission received more than $200 million from liquidated German and Japanese assets. Thus, U.S. war claims were paid in part by German assets that likely included victims' assets.

Restitution efforts of recipient countries were not monitored.

There is evidence that the United States assumed that its western allies to which it restituted looted assets would return those assets to their rightful individual owners (or the heirs of those owners). There is little contemporaneous documentation of efforts by the recipient countries to effect individual restitution and no documentation that the United States monitored the process. None of the national historical commissions consulted by the Commission reported having found evidence of inventories of assets received by their governments from the United States, or of agreements with the United States to effect individual restitution.

Duty was assessed on victims' assets.

The International Refugee Organization of the United Nations was required to pay customs duties of at least $120,000 between 1949 and 1952 on assets brought into the United States to be sold for the benefit of refugees, thereby reducing the funds available to care for those displaced persons.

The $500,000 lump sum settlement of Office of Alien Property claims was inadequate.

Attempts by representatives of victims to achieve a settlement of heirless Office of Alien Property claims began in 1948. At that time, legislation was introduced that valued those claims at $3 million based on extensive research into OAP records by the Jewish Restitution Successor Organization (JRSO), the organization responsible for material claims on behalf of Jewish victims and their heirs. This legislation met with resistance. It was not until October 1962 that Congress amended the Trading with the Enemy Act to authorize the payment of $500,000 out of the War Claims Fund to the JRSO. According to former officials, the JRSO reluctantly accepted the $500,000 as a lump sum settlement of all claims it made for unclaimed property vested in the Office of Alien Property.

Agreements Negotiated by the Commission in the Public and Private Sectors

The Library of Congress has agreed to recognize the provenance of certain books in its collection that had been looted by the Nazis.

As a result of its research into the history of the Jewish Cultural Reconstruction, Inc. (JCR), a successor organization created in 1947 to preserve cultural assets of the Jewish people, the Commission learned that between July 1, 1949 and January 31, 1952 the JCR transferred approximately 158,000 items to libraries in the United States. Among the libraries that received books were Harvard University, Johns Hopkins University, New York University, the University of Iowa, Brandeis University, Hebrew College, and the Jewish Institute of Religion. Several of these are able to identify the books that they received. Others are not.

According to documents examined by the Commission and passed on to the Library of Congress, the JCR sent 5,708 books and periodicals to the Library, of which 107 were defined by the JCR as rare. The Commission also suspected that other items looted by the Nazis had made their way to the Library of Congress through other channels.

On August 6, 1999 Commission staff met with James H. Billington, Librarian of Congress, to alert him to the presence of these books and to discuss appropriate steps to identify and recognize the existence of these books. The Commission and the Library agreed that it would not be feasible to sample the Library's entire collection of over 25 million volumes, thus precluding the possibility of estimating the number of looted books that ended up in the general collection. Instead, they agreed to sample the Library's Hebraic collection of approximately 165,000 volumes—the most likely recipient of JCR books—to try to determine how many JCR books were still in that collection in the Library of Congress.

This procedure sampled the approximately 125,000 items in the Hebraic collection that could have been looted because they were published before 1945 and were in Europe between 1933 and 1945. The survey revealed that nearly 2,300 of the 125,000 items came from the JCR, while 200 more were clearly looted from Jewish victims of the Holocaust and came to the Library by other means.

This effort yielded several important results. First, it added considerably to the Library's own knowledge of the origins of its Hebraic collection. Until the

Commission instigated this exercise, the Library believed that it had few books and periodicals of this nature. The Library now knows that it holds at least 2,300 items from the JCR in its Hebraic collection, and it is reasonable to assume that additional books in other languages were placed in other collections throughout the library.

Second, contrary to what had been previously thought, many of the items received from the JCR are important examples of Hebraica, including numerous Rabbinic texts, *machzors* (holiday prayer books used on the Jewish New Year and Day of Atonement) and other religious volumes. Notably, researchers found nearly all of the 107 books that were designated for the Library of Congress on the JCR's rare book list. The Library also possesses secular items from the JCR, such as a Yiddish translation of Thomas Mann's *Magic Mountain,* that have important historical value.

Finally, the sampling revealed that many of the items received from the JCR did not have the commemorative bookplate that the JCR requested receiving institutions to affix, although the Library still has the bookplates it received 50 years ago from the JCR.

To recognize the unique provenance of the JCR books and other items that were looted by the Nazis, the Library has agreed to establish a "virtual library" of JCR titles and related books.[11] This virtual library will allow the public to search for JCR and related items on-line and to examine the volumes in person in the Library's African and Middle Eastern Reading Room. The Library will also give priority to cataloging any of the remaining books that have been identified as belonging to this collection.

Additionally, the Library is developing a collection "name" field, which will serve to aggregate all the records for the JCR collection within the virtual library. This step will enable users to click on a single link that will lead them to every title in this special collection. The Library will also make this list of titles available to agencies, organizations and individuals involved in the restitution of Holocaust-era assets and will restitute any of these volumes upon establishment of a legitimate claim. The Library will also insert a copy of the original JCR bookplate in each volume from which it was omitted.

The Library will include selected volumes from the collection of JCR and related books in a major permanent exhibition of the Library's international treasures, scheduled to open in February of 2001. The captions used in this section of the exhibit will highlight the unique history of the volumes displayed. Finally, the Library will mount a display of JCR books in the African and Middle Eastern Reading Room in 2002 to mark the 50th anniversary of the completion of the JCR's work.

The National Gallery of Art has agreed to return a painting to its rightful owners.

Shortly after the Commission began operations, its staff contacted National Gallery of Art director Earl A. Powell, III, about obtaining access to the Gallery's documentation for its Holocaust-era art, i.e., works in the collection created before 1945, acquired after 1932 and which were or could have been in Europe

---

[11] For the letters of agreement obtained by the Commission, see Appendix E.

between those dates. Members of the Commission staff met with Gallery staff on June 21, 1999 to share information and to facilitate Commission access to research resources beyond those already available on the Gallery's website.

In February 2000, Commission staff suggested that the Gallery add a "provenance" search field to its website database to allow those using the site to search proper names in the chain of title of Holocaust-era works in the Gallery collection. Because provenance information had already been incorporated into the collection's database, the Gallery was able to quickly add this feature. The "provenance" search feature was unveiled at the Commission's meeting on February 29.

In April 2000, Mr. Powell and his staff met with members of the Commission's Committee on Art and Cultural Property and Commission staff to discuss policies for disclosure of Holocaust-era art of incomplete or questionable provenance and to demonstrate the National Gallery's provenance research procedures.

The National Gallery of Art currently has in its possession 12 paintings that were looted during the World War II era. Of these, 11 were restituted to their original owners after the war. There is evidence that Frans Snyders' *Still Life with Fruit and Game* was looted and not restituted to its rightful owner. The Gallery's investigation into the painting's history revealed that the donor had purchased the work from Baron von Pollnitz, a Luftwaffe officer, who received the painting from Karl Haberstock, a principal Nazi art dealer. The painting came from the collection of the Stern family in Paris and was confiscated by the Nazis. There are no documents that prove how Haberstock acquired the painting.

At the urging of the Commission, the National Gallery of Art had agreed to mount a plaque reflecting the doubtful provenance of this painting. Subsequently, having seen the painting and its provenance on the Gallery's website, the Stern family made a claim for the painting. The Gallery has agreed to return the painting to the family.

The Commission has identified dormant bank accounts and other unclaimed property of Holocaust victims in the United States, and significant members of the banking industry have agreed to endorse suggested best practices for the investigation of bank records regarding such accounts.

To determine whether banks in the United States held accounts of Holocaust victims that became dormant and escheated to the states, the Commission conducted a pilot project matching the names of a limited list of Holocaust victims with a list of escheated property maintained by the State of New York.

In the United States, dormant accounts do not remain in the possession of the bank but rather escheat to the state in which the bank is located. Consequently, the Commission matched the names of Holocaust victims from Holland and Belgium, as well as a list of respondents to the German census of 1939 that required Jews to report their property, against the names of account holders whose accounts had escheated to the State of New York. The Office of the Comptroller of New York State created this database as a public service at the Commission's request.

This procedure matched nearly 400,000 names with over a million unclaimed property records and yielded 18 matches of names of victims with dormant bank accounts in the State of New York. A preliminary search has revealed that the value of these accounts ranges from a few dollars to five thousand dollars.

The Commission has also sought to assess whether people who ultimately became victims of the Holocaust held stocks and bonds issued by American companies. Therefore, the Commission conducted another cross match, comparing the list of Dutch, Belgian and German victims against a database comprised of lists of escheated property from 48 states and the District of Columbia maintained by ACS Unclaimed Property Clearinghouse, Inc., a third-party storage and automation facility operating under contract with many states.[12] ACS performed this cross match as a public service at the Commission's request. The results of this cross match are still preliminary, but indicate that other unclaimed property belonging to Holocaust victims can be identified.

Overall, the demonstration confirmed the need for the use of more sophisticated software that is sensitive to the differences in spelling and pronunciation of common names if the cross match is to capture all of the potential matches and eliminate any false matches. Because the Commission was unable to research each match in depth or to ensure that the databases used were complete, the number of matches obtained should be viewed as a floor, not a ceiling. The Commission's pilot project was intended to demonstrate the feasibility and value of conducting a comprehensive cross match using more complete lists of victims' names and escheated property. That effort was successful, and the Commission hopes to broaden the search for such accounts by repeating this exercise with more comprehensive lists and the participation of more states.

To facilitate additional searches for dormant accounts, the Commission, in discussions with The Chase Manhattan Bank, Citigroup, Inc. and HSBC Bank USA held under the auspices of the New York Bankers Association, has reached an agreement defining suggested best practices to be used by banks when they search for Holocaust assets. These suggested best practices have been unanimously approved by the New York Bankers Association, which has made a significant commitment to assisting in the identification of Holocaust-era assets.[13]

Although both the operation of state-abandoned property laws and the wartime freezing of foreign-owned assets make it most likely that information about Holocaust victims' assets originally deposited in banks will be found in state or federal archives, banks themselves may have information that can assist in identifying or clarifying the fate of such assets.

Under these suggested best practices, banks will first define the universe of accounts to be located to include any account opened at the bank or any of its predecessors in interest before 1945 by a depositor whose address at any time between 1933 and 1945 was in Germany, or a European country occupied by or allied with Germany, and that went dormant after 1933.

Banks will then review all Records (defined as any recording in any form of information about an account in the defined universe) that could contain any information about such accounts, including but not limited to transactional customer records, abandoned property procedures and records, safe deposit box procedures and records, and escheatment procedures and records.

---

[12] California and Indiana did not participate in the database cross match.
[13] For the letters of agreement obtained by the Commission, see Appendix E.

Banks will examine applicable document retention policies, both current and contemporaneous, for possible sources of Records and, notwithstanding the provisions of such policies, determine whether transactional customer records (paper, microfilm, microfiche) exist and review whatever records of the bank and its predecessors in interest still exist. If Records exist, banks will collect and review them and attempt to identify accounts in the defined universe. Records will be maintained in a segregated file.

Banks will contact outside counsel and accounting firms that worked for the bank and its predecessors in interest from 1933 to the present to determine if they have any Records. They will collect and review any such Records and attempt to identify accounts in the defined universe. These Records (or copies thereof) will be maintained in the same file.

Any identification of an account in the defined universe will be reported to the appropriate unclaimed property official of the state to which the account would have escheated. The bank will report publicly on the conclusions of its review, including to the extent possible the number and value (but not the identity of the account holder) of any accounts identified.

The Commission believes that once such a comprehensive search has been completed in accordance with these practices, banks should not be required to make repetitive individual searches.

The museum community has agreed to full disclosure of Holocaust-era works and their provenance.

Holocaust-era cultural property—that is, works created before 1945, transferred after 1932 and before 1946, and which were or could have been in continental Europe between those dates—is found in museums, libraries, galleries, and private collections in the United States.

As early as 1946, the State Department notified museums and other institutions that stolen art was entering the country, but in the years following the war it was not the standard practice for museums, collectors and dealers to investigate the provenance of works they acquired. At the same time, few families whose assets were stolen had the information or the resources—financial or psychological—to locate and pursue claims for lost property.

Although U.S. law provides that good title cannot be conveyed to stolen property, if the current possessor of a stolen work can successfully argue that a claimant's action to recover it is time-barred under a statute of limitations, the goal of restitution can be defeated. Another potential impediment to restitution was raised in a U.S. Government effort to restitute Holocaust-era art by means of a forfeiture action, *United States v. Portrait of Wally*.[14] In that case, a federal district court in New York held that U.S. forces charged with recovering stolen items were acting on behalf of the true owners and that such recovery prohibited continued treatment of the item as stolen property. Nothing in the Commission's research indicates that the U.S. Army was acting on behalf of owners or their heirs.

While most claims for restitution of looted cultural property have been successfully resolved, the process of resolution has sometimes required lengthy and expensive litigation. Because survivors are generally in the last years of their lives,

---

[14] 105 F. Supp. 288 (S.D.N.Y. 2000).

any delays are prejudicial. Claimant and museum representatives agree that alternative dispute resolution mechanisms for such claims would be beneficial.

American museums have committed themselves to provide public access to information about Holocaust-era works in their collections. At the Commission's hearing in New York on April 12, 2000 several museum directors reaffirmed their policies for disclosure of provenance for Holocaust-era works in their collections. The policies were developed separately by the individual museums, and therefore differed in scope and methodology.

In an effort to forge a common policy in response to the Commissioners' concerns, the directors present agreed to full disclosure, which means: (1) all Holocaust-era works will be identified and disclosed and all provenance information in the possession of the museums regarding those works will be disclosed; (2) such provenance information will be disclosed, even where there are no known gaps; and (3) provenance research by museums will be a continuing process with additional information disclosed as it becomes known. They also agreed to restitution where claims are clearly established. Indeed some museums, notably the Seattle Art Musuem, the North Carolina Museum of Art and the Denver Art Museum have returned valuable works in their collections to the heirs of the original owners. The Boston Fine Arts Museum recently settled a claim under a part purchase, part donation agreement with the heirs that allowed the museum to keep the painting. Members of the Commission noted that gaps in provenance do not create a presumption that a work was looted but merely present an opportunity for claimants to come forward with the understanding that they would have to meet the burden of proof currently required by law.

Following discussions with individual museums and their representatives, the American Association of Museums (AAM) and the Association of Art Museum Directors (AAMD), the Commission finds that the museum community is committed to full disclosure as that term is defined above. The Commission acknowledges the commitment of the museum community to full disclosure and restitution as set forth in the letters from the AAM and the AAMD.[15] The Commission recognizes that provenance research is difficult, costly and time consuming, often involving access to records that are hard to obtain or that may be nonexistent, and that few, if any, museums have the resources now to accomplish this.

The museum community has begun to develop tools to achieve full disclosure and will participate in the process of creating a searchable central registry of Holocaust-era cultural property held by American museums, beginning with European paintings and Judaica. This searchable central registry will allow interested parties to access the pool of available information from one Internet site. By taking these steps, the museum community has greatly enhanced the search for truth and justice.

The Commission is also holding continuing discussions with other representatives of interested parties involved in the art trade with the aim of initiating a process that will result in the creation of parallel standards for the conduct of those parties.

---

[15] For the letters of agreement obtained by the Commission, see Appendix E.

The Context of the Commission's Recommendations

A research effort of this scope inevitably identifies new avenues of inquiry that must be left for others to pursue. A number of areas that have been investigated preliminarily by the Commission's staff merit further research. These include:

- the disposition of the assets seized by the Nazis from the Roma and Sinti, disabled or homosexual victims of the Holocaust that came into the possession or control of United States authorities;

- the impact of the Cold War on American policy, including when and how Cold War considerations entered into specific restitution decisions, such as those relating to the return of assets from the Hungarian Gold Train, and the restitution of various libraries to the Baltic states;

- the effect of the creation of the State of Israel during the period in which restitution was being implemented, and its development's effect on decisions regarding the disposition of unidentifiable victims' assets;

- the possibility that looted art from Europe was trafficked through Latin America to the United States both during and after the war, thus escaping the scrutiny of the U.S. Customs Service;

- the possibility that Switzerland became, after the war, a haven for looted art that eventually found its way into American collections;

- the effects of currency reform and exchange controls on restitution; and

- the percentage of victim gold in Reichsbank gold bars.

In addition to identifying such corollary inquiries, the Commission staff also concluded in several instances that further research on particular topics addressed in its report could not be justified because of time and resource constraints. This was particularly the case where the archival records in the United States were incomplete and supplementary information was believed to be available in foreign archives, access to which is often more restricted than in the United States.

Perhaps the most significant example in the area of necessary compromise between research goals and the time and resources available to complete them came in the area of valuation of victims' assets that passed through U.S. hands. The question "How much was, and is, it worth?" appears simple, but is in fact extremely complex. Important but highly technical and difficult questions relating to the effects of currency reform and exchange controls affect the answer. Moreover, in many cases the U.S. documents are inadequate to specify the exact identity or quantity of assets handled (as in descriptions of stocks and securities by their height in inches), making valuation a guessing game at best.

In all of these areas, and others, further research may yield additional valuable information. The Commission believes that an evaluation of the likely returns on further investment in such research should be made, particularly in light of recent developments signaling the opening of access to important new archival sources, primarily in Russia and other countries of the former Soviet Union.

The single most important research task that remains to be undertaken—and one that the Commission firmly believes must be completed—is the integration of this Commission's research findings and those of all the other historical commissions that have been at work on related issues. Such an effort, complex and expensive though it may be, must be made in order to get the full benefit of the extraordinary scope of Holocaust research that has been completed around the world in recent years.

At its first meeting, the Commission determined that research by others into the way victims' assets were handled by the nonfederal sectors was only in its infancy, and that therefore the greatest contribution the Commission could make to this effort was to promote the adoption of standards and best practices that agencies of state and local governments, and private institutions and companies, should follow to pursue their own research into the three asset categories of gold, non-gold financial assets, and art and other cultural property. Because gold was almost exclusively the responsibility of the Federal government, the Commission focused on the role of banks and state governments in handling the accounts (and later escheated assets) of Holocaust victims, and the role of museums, art dealers, auction houses and collectors in transactions involving cultural property that may have been taken from those victims.

Matching records of escheated property with names of victims has demonstrated that additional research has the potential to identify specific assets and their original owners. This could not have been accomplished without the cooperation offered by the New York State Comptroller's Office in automating its unclaimed property records, and by the states and ACS Unclaimed Property Clearinghouse, Inc. The groundbreaking agreement with the New York Bankers Association establishes benchmarks for banks all over the country that will enable government officials, potential claimants, scholars, and other interested parties to judge the commitment of those institutions to identify Holocaust-era assets that may have belonged to victims. The resultant uniformity and transparency in research methodology will be an aid to scholarship as well as to the restitution process.

In the area of best practices, additional standards still need to be developed—for example, for the art trade and for business enterprises whose securities may have been owned by Holocaust victims. A means of monitoring and publicizing compliance with the standards that are developed must also be devised. Where databases are needed, they have to be maintained. Technical assistance resources must be made available.

If coordination of all of these tasks is to be accomplished, two conditions must be met. First, there must be a single institutional focus to coordinate this agenda to prevent the dissipation of responsibility and loss of priority that is the inevitable result of many discrete projects spread among several much larger entities with different missions. Second, the Federal government must continue to provide leadership to assure that these tasks are accomplished. This is not to say that all of these tasks can or should be undertaken by the Federal government—indeed many can only be accomplished by nonfederal entities. The Commission addressed the fundamental question of how the Federal government can best lead and support efforts to be made by a range of institutions, public and private. In fashioning its recommendations to the President, the Commission has made the answer to this question its highest priority.

Recommendations

The Presidential Advisory Commission on Holocaust Assets in the United States makes the following recommendations to the President of the United States, pursuant to the Commission's statutory mandate:

A. *The President should urge Congress to establish a Foundation to promote further research and education in the area of Holocaust-era assets and restitution policy and to promote innovative solutions to contemporary restitution policy issues. The Foundation should be authorized to accept private contributions as well as appropriated funds, and should sunset after 10 years. Contributions to the Foundation should be tax deductible. The President should request Congress to provide a one time appropriation adequate to fully carry out the Foundation's functions.*

The Foundation should coordinate its activities with governmental and nongovernmental organizations and individuals and provide that any of its responsibilities that are ongoing at the time of the Foundation's sunset will devolve to another entity.

Specifically, the Foundation should undertake the following, among other purposes:

1. Provide centralized repositories for research and information about Holocaust-era assets.

- The Foundation should be responsible for the compilation and publication of a report that integrates, synthesizes and supplements as necessary the research on Holocaust-era assets prepared by various countries' commissions on the Holocaust.

- The Foundation should review the degree to which foreign governments have implemented the principles adopted at the Washington Conference on Holocaust-Era Assets and the Vilnius International Forum on Holocaust-Era Looted Cultural Property, and should encourage the signatories that have not yet implemented those principles to do so.

- The Foundation should provide for coordinated and centralized dissemination of information about restitution programs, working with such organizations as the Conference on Material Claims Against Germany and others.

2. Promote the development of tools to assist individuals and institutions to determine the ownership of Holocaust victims' assets.

- The Foundation should make grants to encourage the creation and expansion of mechanisms—including publicizing the availability of such resources—to assist claimants in obtaining speedy resolution of claims. Such grants should not be used for attorneys' fees.

- The Foundation should encourage the use of alternative dispute resolution (ADR) by making grants to enable claimants who cannot otherwise afford such services to make use of them. Such grants should not be used for attorneys' fees.

- The Foundation should provide a grant to an appropriate institution or institutions to establish and maintain a computerized, searchable database of Holocaust victims' claims for the restitution of personal property, giving consideration to the long-term sustainability of the database.

- To implement the agreement with the American Association of Museums and the Association of Art Museum Directors, the Foundation should cooperate with the museum community to provide for the establishment and maintenance of a searchable central registry of Holocaust-era cultural property in the United States, beginning with European paintings and Judaica. This registry, with uniform standards for data inclusion and completeness, will make all object and provenance information accessible by Internet search from a single site. Museums should disclose all currently known object and provenance information as soon as practicable and continue to supplement this information as it becomes available. Congress should provide funds to assist in the establishment and maintenance of the registry.

- The Foundation should support the museum community in its efforts to implement full disclosure of Holocaust-era provenance research, beginning with European paintings and Judaica.

- The Foundation should regularly publish lists of Holocaust-era artworks returned to claimants by museums in the United States.

- The Foundation should cooperate with an appropriate institution, such as the Institute for Museum and Library Services, to fund grants to museums, libraries, universities, and other institutions holding Holocaust cultural property for the conduct of satisfactory provenance research. These awards are to be conditioned on the recipients' acceptance of the standards for provenance research developed in accordance with these recommendations.

- The Foundation should fund a cross match of records developed by the 50 states of unclaimed property from the Holocaust era that has escheated against databases of victims' names, including the database of victims maintained by Yad Vashem, the Holocaust Martyrs' and Heroes' Remembrance Authority in Israel and others. The results should be widely publicized to enable people with legitimate claims to seek return of their assets.

3. Work with the private sector to develop and promote common standards and best practices for research on Holocaust-era assets.

- The Foundation should promote and monitor banks' implementation of the suggested best practices developed in conjunction with the New York Bankers Association.

- The Foundation should monitor the implementation of the Commission's agreement with the museum community regarding full disclosure.

- In cooperation with the private sector, the Foundation should promote the development of common standards and best practices for research by U.S. corporations into their own records concerning the circumstances under which they did business in Germany in the period preceding December 1941.

B. ***The Federal government should promote the review of Holocaust-era assets in federal, state and private institutions, and the return of such assets to victims or their heirs.***

- Building on the Commission's work with the Library of Congress, the National Gallery of Art, and the Army museums, the President should require other federal institutions, including military bases and other installations maintained by the Department of Defense in the United States and abroad, to inspect their holdings for Holocaust-era assets. In the event that an asset located in a federal institution is found to be a looted asset for which no claim by a legitimate owner is known, the asset should be left where it is located and its history acknowledged with immediate appropriate public notice and recognition that remains in place until such time as a successful claim is made with respect to that asset. The federal institution should make diligent attempts to identify the rightful owner or heirs and return the asset.

- The President should commend the Library of Congress for recognizing the unique provenance of the books it received from the Jewish Cultural Reconstruction (JCR) as well as other items that were looted by the Nazis. The Library has agreed to establish a "virtual library" of JCR titles and related books to enable the public to search for JCR and related items on-line; to examine the volumes in person in the Library's African and Middle Eastern Reading Room; to catalogue any of the remaining books that have been identified as belonging to this collection; to develop a collection "name" field to aggregate all the records for the JCR collection within the virtual library; to make this list of titles available to agencies, organizations and individuals involved in the restitution of Holocaust-era assets; and to restitute any of these volumes upon establishment of a legitimate claim. Finally, the Library will include selected volumes from the collection of JCR and related books in a major permanent exhibition of the Library's international treasures, scheduled to open in February 2001. In addition, the Library will mount a display in 2002 to mark the 50th anniversary of the completion of the JCR's work.

- The Foundation should urge other libraries in receipt of books from the JCR to follow the example of the Library of Congress with regard to the identification and recognition of those books that remain in their collections.

- The President should commend the National Gallery of Art for its research into the provenance of Holocaust-era art in its collection. In the event that an asset located in the National Gallery is found to be a looted asset for which no claim by a legitimate owner is known, the asset should be left where it is located and its history acknowledged with immediate appropriate public notice and recognition that remains in place until such time as a successful claim is made with respect to that asset. The National Gallery should make diligent attempts to identify the rightful owner or heirs and return the asset.

- The President should require the Department of Defense to develop, in concert with veterans' service organizations, a program to promote the voluntary return of victims' assets that may have been taken by former members of the armed forces as war souvenirs.

- In light of the success of the Commission's pilot project regarding dormant financial assets, the Federal government should encourage states to automate, in a uniform manner, records of unclaimed property from the Holocaust era that has escheated to them, or that is otherwise the subject of their regulatory jurisdiction.

- The Federal government should encourage private institutions holding Holocaust-era assets to make diligent attempts to locate the rightful owners or their heirs and return any assets for which legitimate claims can be established.

C. *The Federal government should preserve archival records of the Holocaust era and facilitate research into such records.*

- The Federal government should establish an appropriately funded and comprehensive preservation initiative with regard to Holocaust-era records under its control.

- The Federal government should establish and maintain maximum public access to national archives containing documents and other materials related to Holocaust-era assets by providing Federal funds to support the development and publication of research guides and finding aids for Holocaust-era materials by the National Archives and Records Administration (NARA) and other federal and nonfederal institutions.

- The Nazi War Criminal Records Interagency Working Group (IWG) should be fully funded to continue its operations until January 2005.

D. *The Department of Defense should be prepared to address similar issues in future conflicts.*

- The Department of Defense should review existing policies, orders, directives, and regulations governing the control of and accountability for the national and individual property that may come under U.S. military control when the military is deployed on operations in foreign countries to ensure that such policies, orders, directives, and regulations are both adequate and appropriate. The Department of Defense should establish or enhance such policies, orders, regulations, and directives as required to ensure their efficacy.

- The Department of Defense should review the training provided to U.S. service members and Department of Defense civilians regarding the handling, control and accountability of property of foreign governments and their nationals that U.S. forces may encounter during operational deployments. Such training—especially pre-deployment training—should sensitize deploying forces to the moral and legal imperatives associated with the proper handling and safeguarding of national and personal assets consistent with operational requirements.

- The Department of Defense should be encouraged to work cooperatively with the Foundation and other relevant institutions to develop or refine training for U.S. service members and Department of Defense civilians to prepare U.S. forces to meet the challenges and responsibilities while deployed on operational missions overseas when they encounter national and/or individual property. Such training should ensure that deploying U.S. forces understand and can apply the critical lessons learned from their actions during World War II.

E. *The United States should continue its leadership to promote the international community's commitment to addressing asset restitution issues.*

- The United States should establish as a factor in its bilateral relations with nations to which the United States restituted looted assets the identification and publication of information regarding the degree to which the governments of those nations restituted such assets to the rightful owners or their heirs.

- The President should maintain the positions of Special Envoy for Holocaust Issues at the State Department with the rank of Ambassador and Special Representative of the President and Secretary of State for Holocaust Issues. The Office of Holocaust Issues at the State Department should be maintained with adequate resources to assist these positions.

- The President should instruct the Special Envoy for Holocaust Issues at the State Department to continue to encourage foreign governments to make their archives open and accessible and to cooperate with the worldwide archival reproduction program of the United States Holocaust Memorial Museum, as well as to restitute communal and personal property in a nondiscriminatory way.

F. *The President should urge Congress to pass legislation that removes impediments to the identification and restitution of Holocaust victims' assets.*

- The President should urge Congress to amend the Federal Immunity from Seizure Act to provide that an importer of Holocaust-era cultural property seeking immunity from seizure of that property must provide notice of the application to a designated organization representing Holocaust victims and/or their heirs. The application for immunity should state that the works for which immunity is sought are not the subject of a claim listed on the comprehensive claims database proposed in these recommendations.

- The President should urge Congress to amend the National Stolen Property Act to preclude as a defense in a forfeiture action involving the Act that the Holocaust-era art or cultural property lost its status as stolen property (a) when it was recovered by law enforcement or military authorities or (b) when title was transferred in a country whose laws provide that stolen property loses its status as such when a sale or transfer occurs.

- The President should urge Congress to reopen the claims process for victims and their heirs whose property was vested in the Alien Property Custodian but not returned. Congress should authorize the Foreign Claims Settlement Commission to adjudicate any such claims and should provide an appropriation adequate to fund any awards.

Acknowledgments

Many agencies and officials of the Federal government have assisted the Commission. The Commission thanks current members of Congress who have consistently supported its efforts and recognizes the contribution of former Senator Alphonse D'Amato to its creation. The Commission thanks the National Archives for providing work space for our research staff and for the unflagging support of its staff, especially Michael Kurtz and Greg Bradsher. The Commission is grateful to Secretary of the Army Louis Caldera and Assistant Secretary P.T. Henry for their generosity in providing ample work space, computer equipment and other support at Ft. McNair for our staff. We also thank Secretary of the Treasury Lawrence Summers, Attorney General Janet Reno and Director of the FBI Louis Freeh for detailing expert employees to the Commission. The Commission also recognizes the role of Robert G. Waite and William H. Kenety of the staff of the Office of Special Investigations, Department of Justice, in providing us with the results of their research on Jewish books and looted art.

The Commission appreciates the many individuals and organizations in the private sector whose efforts contributed to our work: United Airlines; the Samuel Bronfman Foundation, Inc.; Joseph E. Seagram & Sons, Inc.; the late Dan Dutko and Bill Simmons of the Dutko Group; Ron Birch and Birch, Horton, Bittner and Cherot; Joseph A. Rieser, Jr. and Reed, Smith, Shaw and McClay; Ernst & Young; Abbe Lowell and O'Melveny & Meyers; Stephen E. Herbits and the Herbits Group; Stephen Tractenberg, President, The George Washington University; Sandra K. Stuart and Clark & Weinstock, Inc.; Professor Arthur Kirsch, The George Washington University; Professor James Pustejovsky, Brandeis University; and Professor Ben Shneiderman, University of Maryland. The Commission also thanks Professor Egon Mayer, the Graduate Center, City University of New York, for providing the staff with the results of his research on Kurt Becher. Finally, the Commission is grateful to Barbara S. Kraft for her careful reading of its manuscripts and her valuable editorial advice.

Appendix A

Public Law 105-186
105th Congress

An Act

To establish a commission to examine issues pertaining to the disposition of Holocaust-era assets in the United States before, during, and after World War II, and to make recommendations to the President on further action, and for other purposes.

Be it enacted by the Senate and House of Representatives of the United States of America in Congress assembled,

SECTION 1. SHORT TITLE.

This Act may be cited as the "U.S. Holocaust Assets Commission Act of 1998."

SEC. 2. ESTABLISHMENT OF COMMISSION.

(a) Establishment.—There is established a Presidential Commission, to be known as the "Presidential Advisory Commission on Holocaust Assets in the United States" (hereafter in this Act referred to as the "Commission").

(b) Membership.—

(1) **Number.**—The Commission shall be composed of 21 members, appointed in accordance with paragraph (2).

(2) **Appointments.**—Of the 21 members of the Commission—

(A) eight shall be private citizens, appointed by the President;

(B) four shall be representatives of the Department of State, the Department of Justice, the Department of the Army, and the Department of the Treasury (one representative of each such Department), appointed by the President;

(C) two shall be Members of the House of Representatives, appointed by the Speaker of the House of Representatives;

(D) two shall be Members of the House of Representatives, appointed by the minority leader of the House of Representatives;

(E) two shall be Members of the Senate, appointed by the majority leader of the Senate;

(F) two shall be Members of the Senate, appointed by the minority leader of the Senate; and

(G) one shall be the Chairperson of the United States Holocaust Memorial Council.

(3) **Criteria for membership.**—Each private citizen appointed to the Commission shall be an individual who has a record of demonstrated leadership on issues relating to the Holocaust or in the fields of commerce, culture, or education that would assist the Commission in analyzing the disposition of the assets of Holocaust victims.

(4) **Advisory panels.**—The Chairperson of the Commission may, in the discretion of the Chairperson, establish advisory panels to the Commission, including State or local officials, representatives of organizations

having an interest in the work of the Commission, or others having expertise that is relevant to the purposes of the Commission.

(5) Date.—The appointments of the members of the Commission shall be made not later than 90 days after the date of enactment of this Act.

(c) Chairperson.—The Chairperson of the Commission shall be selected by the President from among the members of the Commission appointed under subparagraph (A) or (B) of subsection (b)(2).

(d) Period of Appointment.—Members of the Commission shall be appointed for the life of the Commission.

(e) Vacancies.—Any vacancy in the membership of the Commission shall not affect its powers, but shall be filled in the same manner as the original appointment.

(f) Meetings.—The Commission shall meet at the call of the Chairperson at any time after the date of appointment of the Chairperson.

(g) Quorum.—11 members of the Commission shall constitute a quorum, but a lesser number of members may hold meetings.

SEC. 3. DUTIES OF THE COMMISSION.

(a) Original Research.—

(1) In general.—Except as otherwise provided in paragraph (3), the Commission shall conduct a thorough study and develop a historical record of the collection and disposition of the assets described in paragraph (2), if such assets came into the possession or control of the Federal Government, including the Board of Governors of the Federal Reserve System and any Federal reserve bank, at any time after January 30, 1933—

(A) after having been obtained from victims of the Holocaust by, on behalf of, or under authority of a government referred to in subsection (c);

(B) because such assets were left unclaimed as the result of actions taken by, on behalf of, or under authority of a government referred to in subsection (c); or

(C) in the case of assets consisting of gold bullion, monetary gold, or similar assets, after such assets had been obtained by the Nazi government of Germany from governmental institutions in any area occupied by the military forces of the Nazi government of Germany.

(2) Types of assets.—Assets described in this paragraph include—

(A) gold, including gold bullion, monetary gold, or similar assets in the possession of or under the control of the Board of Governors of the Federal Reserve System or any Federal reserve bank;

(B) gems, jewelry, and non-gold precious metals;

(C) accounts in banks in the United States;

(D) domestic financial instruments purchased before May 8, 1945, by individual victims of the Holocaust, whether recorded in the name of the victim or in the name of a nominee;

(E) insurance policies and proceeds thereof;

(F) real estate situated in the United States;

(G) works of art; and

(H) books, manuscripts, and religious objects.

(3) Coordination of activities.—In carrying out its duties under paragraph (1), the Commission shall, to the maximum extent practicable, coordinate its activities with, and not duplicate similar activities already being undertaken by, private individuals, private entities, or government entities, whether domestic or foreign.

(4) Insurance policies.—

(A) In general.—In carrying out its duties under this Act, the Commission shall take note of the work of the National Association of Insurance Commissioners with regard to Holocaust-era insurance issues and shall encourage the National Association of Insurance Commissioners to prepare a report on the Holocaust-related claims practices of all insurance companies, both domestic and foreign, doing business in the United States at any time after January 30, 1933, that issued any individual life, health, or property-casualty insurance policy to any individual on any list of Holocaust victims, including the following lists:

(i) The list maintained by the United States Holocaust Memorial Museum in Washington, D.C., of Jewish Holocaust survivors.

(ii) The list maintained by the Yad Vashem Holocaust Memorial Authority in its Hall of Names of individuals who died in the Holocaust.

(B) Information to be included.—The report on insurance companies prepared pursuant to subparagraph (A) should include the following, to the degree the information is available:

(i) The number of policies issued by each company to individuals described in such subparagraph.

(ii) The value of each policy at the time of issue.

(iii) The total number of policies, and the dollar amount, that have been paid out.

(iv) The total present-day value of assets in the United States of each company.

(C) Coordination.—The Commission shall coordinate its work on insurance issues with that of the international Washington Conference on Holocaust-Era Assets, to be convened by the Department of State and the United States Holocaust Memorial Council.

(b) Comprehensive Review of Other Research.—Upon receiving permission from any relevant individuals or entities, the Commission shall review comprehensively any research by private individuals, private entities, and non-Federal government entities, whether domestic or foreign, into the collection and disposition of the assets described in subsection (a)(2), to the extent that such research focuses on assets that came into the possession or control of private individuals, private entities, or non-Federal government entities within the United States at any time after January 30, 1933, either—

(1) after having been obtained from victims of the Holocaust by, on behalf of, or under authority of a government referred to in subsection (c); or

(2) because such assets were left unclaimed as the result of actions taken by, on behalf of, or under authority of a government referred to in subsection (c).

(c) Governments Included.—A government referred to in this subsection includes, as in existence during the period beginning on March 23, 1933, and ending on May 8, 1945—

(1) the Nazi government of Germany;

(2) any government in any area occupied by the military forces of the Nazi government of Germany;

(3) any government established with the assistance or cooperation of the Nazi government of Germany; and

(4) any government which was an ally of the Nazi government of Germany.

(d) Reports.—

(1) **Submission to the President.**—Not later than December 31, 1999,* the Commission shall submit a final report to the President that shall contain any recommendations for such legislative, administrative, or other action as it deems necessary or appropriate. The Commission may submit interim reports to the President as it deems appropriate.

(2) **Submission to the Congress.**—After receipt of the final report under paragraph (1), the President shall submit to the Congress any recommendations for legislative, administrative, or other action that the President considers necessary or appropriate.

SEC. 4. POWERS OF THE COMMISSION.

(a) Hearings.—The Commission may hold such hearings, sit and act at such times and places, take such testimony, and receive such evidence as the Commission considers advisable to carry out this Act.

(b) Information From Federal Agencies.—The Commission may secure directly from any Federal department or agency such information as the Commission considers necessary to carry out this Act. Upon request of the

---

* Date subsequently extended to December 31, 2000 by P.L. 106–155 (106th Cong.)

Chairperson of the Commission, the head of any such department or agency shall furnish such information to the Commission as expeditiously as possible.

(c) **Postal Services.**—The Commission may use the United States mails in the same manner and under the same conditions as other departments and agencies of the Federal Government.

(d) **Gifts.**—The Commission may accept, use, and dispose of gifts or donations of services or property.

(e) **Administrative Services.**—For the purposes of obtaining administrative services necessary to carry out the purposes of this Act, including the leasing of real property for use by the Commission as an office, the Commission shall have the power to—

(1) enter into contracts and modify, or consent to the modification of, any contract or agreement to which the Commission is a party; and

(2) acquire, hold, lease, maintain, or dispose of real and personal property.

SEC. 5. COMMISSION PERSONNEL MATTERS.

(a) **Compensation.**—No member of the Commission who is a private citizen shall be compensated for service on the Commission. All members of the Commission who are officers or employees of the United States shall serve without compensation in addition to that received for their services as officers or employees of the United States.

(b) **Travel Expenses.**—The members of the Commission shall be allowed travel expenses, including per diem in lieu of subsistence, at rates authorized for employees of agencies under subchapter I of chapter 57 of title 5, United States Code, while away from their homes or regular places of business in the performance of services for the Commission.

(c) **Executive Director, Deputy Executive Director, General Counsel, and Other Staff.**—

(1) **In general.**—Not later than 90 days after the selection of the Chairperson of the Commission under section 2, the Chairperson shall, without regard to the civil service laws and regulations, appoint an executive director, a deputy executive director, and a general counsel of the Commission, and such other additional personnel as may be necessary to enable the Commission to perform its duties under this Act.

(2) **Qualifications.**—The executive director, deputy executive director, and general counsel of the Commission shall be appointed without regard to political affiliation, and shall possess all necessary security clearances for such positions.

(3) **Duties of executive director.**—The executive director of the Commission shall—

(A) serve as principal liaison between the Commission and other Government entities;

(B) be responsible for the administration and coordination of the review of records by the Commission; and

(C) be responsible for coordinating all official activities of the Commission.

(4) Compensation.—The Chairperson of the Commission may fix the compensation of the executive director, deputy executive director, general counsel, and other personnel employed by the Commission, without regard to the provisions of chapter 51 and subchapter III of chapter 53 of title 5, United States Code, relating to classification of positions and General Schedule pay rates, except that—

(A) the rate of pay for the executive director of the Commission may not exceed the rate payable for level III of the Executive Schedule under section 5314 of title 5, United States Code; and

(B) the rate of pay for the deputy executive director, the general counsel of the Commission, and other Commission personnel may not exceed the rate payable for level IV of the Executive Schedule under section 5315 of title 5, United States Code.

(5) Employee benefits.—

(A) In general.—An employee of the Commission shall be an employee for purposes of chapters 83, 84, 85, 87, and 89 of title 5, United States Code, and service as an employee of the Commission shall be service for purposes of such chapters.

(B) Non-application to members.—This paragraph shall not apply to a member of the Commission.

(6) Office of personnel management.—The Office of Personnel Management—

(A) may promulgate regulations to apply the provisions referred to under subsection (a) to employees of the Commission; and

(B) shall provide support services, on a reimbursable basis, relating to—

(i) the initial employment of employees of the Commission; and

(ii) other personnel needs of the Commission.

(d) Detail of Government Employees.—Any Federal Government employee may be detailed to the Commission without reimbursement to the agency of that employee, and such detail shall be without interruption or loss of civil service status or privilege.

(e) Procurement of Temporary and Intermittent Services.—The Chairperson of the Commission may procure temporary and intermittent services under section 3109(b) of title 5, United States Code, at rates for individuals which do not exceed the daily equivalent of the annual rate of basic pay prescribed for level V of the Executive Schedule under section 5316 of such title.

(f) Staff Qualifications.—Any person appointed to the staff of or employed by the Commission shall be an individual of integrity and impartiality.

(g) Conditional Employment.—

(1) **In general.**—The Commission may offer employment on a conditional basis to a prospective employee pending the completion of any necessary security clearance background investigation. During the pendency of any such investigation, the Commission shall ensure that such conditional employee is not given and does not have access to or responsibility involving classified or otherwise restricted material.

(2) **Termination.**—If a person hired on a conditional basis as described in paragraph (1) is denied or otherwise does not qualify for all security clearances necessary for the fulfillment of the responsibilities of that person as an employee of the Commission, the Commission shall immediately terminate the employment of that person with the Commission.

(h) Expedited Security Clearance Procedures.—A candidate for executive director or deputy executive director of the Commission and any potential employee of the Commission shall, to the maximum extent possible, be investigated or otherwise evaluated for and granted, if applicable, any necessary security clearances on an expedited basis.

SEC. 6. ADMINISTRATIVE SUPPORT SERVICES.

Upon the request of the Commission, the Administrator of General Services shall provide to the Commission, on a reimbursable basis, the administrative support services necessary for the Commission to carry out its responsibilities under this Act.

SEC. 7. TERMINATION OF THE COMMISSION.

The Commission shall terminate 90 days after the date on which the Commission submits its final report under section 3.

SEC. 8. MISCELLANEOUS PROVISIONS.

(a) Inapplicability of FACA.—The Federal Advisory Committee Act (5 U.S.C. App.) does not apply to the Commission.

(b) Public Attendance.—To the maximum extent practicable, each meeting of the Commission shall be open to members of the public.

SEC. 9. AUTHORIZATION OF APPROPRIATIONS.

There are authorized to be appropriated not more than $3,500,000, in total, for the interagency funding of activities of the Commission under this Act for fiscal years 1998, 1999, and 2000, of which, notwithstanding section 1346 of title 31, United States Code, and section 611 of the Treasury and General Government Appropriations Act 1998, $537,000 shall be made available in equal amounts from funds made available for fiscal year 1998 to the Departments of Justice, State, and the Army that are otherwise unobligated. Funds made available to the Commission pursuant to this section shall remain available for obligation until December 31, 1999.

Approved June 23, 1998.

LEGISLATIVE HISTORY—S. 1900 (H.R. 3662):
CONGRESSIONAL RECORD, Vol. 144 (1998):
    May 1, considered and passed Senate.
    June 9, considered and passed House, amended, in lieu of H.R. 3662.
    June 10, Senate concurred in House amendment.

WEEKLY COMPILATION OF PRESIDENTIAL DOCUMENTS, Vol. 34 (1998):
    June 23, Presidential statement.

Appendix B
Activities of the Presidential Advisory Commission on Holocaust Assets in the United States

Activities of the Commissioners

Commission Meetings

March 16, 1999

Presenters in attendance:

Dr. Greg Bradsher
Director, Holocaust-era Assets
    Records Project
National Archives and Records
    Administration
Washington, DC

Irwin Nack
Investigative Counsel
State of New York Banking Department
New York, NY

June 30, 1999

October 14, 1999

Presenters in attendance:

Dr. Michael Kurtz
Assistant Archivist for Records Services,
    National Archives and Records
    Administration
Chair, Nazi War Criminal Records
    Interagency Working Group
Washington, DC

Dr. Michael Grunberger
Head, Hebraic Section
Library of Congress
Washington, DC

Elizabeth Pugh
General Counsel
Library of Congress
Washington, DC

Frank Mazlewski, Jr.
Administrator
National Association of Unclaimed
    Property Administrators
Wilmington, DE

February 29, 2000

Presenters in attendance:

Richard Ben-Veniste
Nazi War Criminal Records Interagency
    Working Group
Washington, DC

June 28, 2000

Presenters in attendance:

The Honorable Louis Caldera
Secretary of the Army
Washington, DC

July 25, 2000

September 21, 2000

October 19, 2000

Subcommittee Membership

Art and Cultural Property

Senator Christopher J. Dodd
Patrick T. Henry
Representative Rick A. Lazio
Ira H. Leesfield
Dr. Jehuda Reinharz
Margaret M. Richardson
William S. Singer
Stuart E. Eizenstat

Gold

Representative Benjamin A. Gilman
Patrick T. Henry
Ira H. Leesfield
James K. Robinson
William S. Singer
The Reverend Cecil Williams

Non-gold Financial Assets

Roman R. Kent
Miles Lerman
Representative James H. Maloney
Dr. Jehuda Reinharz
Margaret M. Richardson
Patricia S. Schroeder
Representative Brad Sherman
William S. Singer
Neal Wolin

Commission Hearing on Art and Cultural Property, April 12, 2000
New York, NY

Witnesses:

Monica Dugot
Deputy Director
New York State Holocaust Claims Processing
    Office
New York, NY

Gilbert Edelson
Administrative Vice President and Counsel
Art Dealers Association of America
New York, NY

Efroyim Grossberger
Committee for the Search of the
    Gora-Kalwaria Library
Brooklyn, NY

Thomas Kline
Andrews & Kurth, LLP
Washington, DC

Willi Korte
Director
Trans-Art International LC
Washington, DC

Jo Backer Laird
Senior Vice President and General Counsel
Christie's
New York, NY

Glenn Lowry
Director
Museum of Modern Art
New York, NY

Dr. Vivian Mann
Chair, Judaica Department
The Jewish Museum
New York, NY

Philippe de Montebello
Director
Metropolitan Museum of Art
New York, NY

Malcolm Rogers
Director
Boston Museum of Fine Arts
Boston, MA

Stephen E. Weil
Emeritus Senior Scholar
Center for Education and Museum Studies,
    Smithsonian Institution
Washington, DC

Dr. Lawrence Wheeler
Director
North Carolina Museum of Art
Raleigh, NC

Congressional Testimony

House Banking and Finance Committee Hearings on Slave & Forced Labor, September 14, 2000

Testimony by Stuart E. Eizenstat
Deputy Secretary, Department of the Treasury

Senate Foreign Relations Committee Hearings, April 2000

Testimony by Edgar M. Bronfman
Chair, Presidential Advisory Commission on Holocaust Assets in the United States

Senate Foreign Relations Committee Hearings on Slave & Forced Labor, April 2000

Testimony by Stuart E. Eizenstat
Deputy Secretary, Department of the Treasury

House Banking and Finance Committee Hearings on Holocaust-era Assets, February 10, 2000

Testimony by Jonathan Petropoulos
Research Director for Art and Cultural Property, Presidential Advisory Commission on Holocaust Assets in the United States

House Banking and Finance Committee Hearings on Slave & Forced Labor, September 1999

Testimony by Stuart E. Eizenstat
Deputy Secretary, Department of the Treasury

Staff Activities

Research Planning Meeting—March 1, 1999

Attendees:

Dr. Shlomo Aronson
Professor of Political Science
Hebrew University
Jerusalem, Israel

Dr. Greg Bradsher
Director, Holocaust-era Assets Records Project
National Archives and Records
    Administration
Washington, DC

Dr. Jeffrey Clarke
Chief Military Historian
Center of Military History
Washington, DC

Dr. Wesley Fisher
Special Assistant to the Director
United States Holocaust Memorial Museum
Washington, DC

Miriam Kleiman
Cohen, Milstein, Hausfeld, & Toll
Washington, DC

Dr. Sybil H. Milton
Vice President
Independent Commissions of Experts
    Switzerland—Second World War
Chevy Chase, MD

Lynn Nicholas
Author
Washington, DC

R. Cody Phillips
Staff Curator
Center of Military History
Washington, DC

Seymour Rubin
United States Department of State—retired
Washington, DC

Stanley Turesky
Director of Congressional Relations
United States Holocaust Memorial Museum
Washington, DC

Dr. Robert Waite
Office of Special Investigations
Department of Justice
Washington, DC

Dr. Elizabeth White
Senior Historian, Office of Special
    Investigations
Department of Justice
Washington, DC

Robert Wolfe
National Archives and Records
    Administration—retired
Washington DC

Sidney Zabludoff
Independent Researcher
Washington, DC

Meetings and Interviews with:

Zachary Baker
Judaica Hebraica Curator
Stanford University Library
Stanford, CA

Jerome A. Chanes
Associate Executive Director
National Foundation for Jewish Culture
New York, NY

Stephen W. Clark
Associate General Counsel
Museum of Modern Art
New York, NY

Elizabeth A. Croog
Secretary and General Counsel
National Gallery of Art
Washington, DC

Maygene F. Daniels
Chief, Archives
National Gallery of Art
Washington, DC

Dr. Martin Dean
Applied Research Scholar, Center for
    Advanced Holocaust Study
United States Holocaust Memorial Museum
Washington, DC

Gilbert Edelson
Administrative Vice President and Counsel
Art Dealers Association of America
New York, NY

Gerald Feldman
Professor of History
University of California
Berkeley, CA

Benjamin B. Ferencz
former Director General
Jewish Restitution Successor Organization
New York, NY

Bennett Freeman
Deputy Assistant Secretary for
    Democracy, Human Rights & Labor
United States Department of State
Washington, DC

Stuart D. Goldman
Specialist in Russian Affairs,
    Foreign Affairs, Defense, and Trade Division
Congressional Research Service
Washington, DC

Dr. Grace Cohen Grossman
Curator of Judaica and Americana
Skirball Cultural Center
Los Angeles, CA

Ian Hancock
Director, International Romani Archives and
    Documentation Center
University of Texas
Austin, TX

Alan G. Hevesi
Comptroller of the City of New York
New York, NY

Saul Kagan
Corporate Secretary
Conference on Jewish Material Claims
    Against Germany
New York, NY

Dr. Michael Kurtz
Assistant Archivist for Records Services,
    National Archives and Records
    Administration Chair, Nazi War Criminal
    Records Interagency Working Group
Washington, DC

Jo Backer Laird
Senior Vice President and General Counsel
Christie's
New York, NY

Catherine Lillie
General Counsel
New York State Holocaust Claims Processing Office
New York, NY

Dr. Constance Lowenthal
Director
Commission for Art Recovery
New York, NY

Professor Egon Mayer
Director, Center for Jewish Studies,
    The Graduate Center
City University of New York
New York, NY

Shirah Neiman
Deputy United States Attorney
United States Attorney's Office, Southern
    District of New York
New York, NY

Colonel Seymour J. Pomrenze
Former Director, Offenbach Archival Depot
Army of the United States—retired

Dr. Earl Powell, III
Director, National Gallery of Art
Washington, DC

Harry Reicher
Adjunct Professor of Law
University of Pennsylvania Law School
Philadelphia, PA

Dr. Carl J. Rheins
Executive Director
YIVO Institute for Jewish Research
New York, NY

Jonathan Schwartz
Associate Deputy Attorney General
Department of Justice
Washington, DC

Linda Scott
Director of Investor Affairs, Division of
    Investments and Cash Management
Office of the New York State Comptroller
New York, NY

Beverly K. Sheppard
Acting Director
Institute of Museum and Library Sciences
Washington, DC

Alan Shestack
Deputy Director
National Gallery of Art
Washington, DC

Jesse Stiller
Special Adviser for Executive Communications
Office of the Comptroller of the Currency
Washington, DC

Carol Kahm Strauss
Executive Director
Leo Baeck Institute
New York, NY

Gideon Taylor
Executive Vice President
Conference on Jewish Material Claims
    Against Germany
New York, NY

Dr. Sidney Verba
Director
Harvard University Library
Cambridge, MA

Greg Wierzynski
Assistant Staff Director, Committee on
    Banking and Financial Services
United States House of Representatives
Washington, DC

Sid Wolinsky
Director of Litigation
Disability Rights Advocates
Oakland, CA

Nancy H. Yeide
Head, Department of Curatorial Records
National Gallery of Art
Washington, DC

Dr. Gary P. Zola
Executive Director
American Jewish Archives
Cincinnati, OH

Conferences

Vilnius International Forum on Holocaust-Era Looted Cultural Assets, October 2000
Vilnius, Lithuania

Stockholm International Forum on the Holocaust, January 2000
Stockholm, Sweden

> Summit meeting of scholars representing the following governments and organizations:
>
> Executive Council of Australian Jewry (Australia)
>
> Commission for Provenance Research (Austria)
>
> Historical Commission of the Republic of Austria (Austria)
>
> Ministry of Economic Affairs (Belgium)
>
> Institute Terezin Initiative (Czech Republic)
>
> Fact-finding Mission on the Looting of Jewish Assets in France (France)
>
> The Coordinating Office of States for the Return of Cultural Property (Germany)
>
> Jewish Heritage Public Endowment (Hungary)
>
> Hungarian Auschwitz Foundation (Hungary)
>
> Centre of Organizations of Holocaust Survivors in Israel (Israel)
>
> Ministry of Foreign Affairs of Lithuania (Lithuania)
>
> International Commission for the Evaluation of the Crimes of the Nazi and Soviet Occupational Regimes in Lithuania (Lithuania)
>
> Commission on Financial Assets of Victims of the Second World War (the Netherlands)
>
> University of Aveiro (Portugal)
>
> Commission on Jewish Assets in Spain (Spain)
>
> Ministry of Foreign Affairs (Sweden)
>
> Commission on Jewish Assets (Sweden)

Holocaust Research & Holocaust Studies in the 21st Century, December 1999
United States Holocaust Memorial Museum
Washington, DC

37th Annual Conference, National Association of Unclaimed Property Administrators, August, 1999
Des Moines, IA

Seeking Justice for Holocaust Victims, May 1999
Jewish Community Relations Council of the Jewish United Fund of Metropolitan Chicago, Northwestern University Jewish Studies Program, Northwestern University Law School
Chicago, IL

Conference on Entertainment, Arts and Sports Law, January, 1999
American Law Institute-America Bar Association
Los Angeles, CA

Meetings with International Experts

Argentina

Dr. Ignacio Klich
Commission of Enquiry into the Activities of
    Nazism in Argentina
Buenos Aires

Jacob Kovadloff
Commission of Enquiry into the Activities of
    Nazism in Argentina
American Jewish Committee, New York

Austria

Ernst Bacher
Conservator General of the Federal
    Office of Monuments
Commission for Provenance Research

Dr. Reinhard Binder-Krieglstein
Historical Commission of the Republic of Austria

Eva Blimluger
Historical Commission of the Republic of Austria

Dr. Clemens Jabloner
Historical Commission of the Republic of Austria

Hannah Lessing
General Secretary
Viennese Jewish Community

Ariel Muzicant
President
Viennese Jewish Community

Ambassador Hans Winkler
Legal Advisor
Federal Ministry of Foreign Affairs

Dr. Rudolph Wran
Chief, Department of Art and Cultural Affairs
Federal Ministry of Education and Cultural Affairs

Belgium

Nicolas Vanhove
Deputy Counselor, Recovery Unit for
    Despoiled Assets
Ministry of Economic Affairs

Czech Republic

Tomas Jelinek
Office of the President

Tomas Kraus
Federation of Jewish Communities

Dr. Jiri Sousa, CSc.
Department of Subsidiary Historical Disciplines
    and Archival Studies
Charles University,

Dr. Drahomir Jancik, CSc.
Department of Economic and Social History
Charles University

Dr. Eduard Kubu, CSc.
Faculty of Philosophy, Institute of Czech History
Charles History

Estonia

Argo Kuusik
Historical Commission of Estonia

France

Patrice Dreiski
Minister of the Economy and Industry
Fact-finding Mission on the Looting of
    Jewish Assets in France

Norbert Engel
Association of French Museums

Isabelle le Masne de Chermont
Association of French Museums

Professor Adolphe Steg
Deputy Chairman
Fact-finding Mission on the Looting of
    Jewish Assets in France

Annette Wjéviorka
Academic writer
Fact-finding Mission on the Looting of
    Jewish Assets in France

Haim Musicant
Director
Representative Counsel of Jewish Institutions
    in France

Shimon Samuels
European Director
Simon Wiesenthal Center

Claire Andrieu
Fact-finding Mission on the Looting of
    Jewish Assets in France

Jacques Fredj
Director
Center of Contemporary Jewish Archives

Andre Larquie
Director
Fact-finding Mission on the Looting of
    Jewish Assets in France

Germany

Deidre Berger
American Jewish Committee of Berlin

Siegfried Buttner
Archivist
Vice President of the German National Archives

Dr. Michael M. Franz
Project Director
States' Coordination Office for the Return of
    Cultural Treasures

Wilhelm Lenz
German National Archives

Hungary

Balazs Bokor
Ministry of Foreign Affairs

Gabor Kadar
Historian
Jewish Heritage of Hungary Public Endowment

Professor Laszlo Karsai
Leader, Yad Vashem Research Group
University of Szeged

Laszlo Mravik
Art Historian, former leader of research
Directorate of National Cultural Heritage

Ivan Ronai
Directorate of National Cultural Heritage

Agnes Sagvari
Author

Dr. Maria Schmidt
Advisor to the Prime Minister

Gabor Sebes
Director
Jewish Heritage of Hungary Public Endowment

Gyorgy Sessler
Secretary
Jewish Heritage of Hungary Public Endowment

Professor Szablocs Szita
Scientific Director
Auschwitz Foundation

Zoltan Vagi
Historian, Research Fellow
Hungarian Jewish Museum and Archives

Zsolt Visy
State Secretary
Ministry of Cultural Heritage

Gusztav Zoltai
Associate President
Jewish Heritage of Hungary Public Endowment

Israel

Dr. Shlomo Aronson
Professor of Political Science
Hebrew University

Hadassah Assouline
Director, the Central Archives for the History
    of the Jewish People
Hebrew University

Shai Csillag
Center of Organizations of Holocaust
    Survivors in Israel

Dr. Yaacov Lozowick
Director of the Archives
Yad Vashem

Dr. Ronald W. Zweig
Senior Lecturer, Department of Jewish History
Tel Aviv University

Latvia

Aivis Ronis
Latvian Ambassador to the United States

Dr. Rudite Viksne
Researcher, Historical Institute of Latvia
Latvian Historical Commission

Dr. Antonijs Zunde
Associate Professor, Department of Contemporary
    American and Western European History
University of Latvia
Advisor to the Minister of Foreign Affairs

Lithuania

Petras Austrevicius
Government Chancellor
Office of the Prime Minister

Rabbi Andrew Baker
International Commission for the Evaluation
    of the Crimes of the Nazi and Soviet
    Occupational Regimes in Lithuania

Arunas Beksta
Minister of Culture of the Republic of Lithuania

Toma Birmontiene
Director
Lithuanian Centre for Human Rights

Mindaugas Butkus
Head, Division of Americas
Ministry of Foreign Affairs of Lithuania

Darius Degutis
Minister Counselor
Embassy of Lithuania

Alfonsas Eidintas
Ambassador-At-Large
Ministry of Foreign Affairs of Lithuania

Rolandas Kacinskas
Second Secretary
Embassy of Lithuania

Dalia Kuodyte
General Director
Genocide & Resistance Research Center
    of Lithuania

Ronaldas Racinskas
Executive Director
International Commission for the Evaluation
    of the Crimes of the Nazi and Soviet
    Occupational Regimes in Lithuania

Stasys Sakalauskas
Lithuanian Ambassador to the United States

Henrik Schmiegelow
Ambassador and Head of Delegation
Delegation of the European Commission
    to Lithuania

Anthony Spakauskas
Deputy Chief of Mission
United States Embassy in Lithuania

Vygaudas Usackas
Vice Minister of Foreign Affairs of the Republic
    of Lithuania

Sean Wiswesser
Third Secretary
United States Embassy in Lithuania

Emmanuelis Zingeris
Chairman, Commission on Culture & Education
Council of Europe Parliamentary Assembly
Member of Parliament

Markas Zingeris
Research Coordinator
International Commission for the Evaluation of
    the Crimes of the Nazi and Soviet
    Occupational Regimes in Lithuania

Spain

Pablo Martín Aceña
Historian
Spanish Commission on Jewish Assets in Spain

Francisco Ignacio de Cáceres Blanco
Spanish Commission on Jewish Assets in Spain

Enrique Múgica Herzog
Chair
Spanish Commission on Jewish Assets in Spain

Review of Draft Report by Outside Experts

Dr. Jeffrey Clarke
Chief Military Historian
Center of Military History
Washington, DC

Dr. Martin Dean
Applied Research Scholar, Center for
    Advanced Holocaust Study
United States Holocaust Memorial Museum
Washington, DC

Dr. Marion Deshmukh
George Mason University
Fairfax, VA

Dr. Gerald Feldman
Professor of History
University of California
Berkeley, CA

Dr. Peter Hayes
Professor of History
Northwestern University
Evanston, IL

Lynn Nicholas
Author
Washington, DC

Dr. Jonathan Steinberg
Professor of History
University of Pennsylvania
Philadelphia, PA

Dr. Elizabeth White
Senior Historian, Office of Special Investigations
Department of Justice
Washington, DC

Advisory Panels for Asset Groups

Art and Cultural Property

Stephanie Barron
Curator, Twentieth Century Art
Los Angeles County Museum of Art
Los Angeles, CA

Hector Feliciano
Paul Rosenberg &Co.
New York, NY

Sarah Jackson
Historic Claims Director
The Art Loss Register
New York, NY

Ronald Lauder
Chairman
Commission for Art Recovery
New York, NY

Glenn Lowry
Director
Museum of Modern Art
New York, NY

Lynn Nicholas
Author
Washington, DC

Elizabeth Simpson
Bard Graduate Center for Decorative Arts
New York, NY

Craig Hugh Smyth
former Monuments, Fine Arts & Archives Officer

Gold

Dr. Richard Breitman
Professor of History
American University
Washington, DC

Willi Korte
Director
Trans-Art International LC
Washington, DC

Christopher Simpson
Professor of Communications
American University
Washington, DC

Robert Wolfe
National Archives and Records
    Administration—retired
Washington, DC

Non-gold Financial Assets

David Epstein
ACS Unclaimed Property Clearinghouse
Boston, MA

Dr. Gerald Feldman
Professor of History
University of California Berkeley
Berkley, CA

Seymour Rubin
United States Department of State—retired
Washington, DC

Charles Siegman
International Monetary Fund
Washington, DC

Dr. Jonathan Steinberg
Professor of History
University of Pennsylvania
Philadelphia, PA

Appendix C

Staff Contributing to the Commission's Work

Executive

Kenneth L. Klothen . . . . Executive Director

Eugene F. Sofer . . . . Deputy Executive Director

Lynda S. Mounts. . . . . General Counsel

Research Staff

Konstantin Akinsha, Ph.D.. . . . . Deputy Research Director, Art/Cultural Property

John Bendix, Ph.D.. . . . . Senior Researcher

Paul Brown . . . . Researcher

Jill Cooper. Senior Researcher

Joel Davidson, Ph.D.. . . . . Senior Researcher

Colin Fallon, Ph.D.. . . . . Senior Researcher

Abby Gilbert . . . . Researcher (on detail from the Treasury Department)

David Glasner . . . . Researcher

Helen B. Junz . . . . Consulting Research Director, Financial Assets

Marc Masurovsky . . . . Research Director, Gold

Jonathan McMurray, Ph.D. . . . . Senior Researcher

Laura Offen. . . . . Researcher

Jonathan Petropoulos, Ph.D. . . . . Research Director, Art/Cultural Property

Sarah Robinson. . . . . Researcher

M. Erin Rodgers . . . . Researcher

Sebestian Saviano . . . . Researcher

Albert Schmidt, Ph.D.. . . . . Policy Analyst

Allison Shannon. . . . . Researcher

Jerome Simpson . . . . Researcher (on detail from the Federal Bureau of Investigation)

Robert Skwirot . . . . Senior Researcher

Douglas Wilson. . . . . Senior Researcher

Elisabeth Yavnai . . . . Researcher

Temporary Research Assignments

Valerie Bauwens . . . . Researcher

Uri Bitan . . . . Consultant

Aimee Breslow . . . . Senior Researcher

Abraham Edelheit, Ph.D. . . . . Researcher

Charles Fenyvesi . . . . Researcher

Robert Grathwol, Ph.D . . . . Consultant

Donita Moorhus . . . . Consultant

Gregory Murphy . . . . Senior Researcher

Ellen O'Connor . . . . Senior Researcher

Daniel Powers, Ph.D. . . . . Senior Researcher

Jennifer Rodgers . . . . Researcher

Helene Sugarman . . . . Researcher

Irit Tamir . . . . Researcher

Administrative

Margretta Kennedy . . . . Director of Administration

Brenda Jones . . . . Clerk

Stuart Loeser . . . . Commission Relations Coordinator

Katherine Page . . . . Confidential Assistant to
the Executive Director

Linette Wilson . . . . Receptionist

Interns

Ramona Achterberg	Rana Malek
Kelly Calkin	Jeremy Marks
Robert Deutsch	Catherine Nielsen
Daniella Doron	John Nugent
Andrew Eastman	Lauren Oppenheimer
Lisa Fierer	Meredith Perry
Francisco Gonzalez	Ryan Plasky
Monica Hilmer	Nathaniel Robbins
Joshua Katz	Steven Shaw

Appendix D

Commissions of Inquiry into Holocaust Issues

Argentina	Commission of Enquiry into the Activities of Nazism in Argentina (CEANA)
Austria	Commission for Provenance Research Historical Commission of the Republic of Austria
Belgium	Commission on the Study of Assets of the Members of the Jewish Community in Belgium Looted during the 1940-1945 World War
Brazil	Commission for the Investigation of Nazi Assets
Republic of Croatia	Commission for the Investigation of Nazi Assets
Czech Republic	Commission for Holocaust Era Property Issues in the Czech Republic
Estonia	International Commission to Investigate Crimes Against Humanity Perpetrated in Estonia
France	Fact-finding Mission on the Looting of Jewish Assets in France (Mattéoli Commission)
Germany	States' Coordination Office for the Return of Cultural Treasures
Greece	Greek Holocaust Commission
Hungary	Hungarian Historical Commission
Israel	Commission for the Restitution of Jewish Property
Italy	Commission to Reconstruct the Events in Italy Related to the Acquisition of Properties from Jewish Citizens by Public and Private Concerns
Latvia	Latvian Commission on Crimes Against Humanity
Lithuania	International Commission for the Evaluation of the Crimes of the Nazi and Soviet Occupational Regimes in Lithuania
The Netherlands	Commission on Financial Assets of Victims of the Second World War
Norway	Norwegian Holocaust Commission
Portugal	Portuguese Commission on Holocaust Assets
Slovak Republic	Slovakian Holocaust Commission
Spain	Spanish Commission on Jewish Assets in Spain
Sweden	Swedish Commission on Jewish Assets
Switzerland	Independent Commissions of Experts Switzerland—Second World War (Bergier Commission)
	Independent Committee of Eminent Persons (The Volcker Commission)
Turkey	Turkish Commission (Ministry of Foreign Affairs)
United States	Presidential Advisory Commission on Holocaust Assets in the United States

Countries Otherwise Conducting Contemporary Holocaust Research

Albania	Ireland
Australia	Luxembourg
Belarus	Macedonia
Bosnia and Herzegovina	Moldova
Bulgaria	Poland
Canada	Russia
Chile	Slovenia
Cyprus	South Africa
Denmark	Ukraine
Finland	United Kingdom
Iceland	Uruguay

Appendix E

Letters of Agreement

September 29, 2000

Dear Chairman Bronfman:

As you know, over the last year we have worked closely and cooperatively with the Presidential Advisory Commission on Holocaust Assets in the United States, to identify the books, periodicals, and newspapers that were acquired by the Library through the agency of the Jewish Cultural Reconstruction (JCR), as well as through other sources in the immediate aftermath of the Holocaust. I am writing to update you on our progress and our plans.

We are pleased that our collective efforts over the last year and public testimony have confirmed what the Library believed at the outset - that the United States acquisition of unrestitutible Holocaust era books was proper and consistent with the procedures established by the United States Government.

Working diligently, staff of both the Library and Commission located sufficient information to enable the Commission to undertake a sampling of the Library's Hebraic collections. During July, we accorded a team of samplers from the Commission unprecedented and total access to the Hebraic stacks, in compliance with the Library's collections security procedures. Using a sampling method designed by Professor Arthur Kirsch of George Washington University, the team physically examined more than 25,000 Hebraic volumes.

We agree that the JCR collection should be handled in a manner suited to its special provenance. To further the goal of identifying, recognizing, and providing special access to this unique collection, we will establish a "virtual library" of the titles of JCR and related books, which the public will be able to search on-line as well as to examine the volumes in-person in the Library's African and Middle Eastern Reading Room. The Library will also give priority to cataloging any of the books identified as belonging to this collection that have not been fully cataloged; and as we identify additional titles belonging to this collection, we will add a bibliographical note to each cataloging record to describe its special provenance.

In addition, we are developing a collection "name" field, which will serve to aggregate all the records for the JCR collection within the virtual library. This step will enable users to click on a single "icon" or link that will lead them to every title in this special collection. The Library will also make this list of titles available to agencies, organizations, and individuals involved in the restitution of Holocaust-era assets. We expect to complete these preliminary steps shortly, at which point, we will create a test file with prototype records to

2

perform a technical assessment. We also will track and monitor the level of effort, costs and time estimates necessary to complete the entire collection.

The Library also plans to include selected volumes from this collection in a major permanent exhibition of the Library's international treasures, which is slated to open next February in the historic and newly-restored Thomas Jefferson Building. The captions used in this section of the exhibition will note the unique history of the volumes displayed. In addition, we will mount a display of JCR books in our African and Middle Eastern Reading Room in 2002 to mark the 50th anniversary of the completion of JCR's work in 1952.

We look forward to continuing to work with the Commission to educate the public about this important and historic collection. If you have any questions or suggestions, please do not hesitate to contact me at 202-707-5205, or our General Counsel, Elizabeth Pugh, at 202-707-2257.

Sincerely,

James H. Billington
The Librarian of Congress

Mr. Edgar Bronfman
Chairman, Presidential Advisory Commission
    on Holocaust Assets in the United States
901 Fifteenth Street, N.W. - Suite 350
Washington, DC   20005

New York Bankers Association

99 Park Avenue

New York, NY 10016-1502

212.297.1699 Fax 212.297.1658

Michael P. Smith
President

November 14, 2000

Mr. Edgar M. Bronfman
Chairman
Presidential Advisory Commission on
 Holocaust Assets in the United States
901 15th Street, N.W., Suite 350
Washington, D.C. 20005

Dear Mr. Bronfman:

We appreciate the opportunity which you afforded the New York Bankers Association (NYBA), along with three of its member banks (Chase Manhattan Bank, HSBC Bank USA and Citigroup) to work with the Presidential Advisory Commission on Holocaust Assets in the United States (the "Commission") to develop suggested Best Practices for use by United States banks when conducting Holocaust asset research. The Suggested Best Practices Guide which was ultimately developed and jointly agreed to by NYBA, the three named member banks and the Commission, was unanimously ratified by NYBA's Board of Directors chaired by Thomas A. Renyi, Chairman & Chief Executive Officer of The Bank of New York, at its meeting on November 8, 2000.

We applaud the work of your Commission and hope that our efforts have assisted you in realizing your important mission. If you have any questions, please do not hesitate to call me. Thank you.

Sincerely,

Michael P. Smith

AMERICAN ASSOCIATION OF MUSEUMS

EDWARD H. ABLE, JR.
PRESIDENT & CEO

October 20, 2000

Mr. Kenneth Klothen
Executive Director
Presidential Commission on Holocaust Assets in the U.S.
901 15th Street, NW, Suite 350
Washington, DC 20005

Dear Ken:

We are extremely pleased to have been invited to talk with you and members of the Commission today about our common goals. It was good to have had the chance to talk through the details of the Commission's report.

I hope you are left with no doubt that the museum community completely agrees to the goal of "full disclosure" as set forth in the Commission's findings. The American Association of Museums is committed to helping museums achieve this goal through the publication of instructional information on provenance research, dissemination of sample policies and procedures, and development of website standardization and a searchable central registry.

We look forward to working with you on some of these topics as we move forward in this effort.

We have reviewed the text of the draft findings and recommendations related to museums and we support them completely and are prepared to work toward implementing the provisions it includes.

Thank you for the hard work that you, the Commission, and your staff have devoted to this topic and for your support of the museum community's work.

Sincerely,

Edward H. Able, Jr.

cc: Freda Nicholson, Chair, AAM Board of Directors
Katharine Lee Reid, President, AAMD

1575 EYE STREET NW, SUITE 400
WASHINGTON, DC 20005
202.289.1818
FAX 202.289.6578

Association of Art Museum Directors

October 20, 2000

Mr. Kenneth Klothen
Executive Director
Presidential Commission on Holocaust Assets
901 15th Street, NW, Suite 530
Washington, DC 20005

Head Office

41 East 65th Street
New York, NY 10021
Tel 212-249-4423
Fax: 212-535-5039
aamd@amn.org

Washington Office

1319 F Street, N.W., Suite 707
Washington, D.C. 20004
Tel: 202-638-4520
Fax: 202-638-4528
aamddc@amn.org

Dear Ken:

Thank you and the Commission for your continued efforts to resolve one of the most difficult issues of our time – the restitution of Nazi-looted art to its rightful owners. The goal of the AAMD is consistent with the Commission's, but even more importantly is responsive to the obligations we all share to survivors, their families and others who suffered the horrors and injustices of Nazi aggression. Our commitment has long been to focus resources on researching the provenance of our collections following a process that recognizes these individuals as priorities. In that spirit, we have reviewed the Commission's findings and recommendations and are in complete agreement with the goals of full disclosure as set forth in the Commission's findings and we support completely the Commission's findings and recommendations and we commit ourselves to working toward implementing the provisions included in the findings and recommendations.

Since 1998 AAMD members have been researching their collections for gaps in provenance of works that might have been Nazi-looted and have made this research available on their Web sites. A broader assessment of all relevant works acquired by our museums since the beginning of the Nazi era continues, and will ultimately encompass our collections as a whole.

Thank you again. We are especially grateful for your efforts on behalf of the art museum community and your dedication to this cause.

Sincerely,

Katharine Lee Reid
President

Cc: Edward H. Able, Jr. President and CEO, AAM
    Freda Nicholson, Chair, AAM Board of Directors

www.amn.org/aamd

Table of Contents:
Staff Report

Chapter III: Assets in the United States

Chapter IV: Assets in Europe

Chapter V: Restitution of Victims' Assets

Chapter VI: Heirless Assets and the Role of Jewish Cultural Reconstruction, Inc.

Chapter VII: Conclusion

Executive Summary

The primary mandate of the Presidential Advisory Commission on Holocaust Assets in the United States was to "conduct a thorough study and develop a historical record of the collection and disposition of the assets" taken from victims of the Holocaust by Nazi Germany or Nazi-allied governments, "if such assets came into the possession or control of the Federal Government" at any time after January 30, 1933. *Plunder and Restitution: The U.S. and Holocaust Victims' Assets* is the final report of the Commission, including its Findings and Recommendations to the President and the Staff Report to the Commission.

This report identifies several major themes:

- Government officials did not initially distinguish between assets belonging to victims of Nazi persecution and those that did not. In time, the terminology of government policy came to refer to "persecutees," or those who had lost property under duress. While "Holocaust victim" never existed as a legal category, during and after the war the U.S. government devised numerous regulatory and legal distinctions that affected the access of those defined as "enemies," "foreign nationals," "refugees," and the like to their assets. Some of these distinctions helped those we would today call Holocaust victims. The evolution of American thinking led to explicit legal and policy recognition in 1945 and 1946 that "persecutees" and "stateless persons" deserved special status as well as special measures to facilitate recovery of their assets.

- The onset of the war led to aggressive strategic efforts—what *The New York Times* called "a worldwide ring around Nazi attempts to conceal the movement of their assets"[1]—to prevent assets owned by foreign nationals and held in the United States from being used by the Nazis to fuel their war effort.

- Issues the Allies considered more pressing—in particular the imperative to do the maximum economically and politically to win the war, to rebuild the German and European economies after the war, and to wage the Cold War—continually overshadowed concern for restitution.

American policy operated in two arenas: the United States and Europe. In the United States:

- Before, during, and after the war the U.S. government endeavored to deny the enemy control over economic assets being brought into—or already within—its borders. Because the United States took control of so many assets it undoubtedly seized some that belonged to Holocaust victims, though not intentionally.

- U.S. officials were aware of the intensity of Nazi persecution, but it would take until the end of the war before American policy began to accord special status to victims and their assets, because it had seemed consistently more important to defeat the enemy than to aid the victims. In the immediate post-war period, other issues took priority.

- The desire to compensate U.S. citizens for damages suffered overseas competed with the restitution of victims' assets, because both programs drew sums from the pool of seized property. In 1946, however, Congress enacted legislation enabling persecutees to claim property that had been frozen in the United States during the war and, over the next decade, the Office of Alien Property (OAP) carefully examined individual claims to determine the legitimate ownership of assets. But, this resulted in an average delay of more than three years before a victim could recover property.

In Europe:

- As American troops overran large areas of German-occupied territory during the final phases of World War II, they discovered billions of dollars worth of gold, other financial assets and art—much of it looted—left behind by the defeated Nazi regime. U.S. armed forces did not set out to become the guardians of property looted by the Nazis, but circumstances thrust this role upon them.

- American leaders recognized their responsibility to safeguard private property, to prevent its use by the enemy, and to lay the foundation for the eventual return of loot to its rightful owners. Because field units had no systematic method of distinguishing victims' assets from war booty or legitimate German-owned property, the U.S. Army emphasized the collection and control of all asset types.

- Later, when the military occupation government was in full operation, officials made intermittent efforts to segregate obvious victim assets from the general pool of assets under the control of the U.S. military government. Although policies and procedures surrounding collection and protection of assets evolved in response to the circumstances encountered by troops in Europe, U.S. officials often did not follow through in providing the resources necessary to deal adequately with this issue. As a result, policy implementation in the field frequently fell short of fully realizing the U.S. aim to protect property in its care from theft, deterioration, and general destruction.

- Having secured control of innumerable pieces of real estate, cultural artifacts, and financial assets, the United States inaugurated its general restitution program in the summer of 1945. This policy relied on the return of looted assets to the government of the country from which the property had been stolen. By that time, some U.S. officials had begun to recognize victims of Nazi persecution as a distinct category of property claimants. They also recognized that many victims had no country to which assets could be restituted and that it was morally unacceptable to restitute such property to Germany. U.S. officials consulted with the Allies, Jewish organizations, and German officials before implementing plans in Europe to allocate reparations to survivors and restitute looted property.

- To further address the needs of Holocaust survivors, U.S. officials designated the Jewish Restitution Successor Organization (JRSO) to receive non-cultural assets whose original owners could not be identified and employ the proceeds of their sale for the rehabilitation of survivors worldwide. Jewish Cultural Reconstruction, Inc. (JCR) emerged in 1947 to recover cultural property.

Even the impulse to assure restitution of assets falling under U.S. control sometimes delayed restitution to claimants and the successor organizations and had certain unintended consequences:

- The United States insisted that any law providing for restitution in Germany contain a presumption of duress—that is, that persecutees who transferred property after 1935 did so unwillingly, and that current "owners" of such property could be sued to effect the return of property to its original owner. The United States thus forced the creation of a much broader restitution program than initially envisioned by German authorities after the war. This also meant, however, that the promulgation of the restitution law in Germany did not occur until November 1947, more than two years after hostilities ceased.

Not all U.S. authorities recognized persecutees as a special category:

- Much of the documentation created in the immediate postwar era pertaining to restitution does not distinguish between victims' and non-victims' assets. This also meant that, among recovered assets that had been taken from victims by the Nazis, no distinctions were made among assets that had belonged to Jewish, Roma, Sinti, disabled or homosexual victims. Consequently, property that was identifiable as to its country of origin was not further categorized to designate an owner who had been persecuted by the Nazi regime.

- During the period between 1944 and 1947, neither a uniform nor a fixed conception of restitution prevailed among U.S. authorities. The measures envisioned for effecting restitution also shifted over time: while State Department officials initially favored only a modest indemnity payment for dispossessed persecutees, U.S. Military Government authorities promulgated a law in 1947 that promised full restitution of property.

- Sensitivity to survivors, heirs, and the successor organizations attempting to claim property fluctuated in the postwar era as U.S. policies sometimes adversely affected the restitution program. For instance, the decision to return many governing tasks to the Germans in 1945 allowed some who had benefited from Aryanizations—the coerced transfer of Jewish property to non-Jews—to participate in the administration of the restitution program. It took more than a decade for the Congress to pass legislation providing a lump sum settlement of JRSO claims against the Office of Alien Property. In 1962, the JRSO reluctantly accepted $500,000 in that settlement.

Although other policy considerations impeded progress, agencies of the United States government demonstrated a significant commitment to return the property of Holocaust victims after the Second World War.

---

[1] New York Times, June 15, 1941.

Chapter I

The History of the Presidential Advisory Commission on Holocaust Assets in the United States and Its Report

Creation of the Presidential Commission and Its Purpose

After the United States took the lead in prompting other countries to investigate their handling of assets belonging to Holocaust victims, the President and the U.S. Congress recognized the need to examine the American record during and after World War II. In 1998, mindful of the public interest in this unfinished chapter of the Holocaust, the U.S. Congress established the Presidential Advisory Commission on Holocaust Assets in the United States. The vote was not only bipartisan but unanimous. P.L. 105–186 directed the Commission to "conduct a thorough study and develop a historical record of the collection and disposition of the assets" taken from victims of the Holocaust by Nazi Germany or by the governments it controlled, "if such assets came into the possession or control of the Federal Government" at any time after January 30, 1933.

The mandate required study of assets such as gold, non-gold financial assets, and art and other cultural property and instructed the Commission to review work done by others about assets that passed into non-Federal hands. In addition, the Commission was charged to prepare for the President legislative and administrative policy recommendations. *Plunder and Restitution: The U.S. and Holocaust Victims' Assets,* comprised of the Findings and Recommendations of the Presidential Advisory Commission on Holocaust Assets in the United States and Staff Report, fulfills that responsibility.

Twenty-four countries—from Argentina to Sweden, from Lithuania to Portugal—have already created formal government-sponsored commissions to examine their records, and 22 other nations have less formal mechanisms with the same objective. The impetus came from the recognition that with the facts of the Nazi crimes against humanity demonstrated and the imperatives of postwar reconstruction and the Cold War off the agenda, the time had come to find out what happened to the assets of Holocaust victims and to look at this facet of the history of World War II through the prism of their material dispossession.

The Commission determined that in the wartime era at least 70 different Federal departments, agencies, bureaus, and working groups had some responsibility for the development and implementation of U.S. policies regarding Holocaust-era assets. These ranged from the Departments of War, Justice, and Treasury, including the Bureau of Customs, to the Monuments, Fine Arts and Archives Branch of the U.S. Military, the Art Looting Investigation Unit of the Office of Strategic Services (OSS), and many other now obscure wartime working groups in the White House.

Scope of the Report

The Commission, following extensive consultation with the authors of the legislation that created it, along with others in the Congress and the Executive Branch, defined the scope of its historical report and developed key questions: (1) how assets acquired by the Nazis from Holocaust victims throughout Europe came into the control of agencies of the U.S. government; (2) how U.S. agencies came to control victims' assets through measures designed to wage economic warfare; (3) how these agencies handled victims' assets while they remained under U.S. control; (4) how the U.S. government disposed of or restituted the assets; (5) how well the structure controlling the flow of assets actually worked; (6) how restitution policy evolved in its sensitivity to the interests of individual victims; (7) what the role of the U.S. government was in establishing Jewish successor organizations; and, (8) what the role of the successor organizations was in the restitution of victims' assets.

In pursuing these lines of inquiry, the report identifies several themes:

(1) During the war, issues the Allied governments considered more important—in particular the imperative to do the maximum economically and politically to win the war—continually overshadowed concern with restitution. Answers to questions of how to collect, inventory, and control valuables were left unresolved when competing for the attention of military officers. After the war, victims' interests were once again not the priority, as the agenda was dominated by political issues, such as feeding a starving Europe and rebuilding the German and other European economies. Finally, the Cold War affected the readiness of the U.S. authorities to make victims' assets a priority.

(2) The U.S. government's first impulse was strategic in nature: to prevent the use of property by the enemy. Though the onset of the war led to an aggressive effort to prevent assets from being used by the Nazis to fuel their war effort and to exploit certain foreign-owned assets for the benefit of the United States, even here the control exerted was meant to fight enemies, rather than to put friends at a disadvantage. Victims' assets did come into the possession or control of the United States and mechanisms were put in place both during and after the war to address the special problems they presented. These efforts, however, worked imperfectly.

(3) U.S. policies regarding the ownership of the property over which it exercised control evolved. While "Holocaust victim" did not exist as a legal category, during the war the U.S. government devised numerous regulatory and legal distinctions that affected the access to assets by those defined as "enemies," "foreign nationals," "refugees," and the like. Some of these distinctions were to the benefit of those we would call victims today. The evolution in American thinking led

to explicit legal and policy recognition in 1945 and 1946 that "persecutees" deserved special status as well as special measures to recover their assets.

U.S. recognition of the special category of "victim of Nazi persecution" or "persecutee" developed gradually. Government officials did not organize, collect, or sort assets during the war or in its immediate aftermath by what belonged to a victim of Nazi persecution and what did not. While the terminology of the time referred to "persecutees," or those who had lost property under duress, for purposes of the Commission's work victim is defined as an individual who was deprived of his or her civil or political rights on the basis of race, religion, ethnicity, disability, or sexual orientation.

Estimate of Assets in U.S. Possession or Control

The Holocaust was an immeasurable human tragedy and a profound moral failure. It was also the greatest mass theft in history.

Much of the loot collected by the Nazis came into the possession and control of the U.S. government which took control of financial assets in the United States, as well as gold, art and cultural property, and non-gold financial assets in Europe. Within the United States, such control occurred when assets owned by foreign nationals were blocked or seized. That is, assets were either frozen by the Treasury Department, with title left in the hands of the original owners, or seized with title taken by the Treasury or Justice Departments. In Europe, U.S. forces took physical control over most of the assets they found.

A precise accounting of the number and value of assets that came into the possession or control of the U.S. government is impossible. Because of the chaos that characterized the final military campaigns and their immediate aftermath, officials did not always inventory assets in ways that facilitated valuation. When U.S. forces inventoried looted securities, they sometimes listed them by stack height without noting the identity or value of the individual stock certificates. Other inventories identified the number of boxes, crates, or lots—without describing or appraising their contents. U.S. forces were ill-equipped to assess or determine the value of cultural property that they encountered.

The United States did not sort assets according to whether their owner was a victim of Nazi persecution. The Nazis left little evidence of that which they stole from Roma, Sinti, homosexual, disabled, and other victims. This further confounds attempts to quantify the total of the assets ultimately found by the United States as well as the portion of those assets that belonged to these persecuted groups.

The chart below shows the government-controlled assets and their value as estimated in contemporaneous reports by the authorities responsible for their control. It is important to emphasize that victims' assets represent only a small percentage of the totals.[1]

Table 1: Estimated Value of Assets in the Possession or Control of the U.S.

Asset Type	Total Estimated Value
Non-gold Financial Assets, in the United States (1941)	$8,500,000,000[2]
Gold and Non-gold Financial Assets, in Europe (1950)	$343,800,000[3]
Art and Cultural Property, in Europe (1948)	$5,000,000,000[4]

Non-gold Financial Assets in the United States

Foreign-owned financial assets—including cash, bank accounts, securities, and direct investments—that came into U.S. control in the United States were either blocked or vested.

A major problem in estimating their value is that certain types of assets assumed to be foreign-controlled—for example, the contents of safe deposit boxes, copyrights, and patents—were never given dollar values by either the Foreign Funds Control or the Alien Property Custodian. Others were assigned only a nominal value. Of the assets it did value, including businesses and real property, the Alien Property Custodian (APC) vested a total of $241 million. Since the APC also vested large numbers of the nonvalued assets, the total value of assets under the control of APC had to exceed $241 million.

Financial Assets Blocked in the United States

Overall, the 565,000 reports submitted to the Treasury Department for the 1941 Census of foreign-owned assets in the United States show the total value of U.S. assets owned by foreign persons or entities in 1941 to have been $12.7 billion.[5] These reports further show that about two-thirds of this total, $8.5 billion, belonged to 84,000 persons in European countries.[6] The Census data was to include some 30 specified types of property, and the property's value was to be listed in June 1940 and June 1941 dollars. Even assets with values difficult to assess in dollar terms, such as patents or interests in partnerships, had to be reported, as did the contents of safe deposit boxes. However, because the forms filled out by the respondents have since been destroyed, the Commission staff had to rely on much less revealing summary data included in the annual reports compiled by the Treasury Department.

The unblocking of these assets occurred between 1948 and 1962. The majority of them were released outright, while others remained in U.S. control and were vested. In the postwar era, the Foreign Funds Control (FFC) in the Treasury Department wanted to remove restrictions on frozen assets with the least possible delay consistent with the original purpose of preventing their use by the enemy. European governments were given the responsibility to certify that the assets controlled by their nationals were free of enemy taint. By 1949, when the responsibility for the blocked accounts moved from the Department of the Treasury to the Justice Department, about $1 billion remained blocked.[7]

About $15 million in blocked assets was unblocked through two General Licenses issued in June 1953. On June 1, 1953, blocked accounts not exceeding $100 in value were unblocked by General License No. 102, and on June 27, 1953, General License No. 101 removed the remaining controls on blocked property in the United States held by governments or nationals of the "Marshall Plan countries...Switzerland, Liechtenstein, Japan and Western Germany."[8]

After the releases permitted by these General Licenses, the only remaining blocked property belonged to individual citizens or governments of countries under Communist domination. In 1983, the Treasury Department's Office of Foreign Assets Control found that some of these sums remained in the State Abandoned Property Offices of five states: 400 accounts amounting to $900,000 remained from Czechoslovakia, East Germany, and the Baltic states.[9]

Financial Assets Vested in the United States

Executive Order 9567 of June 8, 1945, provided that the liquid assets of Germany and Japan could be seized. Between 1945 and 1953, cash, bank accounts, securities, estates and trusts, life insurance policies and contracts, and other liquid assets were withdrawn from their blocked status under Treasury Department regulation and seized by the APC and its successor organization, the Office of Alien Property (OAP) in the Justice Department. With seizure, title to the properties passed from private or foreign government owners to the United States Government.

Data on the seizure of assets in the United States is found in the reports of the OAP. The data below include the values for seized non-business property through June 1953.

Table 2: Office of Alien Property—U.S. Department of Justice

Total of Seized Non-business Assets as of June 30, 1953		Total of Seized Non-business German Assets as of June 30, 1953	
Cash and Bank Accounts	$45,109,000	Other (Cash and Bank Accounts, Securities, and Insurance Policies)	$102,873,000
Securities	$33,237,000		
Insurance Policies	$3,946,000		
Other	$41,136,000		
Estates and Trusts	$87,792,000	Estates and Trusts	$78,851,000
Real Property	$8,835,000	Real Property	$5,978,000
Total Seized [non-business assets]	$219,965,000[10]	Total Seized [non-business German assets]	$187,709,000[11]

The disposition of seized property included returning the property, returning the proceeds from the sale of the property, or paying compensation for it when it was determined that such "return should be made or such compensation should be paid." Seizure, however, also meant that property could be "administered, liquidated, sold or otherwise dealt with in the interest of and for the benefit of the United States," which permitted a determination that nothing would be returned.[12]

By 1947, the OAP began returning seized property of all kinds—including cash, patents, interests in estates and trusts, copyrights, securities, and real property—to claimant individuals and businesses. By 1958, approximately 3,700 return orders had been issued to divest assets. These returns can be compared to the over 5,000 vesting orders issued during the war and the 14,000 or more issued thereafter to reveal that only about one in five assets seized was returned even by 1958.[13] Of this group, only about 20 percent represented assets seized during the war, as indicated by the dates of the related vesting order numbers.

The Office of Alien Property made the following statement about the effect of postwar vesting on victims' assets: "After the...amendment to the Trading with the Enemy Act in 1946 authorizing the return of vested assets to persecutees of the Nazi regime despite their technical enemy status, this Office took great pains to avoid vesting the property of such persons."[14]

The postwar vesting by the APC, and its successor OAP, explicitly excluded victims' assets, but the Commission staff believes that victims' assets are likely to have been caught up in the pool of assets taken by the 5,000-odd vesting orders from 1942 to 1945. The staff estimates the value of released vested victims' property at $17 million.[15] This figure includes: $15 million[16] estimated to have been released to owners, and $1.5 million[17] that was never claimed and was retained by the APC and transferred to the War Claims Fund. The Commission staff believes that it is likely that this $1.5 million belonged to victims of the Holocaust who could not submit claims for it. Finally, $500,000[18] was turned over by legislation to the Jewish Reconstruction Successor Organization in 1962. By 1954, the War Claims Commission had received a total of $75 million from the disposition of seized German and Japanese assets.

Gold and Non-gold Financial Assets in Europe

The U.S. government came into contact with victims' non-gold financial assets in Europe as well as in the United States. American troops removed caches of gold and non-gold financial assets from Germany and Austria and forwarded them to the Foreign Exchange Depository (FED) in Frankfurt, Germany. U.S. forces sent 121 shipments of monetary gold, non-monetary gold, and non-gold financial assets to the FED between April 1945 and December 1950, when the FED was closed.[19] In addition, one shipment of non-gold financial assets was released directly from the Salzburg Military Government Warehouse to the International Refugee Organization (IRO).

The FED closing report provides the best evidence for estimating the amount and value of gold and non-gold financial assets that passed through the direct control of the U.S. government:

Table 3:
Gold and Non-gold Financial Assets Controlled by the United States in Europe[20]

	FED	Salzburg
Total Value Controlled (including Gold)	$342,823,000	n.a.
Total Restituted to Countries	$65,636,000	n.a.
Total Released to IRO	$808,000	$1,000,000
Total Restituted to Individuals	$656	n.a.
Total FED Incoming Shipments	$297,239,000	n.a.
Direct Restitution (with Silver)	$2,787,000	n.a.
Sent to the TGC from FED	$263,680,000	n.a.
Of this, Prussian Mint Bars	$41,738,000	n.a.

Gold was the most valuable and liquid of the assets encountered by U.S. troops in the spring of 1945. The price of gold was stable at $35 per ounce in otherwise turbulent times. Among the 121 shipments of assets received at the FED, a significant number were known to have included assets of Holocaust victims. In the first year of FED operations, 22 of 77 shipments contained items clearly identifiable as loot taken from victims by Hitler's SS.[21]

Despite the detailed inventories of the FED and the precise estimates of incoming and outgoing shipments at Frankfurt, questions remain about the extent of victims' gold included in the gold that came under U.S. control. A Finance Division officer described the difficulties inherent in any attempt to quantify victims' gold:

> No attempt has been made as yet to evaluate the SS loot but from a cursory inspection of the contents of a few containers, it is apparent that the total value is a very large figure.... Much of the gold bullion cannot be traced, it having been deliberately melted and recast into new bars by its captors.... The questions of restitution and reparations are inextricably conjoined in that all claims for reparations must be reduced by the extent of restitution effected. This necessitates accurate accounting and evaluating of assets which are likely to be the subject of restitutions.[22]

In 1998, following the study on Nazi-looted gold and its restitution coordinated by then Under Secretary of Commerce for International Trade Stuart E. Eizenstat, the Tripartite Gold Commission (TGC) liquidated its accounts (amounting to 5.5 tons in the fall of 1996) and contributed their value to a fund to compensate Holocaust victims.[23] These contributions are supposed to reflect the presence of looted gold in the gold that was shipped to the TGC. The United States pledged an additional $25 million to this fund.[24]

Art and Cultural Property

The restitution records of the Office of Military Government for Germany, United States (OMGUS) and United States Forces Austria (USFA) officials permit the following estimates of the number and value of art and cultural property controlled by U.S. government agencies in Europe.

Table 4: Estimated Restitution of Works of Art and Cultural Objects by the United States, 1945—1948

	Estimated Number of Objects	Estimated Value of Objects
Restitution of Works of Art from OMGUS CCPs to German Owners	3,200,000	$1,500,000,000
External Restitution of Art from OMGUS CCPs	480,000	$500,000,000
Total Works of Art Restituted from OMGUS [25]	3,680,000	$2,000,000,000
Restitution of Books from OMGUS CCPs to German Owners	1,100,000	$30,000,000
External Restitution of Books from OMGUS CCPs	1,500,000	$50,000,000
Total Books Restituted from OMGUS [26]	2,600,000	$80,000,000
Restitution of Works of Art from USFA to Austria [27]	No numbers available	$146,000,000
External Restitution of Works of Art from USFA	No numbers available	$10,000,000
Total Restitutions from USFA	No numbers available	$147,000,000
Total Objects Returned (Art Objects and Books) from OMGUS and USFA [28]	6,280,000 plus unknown number from Austria	$2,947,000,000

The OMGUS art experts gathered this information through 1948 and USFA restitution officials collected it through 1949. OMGUS reported in 1948 that U.S. forces discovered 10.7 million objects with an estimated worth of $5 billion. The same report, however, states that OMGUS restituted $2.1 billion. There is no historical evidence of the methodology used to arrive at either figure, or that the methodology used to arrive at both figures was the same. Of the assets under the control of OMGUS, individual objects had an average value based on category of asset (art object or book) and type of restitution (external or internal) of between $27.27 and $1,041.67. None of the information provided contributes to an evaluation of how many of these assets came from victims.

The Commission staff estimates—based on later restitution records of the American-run central collecting points—that in addition to the restitution figures cited above, between 1948 and 1952, 100,000 art objects were restituted from OMGUS to German owners; 60,000 art objects were externally restituted from OMGUS; 700,000 books were restituted from OMGUS to German owners; and 426,000 books were externally restituted from OMGUS. Including these figures would increase the estimated value of the assets restituted. Using the average values for assets (by category and type of restitution), the values would be increased by $46.9 million for artworks restituted from OMGUS to German owners; $62.5 million for artworks externally restituted from OMGUS; $19.1 million for books restituted to German owners; and $14.2 million for books externally restituted from OMGUS. In sum, this estimate increases the overall total number of objects restituted from 6.3 million objects worth $2.1 billion to 7.5 million objects worth $2.2 billion.

Organization of the Report

This report is organized to answer the questions that Congress posed in the Commission's governing legislation:

- Chapter II, *From Nazi Expropriation to U.S. Control,* sketches the historical context of the 1930s and 1940s, including the Nazi regime's persecution and extermination of vast numbers of persons, the expropriation of their possessions, the development of U.S. policy on the battlefield as the Army discovered caches of looted property, and the competing concerns of the U.S. military as it attempted to maintain law and order and disarm and demilitarize enemy forces while securing and organizing looted assets in preparation for restitution.

- Chapter III, *Assets in the United States,* describes how the U.S. government sought to prevent foreign-owned and foreign-controlled economic and financial assets in the United States from being used by the Nazis to finance their war effort. The United States adopted policies designed to preserve and protect those assets until the war's end, when they were released. Within this framework, the United States moved as early as 1940 to establish effective economic and financial control mechanisms. This chapter focuses on the specific policy areas and tools used to control financial assets already in the United States and those flowing into and out of the country. The pertinent government agencies cast a wide net in their efforts to control these assets and transactions; the assets of the victims of Nazi persecution were, to a certain extent, also caught in this net.

- Chapter IV, *Assets in Europe,* describes the activities of American troops as they liberated large areas of the Third Reich during the final days of World War II in Europe. U.S. troops encountered large quantities of art, gold, and other valuables—looted and otherwise—left behind by the defeated Nazi regime. U.S. forces discovered these assets in salt mines and farmers' fields, as well as in more prosaic locations like banks. Unprepared for the volume, as well as the range and quality of this property, the United States Army had to develop mechanisms to control, inventory, and manage these assets until American officials determined how the assets should be dealt with.

- Chapter V, *Restitution of Victims' Assets,* examines American efforts to restitute property in Europe and the United States. The restitution program began in Germany in the summer of 1945 and became a complex operation, involving numerous intra- and intergovernmental policy discussions, the crafting of legislation to govern restitution by the Military Government, and the creation of special courts to handle the restitution of Aryanized real property. The United States also encouraged the Austrian government to restitute looted property. Within the United States, the end of war permitted the unblocking and defrosting of the assets that had been held by the government since 1940. While the government was aware of the special needs of victims, and enacted legislation to expedite the return of frozen property, the system worked only imperfectly. The bureaucracy in the Office of Alien Property worked very slowly and deliberately and discouraged claimants who would have benefited from a more rapid and compassionate response. On average, the OAP took over three years to resolve victims' claims. It is also clear that the officials heading the War Claims Fund argued forcefully against the use of vested assets to fund the settlement that Congress proposed to reach with the Jewish Restitution Successor Organization (JRSO), until the amount of money involved was minimal. Although much of the documentary evidence pertaining to restitution does not distinguish between victims' and non-victims' assets, wherever possible the focus in this chapter remains on the policies and procedures implemented specifically for victims, their heirs, or the organizations established to receive heirless property.

- Chapter VI, *Heirless Assets and the Role of Jewish Cultural Reconstruction, Inc. (JCR),* describes the activities of the JCR, which was responsible for the distribution of Jewish books and other cultural property to Jewish communities and non-Jewish libraries in the United States.

- Chapter VII, *Conclusion,* identifies the most significant themes of the report and outlines issues for further study that, for reasons of time and cost, the Commission was unable to examine as completely as it would have liked.

Endnotes for Chapter I

[1] For purposes of this report, "Holocaust-era assets" means assets that were in existence between 1933 and 1945, whether or not they belonged to victims. "Victims' assets" is a more limited category comprised of Holocaust-era assets that belonged to victims.

[2] A Treasury Dept. census of foreign-owned assets in the United States as of June 14, 1941 indicated that $8.5 billion was blocked, including $8 billion in foreign-owned assets, and $500 million in assets held by foreign nationals resident in the United States. $4 billion in gold, cash, and bank accounts; $2 billion in securities; and $2 billion in direct investment were blocked as foreign-owned assets. Data taken from U.S. Treasury Department, *Census of Foreign-Owned Assets in the United States* (Washington, DC: Government Printing Office, 1945), VII. Data concerning the assets of foreign nationals resident in the U.S. and for the value of gold, cash, and bank accounts is from the U.S. Treasury Department, *Annual Report of the Secretary of the Treasury on the State of the Finances* (Washington DC: Government Printing Office, 1942), 159. These figures are reported in 1941 dollars.

[3] The exact total in the document is given as $343,823,000. This total includes shipments from the U.S. Zone of Austria and is given in 1950 dollars. Office of Econ. Affairs, Fin. Div., "Foreign Exchange Depository, Status as at C/B, December 15, 1950," NACP, RG 260, Box 400, FED, Disposal Accounts [219600]. The numbers that appear in brackets throughout this report refer to documents compiled and numbered by the Commission in the course of its research.

[4] OMGUS, Prop. Div., "Staff Study on Transfer of Functions and Personnel dealing with MFA&A and Libraries from Property Division to Education and Cultural Relations Division," Sept. 10, 1948, NACP, RG 260, Ardelia Hall Collection, Box 344 [118985–9008]. This report values the objects discovered in repositories (which it numbers at 10.7 million) but does not provide a methodology for the valuation nor does it specify whether it includes objects in Germany or Austria, or both. The figure is reported in 1948 dollars.

[5] *Census of Foreign-Owned Assets*, 1945, 14–15.

[6] *Census of Foreign-Owned Assets*, 1945, 14; and *Annual Report of the Secretary of the Treasury*, 1942, 159.

[7] *Annual Report of the Secretary of the Treasury*, 1949, 99; Memo from Robert J. Schwartz, Treas. Dept. to Donald Sham, OAP, Justice Dept., Feb. 2, 1949, NACP, RG 131, Entry 66–A–816, Box 53, File TFR 600. Figure for estimated total blocked as of June 1, 1948 from all reports submitted through Jan. 14, 1949 is given as $981 million.

[8] U.S. Justice Dept., *Annual Report of the Attorney General of the United States*, 1953, 65 [333621–634].

[9] Office of Foreign Assets Control, U.S. Treas. Dept., *Blocked Foreign Assets in the United States: Summary Report of 1983–84 Census of Blocked Property*, May 1985, 18, 20, 22, 24, 26.

[10] *OAP Annual Report*, 1953, Table 3, 14. Other data are calculated from the table.

[11] *OAP Annual Report*, 1953, Table 3, 14, Table 6, 18. Other data are calculated from this table.

[12] Specimen copies of vesting orders from 1942 and 1943 can be found in Otto Sommerich, "Recent Innovations in Legal and Regulatory Concepts as to the Alien and his Property," *American Journal of International Law* 37 (1942), 67, and in Martin Domke, *Trading with the Enemy in World War II* (New York: Central Book Co., 1943), 467–68.

[13] APC *Annual Report* 1945, 9 [322954–3090]; OAP *Annual Report* 1958, 82 [324619–718]; OAP *Annual Report* 1953, 147 [324089].

[14] Letter from Paul Myron, Dept. Dir., OAP to Congressman Arthur G. Klein, Aug. 10, 1956, The Jacob Rader Marcus Center of the American Jewish Archives (AJA), World Jewish Congress (WJC) Papers, Box C294 [116923–925].

[15] Ibid. The Commission staff calculated this figure by taking 22 percent of the total of 11,000 JRSO claims for heirless property vested by the APC between 1942 and 1946 plus the few OAP orders vesting persecutee property between 1946 and 1953 (2,420 claims) and multiplying by the average value of the JRSO claims ($7,240) for a total of $17,520,800.

For derivation of 22 percent see "Assets Under U.S. Government Control in the United States: Policy and Practice, Annex I— OAP Claims Survey: Results and Analysis," August 7, 2000, 2–3, Washington National Records Center (WNRC), Suitland, MD, RG 131 — Acc. 65F1063, FFC, Vesting Orders Number 1–19, 312 issued between March 1942 – April 1953. Twenty-two percent was the same percentage found by the OAP in their investigation of 808 JRSO claims filed regarding owners originating in Germany.

[16] Calculated by multiplying the average value of persecutee claims ($7,420) by the number of persecutee claims (1,293) attached to the vested property in the 754 vesting orders (out of 11,000 filed) that the JRSO judged to be relevant to pursue for heirless assets ($7,420 x 1,293 = $15.5 million).

[17] Derived by subtracting the estimated number of victims' assets released to owners and the $500,000 given the JRSO ($15.5 million + $.5 million = $16 million) from the estimated total of victims' assets ($17.5 million) = $1.5 million. The total of $1.5 million that was transferred to the War Claims Fund can be calculated from a different perspective. Once again applying the random sample results of 22 percent to the 1,293 relevant JRSO claims, 284 JRSO eligible claims for heirless property are derived. Multiplying the 284 claims by the average amount of one claim derived from the random sample study, $7,420, one gets $2,056,160 (284 x $7,240 = $2,056,160). This total is virtually the same figure that the JRSO arrived at in a very different investigation of the OAP vesting orders.

[18] Lump sum settlement for heirless property vested by the APC (1942–1946) agreed to between the Jewish Restitution Successor Organization (JRSO) and the OAP, Justice Dept. in P.L. 87–846, Oct. 22, 1962, 76 Stat. 1114–1115.

[19] "Register of Valuables in the Custody of the Foreign Exchange Depository," NACP, RG 260, Fin. Div., Box 469 [114094–109].

[20] Office of Econ. Affairs, Fin. Div., "Foreign Exchange Depository, Status as at C/B, December 15, 1950," Disposal Accounts, NACP, RG 260, FED, Box 400 [219600]. The total includes shipments from the U.S. Zone of Austria.

[21] "Data re: S.S. Loot," NACP, RG 260, Fin. Div., Box 50, Gold and Silver (Hungarian Restitution) [305154–156].

[22] Memo from Capt. Paul S. McCarroll to Exec. Officer, Fin. Div., OMGUS, USFET, "Foreign Exchange Depository," Jan. 24, 1946, NACP, RG 260, FED, Box 399, History of FED [227403–406].

[23] Ambassador Louis Amigues, "The Closing of the Tripartite Gold Commission for the Restitution of Monetary Gold," *Proceedings of the Washington Conference on Holocaust-Era Assets* (Washington, DC: U.S. Government Printing Office, 1998), 64–65.

[24] Stuart E. Eizenstat, "Review of Gold issues, Research and Resolution," *Proceedings of the Washington Conference on Holocaust-Era Assets*, 62.

[25] OMGUS, Prop. Div., "Staff Study on Transfer of Functions and Personnel dealing with MFA&A and Libraries from Property Division to Education and Cultural Relations Division," Sept. 10, 1948, NACP, RG 260, Ardelia Hall Collection, Box 344 [118985–9008] [hereinafter the "Staff Study"].

[26] "Staff Study," Sept. 10, 1948, NACP, RG 260, Ardelia Hall Collection, Box 344 [118985–9008].

[27] Rpt. of the U.S. High Commissioner for Austria, Vols. 45, 46, 47, 3 Q 1949, July 1949, "Estimated Value of Completed Restitutions from U.S. Zone Austria and U.S. Vienna Area as of 31 July 1949 (in dollars)," NACP, RG 84, Entry 2082, Box 5 [119041]. Many works of art discovered in Austria were transferred to Munich for identification and restitution (such as the nearly 27,000 from the Alt Aussee mine that went to the Munich CCP). Other works remained in Austria, from where they were restituted. No information is available concerning the number of artworks or books restituted by USFA. The only numbers available report that 5634.50 metric tons of art were restituted, of which 3576.25 metric tons (63.5%) were restituted to Austria. The figure as stated in the report for restitution of art assets to Austria is $145,628,800; for restitutions to other nations, the figure stated in the report is $9,662,990.

[28] This number reflects the addition of the total number of art objects and books restituted externally and to German owners from the OMGUS operated Central Collecting Points. The estimated total value reflects the value of the restitutions made by both OMGUS and USFA.

Chapter II

From Nazi Expropriation to U.S. Control

Introduction

As the harsh winter of 1944–45 turned to spring, World War II drew to a close in Germany with American troops making a series of gruesome discoveries. On April 4, 1945, units of the 4th Armored Division and the 89th Infantry Division of the U.S. Third Army entered the concentration camp at Ohrdruf, near Weimar, and the soldiers were overwhelmed by the terrible odor of decaying flesh. No briefing about Nazi atrocities could have prepared them for what they saw: railroad cars packed with corpses, piles of incinerated skeletons, and emaciated prisoners unable to make their way out of their squalid barracks. Over the next four weeks, other American troops liberated more concentration camps, parts of a vast network built to imprison Jews and other enemies of Nazi Germany.[1] "It is not an exaggeration to say that almost every inmate was insane with hunger," reported Captain J.D. Pletcher of the 71st Division Headquarters after his visit to Gunskirchen, a subcamp of Mauthausen.[2] Supreme Commander Dwight Eisenhower, who entered Buchenwald the day it was liberated, later noted: "I never at any time experienced an equal sense of shock."[3]

Nazi policies of discrimination, persecution, and extermination had an economic agenda, as well. Allied units advancing through German territory came upon large stores of valuables, such as gold, artwork, the currency of several countries, securities, and precious metals, that the Nazis had stolen and then stashed away in concentration camps, barns, mines, castles, trains, factories, banks—wherever they thought they could find them again at an opportune moment. Following Germany's unconditional surrender on May 8, 1945, the Allies banned Hitler's Nazi Party, confiscated its assets, and supplanted its authority over Germany and Austria. The victorious Allies promptly took control of assets stripped from victims of the Nazi regime and from the countries invaded by Germany as well as legitimate German property kept safe from Allied bombers.

Nazi Victimization

"The Science of Race"

Total control over the instruments of state between January 1933 and May 1945, and the suspension of most constitutional constraints on executive powers, enabled the Nazis to extort and steal the properties of their enemies. The methods used by the Nazis against their internal and external enemies built upon their racist ideology and brought unprecedented material devastation and human suffering, victimizing millions of people across Europe.

The Nazi ideology exalted a mythical "master race," of which the Aryan Germans were the superior example. This "culture-creating" race also included the English, Dutch, and Scandinavians. "Culture-bearing" races (Asians, Latins, and Slavs) had little to offer. The "culture-destroying" races included "Gypsies, Negroes, and Jews" and were considered subhuman.[4] Each race struggled to survive and expand, and the Nazis believed Germany's biologically defined destiny was to expand to the east, taking living space (*Lebensraum*) from "inferior" races such as the Poles or Russians.[5] Roma and Sinti (then known as Gypsies) and Germans who were mentally and physically disabled were early targets of Nazi persecution on "racial" grounds. Political opponents, members of religious sects that declined to pledge unconditional allegiance to the regime (Christian Scientists, Jehovah's Witnesses), as well as Freemasons and homosexuals, were victims of Nazi persecution.[6]

In this ideology, the "master race" was in a battle for world domination with its chief enemy, the Jews, who, aware of their "inferiority," used every foul means to subdue the Aryan race. Nazi ideology associated democracy, socialism, capitalism, liberalism, modernism in art, and prostitution with the Jews and postulated that Jews, if not segregated and eventually removed from Germany, would further infect German culture, increase control over Germany's finances, and pollute German blood through miscegenation. The end result of the Jewish infiltration would be a Bolshevik dictatorship that would extinguish the German race.[7]

Once Hitler became chancellor, Nazis and their sympathizers subjected Jews to commercial boycotts as well as scattered acts of violence. Because violent actions often destroyed property and prompted criticism from abroad, they hurt the German economy. Nevertheless, the Nazi regime was determined to profit from dispossessing its enemies, and it prepared a comprehensive strategy of plunder.[8]

Discrimination and Plunder Become Law

The first part of that strategy was the removal of opponents from public life. As early as March 1933, Nazi officials established a concentration camp at Dachau to intern communists, social democrats, and members of trade unions. Jews with similar political beliefs were among the first wave of prisoners. In later years the Nazis built hundreds of concentration camps and interned Jews (from Germany and elsewhere) regardless of their politics, as well as Sinti and Roma, homosexuals, Jehovah's Witnesses, prisoners of war, Poles, and others. One month after the Nazis inaugurated the Dachau camp, the racism of this once fringe group gained its first foothold in the German legal system with the enactment of the Law for the Restoration of the Professional Civil Service of April 7, 1933. The law dismissed Jewish civil servants from state employment, with few exceptions.

Corollary laws disbarred Jewish judges and dismissed Jewish tax advisors. Hitler and his party were taking the first steps toward their goal of a Germany free from Jewish influence.[9]

From 1933 on, the Nazi regime supplemented unofficial acts of repression with official discriminatory decrees. Other policies followed to expropriate Jewish assets, to deprive Jews of their livelihoods, and to force them out of Germany. The process was gradual but inexorable, provoking the emigration of between 100,000 and 170,000 German Jews between 1933 and 1938, half of whom might have had significant assets. As Jews emigrated, the Nazis also attempted—by whatever means—to transfer their assets into non-Jewish hands.[10] One mechanism was the Transfer (Ha'avara) Agreement of August 28, 1933, originally negotiated between Germany and some of the Zionist leaders. Under the controversial agreement—criticized by many Jews who urged a boycott of Germany instead—20,000 Jews emigrated to Palestine between 1933 and 1941 after depositing funds in a German-based account. Once there they were to be reimbursed from the proceeds of the sale of German goods in Palestine.[11]

In 1934, the Nazis increased the tax on Germans applying for emigration, and two years later they restricted the export of securities. Other devices to wrest assets from Jews fleeing Germany included blocking accounts, manipulating exchange rates, confiscating insurance monies, forcing Jews to pay "atonement" fines, taxing them on their "right" to sell their property, and making them pay into a fund to support the emigration of poor Jews.[12]

The onslaught on German Jews was relentless and systematic. The Nazi Party used citizenship "experts" in the Reich Interior Ministry to write the Law for the Protection of German Blood and Honor and the Reich Citizenship Law. Following Hitler's orders, in 1935 the Nazi-controlled Reichstag (parliament) adopted these laws, known as the Nuremberg Laws. They identified the Jews, as those against whom official discrimination could and would be directed, to segregate them from German society and state citizenship.[13] Accompanying regulations also included an elaborate scheme to officially define "Jew." By adding up Jewish ancestors, the laws assessed a person's "degree" of Jewishness. For instance, individuals with two Jewish grandparents were Jews if they professed the Jewish religion or if they were married to a Jew; if neither condition was met they were considered of "mixed Jewish blood."[14] Among other things, the legislation banned marriage and extramarital relations between Germans and Jews and forbade Jews to hoist the German flag and to display the colors of the Reich.[15]

The Nuremberg Laws served as the prototype for the racial persecution of Sinti, Roma, and others defined as "non-Aryans." By 1939, the Nazis targeted social and political groups through more than 400 discriminatory laws, decrees, regulations, and amendments.[16] Promulgated by executive decisions, these measures tended to be couched in vaguely worded measures of crime prevention or public health. Invariably they were punitive, restrictive, or confiscatory in nature and unmistakably designed to segregate "asocial" elements from the ethnic German community.[17] Once the Nazi regime had defined its enemies, they could be easily identified and their assets targeted for confiscation.

Jewish business proprietors were vulnerable to Nazi extortions and Jewish-owned businesses were subjected to "Aryanization"—that is the process of transferring ownership to non-Jewish hands. After 1933, many pressures drove Jewish owners to sell their businesses—German boycotts, refusals by Germans to pay business debts to Jews, official harassment, the denial of credit by banks, threats issued to business owners when taken into what the police called "protective custody" and imprisoned, and the business owners' desire to raise the necessary cash to emigrate.[18] By 1935, as many as a quarter of Jewish businesses, particularly in rural areas and small towns, might already have closed or been sold.[19] While details of many of these transactions are no longer available, it is clear that Aryanization first struck at Jewish shopkeepers, while the larger Jewish enterprises—textile firms, department stores, banks heavily involved in export financing—were among the last to be sold or transformed into limited partnerships or other forms of enterprise.[20] Of an estimated 100,000 Jewish enterprises of all kinds in 1933, only about 40,000 remained by November 1938 when the Nazi government prohibited Jewish ownership of retail businesses.[21]

The Nazi regime promptly and efficiently exported its racial policies and its institutional framework to each territory it absorbed into the Reich. On March 12, 1938, Nazi Germany celebrated its first large acquisition as its army marched into Austria and attached it to the Reich. The *Anschluss* (annexation) absorbed Austria's nearly 200,000 Jews, whose wealth totaled an estimated 2.5 billion Reichsmarks.[22] Up to the outbreak of the war the following year, the Nazis offered exit visas to Austrian Jews but only in exchange for everything they owned. Officials in Austria wasted no time in targeting Jewish wealth for confiscation. Austrian Nazis surpassed the Germans in looting property from Jewish shops and homes, including household goods, libraries, and valuable paintings, and "revealed a degree of vicious anti-Semitism which surprised even the Germans."[23]

On April 26, the official Nazi newspaper *Völkischer Beobachter* declared: "The Jew must go—and his cash stays here!"[24] The newspaper referred to the decree promulgated that day requiring all Jews in the Reich to register all their domestic and foreign property worth more than 5,000 Reichsmarks.[25] Although ostensibly the decree was to ensure the utilization of assets for the Reich, its ultimate purpose was to exclude Jews from the economy.[26] In November 1938, the Nazis assessed the value of all Jewish assets in the Reich, now including Austria, at 8.5 billion Reichsmarks, of which RM 1.4 billion were debts and other liabilities. The assets included business capital, real estate, and financial assets—including pensions, salaries, insurance, bank notes, securities, and other "vulnerable assets . . . readily seizable."[27]

The situation for Jews in Nazi Germany grew worse in the autumn of 1938. On November 7, Herschel Grynszpan, a young Jew distressed by the mistreatment of his parents by the Nazis, assassinated Ernst vom Rath, the Councilor of the Legation at the German Embassy in Paris. To retaliate, Nazi leaders urged their supporters throughout the Reich to take to the streets on November 9 and burn synagogues, break into Jewish apartments, and wreck Jewish-owned shops.[28] During the three days of the pogrom, ninety-one Jews perished, including many suicides.[29] The Nazis also imprisoned over 35,000 Jews in concentration camps.[30] The depredations of *Kristallnacht*, the "Night of Broken Glass" (so-named for the smashed window panes on the streets), marked a new era of official violence against Jews. Jews were ordered to clean up and make repairs and were barred from collecting insurance for the damages.

Although still maintaining the pretensions of *Rechtsstaat*, the vaunted Germanic concept of "a state ruled by law," the ostensibly legal transfer of property and enterprises into non-Jewish hands differed little from expropriation and theft, for example, the "Atonement Tax" imposed in the wake of *Kristallnacht* was the largest single tax or fine on Jews and raised more than 1.1 billion Reichsmarks from the Jewish community in Germany by confiscating payments from insurers that were intended to compensate property owners for their damages.

The Nazi momentum seemed unstoppable. In October 1938, the Reich expanded again, following the agreement at Munich (between Germany, France, Great Britain, and Italy) that forced Czechoslovakia to surrender control of the Sudetenland to Germany. In March 1939, Czechoslovakia ceased to exist when Germany occupied Bohemia and Moravia and established the puppet state of Slovakia. That September Germany attacked Poland, which led to declarations of war by France and Great Britain. In 1940, the Nazi armies went on to invade and defeat Denmark, Norway, Luxembourg, the Netherlands, Belgium, and France; the following year they turned south into Greece and Yugoslavia, creating the puppet state of Croatia in the process. Germany now controlled most of western and central Europe, with its allies—Italy, Bulgaria, Hungary, and Romania— holding much of the rest.

By the summer of 1941, the Reich acquired additional resources and laborers but also more "undesirables." With varying degrees of success, Nazi Germany bullied its allies, the puppet states, and the governing agencies in occupied countries to impose laws to exclude Jews from economic and public life and, eventually, to assist Germany in the deportation of the Jewish population and the seizure of its wealth. Two countries resisted: Denmark, German-occupied but with its prewar government in place, and Finland, a future German ally against the Soviet Union. The others, including allies, wavered between compliance with and resistance to German pressure to deal harshly with their Jewish populations. Although Bulgaria, Hungary, Romania, and Slovakia were "avid expropriators" of Jewish assets, they often fell short of "the German standard" in dealing with Jews.[31]

As soon as they occupied an area, Nazi officials began identifying and confiscating assets, creating what has been called a "plundering bureaucracy" for art and cultural property to supplement the organizations and laws concerned with expropriating financial holdings.[32] For instance, in Poland Nazis stripped the Catholic Church of most of its regalia and treasure. In France, German embassy staff collected Jewish artwork. The occupation authorities in the Netherlands required Jews to turn over their jewels, precious metals, and other valuables.

A host of agencies, some under the leadership of high-level Nazi party members such as Hermann Goering and Joachim von Ribbentrop, arose specifically to confiscate assets. Hitler himself created an organization to collect artwork for his pet project, a grand museum in Linz. The quasi-commercial *Dienststelle Mühlmann* served as a clearinghouse for confiscated artwork. A key instrument of plunder was the special party agency *Einsatzstab Reichsleiter Rosenberg* (ERR). These organizations competed with one another to loot archives, libraries, artwork, and cultural objects from the "enemies" of National Socialism. In their rush to plunder, the Nazis did not limit themselves to cultural items. For instance, between January 1942 and August 1944, the ERR raided 71,619 Jewish dwellings in the western occupied territories, packed up household property worth RM 1.5 billion, and transported it—in 29,436 railroad cars full of containers sometimes marked "Jewish goods"—to the Reich. The special operation also netted RM 11.7 million in currency and securities from Jewish residences.[33]

Devices of Extermination

After September 1939, the brutal persecution of Jews and other "enemies" paralleled Nazi Germany's widening war of aggression against most of the rest of Europe. Although in 1939 the Nazis still encouraged Jewish emigration from Germany, by 1940 they were instead forcibly deporting victims to occupied Poland. Germans took over the property left behind, including the contents of tens of thousands of apartments as well as the dwellings themselves.[34] To maximize the amount of property abandoned in the confusion and available for confiscation, secret Nazi plans called for abruptly transferring Jews into ghettos.

By the end of 1941, the Nazis had established major Jewish ghettos in Warsaw, Cracow, Lodz, Lublin, and Lvov; they would establish hundreds more throughout Eastern Europe.[35] In October 1941, the German Security Police sent 20,000 Jews from Germany, Austria, and Luxembourg and 5,000 Roma and Sinti to Lodz.[36] The process of liquidating the ghettos began in the spring of 1942.

The German invasion of the Soviet Union on June 22, 1941, marked yet another phase of the victimization policy. Agencies such as the *Sonderkommando Ribbentrop* followed the German troops and plundered art, cultural objects, and books.[37] More sinister were mobile units—*Einsatzgruppen*—that also accompanied German troops and killed Jews and Communists on the eastern front.[38] According to a directive of June 3, 1941, from German Army Headquarters entitled "Guidelines for the Conduct of Troops in Russia," the struggle demanded "ruthless and energetic measures against Bolshevik agitators, guerrillas, saboteurs, [and] Jews."[39] In practice, "ruthless" measures resulted in the death of large numbers of Soviet prisoners of war and civilians. From 1941 to 1943, the Order Police (*Ordnungspolizei*) together with the Security Police (*Sicherheitspolizei*) deported Poles from annexed territories and shot hundreds of thousands of Jews and partisans in the Soviet Union and Poland. Some police units stripped Polish Jews of their valuables before deporting them from Polish ghettos to newly established camps at Treblinka and Majdanek.[40]

On January 20, 1942, Nazi leaders met in a villa in the Berlin suburb of Wannsee to coordinate a "Final Solution of the Jewish Question." During discussions they expressed pride in the ongoing expulsion of Jews from German life and decided on more deportations to the east. But they also planned to force able-bodied Jews to build roads, "in the course of which doubtless many will be eliminated by natural causes." Those that survived, who would "undoubtedly consist of the most resistant portion," would have to be "treated accordingly" since they "would, if released, act as a seed of a new Jewish revival."[41]

"Treated accordingly" meant execution by firing squad or death by gassing, the latter a technique adapted from the Nazi's so-called euthanasia program. In November 1941, the Nazi regime began building the first extermination centers at Chelmno and Belzec. Belzec opened in March 1942, soon to be followed by Sobibor, Treblinka, Majdanek, and Auschwitz.[42] By this time, emigration was no longer possible for Jews in German-occupied Europe or Jews in Germany, and deportations to the "east"—a euphemism for the killing centers—intensified.[43] Before the death camps ceased operations, an estimated 2.7 to 2.9 million people died at these six locations.[44]

The deportees carried with them a strictly limited number of possessions, usually in one small suitcase per person. The Nazi officers in charge of the concentration and death camps—members of the SS (*Schutzstaffel*), Heinrich Himmler's elite police and guard organization—carefully collected every small item. Between April 1942 and December 1943, for example, the Reich collected assets with a total value of 178.7 million Reichsmarks from victims of the camps in the Lublin area. The majority of the valuables consisted of German, Polish, and foreign currency and coins; the loot also included precious metals, jewelry, household items, and fabric. At Auschwitz confiscated valuables included the gold fillings that the Nazis had extracted from the mouths of their victims.[46]

Between August 26, 1942, and January 27, 1945, the SS made 78 deliveries to the Reichsbank in Berlin of property it had confiscated from victims of Auschwitz and Lublin, with a total value estimated between 36 million and 50 million Reichsmarks. The bank acted as trustee for some of the loot and disposed of the rest, depositing the proceeds in an account in the name of the Ministry of Finance, to help fund Germany's war effort. The Reichsbank purchased outright the foreign bank notes, gold, and securities; it enlisted the services of the Prussian State Mint and the firm of Degussa to smelt jewelry, broken gold, and dental gold; and it sold jewelry and other items to the Berlin Pawnbroker Office. The Reichsbank disposed of 43 shipments of SS loot for an estimated 24 million Reichsmarks. After the Allies bombed the bank building in February 1945, bank officials stashed the contents of the vaults in mineshafts near Merkers in western Thuringia.[47]

Having confiscated items from prisoners, camp officials promised those strong enough to work a "reprieve" from death. An April 30, 1942 directive instructed camp officials to exploit their prisoners as slave labor for the Reich without regard to health and life, essentially a process of "extermination through work."[48] In other words, those who were spared from gassing were to be worked to death.

United States Engagement

Overcoming Isolationism

The horrors perpetrated by Nazi Germany during the 1930s drew little attention or calls for action in the United States. Domestic problems—in particular unemployment and the sagging economy of the Great Depression—loomed far larger in the early 1930s than international concerns. Many felt that it was risky and unnecessary to become embroiled abroad when the nation's strength was so sapped. In 1932, when unemployment stood at 13.7 million in the United States, the isolationist Senator William E. Borah wrote that Americans should "look after our own interests and devote ourselves to our own people."[49] This political isolationism grew out of a strong sense of nativistic nationalism, an attitude of "America for Americans." The attitude overlapped with and only thinly disguised anti-immigrant and anti-Semitic sentiments prevalent in broad strains of American society, including some members of Congress and the State Department who could tie up any political initiatives to aid Jewish refugees before and during the war.[50] Between 1938 and 1941, one-third to one-half of Americans questioned in public opinion polls believed that Jews had "too much power in the United States," especially in "business and commerce" and in "finance."[51] Furthermore, popular distrust of banks, big business, and munitions manufacturers, all of which were perceived as profiting from continuing foreign trade (if not actively promoting war), supported inward-looking attitudes.[52]

President Franklin D. Roosevelt reflected national sentiment in August 1936, when he declared that, "we shun political commitments which might entangle us in foreign wars."[53] Until 1938, Roosevelt's efforts focused on ways to undermine aggressor nations by encouraging disarmament and by restricting trade, as well as by suggesting blockades or other ways of controlling the seas. His efforts were stymied by the Congressional passage of the Neutrality Acts (1935–37) that mandated arms embargoes and prohibited loans to all belligerents, making it impossible to favor those considered allies. It remained possible to supply food, raw materials, and manufactured goods as long as a country paid for them in cash and carried them away on foreign ships. While the United States remained officially neutral until 1941, this allowance permitted a transatlantic trade with Great Britain to flourish.[54]

In 1936, President Roosevelt said, "I can at least make certain that no act of the United States helps to produce or to promote war," implying that provocative acts by other nations were a different matter.[55] During his reelection bid in 1940, still under pressure from the political isolationists, Roosevelt declared that American "boys are not going to be sent into any foreign war." On other occasions, however, he added a key qualifier, "except in case of attack."[56]

Even before the election, he and his advisors began planning to extend aid to Great Britain. With Nazi Germany in control of the entire continental coastline from southern France to the north of Norway and threatening Great Britain, Roosevelt considered such support in America's self interest. "If my neighbor's house catches fire," Roosevelt said, "and I know the fire will spread to my house . . . and I don't pass my garden hose over the fence to my neighbor, I am a fool." With that analogy, Roosevelt gained public approval of his Lend-Lease policy.[57]

The passage of the Lend-Lease bill in March 1941 was a turning point in the country's greater involvement, permitting the United States to lend or lease to Great Britain—the only Western European power left to oppose Nazi domination—the weapons, munitions, food, or other supplies needed to fight Hitler without requiring payment in return. The measure, Roosevelt said, was "key to the security of the Western Hemisphere" and to the security of the United States.[58] The Japanese attack on Pearl Harbor on December 7, 1941, finally ended American political and military isolation. Three days after declaring war on Japan, the United States also found itself at war with Japan's allies, Germany and Italy, known collectively as the Axis Powers.[59] The United States' entry into the European conflict after Hitler's declaration of war on the United States on December 11 resulted in the formal alliance with Great Britain and the Soviet Union that eventually crushed Nazi Germany.

The Grand Alliance

Roosevelt chose to give the war in Europe strategic primacy, but he still had to weigh that priority against the demands of the war in the Pacific, in which the Soviet Union was reluctant to get involved. During World War II the western powers—the United States and Great Britain—and the Soviet Union worried that their Grand Alliance to defeat Nazi Germany might split, that Hitler might succeed in reaching a separate agreement with one or the other. In such a scenario, the Germans could have marshaled their forces on one front and possibly reversed the tide of the war. The success of the Big Three in maintaining the coalition—in doubt until the last months of the war—ensured the joint victory that gave U.S. forces and agencies the opportunity to recover and later dispose of victims' assets in the territories that they occupied.

Beginning in 1942, the Soviets pressed the western Allies for a second front against the Germans in Europe. The Soviet Union's leaders dismissed Allied operations in the Mediterranean Theater as providing little relief in the east. In June 1944, the western Allies invaded Normandy, and officials both in the United States and in Great Britain began considering how the map of postwar Europe (and the world, for that matter) might look, and several had substantial concerns about Soviet designs in the east. In 1944 the State Department's leading expert on the Soviet Union, George Kennan, believed it time for a "full-fledged and realistic political showdown with the Soviet leaders" to discuss their territorial intentions.[60] In May 1945, the European war came to an end, with Germany invaded from the east by the Soviet Red Army and from the west by the combined forces of the United States and Great Britain, aided by Free French Forces.

The final movement of western forces through Germany and into Austria and Czechoslovakia brought American soldiers into positions to discover and impound caches of enormous wealth that the Nazis had looted from victims all over Europe. The endurance of the Grand Alliance (or "Strange Alliance," as it has also been dubbed),[61] which linked the Soviet Union with the western powers, created the conditions that placed many of these treasures, including assets originally owned by victims of the Holocaust, in American hands. In the months following Germany's defeat, the alliance collapsed, dissolving into a Cold War that further complicated European reconstruction and the restitution of Nazi loot to the original owners or their heirs.

The case of Hungary demonstrates these complications. In the first flush of victory, the U.S. government declared as "war booty" goods that the Hungarian or the German government transported to the Reich to evade capture by Soviet forces. In the list were items such as the gold reserves of the Hungarian National Bank, rolling stock, medical supplies of the retreating Hungarian army, and several hundred pedigreed horses. Noting the collapsed economy and the fragility of an emerging democracy, U.S. diplomats and military officers assigned to Hungary began recommending soon after their arrival that Washington comply with requests for restitution.

Little by little and item by item, the American government relented on the subject of war booty. On June 15, 1946, the Departments of State and War decided that "restitution improves the political stability of the U.S. relations" with the countries so favored.[62] As the Cold War replaced the Grand Alliance, American policymakers reacted to communist propaganda that claimed that U.S. occupation forces in Germany were holding back Hungarian goods in order to harm Hungary. A little more than a year after the war ended, the U.S. government position shifted to favor of wholesale restitution in the hope that it would contribute to Hungary's economic reconstruction and political stability.

The United States went out of its way to dramatize its change of mind. On August 6, 1946, U.S. Minister Arthur Schoenfeld welcomed the train carrying the bullion of the Hungarian National Bank, worth $32 million, and expressed the hope that it would help stabilize the economy and "rebuild Hungary on democratic lines." Schoenfeld stressed that the gold, shipped to Germany during the last phase of the war, was captured by the U.S. Army as war booty and as such, the

American government was entitled to possession, yet decided to return it to Hungary. Upon receipt of the Hungarian National Bank gold, Finance Minister Gordon delivered an address "which was very complimentary to the United States."[63]

On December 22, 1946, General George Weems, U.S. representative on the ACC for Hungary, was present at Budapest's Eastern Railway Station to welcome the return from Austria of "a heated train of carefully crated fine art," originally from Hungarian museums.[64] Additional assets restituted a few weeks earlier included barges, passenger ships, and the pedigreed horses.

Occupation and Stabilization

Civil Life in Chaos

World War II caused unprecedented destruction and an estimated 60 million deaths worldwide, military and civilian, including approximately six million murdered because they were Jews.[65] The fighting displaced millions of people, and the postwar settlements displaced millions more.[66] With the infrastructure that sustained civilian life paralyzed or destroyed in much of Europe, the U.S. Army faced occupation duties that called for skills dramatically different from those it had applied to winning the war.

In the final months of the war, retreating Germans devastated northern France and Belgium: broken dikes in the Netherlands caused widespread flooding. Milan and Turin—Italy's traditional centers of economic strength—lay prostrate. In central Europe, bomb craters, denuded countryside, and heaps of rubble and debris replaced urban, residential, and agricultural centers.[67]

In May 1945, U.S. troop strength in the European theater stood at just over three million. By July 1945, the general population under direct U.S. Army control had grown to a staggering 22 million—19 million in Germany and nearly three million in Austria. Within its zones in Germany and Austria, the U.S. Army housed and fed five million people—displaced persons in camps, prisoners of war, and U.S. troops.[68] The war had destroyed nearly 20 percent of the housing in Germany; many of the standing structures were uninhabitable. Pressures to locate civilian housing only increased with the arrival of refugees—92,000 in Frankfurt alone between May and August 1945. Over the following year Frankfurt saw an additional 1,000 former soldiers and air raid evacuees return each week.[69]

The threat of famine haunted postwar Europe. The war had eroded the farm economy: machinery, fertilizers, and seed were destroyed and breeding livestock killed. Grain production in France was less than half of its prewar levels. Limited food supplies necessitated mandatory rationing. The commander of the U.S. Military Government in Germany from 1945 to 1949, General Lucius D. Clay, later recalled that "for three years the problem of food was to color every administrative action" taken in Germany.[70] Yet food was not the only necessity in short supply: clothing and shoes were scarce; tools, coal, and domestic amenities were largely unavailable. German civilians burned any flammable substance they could find to survive the harsh winters of 1945–46 and 1946–47.

Most shops remained empty, making it nearly impossible to purchase legitimately such commodities as fabric, soap, light bulbs, or window glass. Nearly one-third of the goods still being produced in Germany at war's end found their way onto the black market. Although trading on the black market was a court-martial offense, soldiers actively bartered or sold army-issue cigarettes, which quickly became the preferred currency on the black market. A first lieutenant selling his entire cigarette allowance stood to pocket six times his annual salary in four months.[71] At times, using the black market became the only means of carrying out military assignments.[72]

Well aware of the dominating influence of food concerns, General Clay realized that the United States "could not hope to develop democracy on a starvation diet."[73] To improve the material situation of the population of the U.S. Zone, military commanders began to distribute seed and fertilizer as early as the summer of 1945. The 12th Army Group released 400,000 German prisoners of war for employment in farm labor. In June 1945 Supreme Headquarters Allied Expeditionary Force (SHAEF) ordered 650,000 tons of wheat for import into the American Zone.[74]

Having won the war, the U.S. Army in Germany changed its objectives drastically in May 1945 to focus on bettering the lives of civilians under its care. It had to marshal personnel and equipment to revitalize national civilian infrastructures in both liberated and occupied countries. Accordingly, army units shifted their mission from combat to control and governance. Troops maintained law and order, disarmed and demilitarized a population they feared might be belligerent, and organized the U.S. military government in Germany and Austria. These concerns all competed with the task of securing and organizing looted assets in preparation for their restitution. The continuing war in the Pacific theater also led the Army to extract troops from Europe to deploy in the war against Japan—still intense in May 1945—or return them to the United States for demobilization.[75]

The task of redeployment demanded a prodigious effort in the first months after the war ended in Europe. It required the reduction of troop strength in Europe by hundreds of thousands, shipping men and material to the Pacific, and "readjusting" the total combat force to allow the soldiers with the longest service in combat and with dependent children to return to the United States. The original War Department plan had called for reducing troops in the European theater from 3.1 million in May 1945 to about 400,000 in 18 months, meaning that more men would be shipped out each month than the maximum number arriving in any one month during the war. The redeployment effort had to be coordinated and accomplished even though the most experienced personnel were simultaneously leaving Europe. By comparison, the replacements arriving in Europe tended to be unskilled and less well-trained.[76]

Redeployment hindered the effort to collect, control, and distribute victims' assets and other valuables. More immediate problems for the military took precedence, the most important of which was the provision of basic necessities—food, lodging, and clothing—to the population under its authority. Material conditions improved only slowly.

U.S. Command Structure

Germany

In 1943, the U.S. Army created a command element known as the Civil Affairs and Military Government Division (G–5). Attached to SHAEF, the G–5 Division was to organize military government in occupied territory, which included establishing property and financial controls and caring for and repatriating uprooted and dispossessed persons. In time G–5 duties included securing, safeguarding, and registering looted assets.[77]

G–5 detachments accompanied the troops liberating Europe and were responsible for setting up rudimentary military governments.[78] Never in one place for long, the G–5 detachments were often the first units to come into contact with Nazi plunder and assume responsibility for victims' assets.

Chaos on the ground had its parallel in the military structure. The United States Group Control Council (Germany) (USGCC) was established as a U.S. organization on August 9, 1944, with a mission almost identical to that of the G–5 Division. The USGCC was subordinate to SHAEF until the combined command terminated in July 1945.[79] Originally, the USGCC included only three divisions responsible for German disarmament and demilitarization, the repatriation of Allied prisoners of war, intelligence collection, as well as economic and political matters. In November 1944, USGCC was reorganized into twelve divisions including a Reparations, Deliveries, and Restitution division. A Monuments, Fine Arts, and Archives Subcommission (MFA&A), formerly a part of SHAEF, became a branch of this new division under USGCC.[80] The mission of MFA&A was to prevent damage to monuments, buildings, statues, and artworks while warfare raged; to identify, inventory, and safeguard cultural artifacts and property coming under U.S. Army control; and to restitute such items in the immediate postwar era. No comparable unit existed for gold or other financial assets.

On July 1, 1945, an independent American command, U.S. Forces, European Theater (USFET), was established and SHAEF was dissolved.[81] Eisenhower headed USFET until November 11, 1945, when General Joseph T. McNarney took command. Lieutenant General Lucius D. Clay, who later assumed a critical role in the restitution process, became SHAEF Deputy Military Governor in March 1945 and continued in that position under USFET. In 1947, Clay became Commanding General of the European Command (EUCOM, the successor to USFET), a position that he held well into 1949. From October 1945 to late 1949, Clay commanded the Office of Military Government for Germany, United States (OMGUS).

The USFET commanding general served as the U.S. representative to the Allied Control Council (ACC). The ACC served as a quadripartite commission, comprised of the commanders-in-chief of the Allied armed forces and a French representative. The commanders of the four occupying armies exercised complete authority within their zone. The ACC had a dual mission to administer Germany as a single economic unit and to establish a subsistence level for industrial production. As serious disagreements over economic policy and the reparations issue arose, however, the ACC became more a negotiating than a governing body.[82] Although it enacted legislation, the ACC was unable to enforce its decisions.

Presidents Roosevelt and Truman agreed that civilian authorities were better suited to governing and should relieve military forces of their political control of conquered territories.[83] War Department officials and commanding generals also disliked the idea of turning soldiers into governors.[84] Secretary of War Henry Stimson and Assistant Secretary John J. McCloy both envisioned a "short military occupation with minimal political responsibilities."[85] In 1943, Army Chief of Staff General George C. Marshall instructed the commander of the Civil Affairs Division—the agency within the War Department charged with coordinating policy for liberated and occupied territories—to focus on getting out of planning for the occupation, emphasizing that "we have never regarded it as part of the proper duty of the military to govern."[86]

On September 29, 1945, the Army redesignated USGCC as OMGUS. At the same time G–5, still part of the USFET general staff, became Office of Military Government for Germany, U.S. Zone (OMGUSZ). MFA&A became a section of the OMGUS Economics Division, Restitution Branch.[87] This restructuring removed the dual system of military government, replaced it with an increasingly centralized operation, and allowed Clay progressively to remove most of the military personnel from the military government.[88] The overlapping military alignments complicated the conduct of military government, including the management of assets seized from the Nazis.

OMGUS served as a de facto government in the U.S. Zone, largely replicating the structure of prewar German administration. Clay made explicit his intention to hold elections in the U.S. Zone by 1946. As early as August 1945, Clay encouraged the Germans to form parties, hold elections, and operate courts. Although OMGUS retained ultimate authority to intervene, for the most part it played a supervisory role and progressively withdrew from the day-to-day operations of government. American civilians replaced military personnel in the administration of German affairs before turning their tasks over to German officials.[89] From 1946, OMGUS existed to advise and observe the new German civil government.[90]

On September 21, 1949, the Office of the U.S. High Commission for Germany (HICOG) replaced OMGUS, signaling the final shift of responsibility from a military to a civilian agency.[91] The first High Commissioner, John J. McCloy, played an important role in the restitution of assets confiscated by the Nazis, encouraging the German government to provide restitution of its own accord (*Wiedergutmachung*) and to assist its Jewish community and the Jewish Restitution Successor Organization (JRSO).[92] In McCloy's opinion, these actions were necessary to bring about the political and "moral integration" of Germany into postwar Europe.[93]

Austria

As had been done in Germany, Austria was occupied by Allied troops and divided into four zones of control governed by the United States, France, the Soviet Union, and the United Kingdom, respectively. Unlike Germany, political and economic authority in Austria quickly returned to the Austrians—a consequence of the 1943 Moscow Declaration. The Allies agreed that Austria, as the first victim of Nazi aggression, should be occupied, but not treated as a defeated enemy.[94] The four powers retained a military presence in Vienna and in their four zones, and, in June 1946, recognized an autonomous Austrian national government. The peace treaty officially ending the occupation was signed in May 1955.

In July 1945, U.S. Forces Austria (USFA) was established and placed under the command of General Mark W. Clark. USFA operated under the authority of the Joint Chiefs of Staff in Washington, as did its USFET counterpart in Germany.[95] USFA established headquarters in Salzburg on August 10, 1945, and although an equivalent to USFET as a command, it depended upon USFET headquarters in Frankfurt for supply and administration. The United States Allied Council for Austria (USACA)—comprised of the commanding officers from each occupied zone—mirrored the United States Group Control Council (USGCC) in Germany.

The U.S. Army and the Discovery of Assets

As Germany's eventual defeat appeared imminent, German officials sought to protect assets from destruction or seizure by enemy armies. Allied ground and air attacks increased steadily, and those in charge of national treasures—including plunder—began hurried attempts to move valuables and hoards of loot to safety, shipping most of them to isolated areas in southern Germany and western Austria. Because American armies advanced into precisely these areas in early 1945, American soldiers uncovered many of these caches of valuables.

Initially, the task of safeguarding, cataloging, and restituting looted assets fell to specialized units of the U.S. Army. G–5 personnel and more specialized detachments assumed responsibility to protect these assets from combat damage and the elements, and also to prevent theft and destruction by American soldiers, DPs, and German civilians.[96] In April 1945, military authorities established the Foreign Exchange Depository (FED) in Frankfurt as a site for holding gold and financial assets. Throughout the spring of 1945, SHAEF established collecting points in Germany and Austria within the U.S. Zones to serve as depots for other assets.

G–5 detachments shouldered awesome military, civil, and humanitarian responsibilities with little time in which to carry them out. Safeguarding assets constituted only one of the many responsibilities facing G–5 personnel, who were also charged with establishing civic order and government. Despite the fact that many Germans with administrative experience had served as civilian officials under Hitler or had been members of the Nazi Party, G–5 personnel had to rely on them to implement the policies of the Military Government. Frequently combat had destroyed the offices that housed local civilian government, and G–5 detachments confiscated or requisitioned public and private buildings to take their place. They also restored utilities and basic services. G–5 detachments repaired or arranged for the repair of damaged roads and railroad tracks to allow for shipments of military equipment, medical supplies, food, and coal to the armies. They prevented the outbreak of deadly diseases, fed and provided shelter for displaced persons of various backgrounds, dismissed and appointed civilian officials according to strict denazification guidelines, organized German police to help keep order, and removed all obstacles in the way of the war effort. Highly mobile and severely understaffed, G–5 had to meet immediate needs in a chaotic environment.[97]

Managing Refugees and Displaced Persons

SHAEF used the term "refugee" to designate civilians temporarily homeless within their national borders and "displaced persons" (DPs) civilians outside their native countries. Then, as now, the word "uprooted" incorporated both categories.[98] U.S. occupation authorities looked upon the masses of the uprooted in Germany and Austria as almost as much of a potential threat to postwar stability as resurgent Nazis. The number of refugees at war's end presented the U.S. Army with one of its most significant challenges.

The uprooted people not only included those who had been imprisoned in camps and worked as forced laborers for the Reich and German industries, but also liberated prisoners of war (POWs), evacuees, members of the Nazi Party, and many others.[99] Ethnic Germans expelled from Eastern Europe and the Baltic region, and those fleeing from the Soviet area of occupation into the western zones, soon added to this mix of victims, non-victims, and perpetrators.

According to General Clay, Allied forces advancing into Germany encountered almost 6.5 million uprooted persons, the vast majority brought into Germany for forced labor.[100] Employing a kind of "hurry-up humanitarianism,"[101] the U.S. military government repatriated more than four million of these DPs and refugees by the end of July 1945, including at least one million Russians and more than 500,000 French.[102] Despite these efforts, nearly 40 percent of the population in Germany in May 1945 qualified as DPs or refugees; by August approximately 25,000 to 30,000 people fleeing Eastern Europe were arriving daily in Berlin, and by the end of the year, nearly one-third of the residents of Bavaria, Lower Saxony, and Schleswig-Holstein were uprooted persons.[103] British estimates placed more than seven million refugees and DPs or the three western zones (16 percent of the population) by October 1946. In the 1950 census, the newly created Federal Republic of Germany counted 9.6 million people (around 20 percent) who had arrived during or after the war, many of them political refugees from the east.[104]

In December 1944, SHAEF had directed military commanders to locate, register, care for, and control non-enemy displaced persons, to move the DPs away from combat areas, to segregate them from enemy or ex-enemy persons, and to provide adequate humanitarian and medical assistance. SHAEF also expected the commanders to cooperate with repatriation officials for the speedy return of DPs to their country of origin.[105] During the last months of the war and the first months of peace, allied military forces assumed primary responsibility for the uprooted.

Despite the chaos surrounding them, Allied forces quickly implemented this policy. Thousands of civilians, speaking a variety of languages, required urgent care in bombed-out villages and cities. They were housed in former army posts, suburban dwellings, castles, and even former Nazi concentration camps where soldiers supplied food and clothing, repaired buildings, restored water and electricity, constructed latrines, and provided medical services.[106]

Although Allied military forces exercised primary responsibility for the DP camps, the United Nations Relief and Rehabilitation Administration (UNRRA) , a civilian entity, aided efforts from 1943 to 1947. Forty-four nations, including the United States, Great Britain, and the Soviet Union, founded UNRRA in 1943 to care for "victims of war in any area under the control of any of the United Nations [the Allies] through the provision of food, fuel, clothing, shelter and other basic necessities, medical and other essential services."[107] By the end of June 1945, 322 UNRRA teams helped Allied forces administer the DP camps.[108] The United Nations Organization established the International Refugee Organization (IRO, preceded by an initial preparatory commission, the PCIRO) to replace UNRRA. In July 1947, the IRO assumed all UNRRA personnel and equipment, and inherited total responsibility for over 700,000 persons displaced by the war and its aftermath.[109] The IRO also superseded the Inter-Governmental Committee on Refugees (IGCR)—a nonmilitary agency that had existed since 1938—in assisting the resettlement of stateless persons and DPs.[110] During its five-year existence, the IRO worked to repatriate and resettle approximately one million displaced persons and refugees.[111] Although by the early 1950s, Europe's DP camps still contained several hundred thousand people, the IRO disbanded in 1952.[112]

The American Jewish Joint Distribution Committee (AJDC)—an organization founded in 1914 to embody "whatever American Jewry was willing to do for its fellow Jews overseas"—held immense significance for many Jewish DPs. Between 1946 and 1950 the AJDC spent $280 million to help DPs. Initially, the AJDC provided medical services and helped locate relatives, but eventually the organization supplied food, clothing, and other goods. The AJDC also borrowed over 21,000 Jewish books from military authorities to be distributed by the UNRRA in DP camps. Beyond the material assistance that the AJDC provided, it established a Branch for the Restitution of Jewish Property in March 1947 to cooperate with OMGUS on the implementation of policies regarding the disposition of victims' assets in Germany.[113] These several organizations—UNRRA, IGCR, IRO, and AJDC—all dealt with victims and, in some instances, with victims' assets.

The U.S. Army identified DPs by nationality,[114] grouping Jews and other victims with their fellow nationals. German Jewish refugees and others displaced from countries allied with Germany during the war—Austria, Bulgaria, Hungary, Italy, and Romania—fell under the designation of "enemy nationals." Jews were often denied the status of United Nations displaced persons, which entailed greater privileges. Allied policy further disadvantaged Jews by not recognizing religion as a factor in determining the level of care needed by the uprooted.[115] As a result, Jewish DPs, including former camp inmates, were often placed in difficult situations, forced to live in camps with refugees from the Baltic states, Poland and elsewhere. Many of the other DPs had espoused anti-Semitic views and, in some cases, had even collaborated with the Nazis.[116]

Between May and November 1945, the U.S. Army repatriated more than 2.3 million displaced persons from the areas that it controlled, leaving about 475,000 still in its zone.[117] In January 1946, the U.S. Zone officially contained 36,000 Jewish DPs; by October the number had climbed to 141,000, the increase attributed to an influx of refugees called "infiltrees" from Soviet-occupied Europe.[118] As late as May 1948, more than 124,000 Jews sought refuge in the U.S. Zone.[119]

The U.S. Military Government's initial failure to acknowledge the unique situation of Jewish survivors meant that military personnel responsible for caring for the displaced population were often unapprised of their special needs and problems. Anti-Semitism in the armed forces sometimes manifested itself in hostility toward and mistreatment of Jewish DPs.[120] Reports of deplorable conditions for Jews and other concentration camp survivors in the DP camps motivated President Harry Truman to ask Earl G. Harrison, Dean of the University of Pennsylvania Law School and former Commissioner on Immigration and Naturalization under President Roosevelt, to visit DP centers and to file a report. After an intensive inspection of several camps during the summer of 1945, Harrison informed the President in early August that, indeed, surviving Nazi persecutees suffered under U.S. supervision, and remained confined to areas surrounded by barbed wire and armed guards, often in former concentration camps. In summary, Harrison reported, "As matters now stand, we appear to be treating the Jews as the Nazis treated them except that we do not exterminate them."[121] As a consequence of the Harrison report, the U.S. military provided separate DP camps and increased rations for Jews, and the War Department appointed an advisor to the military governor on Jewish affairs, a position that endured to the end of 1949.[122]

Jewish repatriates also confronted anti-Semitic attitudes and policies in their native lands. In August and September 1945, the *New York Times* reported that initial efforts undertaken by Jews to recover looted possessions from local government officials in Slovakia and Austria, and also in Germany, remained fruitless.[123] Worse yet, Jews sometimes became the targets of overt discrimination and physical assaults. On December 10, 1945, the *New York Times* described how in Poland "Jews are receiving threatening letters warning them to get out."[124] In July 1946, 42 Jews were killed in Kielce, spurring Jewish migration from Poland shortly afterwards.[125] Even with the end of the Nazi regime, Jewish refugees, DPs, and repatriates continued to suffer from discrimination and violence.

Policy Versus Implementation

The measures U.S. occupying forces took to establish and maintain control of Germany in 1945 stemmed from a wide array of individual and institutional perspectives. President Roosevelt, President Truman, the State Department, War Department, and Treasury Department all held conflicting views on how best to administer defeated Germany, leading one scholar to interpret the actions of those years as "improvising stability and change."[126]

In the summer of 1944, the White House had yet to formulate specific policy guidelines on postwar Germany. In their absence, SHAEF developed its own set of directives as American troops prepared to invade and occupy Germany. The resulting "Handbook for MG [Military Government] in Germany" provided orders for denazification and demilitarization, but failed to satisfy those American officials who sought thorough punishment of Germany.[127] Chief among those criticizing the "Handbook" was Treasury Secretary Henry Morgenthau who advocated a much harsher proposal that envisioned the deindustrialization and "pastoralization" of Germany. The "Morgenthau Plan," as the proposal came to be known, briefly won Roosevelt's approval in autumn 1944. "We have to be tough with Germany," Roosevelt said, but other Cabinet officials, such as Secretary of War Henry Stimson and Secretary of State Cordell Hull, found the Morgenthau Plan vindictive and brutal, and Stimson argued to Roosevelt that it was a "crime against civilization itself."[128] Roosevelt moved away from the Morgenthau Plan, but the spirit of being "tough with Germany" nevertheless influenced a later short-term directive concerning occupation issued in 1945 by the Joint Chiefs of Staff (JCS).

JCS 1067, as the directive was known, instructed occupiers to control the German economy "only to the extent necessary to meet the needs of the occupation forces or to produce the goods which would prevent disease and unrest, which might endanger the occupying forces."[129] Occupation officials were to demilitarize Germany, dissolve the Nazi Party, monitor the press and the educational system, decentralize the German government, assist with reparations, and try war criminals. In the retrospective opinion of General Clay, Commander of the Military Government in Germany (OMGUS) between 1945 and 1949, JCS 1067 "specifically prohibited us from taking any steps to rehabilitate or maintain the German economy except to maximize agricultural production."[130] However, SHAEF could not officially implement JCS 1067 without British agreement, and that was not immediately forthcoming.[131] Moreover, eight different versions of this directive appeared between the early draft in September 1944 and April 1945 when it was issued to Eisenhower.[132] At the Potsdam Conference in the early summer of 1945, the Allies modified the stringent economic conditions set forth in it. The Americans, and General Clay in particular, began to worry about how much material they would need to furnish, at the expense of the American taxpayer, to prevent widespread starvation and the total collapse of the German economy.

At both the Yalta and Potsdam conferences the three Allies—the United States, Great Britain, and the Soviet Union—agreed that Germany should retain enough of its productive capacity to rebuild a viable peacetime economy and to pay reparations. To address the latter, the Allies began an inventory of industrial plants with an eye not only to their closure if they had produced war material, but also to their use as partial reparations payments once the plants had been dismantled and moved out of Germany. Initially the United States and Great Britain considered expropriating 1,500 to 2,000 industrial plants, but by the end of 1947, only 682 plants (mostly in the British Zone) were still under consideration as "surplus and available for reparations." Only 40 factories had been dismantled and removed by that time from either the American or British zones. France pursued its own policy. Cold War tensions with the Soviets were rising as well, partly because Soviet leaders were unwilling to treat Germany as a single economic unit despite the Allied agreement at Potsdam to do so, and partly over the the Soviet actions regarding reparations. The State Department realized that by 1948 the Soviets had removed and shipped to the east an unknown amount of capital equipment from their zone, lowering Germany's productive capacity.[134]

As early as 1946, it became evident that the postwar British and American goal of rebuilding the German economy was at odds with shutting down and removing industrial facilities and at odds with Soviet and French policies regarding the economic treatment of Germany. General Clay's cessation of dismantling industrial plants as part of reparations' transfers to other zones illustrates this clearly.[135] U.S. Secretary of State James Byrnes emphasized the position of the United States at a July 1946 meeting of the Council of Foreign Ministers. Either the four powers had to treat Germany as an economic whole or the United States would have to merge its zone with that of any other power to accomplish rationalization and economies of operation. Only the British accepted, and on January 1, 1947, the British and American zones merged to form the new administrative unit known as Bizonia.

The creation of Bizonia underscored crystallization of a new approach by the United States toward Germany. Secretary Byrnes outlined the new thinking in a speech in Stuttgart in September 1946, in which he asserted that the policy of distrust and nonfraternization of the early months of the occupation had now given way to an attitude of friendship. He urged that levels of German production be raised immediately if the four powers intended to continue to take reparations from current German production. Finally, he suggested that the governing powers in Germany had to introduce an all-German currency reform as an essential step to the restructuring of the German economy.[136] A year later, in August 1947, the State and War Departments issued a joint communiqué reemphasizing the policy: "The old plan provided for very sharp cuts in production capacities... from which the bulk of reparations were to be obtained. It is impossible to provide a self-sustaining economy in the bizonal [U.S. and British] area without materially increasing the levels in these industries."[137]

About the same time, the British and Americans began discussions with French representatives for the creation of a trizonal government.[138] By the spring of 1948, these discussions had merged with discussions leading to currency reform for Germany in June 1948 and to the re-establishment of an autonomous

German government, albeit with certain powers still reserved for the three occupying powers.[139]

The increasing political difficulties of cooperating with the Soviets in the various four-power decision-making bodies governing Germany concealed a fundamental dilemma between the desire to limit Germany's capacity to produce industrial goods—production capacity that might be converted to wartime uses—and the desire to rebuild the German economy within Europe, a goal that grew out of memories of the tangled politics, economics, and psychology that surrounded the failed economic reconstruction of Europe after World War I. By 1948, the western powers had resolved the dilemma in favor of rebuilding Germany. Ultimately, the countercurrents that characterized American policy towards Germany between 1944 and 1947 accorded U.S. military leaders great flexibility to interpret, improvise, and implement according to their own perceptions of the day-to-day situation that they faced.

Control of Victims' Assets In The United States

The invasion and occupation of Germany and Austria did not represent the first American opportunity to take control of Nazi assets. Even before the United States entered the war in Europe, it had sought to deny certain assets potentially available to support the Axis war effort.

The United States Treasury Department and Frozen Assets

Beginning on April 10, 1940, the United States took steps to protect assets in the United States belonging to friendly aliens and to prevent their use by the Axis powers. The blocking or "freezing" of property meant that its title remained with the private owner, but U.S. authorities controlled transfers and other dealings affecting the property. By June 1941, the U.S. government had "frozen" the assets of twelve invaded European countries and their citizens. On March 11, 1942, President Roosevelt established the Office of Alien Property Custodian, which was empowered to "direct, manage, supervise, control or vest alien property." When a property was "vested" the United States assumed its title. The Custodian also had authority to seize and profit from business enterprises, patents, trademarks, and copyrights.[140]

The Bureau of Customs, Import Prohibitions, and the Post Office

The U.S. Bureau of Customs and the Post Office also acted as mechanisms to detect foreign and enemy assets nationwide. In cooperation with the Treasury Department they monitored the import and export of securities, currency, and foreign exchange and delivered seized securities and currency to the Federal Reserve Bank.[141] The Customs Bureau also cooperated with Foreign Funds Control (FFC) and the State Department to oversee the importation of gold, diamonds, postage stamps, and artwork.[142] The FBI also played a role. In one case in September 1945, the State Department asked the FBI to determine whether artworks that Customs had recently seized in New York City had been looted.[143]

In compliance with the Tariff Act of 1930, the U.S. Bureau of Customs regulated the importation of all works of art into the United States. Although artwork could be brought in duty free, the importer had to declare the objects and their true value at the time of entry or risk their forfeiture. During the war Customs tightened its controls. A Treasury Department decision on July 8, 1944, gave Customs the power to detain any artworks entering the United States and required importers to obtain an import license and file a report on the nature of the work and the circumstances of its acquisition.

Customs regulations authorized the U.S. Post Office to investigate all foreign mail parcels. U.S. personnel stationed abroad could send (with a required declaration) gift parcels valued at no more than $50. The Post Office could inspect any parcel lacking a proper declaration or appearing to surpass the value limit.[144] The Bureau of Customs and the Post Office had mechanisms in place to intercept illegal transfers, including those parcels sent by U.S. personnel overseas.

The Cold War and The Jewish State

The beginnings of the Cold War and the formation of a Jewish state in Palestine affected how the United States handled victims' assets. Between 1945 and 1948, the Grand Alliance between the United States and the Soviet Union fell apart. On March 5, 1946, former British Prime Minister Winston Churchill spoke of an "iron curtain" descending across Europe from the Baltic to the Adriatic. The American journalist Walter Lippmann later characterized this developing struggle between the United States and the Soviet Union as a "Cold War."

The United States only gradually assumed a leadership role in this evolving conflict. Even though the American public hoped for a prompt demobilization of its armed forces and a return to a normal, peacetime existence, the U.S. government remained engaged in European and regional affairs. In March 1947, to counter Soviet threats and communist insurrections in Europe, President Truman sent a message to Congress pledging U.S. support "for free peoples who are resisting attempted subjugation by armed minorities or outside pressures."[145] Truman expressed his willingness to extend assistance to similarly threatened nations marking a change of course from the earlier isolationist stance taken by the United States.

The European Recovery Program (ERP), outlined by Secretary of State George C. Marshall in 1947, marked another step in the American path to world leadership. The "Marshall Plan" offered American economic aid to all European countries willing to cooperate in the economic reconstruction of Europe as a whole. The proposal represented an invitation to Western European nations to create a new alignment based on shared economic principles.

In 1947 and 1948, Communist parties, with Soviet support, seized government control in Poland, Hungary, and Czechoslovakia. In March 1948, President Truman urged Congress to reinstate peacetime conscription for military service, affirming American participation with Western European states in a common military defense. These steps confirmed a new direction in American foreign policy—resistance to and "containment" of Soviet power in Europe and around the globe.

These newly formed ties between the United States and Western Europe were tested in June 1948 in Berlin. Although the city remained an island in the Soviet occupation zone, each of the four powers occupied a sector of the city and established military government there. As postwar tensions increased among the occupying powers over Germany's future the Soviet Union seized the opportunity to test western resolve by blocking land access to Berlin from the three western zones of Germany. Short of confronting the Red Army, the West could only gain access to Berlin through established air "corridors." Nonstop flights to Berlin from western occupation zones delivered foodstuffs and other necessities, keeping the people of Berlin alive. The "Berlin Airlift" of 1948 showed the Western determination to prevail, and led the Soviets to eventually rescind their land blockade.

In devising pragmatic solutions to address immediate problems, U.S. officials remained committed to revitalizing Europe and avoiding an armed conflict with the Soviet Union. A deepening mistrust of communism and the Soviet Union enveloped leadership circles in American society, government, and business and prompted policymakers to deny the Soviets any advantage. The Cold War shaped attitudes in the United States, and, at times, interfered with the restoration of looted assets to individuals whose property—if returned to the country of origin—might once again be subject to expropriation.

Before World War II, underdeveloped and strife-torn Palestine was not a magnet for the majority of European Jews fleeing Hitler's Germany. Though British opposition to a Jewish influx further discouraged potential immigrants, Jewish leaders decided by early 1944 that any mass postwar migration would have to be to Palestine, with or without British approval.[146] The war did not change British visa policies, but restrictions on emigration from DP camps to the United States (and to a lesser degree to Canada, Australia, and Brazil) persuaded many uprooted Jews to decide in favor of Palestine.[147]

After the creation of the State of Israel in 1948, U.S. policy to turn over heirless assets to Jewish organizations played a role in building the new state. It facilitated the rapid resettlement of hundreds of thousands of refugees. Between 1947 and 1953, the American Jewish Joint Distribution Committee (AJDC) and the Jewish Agency for Palestine (JA) received over $10 million to resettle 120,000 DPs in Israel.[148] Had these funds not been available, the activities by the AJDC, JA, and other organizations supporting the resettlement of DPs would have been made considerably more difficult, if not impossible.

Summary

As soon as it gained power in 1933, the Nazi Party began to turn into laws and policies the racial ideology Adolf Hitler proposed in *Mein Kampf*. Implementing "the natural law" based on the "supremacy" of the Aryan master race and the "inferiority" of other races that must be wiped out, the Reich's policies on Jews escalated from forced emigration to "Aryanization" of business enterprises to the "Final Solution" of genocide. But whether uprooting or exterminating entire categories of people, Nazi officials also took great care in first stripping them of whatever they owned.

By 1945, few Americans questioned why the United States had been at war with Nazi Germany. The extent of the Nazis' unimaginable atrocities became known when soldiers and civilians touring the camps reported back home. In the 1930s, however, Americans had been preoccupied with domestic issues, most notably the economic hardships of the Great Depression. Throughout the 1930s Americans resisted political involvement in European affairs. Isolationist policies prevailed until a concurrence of foreign events and the perseverance of an astute American president moved the government to assist European nations as they fell prey to German military might. Despite its awareness of the Nazi campaign of terror on the European continent, it was a surprise attack by Japan that moved the United States from neutrality to war.

In the aftermath of the war, U.S. officials took steps to bring order to a devastated European society and economy. In Germany and Austria, occupying forces repaired roads, railways, waterways, housing, and other infrastructure while providing care for the millions of refugees and victims of Nazism. The United States came into possession of victims' assets in a variety of ways, partly through Treasury Department action to freeze foreign assets, in part through discovery and seizure by invading troops. The question of how to return valuables to their rightful owners had to vie for the attention of occupation officials and policy planners in Washington with the problems of providing food, shelter, medicine, and other necessities to Nazi victims and other displaced persons in the former Reich.

During the war, officials in Washington addressed the subject of property looted by the Nazis as one among the many problems spawned by the conflict. After achieving victory in Europe, they confronted the complicated and challenging tasks of occupation and restitution. The President and the Departments of War, State, and Treasury struggled to formulate the policies guiding military and civilian government of Germany—including a policy for the restitution of victims' assets—without the advantage of either precedents in international law or even clear understanding of the situation of victims.

Lacking clear guidelines from Washington, the U.S. Army issued its own directives to manage the occupation in Germany and Austria. The Army took the lead to create order out of chaos, to care for those persecuted by the Nazis, and to return stolen property. Only later did other governmental and international agencies follow the Army's lead as custodians of victims' assets in Europe.

The Nazi campaign against Jews and other "non-Aryans" began with discriminatory legislation in 1933 and ended with the regime's collapse in 1945. The extensive material damage and enormous human suffering caused by the war made the occupation, the reconstruction of civil society, and the re-creation of a viable international order, a seemingly impossible program for the victors.

Endnotes for Chapter II

[1] Robert H. Abzug, *Inside the Vicious Heart: Americans and the Liberation of Nazi Concentration Camps* (New York: Oxford Univ. Press, 1985), 27, 30; Gerhard L. Weinberg, *A World At Arms: A Global History of World War II* (New York: Cambridge Univ. Press, 1994), 834.

[2] Michael Berenbaum, ed., *Witness to the Holocaust* (New York: Harper Collins, 1997), 308-10.

[3] Dwight D. Eisenhower, *Crusade in Europe* (Garden City, NY: Doubleday, 1948), 408–9.

[4] Leon Baradet, *Political Ideologies*, 5th ed. (Englewood Cliffs, NJ: Prentice Hall, 1994), 246.

[5] Lucy S. Dawidowicz, *The War Against the Jews, 1933–1945* (New York: Holt, Rinehart & Winston, 1975), 90–91; Alan Bullock, *Hitler: A Study in Tyranny* (New York: Harper, 1964), 399.

[6] See Michael Berenbaum, ed., *A Mosaic of Victims: Non-Jews Persecuted and Murdered by the Nazis* (New York: New York Univ. Press, 1990); Guenter Lewy, *The Nazi Persecution of the Gypsies* (New York: Oxford Univ. Press, 2000).

[7] Bullock, *Hitler*, 365, 407.

[8] Avraham Barkai, *From Boycott to Annihilation: The Economic Struggle of German Jews, 1933–1943*, trans. William Templer (Hanover, N.H.: Univ. Press of New England, 1989), 56–57; Richard Breitman, *Official Secrets: What the Nazis Planned, What the British and Americans Knew* (New York: Hill & Wang, 1998), 20–21.

[9] Uwe Adam, *Judenpolitik im Dritten Reich* (Düsseldorf: Droste Verlag, 1972), 310; Raul Hilberg, *The Destruction of the European Jews* (New York: Holmes & Meier, 1985), 27–28; Raul Hilberg, *Perpetrators, Victims, Bystanders: The Jewish Catastrophe 1933–1945* (New York: Harper Collins, 1992), 12–13.

[10] Helen Junz, "How the Economics of the Holocaust Add" (Appendix S), in Report of the Independent Committee of Eminent Persons (Volcker Commission, 1999), A–171. See Hilberg, *Destruction of the European Jews*, Ch. 2 & Ch. 3.

[11] Edwin Black, *The Transfer Agreement: The Untold Story of the Secret Agreement Between the Third Reich and Jewish Palestine* (New York: Macmillan Publishing Co., 1984), 231–32, 249, 256–59, 268, 379. Another 40,000 Jews emigrated through indirect aspects of the transfer agreement.

[12] Christopher Kopper, *Zwischen Marktwirtschaft und Dirigismus. Bankenpolitik im "Dritten Reich" 1933–1939* (Bonn: Bouvier Verlag, 1995), 266–67; Junz, "Economics of the Holocaust," A–201; Barkai, *From Boycott to Annihilation*, 100.

[13] Andreas Rethmeier, *"Nürnberger Rassegesetze" und Entrechtung der Juden im Zivilrecht* (Frankfurt am Main: Peter Lang Verlag, 1995), 88–100.

[14] For a description of Nazi racial decrees and attempts to define who was Jewish, see Hilberg, *Destruction of the European Jews*, 27–37.

[15] *Reichsbürgergesetz vom 15. September 1935; Gesetz zum Schutze des deutschen Blutes und der deutschen Ehre vom 15. September 1935; Gesetz zum Schutze der Erbgesundheit des deutschen Volkes vom 18. Oktober 1935* (Munich: C. H. Beck'sche Verlagsbuchhandlung, 1936), 31–37; Dawidowicz, *War Against the Jews*, 67.

[16] Arnold Paucker et al., *Die Juden im nationalsozialistischen Deutschland* (Tübingen: J. C. B. Mohr, 1986), 105.

[17] Michael Burleigh & Wolfgang Wippermann, *The Racial State: Germany, 1933–1945* (New York: Cambridge Univ. Press, 1991), 49; Guenter Lewy, "The Travail of the Gypsies" *The National Interest* (Fall 1999): 82.

[18] Karl Schleunes, *The Twisted Road to Auschwitz. Nazi Policy Toward German Jews 1933–1939* (Urbana: Univ. of Illinois Press, 1990), 143.

[19] Barkai, *From Boycott to Annihilation*, 70.

[20] Ibid., 72–77.

[21] Paucker et al., *Die Juden im nationalsozialistischen Deutschland, 156;* Barkai, *From Boycott to Annihilation*, 111.

[22] George Weis, "Report on Jewish Heirless Assets in Austria," Dec. 4, 1952, 9–11, NACP, RG 59, Recs. of the Officer in Charge of Italian & Austrian Affairs, Lot File 58D223, Entry 1284, Box 8, File 586 [319306–317; 319342–343]. In 1939 the agency established to record Jewish wealth in Austria reported a total of RM 2.04 billion. The Weis report adjusts this figure to RM 2.5 billion for several reasons, including probable undervaluation of assets reported by Jews and the Austrian agency's use of only about 48,000 of an estimated 62,000 reports eventually filed. The Reichsmark figure equates to either $750 million, converted from marks to Austrian schillings to dollars, or just over $1 billion, converted from marks to dollars ($8.8 billion or $11.8 billion in 1999 values).

[23] Lynn Nicholas, *The Rape of Europa. The Fate of Europe's Treasures in the Third Reich and the Second World War* (New York: Alfred A. Knopf, 1994), 38–44.

[24] Cited in Robert Wistrich, *Austrians and Jews in the 20th Century* (New York: St. Martin's Press, 1992), 208.

[25] George Weis, "Report on Jewish Heirless Assets in Austria," Dec. 4, 1952, 4, 9–10, NACP, RG 59, Recs. of the Officer in Charge of Italian & Austrian Affairs, Lot File 58D223, Entry 1284, Box 8, File 586 [319310–316 of 319306–317].

[26] Barkai, *From Boycott to Annihilation*, 118.

[27] Junz, "Economics of the Holocaust," A–166; Barkai, *From Boycott to Annihilation*, 113.

[28] Anthony Read & David Fisher, *Kristallnacht: The Nazi Night of Terror* (New York: Random House, 1989).

[29] *Encylopaedia Judaica*, vol. 12 (Jerusalem: Keter Publishing House, 1972), 1279.

[30] Martin Gilbert, *Atlas of the Holocaust* (New York: William Morrow & Co., Inc., 1993), 28.

[31] Adam, *Judenpolitik im Dritten Reich*, 310; Hilberg, *Destruction of the European Jews*, 168–69. See especially Hilberg, *Perpetrators,* 75–86; the quoted phrases are on pages 76–78.

[32] Jonathan Petropoulos, *Art and Politics in the Third Reich* (Chapel Hill: Univ. of North Carolina Press, 1996), 129, 141.

[33] Ibid., 126–50; Nicholas, *Rape of Europa*, 44–49, 64, 98, 137–140. The *Dienststelle* (agency) *Mühlmann* was named after Kajetan Mühlmann, a party functionary and assistant to the Reichskommissar for the Netherlands, Arthur Seyss-Inquart; and the ERR after Alfred Rosenberg, the party's ideologue. See Tuviah Friedmann, *Das Vermögen der ermordeten Juden Europas* (Haifa: Institute of Documentation, 1997); Wolfgang Dressen, *Betrifft: "Aktion 3"— Deutsche verwerten jüdische Nachbarn* (Berlin: Aufbau-Verlag, 1998), 45–61. This particular aspect of the ERR's activities was known as the *Möbel-Aktion*, literally "furniture operation."

[34] Hilberg, *Destruction of the European Jews*, 160–162; Hilberg, *Perpetrators,* 15, 196–97.

[35] Barkai, *From Boycott to Annihilation*, 175; Hilberg, *Destruction of the European Jews*, 74–84.

[36] Breitman, *Official Secrets*, 72; Hannah Arendt, *Eichmann in Jerusalem* (New York: Penguin, 1982), 93–95.

[37] Petropoulos, *Art and Politics*, 145–150. The *Sonderkommando* (special command), as it was informally known, was named after its leader, Foreign Minister Joachim von Ribbentrop.

[38] Hilberg, *Destruction of the European Jews*, 99–103, 125.

[39] Falk Pingel, *Häftlinge unter SS-Herrschaft* (Hamburg: Hoffman und Campe, 1978), 119–22; Dawidowicz, *War Against the Jews*, 123–25; Richard Breitman, *The Architect of Genocide: Himmler and the Final Solution* (Hanover, N.H.: Univ. Press of New England, 1991), 149–50.

[40] Christopher R. Browning, *Ordinary Men: Reserve Police Battalion 101 and the Final Solution in Poland* (New York: HarperCollins, 1992), 9–25, 109, 134.

[41] The quotations from the protocol appear in Dawidowicz, *War Against the Jews*, 106. For the Wannsee Conference see Christopher Browning, *Nazi Policy, Jewish Workers, German Killers* (Cambridge: Cambridge Univ. Press, 2000), 26–57, and Hilberg, *Destruction of the European Jews*, 165–68.

[42] Hilberg, *Destruction of the European Jews*, 228–30; Gudrun Schwartz, *Die national-sozialistischen Lager* (Frankfurt am Main: Campus, 1990), 210–16.

[43] Adam, *Judenpolitik im Dritten Reich*, 310.

[44] Hilberg, *Destruction of the European Jews*, 225–228, 239–240; Schwartz, *Die national-sozialistischen Lager*, 212–16.

[45] Friedmann, *Das Vermögen der ermordeten Juden Europas*, 9–13.

[46] Hilberg, *Destruction of the European Jews*, 249.

[47] Col. Bernard Bernstein, "SS Loot and the Reichsbank," Oct. 30, 1945, Part B–I 1–2, Part B–II 1–4, NACP, RG 260, Office of the Adj. Gen., Gen. Corresp. & Other Recs. "Decimal File," Box 8, File 004.2 [216036–046]; Monthly Rpt., Part III "Further Evidence on Disposition of SS Loot by Reichsbank," May 1945, NACP, RG 260, FED, Central Files 1945–50, Box 423, File 940.304 [220381–386]. U.S. officials in 1945 equated the 23.9 million "gold RM" accruing from the 44 shipments to $9.56 million. See also Memo from Keating, OMGUS, to AGWAR for WDSCA, no date [ca. July 1947], NACP, RG 260, Recs. of the Office of Finance Adv., FED, Box 160, Currencies Rest. [329606–608].

[48] Bernd Klewitz, *Die Arbeitssklaven der Dynamit Nobel* (Schalksmühle: Verlag Engelbrecht, 1986), 432–34.

[49] Thomas Guinsburg, *The Pursuit of Isolationism in the United States Senate from Versailles to Pearl Harbor* (New York: Garland Publishing, 1982), 135.

[50] On nativistic nationalism and its relationship to anti-Semitism see David S. Wyman, *Paper Walls: America and the Refugee Crisis, 1938–1941* (New York: Pantheon Books, 1968, 1985), 10–14, 82–92.

[51] David S. Wyman, *The Abandonment of the Jews: America and the Holocaust, 1941–1945* (New York: Pantheon Books, 1984), x, 14–15. See also Deborah E. Lipstadt, *Beyond Belief: The American Press and the Coming of the Holocaust, 1933–1945* (New York: The Free Press, 1986).

[52] Manfred Jonas, *Isolationism in America 1935–1941* (Ithaca: Cornell Univ. Press, 1966), 26.

[53] *New York Times*, Aug. 15, 1936, reprinted in Paul Holbo, *Isolation and Interventionism, 1932–1941* (Chicago: Rank McNally & Co., 1967), 17. See also H. Schuyler Foster, *Activism Replaces Isolationism: U.S. Public Attitudes 1940–1975* (Washington, D.C.: Foxhall Press, 1983).

[54] Ronald Powaski, *Toward an Entangling Alliance. American Isolationism, Internationalism and Europe, 1901–1950* (New York: Greenwood Press, 1991), 58–88.

[55] *New York Times*, Aug. 15, 1936, reprinted in Holbo, *Isolation and Interventionism*, 17.

[56] Holbo, *Isolation and Interventionism*, 51.

[57] Warren F. Kimball, *The Most Unsordid Act: Lend-Lease 1939–1941* (Baltimore: Johns Hopkins Univ. Press, 1969), 77.

[58] Powaski, *Toward an Entangling Alliance*, 95.

[59] Ibid., 110.

[60] Stephen E. Ambrose, *Rise to Globalism. American Foreign Policy Since 1938*, 8th rev. ed. (New York: Penguin Books, 1997), 27–31.

[61] Ibid., 15.

[62] Cable from Depts. of State, War and Navy to USFET, Frankfurt, OMGUS Berlin, ACC Vienna, and ACC Budapest, Hungary, June 15, 1946, NACP, RG 338, Entry 11017, Box 53 [124725–726].

[63] Cable from OMGUS, Econ. Sec., MTOUSA signed Weems to OMGUS Berlin, Econ. Div., no date, NACP, RG 338, Entry 11017, Box 55 [124727–729].

PLUNDER AND RESTITUTION: The U.S. and Holocaust Victims' Assets **SR–37**

[64] Rpt. U.S. Naval Member, ACC, Budapest Hungary, "Danube Shipping, Restitution of Hungarian Vessels," Dec. 20, 1946, NACP, RG 338, Entry 11017, Box 39 [124730–734].

[65] Weinberg, *World at Arms*, 894–95. Peter Calvocoressi and Guy Wint, *Total War. Causes and Courses of the Second World War* (New York: Penguin Books, 1979), 551–53, estimate the global death toll at 50 million.

[66] Weinberg, *World at Arms*, 894–95. Calvocoressi & Wint, *Total War*, 551–53.

[67] For this and subsequent paragraphs describing Europe in 1945 see Walter Laqueur, *Europe since Hitler: The Rebirth of Europe* (New York: Penguin Books, 1982), 15–20. See also Alfred Grosser, *Germany in Our Time: A Political History of the Postwar Years* (New York: Praeger Publishers, 1971), 35ff.

[68] Population figures for Germany come from Oliver J. Frederiksen, *The American Military Occupation of Germany 1945–1953* (Darmstadt, Ger.: Historical Div., HQ, U.S. Army, Europe, 1953), 12, 50, 119; for Austria from "A History of the United States Allied Commission, Austria," no date [ca. July 1945], para. 100, NACP, RG 260, USACA, Files of the Dir., Entry A/B/C, Box 45 [212935 of 212856–957].

[69] Rebecca Boehling, *A Question of Priorities: Democratic Reform and Economic Recovery in Postwar Germany* (Providence: Berghahn Books, 1996), 80–81, 90, 106.

[70] Lucius D. Clay, *Decision in Germany* (Garden City, NY: Doubleday & Co., Inc., 1950), 263.

[71] A. J. Ryder, *Twentieth-Century Germany: From Bismarck to Brandt* (New York: Columbia Univ. Press, 1973), 467.

[72] Response of Maj. Gen. Robert J. Fleming to letter from Karl C. Dod, Oct. 18, 1973, Office of Hist., HQ, U.S. Army Corps of Engineers, Research Collections, Mil. Files, XI, Box 3, File 3 [122866–875].

[73]Clay, *Decision in Germany*, 266.

[74] Earl F. Ziemke, *The U.S. Army in the Occupation of Germany, 1944–1946* (Washington, D.C., Center of Mil. History, 1975), 274–75.

[75] For an extensive discussion of the army's shift from combat to demobilization and redeployment, see Robert P. Grathwol & Donita M. Moorhus, "Building For Peace: U.S. Army Engineers in Europe, 1945–1991," (Office of Hist., HQ, U.S. Army Corps of Engineers, 1999), 16–33.

[76] Ibid., 17; Ziemke, *The U.S. Army in the Occupation of Germany*, 320, 328–29, 334–36, 422–24.

[77] Ziemke, *The U.S. Army in the Occupation of Germany*, 164.

[78] Klaus-Dietmar Henke, *Die amerikanische Besetzung Deutschlands* (Munich: Oldenbourg, 1996), 240. Frederiksen, *The American Military Occupation of Germany*, 9.

[79] Christoph Weisz, *OMGUS-Handbuch. Die amerikanische Militärregierung in Deutschland, 1945–1949* (Munich: Oldenbourg, 1994), 11.

[80] Ziemke, *The U.S. Army in the Occupation of Germany*, 56. Although the entity responsible for monuments, fine arts, and archives changed names, organization, and reporting responsibility several times during and after the war, for consistency this report often uses "MFA&A" to refer to any of the iterations of this organization.

[81] Frederiksen, *The American Military Occupation of Germany 1945–1953*, 23.

[82] Ziemke, *The U.S. Army in the Occupation of Germany, 1944–1946*, 344.

[83] Ibid., 13; Earl F. Ziemke, "Improvising Stability and Change in Postwar Germany," in Wolfe, *Americans as Proconsuls: United States Military Government in Germany and Japan, 1944–1952*, (Carbondale: Southern Illinois Univ. Press, 1984), 59.

[84] See Harry L. Coles & Albert K. Weinberg, *Civil Affairs: Soldiers Become Governors* (Washington, D.C.: Office of the Chief of Mil. Hist., Dept. of the Army, 1964).

[85] Boehling, *Question of Priorities*, 18.

[86] Cited in Edward N. Peterson, *The American Occupation of Germany: Retreat to Victory* (Detroit: Wayne State Univ. Press, 1977), 33.

[87] *Report of the American Commission For the Protection and Salvage of Artistic and Historic Monuments in War Areas*, (Washington, DC: Government Printing Office, 1946), 123–24.

[88] Ziemke, *U.S. Army in the Occupation of Germany*, 401–02, 432. OMGUSZ and OMGUS merged on April 1, 1946.

[89] John Gimbel, "Governing the American Zone of Germany," in Wolfe, ed., *Americans as Proconsuls*, 94.

[90] Peterson, *The American Occupation of Germany: Retreat to Victory*, 93.

[91] Frederiksen, *The American Military Occupation of Germany*, 149, 198; Boehling, *Question of Priorities*, 46.

[92] Thomas Alan Schwartz, *America's Germany: John J. McCloy and the Federal Republic of Germany* (Cambridge: Harvard Univ. Press, 1991), 177–180.

[93] Ibid.,176.

[94] Kurt Tweraser, "Von der Militärdiktatur 1945 zur milden Bevormundung des 'Bargaining-Systems' der fünziger Jahre" in Alfred Ableitinger, Siegfried Beer, Eduard Staudinger, eds., *Österreich unter alliierter Besatzung 1945–1955* (Vienna: Böhlau Verlag, 1998), 302; also see U.S. State Dept. and Senate Committee on Foreign Relations, *A Decade of American Foreign Policy: Basic Documents, 1941–1949* (Washington, D.C.: Government Printing Office, 1950).

[95] *The First Year of the Occupation, Occupation Forces in Europe Series, 1945–1946*, Vol. 1 (Frankfurt: Office of the Chief Hist. EUCOM, 1947), 87 [122880].

[96] Ziemke, *The U.S. Army in the Occupation of Germany*, 199, 250–251.

[97] Ibid., 402.

[98] "A View of the Jewish Problem from the Pentagon and State Department," transcription of memoirs taped by Herbert A. Fierst, 87–98. Also interviews with Herbert A. Fierst.

[99] Malcolm J. Proudfoot, *European Refugees: 1939–52* (Evanston: Northwestern Univ. Press, 1956), 115.

[100] Clay, *Decision in Germany*, 231.

[101] Carl Friedrich et al., *American Experiences in Military Government in World War II* (New York: Rinehart & Co., 1948), 180.

[102] Harold Zink, *American Military Government in Germany* (New York: Macmillan, 1947), 107.

[103] Horst Pötzsch, *Deutsche Geschichte nach 1945 im Spiegel der Karikatur* (Munich: Olzog, 1997), 22.

[104] Robert Moeller, ed., *West Germany under Construction* (Ann Arbor: Univ. of Michigan, 1997), 54.

[105] Proudfoot, *European Refugees*, 147–48.

[106] Ibid., 171.

[107] From Article I of the UNRRA constitution, cited in George Woodbridge, *UNRRA: The History of the United Nations Relief and Rehabilitation Agency* (New York: Columbia Univ. Press, 1950), 4. The term "United Nations" used repeatedly in this report and in wartime documents refers to the 26 nations (including the United States, Great Britain, the Soviet Union, China, and most Latin American countries) that pledged in the "Declaration of the United Nations," published on Jan. 1, 1942, to fight "to defend life, liberty, independence, and religious freedom and to preserve human rights and justice in their own lands as well as in other lands, and that they are now engaged in a common struggle against savage and brutal forces seeking to subjugate the world." These "United Nations" are to be distinguished from the United Nations Organization founded in San Francisco in 1945. See Carroll Quigley, *The World Since 1939: A History* (New York: Macmillan Co., 1968), 95–96.

[108] The military set up camps and brought in supplies, while the UNRRA provided administrators with various specialties. See Mark Wyman, *DPs: Europe's Displaced Persons, 1945–1951* (Ithaca: Cornell Univ. Press, 1989), 46.

[109] Proudfoot, *European Refugees*, 407.

[110] Frederiksen, *The American Military Occupation of Germany*, 78-79.

[111] *Memo to America: Final Report of the United States Displaced Persons Commission* (Washington, DC: Government Printing Office, 1952); Rene Ristelhueber, "The International Refugee Organization," *International Conciliation* 470 (April 1951): 222. Resettlement meant relocation of DPs in areas other than their native land.

[112] Ristelhueber, "International Refugee Organization," 436.

[113] Yehuda Bauer, *Out of the Ashes* (Oxford: Pergamon Press, 1989), 120–24, 203, 213–14, 256, 273; Memo from Lester K. Born to Col. J. H. Allen, "Loan of Jewish Books from Offenbach Archival Depot," Feb. 27, 1947, NACP, RG 260, Prop. Div., Box 722 [120262–268].

[114] Leonard Dinnerstein, "The U.S. Army and the Jews: Policies Toward The Displaced Persons After World War II," in Michael R. Marrus, ed., *The End of the Holocaust*, vol. 9 of *The Nazi Holocaust: Historical Articles on the Destruction of European Jews* (London: Meckler, 1989), 513–515.

[115] Dinnerstein, "U.S. Army and the Jews," 513–515; Abzug, *Inside the Vicious Heart*, 151.

[116] Abzug, *Inside the Vicious Heart*, 151.

[117] Frederiksen, *The American Military Occupation of Germany*, 75.

[118] Angelika Königseder & Juliane Wetzel, *Lebensmut im Wartesaal. Die jüdischen DPs (Displaced Persons) im Nachkriegsdeutschland* (Frankfurt am Main: Fischer, 1994), 47, and Frederiksen, *The American Military Occupation of Germany*, 77.

[119] Frederiksen, *The American Military Occupation of Germany*, 80.

[120] Wyman, *Abandonment of the Jews*, 13–14.

[121] Report of Earl G. Harrison to President Harry Truman, Aug. 1945, reprinted in Leonard Dinnerstein, *America and the Survivors of the Holocaust* (New York: Columbia Univ. Press, 1982), 300–301; Bertram Hulen, "President Orders Eisenhower to End New Abuse of Jews," *New York Times*, Sept. 30, 1945, reprinted in Robert Hilliard, *Surviving the Americans: The Continued Struggle of the Jews After Liberation* (New York: Seven Stories Press, 1997), 214–216.

[122] Ziemke, *U.S. Army in the Occupation of Germany*, 417; Frederiksen, *The American Military Occupation of Germany*, 195, 198.

[123] "Anti-Semitism Rife in Central Europe," *New York Times*, Sept. 9, 1945; "Jews in U.S. Zone of Reich Find Conditions Improving," *New York Times*, Aug. 26, 1945.

[124] "Poles are Accused of Anti-Semitism," *New York Times*, Dec. 10, 1945.

[125] See Michael C. Steinlauf, *Bondage to the Dead: Poland and the Memory of the Holocaust* (Syracuse: Syracuse Univ. Press, 1997).

[126] Ziemke, "Improvising Stability and Change in Postwar Germany," 52–66.

[127] Boehling, *Question of Priorities*, 27.

[128] Cited in Peterson, *American Occupation of Germany*, 38–39.

[129] Clay, *Decision in Germany*, 17.

[130] Cited in Clay, *Decision in Germany*, 18; Ziemke, *The U.S. Army in the Occupation of Germany*, 104.

[131] Ziemke, *The U.S. Army in the Occupation of Germany*, 58–60, 106. See also Boehling, *Question of Priorities*, 28.

[132] Peterson, *American Occupation of Germany*, 42.

[133] U.S. State Department, *Germany 1947–1949: The Story in Documents* (Washington: Government Printing Office, 1950), 413–14; Wolfgang Benz, *Die Geschichte der Bundesrepublik Deutschland* (Frankfurt au Main: Fischer Verlag, 1989), 73–74; Conrad Latour & Thilo Vogelsang, *Okkupation und Wiederaufbau. Die Tätigkeit der Militärregierung in der amerikanischen Besatzungszone Deutschlands 1944–1947* (Stuttgart: Deutsche Verlags-Anstalt, 1973), 159–61.

[134] U.S. State Department, *Germany*, 422.

[135] Gimbel, *The American Occupation of Germany: Politics and Military, 1945–1949*, (Stanford: Stanford Univ. Press, 1968), 25–28–56–58, and passim.

[136] Ibid., 85–90.

[137] See "Revised Plan for Level of Industry in the Combined U.S.-U.K. Zones of Germany" in U.S. State Department, *Germany*, 358.

[138] Gimbel, *The American Occupation of Germany*, 195–98.

[139] Gimbel, *The American Occupation of Germany*, 198–225; Clay, *Decision in Germany*, 205–207.

[140] Isadore Alk & Irving Moskovitz, "Removal of United States Controls Over Foreign-Owned Property," *Federal Bar Journal* 10, no. 1 (Oct. 1948): 4; Frederick Eisner, "Administrative Machinery and Steps for the Lawyer," *Law and Contemporary Problems* 11, no. 1 (1945): 66; Greg Bradsher, *Holocaust-Era Assets: A Finding Aid to Records at the National Archives at College Park, Maryland* (Washington, D.C.: NARA, 1999), 1056.

[141] "General Information on the Administration, Structure and Functions of Foreign Funds Control, 1940–1948," no date [ca. 1948], Ch. 5, 13–14, NACP, RG 56, Entry 66A816, Box 47 [331487–488]; U.S. Treas. Dept., *Documents Pertaining to Foreign Funds Control* (Washington: U.S. Treas. Dept., 1940), 14.

[142] Harry M. Durning & Gregory W. O'Keefe, "Directory of War Time Activities within Collection District No. 10, Port of New York," Nov. 1942, 33, Historian's Office, U.S. Customs Svc. [330859].

[143] Rpt. of James F. Gardner, FBI, Sept. 12, 1945, FBI Files [349172]. The FBI investigated these paintings and concluded that there was no evidence that they had been in Germany in recent years. Nor was there any evidence of Nazi ownership.

[144] Treasury Decision #49755, Art. 371 (C), in *Treasury Decisions Under Customs and Other Laws, July 1938–June 1939* (Washington, DC: Government Printing Office, 1940), 283–84.

[145] This principle became known as the "Truman Doctrine."

[146] Abraham J. Edelheit, "The Holocaust and the Rise of the State of Israel: A Reassessment Reassessed," *Jewish Political Studies Review*, vol. 12, 97–112.

[147] Peter Duignan & L.H. Gann, *The Rebirth of the West. The Americanization of the Democratic World, 1945–1958* (Cambridge: Blackledge, 1992), 314–15.

[148] "IRO Financial Transactions with Voluntary Agencies," Jan. 13, 1953, American Jewish Joint Distribution Committee Archives AR45/64, File 3840 [124711–720].

Chapter III

Assets in the United States

Introduction

Before, during, and after the United States entered the war, the U.S. government endeavored to deny Germany control over economic assets in, or being brought into, the United States.[1] Because the United States took control over so many assets, it undoubtedly seized some that belonged to Holocaust victims, though unintentionally. While U.S. officials were not oblivious to the intensity of Nazi persecution, it would take until the end of the war before policy began to accord special status to victims and their assets. Even in the immediate postwar period, other issues took priority, and it seemed consistently more important to fight the enemy than to aid the victims.

When the Germans invaded a country, the U.S. government assumed that the assets of that country, including those located in the United States, would be used to help the Axis powers and acted to block them. The Treasury Department immobilized foreign-controlled assets while the Alien Property Custodian (APC) seized assets. While the former practice left title with the original owner, the latter transferred title to the U.S. government.

Foreign Funds Control and the "Freezing" of Assets

Freezing Foreign-owned Assets

Germany invaded Denmark and Norway on April 8, 1940, and the United States quickly responded to the aggression. In an attempt to keep the Germans from taking control of Danish and Norwegian assets held in the United States, Executive Order 8389 "froze" all financial transactions involving Danes and Norwegians. The freezing order prohibited, subject to license, credit transfers between banking institutions within the United States and between the United States and foreign banks, payments by or to banking institutions in the United States, all transactions in foreign exchange, the export of gold or silver coin or bullion or currency, and all transfers, withdrawals or exportations of indebtedness or evidences of ownership of property by any person within the United States. It also prohibited acquiring, disposing, or transferring any security bearing foreign stamps or seals, and gave the Secretary of the Treasury the power to investigate, regulate, or prohibit the mailing or importing of securities from any foreign country.[2] The executive order provided that willful violation could carry a $10,000 fine, 10 years imprisonment or both.[3]

The rapid U.S. response was possible only because of long preparation. In issuing Executive Order 8389, the President acted on the basis of the Trading with the Enemy Act of 1917, as amended by Congress in 1933, which provided him with the authority to:

> investigate, regulate, or prohibit . . . by means of license or otherwise any transactions in foreign exchange, transfers of credit between or payments by banking institutions . . . and export, hoarding, melting, or earmarking of gold or silver coin or bullion or currency by any person within the United States or any place subject to the jurisdiction thereof.[4]

The U.S. government had first considered the use of such economic weapons in 1937. In response to the Japanese bombing and sinking of the American gunboat Panay in Chinese waters, Herman Oliphant, General Counsel in the Treasury Department, suggested to Treasury Secretary Henry Morgenthau that foreign exchange controls and a system of licenses for financial transactions could be instituted against the Japanese.[5] Tensions with Japan subsequently eased and Oliphant's proposals were shelved. But in 1938, after the German annexation of the Sudetenland, reports circulated that the Germans were forcing Czechs to turn over all assets they held in the United States. Such information prompted the Treasury to revisit Oliphant's proposals.

Subsequent German actions, including the occupation of the Czechoslovakian lands of Bohemia and Moravia, further increased support within Treasury for the imposition of freezing controls. Treasury also took the step of verifying with the Justice Department the legality of such controls in the absence of a state of war.[6] Although the United States ultimately decided not to respond to Germany's actions in 1938 and 1939, Treasury was prepared to act quickly in April 1940.

As Germany continued its invasions, the U.S. government successively froze assets, country by country, over the European continent. Thus, on May 10, 1940, FFC extended freezing controls to cover the Netherlands, Belgium, and Luxembourg.[7] The assets of France and Monaco (June 17), Latvia, Estonia, and Lithuania (July 10), and Romania (October 9) were subsequently frozen that year.[8] By the end of April 1941, the United States added Bulgaria, Hungary, Yugoslavia, and Greece to the list.[9]

The further extension of controls to belligerents and neutrals remained controversial. While Treasury favored a rapid extension of controls, the State Department, concerned about maintaining America's status as a neutral as well as U.S. diplomatic privileges, objected.[10] Assistant Secretary of State for Economic Affairs Dean Acheson noted that "from top to bottom our [State] Department, except for our corner of it, was against Henry Morgenthau's campaign to apply freezing controls to Axis countries and their victims."[11]

Eventually, the course of the war dictated a shift in U.S. policy. On June 14, 1941, through Executive Order 8785, the United States extended freezing controls to cover all of continental Europe, including "aggressor" nations and annexed or invaded territories (Germany and Italy; Danzig, Austria, and Poland) as well as neutral nations, small principalities, and countries not previously included (Spain, Sweden, Portugal, and Switzerland; Andorra, San Marino, and Liechtenstein; Albania and Finland). Turkish assets were never blocked, and Soviet assets were only blocked for a relatively short time until Germany invaded Russia in June 1941.[12] As the United States moved from being a neutral to a belligerent, the role of FFC, an administrative agency within the Treasury Department, expanded.

Assets within the United States

Census of Foreign-owned Assets in the United States (1941)

On June 14, 1941, amended regulations under Executive Order 8389 called for a census of foreign-owned assets.[13] Every person in the U.S. (including corporations and foreign nationals) was required to report all property held for or owned by a foreign country or national. The Treasury Department reasoned that no one could foresee which nations might yet be overrun, that title changes could occur anywhere, and that compiling comprehensive records of who controlled which assets was vital.[14] Treasury was subsequently unwilling to share the information it had gathered even with friendly foreign governments or American creditors.[15]

The census form listed some thirty types of property: bullion, currency and deposits; domestic and foreign securities; notes, drafts, debts, claims; miscellaneous personal property such as bills of lading, commodity options, merchandise for business use, jewelry, machinery, objects d'art; real property and mortgages; patents, trademarks, copyrights, franchises; estates and trusts; partnerships; and insurance policies and annuities. The value of each asset both in June 1940, and in June 1941, had to be provided, as did extensive information about the persons with an interest in the property (including citizenship, address, date of last entry into the United States, visa type, and alien registration number), to enable the government to trace transfers and changes in the assets. Property whose total value was less than $1,000 did not have to be reported unless its value could not be ascertained, but even assets with values difficult to assess in dollar terms, such as patents or interests in partnerships, had to be reported as did the contents of safe deposit boxes.[16]

The census revealed that earlier U.S. government estimates, which have been destroyed, had often been inaccurate.[17] Generally, Axis holdings had been underestimated while the holdings of German-occupied countries (particularly France and the Netherlands) had been overestimated. A sizeable portion of foreign-owned assets proved to be in the hands of British and Canadian investors. The census showed as well how dominant New York was as a financial center: two-thirds of all reports, and more than three-quarters of all bank and broker reports were filed in the New York district.[18]

Overall, the 565,000 reports submitted showed the total value of U.S. assets owned by foreign persons or entities in 1941 was $12.7 billion. About two-thirds, or $8.1 billion, of the $12.7 billion total reported belonged to 84,000 persons located in European countries,[19] and other than the large United Kingdom ($3.2 billion) holdings, the only other European countries with holdings near $1 billion were Switzerland ($1.2 billion), France ($1 billion), and the Netherlands ($977 million).[20]

But Treasury Department fears that Germany might be able to exploit the assets from occupied territories were warranted. The total value of foreign-controlled U.S. assets just from West European countries that were overrun or defeated in 1940—Denmark ($48.1 million), Norway ($154.7 million), the Netherlands ($976.7 million), Belgium ($312.7 million), Luxembourg ($33.4 million), France ($1 billion), and Monaco ($15.5 million)—amounted to $2.5 billion, or more than twelve times Germany's 1941 U.S. holdings of $198 million.[21] The following table shows the geographic origin of the funds, according to the census:

Table 5: Value of Foreign-Owned United States Assets
(by continent and country of reported address of the owners, as of June 14, 1941, in millions of dollars)

Continent With largest countries in region		Values
Europe		**8,128**
of this, United Kingdom	3,239	
of this, Switzerland	1,211	
of this, France	1,041	
North America		**1,743**
of this, Canada	1,709	
Asia		**1,257**
of this, China	356	
of this, Philippine Islands	277	
of this, Japan	161	
South America		**673**
of this, Argentina	233	
of this, Brazil	134	
Central America		**385**
of this, Panama	170	
of this, Mexico	160	
West Indies and Bermuda		**306**
of this, Cuba	172	
Africa		**163**
of this, South Africa	57	
of this, Belgian Africa	50	
Oceania		**68**
of this, Australia	55	

Only 21 percent of the foreign-owned U.S. assets were owned by individuals: corporations owned 63 percent, and governments 16 percent. Among individuals, securities ($808 million), estates and trusts ($799 million), and deposits ($505 million) predominated, though all three combined amounted to only 16.5 percent of all foreign-owned assets. Corporate holdings in deposits ($2.8 billion), interests in enterprises ($2 billion), and domestic securities ($1.8 billion) were far larger. Of the foreign-owned American securities 75 percent were held by persons in only five countries (the United Kingdom, Canada, Switzerland, the Netherlands, and France), with the majority (70 percent) in common stock, and far less (12 percent and 8 percent, respectively) in preferred stock and corporate bonds. Only about 30 percent of these securities belonged to individuals, while 65 percent belonged to corporations.[22]

At the wealthy end of the spectrum, 9,255 "persons" (including corporations), who held total assets greater than $100,000 each, accounted for fully 88 percent ($11.2 billion) of the $12.7 billion total. At the other end, the Census reported 112,399 "persons" with a range of assets of less than $10,000 each, accounted for only 3.3 percent ($427 million) of the total foreign-owned assets counted. In fact, "small holdings of less than $5,000 accounted for…58 percent of the number of persons, and close to 90 percent of them were individuals."[23]

Looted Assets and the U.S. Market

Though FFC wanted to prevent the enemy from using assets in the United States, it did not want to hinder legitimate business, and therefore developed a licensing system to monitor and regulate transactions. Controlling readily convertible and transportable assets, in particular securities, currency, and gold, called for different measures.

Securities. Treasury's General Ruling 2, "Transfer of Stock Certificates and Custody of Securities," issued nine days after the proclamation of Executive Order 8389, prohibited transfers of securities involving Danish or Norwegian nationals. The ruling had limited impact since the combined value of U.S. domestic securities held by Danes and Norwegians amounted to only $16.6 million.[24] However, the German invasion of the Netherlands, Belgium, and Luxembourg in May 1940 substantially increased the stakes, as securities worth $358.2 million were in danger of falling under German control. Dutch owners held 89 percent of these securities, and as many as half of the securities were thought to be in the form of readily convertible corporate bearer bonds.[25] "Unless a way could be found to prevent the liquidation of securities seized by the invaders," a Treasury Department summary noted in mid-1942, "tremendous losses would accrue to their legitimate owners, and a tremendous asset would be given to the war effort of the Axis."[26]

Initially, FFC recommended the destruction of securities that were at risk of German seizure. In the Netherlands, many owners resisted this approach, for fear of not being able to replace the securities at a later date. The Dutch government also informed the State Department that owing to the military situation it was simply too late to undertake any financial measures at all and that not enough personnel was available to destroy all the securities. In desperation, FFC sent a cable with the instruction to take the securities and "dip them in red wine,"[27] thereby making them immediately identifiable in case they were looted.

Such expedients were insufficient to keep Germany from exploiting looted securities registered in the name of an individual. On June 3, 1940, the Treasury Department issued General Ruling 3, extending the freezing control to prohibit the acquisition, transfer, disposition, transportation, importation, exportation, or withdrawal of any securities that were registered in the name of a national of a blocked country. The ruling prohibited U.S. registrars or transfer agents from changing the name in which the security was registered, even if a legitimate transfer of title had taken place before the German invasion.[28]

While General Ruling 3 blocked the transfer of enemy-captured registered securities, it did not fully address the direct importation of bearer securities into the United States. To attack this problem, FFC determined that an import inspection system was necessary. On June 6, 1940, it issued General Ruling 5 on the "Control of Imported Securities," prohibiting "the sending, mailing, importing, or otherwise bringing into the United States" of securities. If any securities were physically brought into the country, they were to be immediately turned over to a Federal Reserve Bank.

For implementation, FFC relied heavily upon other agencies, in particular on the Customs Service and the Post Office. Customs inspectors met, questioned, and searched incoming passengers to determine whether they were carrying securities, while postal inspectors examined the incoming mail to make sure that stocks and bonds did not enter the country surreptitiously.[29] Once the Federal Reserve Bank took possession of securities, "they could be released only upon proof, judged sufficient by the Treasury Department, that no blocked country or national thereof had any interest in such securities since the date of the freezing order."[30]

Imported securities that could not be released remained in the custody of the Federal Reserve Bank. Yet to prevent undue hardship, the Treasury Department issued General Ruling 6 on August 8, 1940, allowing such surrendered securities to be moved from the Federal Reserve Bank into special blocked accounts (called "General Ruling 6 Accounts") in domestic U.S. banks. This arrangement permitted the completion of certain basic transactions. Dividends from these securities, for example, and even the proceeds from the sale of these securities, could be accrued in these blocked bank accounts, as well as taxes and bank charges deducted.

Unregistered (or bearer) securities falling into enemy hands were particularly troublesome, not only because they had been used extensively before the war by German cartels as a means to hide ownership, but also because General Ruling 3 did not apply to them and General Ruling 5 only applied to blocked countries. Thus, between the time General Ruling 5 was issued in June 1940 and the extension of freezing controls to the neutrals in June 1941, it was possible for Swiss, for example, to continue to export securities to the United States. Then there were the issues of controlling foreign securities that had been issued in and were payable in the United States, and preventing blocked nationals from acquiring controlling interests in U.S. corporations by buying their stocks and bonds.

The Treasury Department addressed many of these problems through certification, an expedient somewhat similar to the European practice of affixing tax stamps to legitimately acquired securities. Treasury's certification (using Form TFEL–2) could be attached to securities "if the owners could prove that they were free from any blocked interest."[31] Treasury also applied this device to securities issued in blocked countries but payable in the United States.[32] Because securities looted abroad might be sold to persons resident in the United States, the freezing order prohibited such acquisitions or transfers as long as these securities were not in the United States. By 1943, this prohibition was relaxed so as to permit the acquisition of securities in Great Britain and Canada, as well as to a more limited extent from within the generally licensed trade areas.[33]

Currency, Dollar Checks, and Drafts. In the process of trying to prevent securities from entering the country, U.S. Customs also discovered that currency, particularly dollars, was being brought into the United States, amounting to $3 million worth in Fiscal Year 1943 alone.[34] In 1940 and 1941, the United States was still neutral and no mechanism was in place to impound currency. Foreign Funds Control therefore asked the Collector of the Customs simply to keep a record of the amount of currency arriving and to send a monthly report to the Treasury Department listing sender and recipient. By 1942, the United States was a belligerent and General Ruling 6A, issued in March 1942, added "currency" to the definition of "securities or evidences thereof," thereby enabling FFC to apply similar controls.[35] The operating presumption of the Treasury Department was that dollars imported directly from Europe had been looted.[36] Only currency imported from Canada, Great Britain, Newfoundland, or Bermuda escaped the wartime currency import restrictions.[37]

Controlling the direct importation of securities or currency did not address yet another problem: censorship offices in both the United States and Great Britain were discovering that "substantial amounts of funds" were flowing between Europe and the Western Hemisphere in the form of dollar-denominated checks and drafts.[38] U.S. funds were entering blocked European countries, and dollar checks were being resold in neutral countries. The U.S. Legation in Switzerland, for example, reported that Germany had obtained about $12 million in this fashion, noting that German agents were trying to sell such checks and drafts in neutral countries at a discount in order to acquire Swiss francs and Portuguese escudos.[39] General Ruling 5A (July 7, 1943) thus required a license to collect payment on these kinds of checks, a control that worked in both directions.[40] Checks, drafts, notes, securities, or currency could not be exported to any blocked country unless under license, and all checks or drafts imported after August 25, 1943, had to be sent to the Federal Reserve Bank of New York. There they were held indefinitely, with licenses for their release only granted in very unusual circumstances.[41]

Gold. Whether the U.S. government knowingly traded in gold looted from victims begs the prior question of the nature of the gold trade. U.S. policies on gold long predated the war, and the war did not substantially alter them. Until 1934, U.S. currency could be redeemed in gold coin, and by statute the Treasury had to maintain a minimum amount of gold to make redemptions possible. Economic expansion in the 1920s had increased the domestic demand for currency, which increased the purchase of gold from abroad, and turned the United States into "a gigantic sink for the gold reserves of the rest of the world."[42] Having gold (in Fort Knox, for example) helped maintain public confidence in the currency.[43]

The economic crisis of the Depression led to passage of the Gold Reserve Act of January 30, 1934, prohibiting the private trade in gold and giving the Treasury Secretary the authority to control all future dealings in gold, including setting the conditions under which gold could be held, transported, melted, treated, imported, and exported, as well as allowing him to "purchase gold in any amounts, at home or abroad...at such rates and upon such terms and conditions as he may deem most advantageous to the public interest."[44] Immediately after passage of the act, President Roosevelt revalued gold, fixing its price at $35/oz. (substantially up from its previous $20.67/oz. price). In effect, this gave the Treasury a paper profit of almost $3 billion, $2 billion of which went into a Stabilization Fund authorized to deal in gold and foreign exchange with an eye to influencing the value of the dollar by buying and selling on the open market.[45] The Treasury Secretary thus was given both full power to buy gold and substantial funds to do so.

The consequences of the Gold Reserve Act and the revaluation were immediate. Gold held privately (and by banks) in the United States was turned in to the Treasury Department and added $2.4 billion to its ledgers in 1934 alone,[46] and the increase in the price the United States would pay stimulated mining to such an extent that during the six years after 1934, world gold production rose by two-thirds and U.S. domestic production more than doubled.[47]

More importantly, these U.S. changes drew capital from Europe, perhaps in part due to the new price, but certainly because of "the growing threat of Nazism in Hitlerite Germany."[48] In only six weeks from February 1 to March 14, 1934, more than half a billion dollars' worth of gold was imported by the United States, and by 1936, an estimated $3 billion worth of gold had come from France.[49] Gold hoarded in England came onto the London market in 1936 and 1937, and from August 1938 to May 1939 alone, about $3 billion worth of gold came to the United States, $2 billion of which was from the United Kingdom, and perhaps $670 million of that U.K. gold had been transshipped from other countries.[50] In fact, from February 1934 until October 1942, "a phenomenal gold movement" to the United States began, with gold stock increasing "every single month for 8 _ years" (an average yearly increase from 1934 to 1938 of $1.5 billion worth of gold) in the end amounting to $16 billion worth of gold flowing into the United States.[51]

The following table, prepared by the Treasury Department in answer to an inquiry from Senator William Knowland in 1952, lists yearly gold flows to and from the United States:

Table 6: U.S. Gold Flows, 1934–1945[52] *(in millions of dollars at $35/oz.)*

Year	U.S. Gold Purchases[1]	U.S. Gold Sales[2]	Change in in Gold Stock[3]	Percent Change in Gold Stock	Gold Held[4] (in billions)
1934	1,147	24	1,241	15	8.26
1935	1,854	125	1,865	18	10.12
1936	1,150	14	1,299	11	11.42
1937	1,601	427	1,367	11	12.79
1938	1,752	140	1,802	12	14.59
1939	3,267	263	3,208	18	17.80
1940	4,156	144	4,242	19	22.04
1941	986	463	719	3	22.76
1942	346	486	−23	−.01	22.73
1943	32	795	−758	−3	21.98
1944	50	1,373	−1,349	−6.5	20.61
1945	396	857	−548	−3	20.08

Notes:

1. purchases of foreign gold (1933–1944) include gold from foreign governments, private holders, mines, refiners and others

2. sales data (1934–1939) include some made to non-governmental buyers in the UK and French gold markets

3. discrepancies between the sum of purchase minus sales and the total listed under Change in Gold Stock are due to omission of data on domestic net receipts (newly mined domestic gold, domestic coin, and secondary gold, less sales to domestic industry). Prewar, the mean value was +176, range +118 (1934) to +231 (1940); during the war the mean value was +45, range −66 (1945) to +196 (1941)

4. total gold stock includes gold in the Exchange Stabilization Fund

Unmistakably, gold was fleeing Europe before the war, and Europeans were receiving dollars for it. However, most gold was not coming directly from the Axis powers. A table prepared in connection with Stabilization Fund hearings in 1941 showed that from 1934 through 1940, the U.S. imported only $94,000 worth of gold from Germany, $60.5 million from Italy and $692.5 million from Japan.[53] Relative to the increase in the U.S. gold stock from 1934 to 1940, all gold imported from Germany, Italy and Japan combined ($753 million) accounted for less than 5 percent of the total increase in the U.S. gold stock. In fact, three-quarters of the gold imported by the U.S. in 1940 came from only three countries: Canada (55 percent), the United Kingdom (14 percent) and France (5 percent).[54]

The volume of gold coming in troubled Treasury, which held internal discussions about embargoes or other means to stem the flow. But Henry Dexter White, head of the Division of Monetary Research, wrote to Secretary Morgenthau in May, 1939, that "there is very little we can do to reduce gold imports—except promote recovery here."[55] White himself regarded gold as "the best medium of international exchange yet devised," one that served to insulate the U.S. domestic economy from foreign economic changes, and the medium of exchange par excellence since "every country in the world will sell goods for gold and no country will refuse gold in settlement of debt or in payment for services rendered."[56]

White was well aware that it was "the fear of war abroad with its concomitant likelihood of depreciation, strict exchange controls, and possible inflation or confiscation" that was prompting the massive inflow, and that people wanted to protect assets abroad from sequestration or wanted to buy American currency since that allowed them to "have funds in the form that can be easily hidden" from their governments.[57] Eighty percent of the inflow was being put into short-term balances, suggesting that the dollars received for gold were being temporarily parked in U.S. accounts, some of which were probably then frozen.

The German invasion of France, Belgium and the Netherlands in May of 1940, prompted Mr. Pinsent, Financial Counselor at the British Embassy, to send a note to the Treasury Department to inquire of Mr. Morgenthau "whether he would be prepared to scrutinize the gold imports with a view to rejecting those suspected of German origin," as Pinsent explicitly feared that the private hoards of Dutch and Belgian gold might fall into German hands.[58] In a June 4, 1940 memo, Henry Dexter White explained why the U.S. Treasury did not raise questions about the origin of "German" gold.

First, such gold could readily lose its identity by being used as payment in third countries. If Germany looted gold and resold it, the global cooperation needed to stop this movement simply did not exist. Second, Treasury had consistently taken the position before Congress that "it cannot effectively distinguish gold originating from any one foreign country."[59] Third, Germany could claim its gold shipments were of its own prewar stocks, meaning gold would have to be refused not for its title but for political reasons. Fourth, discriminating against gold from Germany "will intensify Germany's propaganda against the usefulness of gold." The most effective contribution the United States could make to keep gold as an international exchange medium, White argued, "is to maintain its inviolability and the unquestioned acceptance of gold as a means of settling international balances."[60]

Indeed, six months later White would scornfully write of his "adamant opposition to give even serious consideration to proposals coming from those who know little of the subject that we stop purchasing gold, or that we stop buying the gold of any particular country, for this or for that or for any particular reason."[61] In early 1941, White was asked again, through an internal Treasury memorandum, to consider the question "whose gold are we buying?"[62] but from his memos it is clear that the answer was an "unquestioned acceptance of gold," regardless of origin.

Licensing

Following application by an individual or business, Treasury issued licenses that could be either Specific (governing a particular transaction) or General (covering broader categories of transactions). General Licenses removed the need for FFC to investigate every transaction, and such licenses were functionally differentiated to apply to persons, geographic regions, or particular types of transactions. Entire categories of transactions were deemed acceptable, such as the payment of interest on securities, managing or liquidating property to meet expenses and taxes, servicing life insurance policies, and even sending remittances to persons in territories occupied by the enemy, though Treasury placed restrictions on those remittances and the amounts could not come from blocked accounts.[63]

Under "persons," Treasury designated individual nationals of blocked countries who had been residents of the United States for a certain period of time as "generally licensed nationals." These persons, as well as all residents in the United States, regardless of nationality or length of residence, could obtain a certain amount of money for living expenses, even from blocked accounts.[64] Treasury also designated certain regions as "generally licensed trade areas." Such a designation permitted transactions to occur without restriction. In a modified example of this approach, Treasury granted general licenses to the four neutral countries (Switzerland, Sweden, Spain, Portugal), with provisos that transactions be certified by government, central bank, or designated agent, and that these transactions were not carried out on behalf of a blocked country or national. Under such a license, a Swiss national in Switzerland could

> transfer funds from his account in a bank in New York to Credit Suisse in Switzerland to be used for the payment of goods which he is going to purchase in Switzerland. On the other hand, a German citizen in Switzerland...cannot...transfer funds in this manner for the same purpose.[65]

Yet Treasury wanted to disrupt economic life as little as possible, and during the war it approved 83 percent of all applications to conduct financial transactions under the freezing order.[66] According to the Treasury Department, "from January 1942 to March 1945, transactions in assets totaling over $10 billion were authorized by specific license."[67] This $10 billion represented 78 percent of the total amount of foreign-owned assets reported in the 1941 Census ($12.7 billion), and suggests Treasury's main concern was for the 20 percent or so of assets that were suspected of being under enemy control.

In spite of its generally positive approach, Treasury was ready to exert more onerous controls particularly over businesses owned by or which had close ties to enemy companies. Before 1933, German companies had commercial arrangements with American companies, such as exclusive sales contracts and patent-sharing, or had established subsidiaries in the United States, and while some of these involved legitimate business practices, others used mechanisms that lent themselves to concealment.[68] For example, shares of stock that represented majority ownership and control of an American company would be transferred to holding companies in various countries in the form of bearer shares. Because the holding company's stock was both frequently traded, including to other holding companies, and ownership was anonymous, it was not possible to establish who actually controlled the shares.[69] The Treasury Department also feared that German interests might use Swiss or Dutch companies as fronts for clandestine operations inside the United States.

Treasury possessed a variety of means to control blocked businesses. Its reporting requirements obliged such businesses to file affidavits containing detailed information about their organization, directors and officers, their relationships to other enterprises, their principal customers and their capital structure. Armed with this information, Treasury could determine whether or not to license a given business to continue operations. As a condition for granting such licenses, Treasury could mandate changes in organizational structure, require that executives or employees be dismissed, or make the enterprise break off relations with certain customers. Treasury could also deny the renewal of a license.[70] More intrusively, government "intervenors" could be placed directly inside firms to supervise or reorganize the business, including severing contracts and preventing trades, or liquidating stock. By withholding a license, Treasury could prevent a company owned or controlled by an Axis power from operating at all and could force a sale of its assets: government representatives would be placed on the premises to supervise the liquidation. By mid-1942, Treasury had liquidated about 500 enterprises, many of them banks and insurance companies,[71] and the funds remaining from the sales, after creditors had been paid, went into blocked accounts.[72]

In short, exerting control over foreign funds entailed a variety of discrete if interconnected acts. The basic policy decision to freeze assets predated the U.S. declaration of war, but each German act to invade or control new territory engendered a new response from Washington as well as an additional presidential executive order. For Treasury to exert control over foreign-controlled assets necessitated first gathering detailed information about the extent and ownership of such assets through a census. Then a licensing system to allow scrutiny of asset transactions had to be devised and implemented. In practice, the vast majority of transactions were permitted, albeit Treasury had at its disposal intrusive control measures when it suspected enemy interests might be involved in a transaction.

Readily fungible assets like bearer securities and gold were particularly troublesome, as the U.S. wartime expedient of certifying the legitimacy of transactions in such assets obscured their looting by Germans, or the duress under which such assets had changed hands (or been converted to cash) in Europe. The restitution of such assets even to their countries of issue would remain a contentious matter long after the end of the war. Yet in all of this, the U.S. concern was to keep property out of the hands of the enemy, and if possible even to preserve the property and rights of legitimate asset holders. Legitimate asset holders may well have included victims, though the focus was on the enemy, and explicit distinctions between victim and non-victim were rarely drawn during the war.

Aliens, Nationals, Enemies, Friends

The specific concern for victims was obscured, though not entirely absent, during the war because political interests and overlapping definitions were at play in domestic law and policy. Treasury was concerned about foreign enemies trying to liquidate assets in the United States, but the Justice Department cared about enemies in (or trying to enter) the country to subvert the U.S. war effort. As one consequence of these differing concerns, definitions of "enemy" varied from one act to another, in turn creating contradictory regulations that had the effect of increasing the discretionary power of government.[73]

Victims and non-victims alike faced a patchwork of policy and regulations. For an individual, much depended upon whether he or she was classified as enemy or friendly alien, naturalized or non-naturalized, resident or refugee, or as domiciled in the United States or abroad. Yet cutting through these categories were high-level political and legal judgments that certain groups posed no threat, that demonstrated loyalty meant more than formal citizenship, and that even stateless refugees had legal rights. In short, those who had been victimized abroad found themselves categorized in the United States in ways that limited their liberty, including access to their assets, but they could equally well find that some of the very distinctions that were drawn for other wartime purposes worked to their benefit.

Numbers and Definitions

The U.S. government's 1940 Alien Registration Program found 4.9 million aliens in the United States, more than 70 percent of whom (or 3.4 million) had arrived before 1924. About 73 percent of these 4.9 million were from "Europe."[74] The five largest nationality groups, accounting for 60 percent of the European total were, in descending order, Italians, Poles, Russians, Germans, and British. Thus, at the beginning of World War II there was a substantial cohort of long-term resident aliens who had come from Europe.

As for those from Axis countries, the 1940 Census found 1.2 million residents of German birth, 1.6 million of Italian birth, and 127,000 of Japanese birth. In each group, only a minority were not naturalized American citizens.[75] The same was true of individuals from Axis-invaded countries: a 1942 tally found that only 36 percent of the 2.3 million foreign-born residents from these countries were still aliens.[76] A 1942 estimate put the number of refugees from Europe who had arrived in the United States since 1933 at 250,000.[77] Within the United States, of those born in Axis countries, only about one-third still had Axis citizenship.

But executive orders made it unclear whose assets were meant to be controlled. The first freezing order in 1940, applied to "nationals" of a blocked foreign country, with "national" defined as "any person who has been domiciled in, or a subject, citizen, or resident of a foreign country at any time on or since the effective date of this Order."[78] German Jews and some other refugees made stateless by the Nazis did "not cease to be nationals of such country merely by reason of such cancellation or revocation of citizenship," at least so far as Treasury was concerned.[79] But the freezing order also gave the Secretary of the Treasury full power to determine "that any person is or shall be deemed to be a 'national' within the meaning of this definition."[80] Thus a "national" by the first two statements might be defined by the criteria of former or present foreign domicile and foreign citizenship (even if revoked), yet by the third statement a national could be defined simply through the discretionary power of the Secretary. Subsequent executive orders did not clarify matters. They defined "national" to include foreign nationals who were resident in the United States as in June 1941, or, as in July 1942, defined "national" as "any person in any place under the control of a designated enemy country" with which the U.S. was at war.[81] The first appeared to make citizenship key regardless of domicile, while the second seemed to make both citizenship and domicile irrelevant since it was enemy control that mattered. By contrast, Treasury's General License No. 42 declared that any individual residing in the United States as of February 23, 1942 (including a stateless refugee) was a generally licensed national. Not only did this allow for liberties over assets, it meant that domicile rather than citizenship mattered.[82]

There are several explanations for this apparent arbitrariness. First, definitions are confined to the act or regulation in which they appear, and Treasury's interpretations do not appear to have tracked executive orders. Second, contradictions in definitions permitted a kind of "ad hoc blocking" to be imposed if necessary.[83] Third, the point of freezing was to control a potential problem rather than to prohibit all trade. Foreign Funds Control "never intended to subject all individuals within the United States who were nationals as defined in the Order" to its control but rather to draw a distinction between the smaller group of those suspected of "carrying on activities inimical to the public interest" and the much larger group of those "whose activities were clearly above suspicion."[84]

Alien Enemies: Restrictions and Rights

The freezing orders and Treasury interpretations define "nationals"—not "enemies." Understanding the difference prompted one commentator in 1943 to note that "Congress may want to make a distinction in favor of those German nationals who are the enemy's most cruelly persecuted victims and to whom it must seem a bitter irony to find themselves treated as our enemies."[85] The reason for this assertion was that the Alien Enemy Act of 1940 had declared that all resident natives, citizens, denizens, or subjects of a country with which the United States is at war and who are not naturalized are liable to be apprehended, restrained, secured, and removed as "alien enemies" in or from the United States.[86] That included Germany's "most cruelly persecuted victims" who had fled to the United States as refugees. The Trading with the Enemy Act had by contrast defined an "enemy" as a person resident within the territory with which the United States is at war, which meant that "enemy" was defined as a nonresident of the United States.[87] As a consequence, "alien enemies in this country [U.S.] are not considered enemies for the purpose of trading with the enemy measures."[88]

In December 1941, President Roosevelt issued three proclamations placing restraints on aliens of German, Italian, and Japanese nationality. The restrictions included prohibitions on owning cameras, short wave radios, firearms and explosives, exclusion from living in certain areas, travel restrictions (alien enemies were not permitted to take airplane flights and needed written authorization for trips outside their district), restrictions on changing name, residence, or employment, and a requirement to apply for and carry identification certificates at all times.[89]

Though the intent of these restrictions was clearly to restrict subversion, the difficulty, as the Commissioner on Immigration and Naturalization Earl Harrison noted in April 1942, was that "alien enemies" thereby included

> persons who have actually fought in battle against Hitler forces; it includes a great many who have bitterly opposed Hitler and Nazism and Fascism in civilian life for years; it includes many who have been in foreign concentration camps, had their property appropriated and their German citizenship revoked; it includes some who...[have] been classified as friendly aliens in England; it encompasses many who do not recall any country other than the United States and whose American born children are now serving in the American army.[90]

Others, too, reiterated Harrison's point at the time.[91] The implication was that nominal citizenship mattered much less than loyalty to the United States, particularly if it was "honestly-determined loyalty of the individual rather than his assumed loyalty."[92]

The category of "enemy alien" also was not as comprehensive as it might have been. Austrians, Austro-Hungarians, and Koreans, for example, were not defined as alien enemies, nor were former Germans, Japanese, or Italians who had become naturalized citizens of neutral or friendly countries.[93] Executive Order No. 9106 (March 20, 1942) excepted persons Attorney General Francis Biddle had certified, after investigation, as loyal to the United States, specifically for the purpose of allowing such persons to apply for naturalization.[94] On Columbus Day (October 14) in 1942, Biddle also announced that the more than 600,000 resident Italian aliens would henceforth be exempt from the restrictions placed on enemy aliens, and subsequently issued the relevant orders making it so.[95]

Soon after Pearl Harbor, Attorney General Biddle made several strong statements in favor of tolerating "all peaceful and law-abiding aliens," reassuring noncitizens that the U.S. government would not interfere with them "so long as they conduct themselves in accordance with the law."[96] Common law and legal precedent established the general rule that for aliens, "lawful residence implies protection, and a capacity to sue and be sued" unless that right was expressly withheld by law.[97] This general rule was reaffirmed in the case of Kaufmann v. Eisenberg and City of New York (1942)[98] with the words "the right of a resident enemy alien to sue in the civil courts like a citizen has been accorded recognition under the generally accepted rule," a ruling reaffirmed by Attorney General Biddle who stated in a Justice Department press release that "no native, citizen, or subject of any nation with which the United States is at war and who is resident in the United States is precluded by federal statute or regulations from suing in federal or state courts."[99] Thus, even those formally designated as "enemy aliens" could have their day in court.[100]

Despite long residence in the U.S. or demonstrated loyalty, even some "friendly aliens" saw their property confiscated.[101] However, their right to just compensation, in keeping with the Fifth Amendment, had been affirmed several times by the Supreme Court in the 1930s and was reiterated after World War II.[102] Lower courts clearly affirmed the right of friendly aliens to be given the same treatment as citizens, to recover their property in kind or sue for its return,[103] or be provided administrative means to do so.[104] Thus, being defined as "friendly" rather than "enemy" was important for the recovery of assets, and all "aliens" had recourse to the courts.

Aliens and Real Property

Though the Treasury Department granted "generally licensed" status to resident aliens in February 1942, New York and some other states reserved to themselves the power to escheat property, which meant the state took control over real property upon the death of the owner, particularly if there were no heirs to claim it.[105] Under Section 10 of New York's Real Property Law (1913), a statutory provision held that "alien friends are empowered to take, hold, transmit and dispose of real property within this state in the same manner as native-born citizens,"[106] and Judge Benjamin Cardozo in Techt v. Hughes (1920) subsequently defined "alien friends" as "citizens or subjects of a nation with which the United States is at peace."[107] That explicitly excluded citizens of countries with which the United States was at war,[108] so that a real property title held by an "alien enemy" in 1942 would "upon his death immediately escheat" as long as there were no heirs.[109] The New York Public Lands Law had "provided machinery whereby the putative 'heirs' of an alien enemy may secure, at a very favorable price, a release of escheated lands."[110]

But all was not as it appeared, and key political figures were quite aware of predicaments stateless refugees could face. Already on July 1, 1942, New York State Attorney General Bennett, in an informal letter opinion to the Jewish Agricultural Society, Inc., suggested that those deprived of German citizenship by German law should be regarded as "alien friends."[111] By March 22, 1944, the New York State Legislature had abolished the disabilities "alien enemies" had under the New York Real Property Law by the simple expedient of deleting the word "friends" from the statute.[112] In making this change, the legislature may have been responding to the many long-term resident aliens in the state who "were unquestionably 'alien friends' " but were facing an inheritance law that was at best "only a dubious means of enriching the state at the expense of harmless and innocent people."[113] The result of the legislative change was to permit all aliens to hold and will to heirs real property in the same manner as citizens.[114] While this may not have prevented the escheating of Holocaust victim property when there were no heirs, it also indicates that even during war, states removed some of the legal disabilities aliens faced. Inheritance, of course, became complex when it was a matter of alien heirs resident in the United States from decedents who were citizens of enemy or enemy-occupied countries, though authentication systems for foreign records were developed even in the New York State court system.[115]

Victims in Europe

FFC took positive steps to assist victims in Europe. In 1942, initial inquiries about licenses were made

> for the purpose of providing funds for getting persons out of enemy or enemy occupied areas.... Thereafter we [FFC] approved applications for licenses to effect remittance in reasonable amounts to neutral areas on behalf of prospective emigrants from enemy territory.... During 1943, we were receiving reports of the character of the German treatment of refugees, particularly Jews, throughout the areas under their control.[116]

Despite Treasury restrictions under General Ruling 11 that explicitly prohibited communication with enemy territory as well as financial transactions with those in enemy territory, FFC "re-examined our general trading with the enemy policy...to permit operations designed to bring relief to particularly oppressed groups in enemy territory."[117] These included funding underground organizations, supporting U.S. organizations that could conduct relief operations in enemy territory, and establishing safeguards to keep funds from falling into enemy hands. "In view of the policy of the enemy to annihilate certain minority groups either by slaughter or starvation, operations to bring relief [would further the] fundamental objectives of the United Nations." Accordingly, FFC decided it "should permit certain responsible groups to enter into arrangements to bring some relief to groups in enemy territory."[118] FFC thus authorized the Legation in Bern to give the World Jewish Congress a license permitting it to obtain local currency to help in the evacuation of refugees, and allowed it to communicate with enemy territory. This license was subsequently amended to permit acquiring currency "from persons in enemy or enemy-occupied territory against payment in free currency rates" in order to "assist in the evacuation of victims of Nazi aggression," a policy cleared through "Treasury and other Departments of the [U.S.] government."[119] The Treasury Department deliberately made an exception to its restrictive policies in order to provide aid to victims.

"Vesting" Assets and the Office of Alien Property Custodian

Creation of the Office of Alien Property Custodian

Vesting

Congress considerably expanded the President's regulatory power when it passed the First War Powers Act on December 18, 1941, giving the Chief Executive the power to "vest" (seize, or take over the title to) the property—including businesses—of any foreign country or national.[120] While the power to freeze left the title with the original owners, with "vesting," title passed into the hands of the U.S. government, with the declaration that seized property could be used for the benefit of the United States.[121] The Office of Alien Property Custodian (APC) would be given far more direct power over businesses than the Department of the Treasury had been granted, though it would be exercised over far fewer businesses.[122]

President Roosevelt could not easily bring APC to life because the precedent was inauspicious. An Alien Property Custodian had been appointed during World War I, but the office had been scandal-ridden, and one custodian had even gone to prison in the wake of a postwar congressional investigation.[123] The first Custodian's Office was abolished in May 1934, but its remaining functions were still being carried out by the Alien Property Division in the Justice Department in early 1941.[124] The Attorney General lobbied Roosevelt to have a new custodian appointed in the Justice Department, but the Secretary of the Treasury did not want the functions of FFC to be undermined, and any new custodian would also have to take over the alien property issues that still remained from World War I. The APC was finally launched as an independent agency on March 11, 1942 by Executive Order 9095. It was placed in the Office for Emergency Management of the Executive Office of the President and its function was to seize or vest and take over the ownership of certain types of enemy property that was not already frozen or blocked and regulated by the Treasury Department.

The Process of Vesting

Within APC, an Investigations Division looked for property that should be seized.[125] Much of its information came at first from Treasury's 1941 Census of Foreign-Owned Assets, though the Custodian's office also relied on the Justice Department, OSS and other intelligence agencies, the Securities and Exchange Commission, and the Patent Office.[126] The Investigations Division then made recommendations to the Executive Committee, chaired by the Deputy Custodian, and that committee made recommendations to the custodian. The final decision to vest lay with the custodian.

If a vesting order was issued and published in the Federal Register, that transfer of title was immediately and summarily effectuated.[127] Vesting, however, was not the only option available, for the custodian could also provide for "direction, management, supervision, and control" without transferring ownership, an option particularly suited for the vesting of business enterprises. General Orders, usually relating to specific classes of property, were also issued, requiring specific action on the part of persons who held an interest in the asset in question.[128]

The Custodian's Office also established mechanisms so that if a mistake was made in the decision to vest, "every American and friendly alien [was] given opportunity to show that his rights [had] been infringed."[129] The operating principle was that "mistakes against our friends could be corrected, but mistakes in favor of our enemies might be fatal."[130] Any person other than "a national of a designated enemy country" could assert and file a claim with the Alien Property Custodian, requesting a hearing within a year from the time the vesting order was issued. Claims were heard by the Vesting Property Claims Committee. The committee, set up on July 22, 1943, found itself busy, processing more than 2,000 claims within a year of its establishment.[131] Once the committee had reviewed a claim, it passed its recommendations to the Alien Property Custodian. Some contemporaries remarked that because the custodian had appointed the committee members, this process made him "judge and defendant in his own case."[132] Others, however, believed that the procedure met "the basic constitutional requirements for administrative review."[133]

What would become of property taken under control was not always clear, and the wording of the vesting orders themselves left open what would happen to the property. The orders read that property and its proceeds "shall be held in a special account pending further determination of the Alien Property Custodian." That determination might include returning the property, returning the proceeds from the sale of the property, or paying compensation for it "if and when it should be determined that such return should be made or such compensation should be paid." Vesting, however, could also mean property could be "administered, liquidated, sold or otherwise dealt with in the interest of and for the benefit of the United States," and that could mean a determination that nothing would be returned.[134] It was also possible to interpret the power to vest merely as an act of custody. The press release accompanying Vesting Order No.1 (Feb. 16, 1942) stated that vested property was to be considered as "sequestered."[135] The precedent of World War I could be read two ways as well, either implying confiscation—

since the Supreme Court had held in 1924 that the end of World War I did not bring with it a right to have property returned[136]—or implying a return of the proceeds, since alien properties had been sold but most of the proceeds subsequently returned to the former owners.[137] The ultimate disposition of vested property remained unclear during the war, and in any case was a matter for Congress to decide.

Faced with this uncertainty over eventual disposition, the Alien Property Custodian equivocated.[138] In the case of vested businesses, some were sold but others were run as going concerns, sometimes with salaried employees of the APC acting in supervisory or directorial capacities, as much for lack of skilled and competent managers as out of fear of enemy influence. On the other hand, the Custodian's Office really did not want to assume the direct responsibility for everything from methods of production to labor relations, arguing that "activities of this character are foreign to the effective operation of the Custodian's Office as an agency of the government."[139] Assets were also treated selectively, since not all assets were readily convertible into cash, or even if they were, equally valuable. Thus, patents were ordinarily vested but mortgages and life insurance policies were not. The general rule of selling vested property at public sales (by General Order 26, of June 9, 1943) by sealed written bids was hedged with all kinds of exceptions: property worth less than $10,000 might be sold privately or not advertised for sale; brokers might be used in exceptional circumstances; some classes of persons (such as those on the Proclaimed List) would not be permitted to buy; perishable commodities or property that was expensive to retain might be disposed of through privately arranged sales; and some property could not find willing buyers at the assessed value.

The most useful and pragmatic solution, the APC argued, was to convert vested property (other than patents and copyrights) into cash and hold it in separate accounts, pending Congressional decision about settlement, and the decision to sell at the best price was compatible with a decision to provide full compensation since "the original owners are in general interested not in specific pieces of property but in the economic value of their property as a source of income."[140] Whether this assumption was justified, at least in 1944, "it seems certain...that provisions will be made for the return of property to nationals of non-enemy countries."[141] The provision of separate accounts of course also made it easier to return vested property.

Evaluating the Property Taken Under Control

Because so much property in so many different asset categories was seized from enemy nationals for the war production effort, it is likely that some victims' assets were inadvertently taken in the process. Knowing the extent of the value of all assets taken was important at the time: it provided a basis for Congressional decisions about future disposition. For individuals or companies whose assets were seized, the value would become part of the claim for return that could be filed, including for the return of property seized in error. The vesting program is also one of the instances where the property of individuals was taken by the U.S. government, though there is evidence that some of that property was also returned. That intellectual property formed a large part of the assets seized adds still another dimension.

In many ways, the APC resembled a holding company, not only because it controlled assets of considerably greater value than its ownership equity in them, but also because of the wide variety of property involved.[142] The Custodian was the majority stockholder of corporations producing cameras, dyestuffs, potash, pharmaceuticals, scientific instruments, and alcoholic beverages, but was also in charge of guardianship estates of Japanese children born in the United States who had been sent to Japan for their education. The Custodian's Office held the largest patent pool in the country, and it vested over 200,000 copyrights during the war. It also controlled dairies, banks, and retail stores. It was the successor to the enemy heirs of more than 2,000 American residents whose estates held cash, real property, jewelry, securities, and other valuables, but it was also in charge of "bankrupt enterprises, damaged merchandise, rural wasteland, and bad debts."[143]

Copyrights, Trademarks, and Patents

Copyrights, trademarks, and patents are structurally similar, as they protect an exclusive legal right, whether to make, use, or sell an invention (in the case of a patent), to reproduce, publish, and sell a literary, musical, or artistic work (in the case of a copyright), or to reserve the use of the owner as maker or seller (in the case of a trademark). Put more precisely, at least in the case of a patented invention, it "confers the right to secure the enforcement power of the state in excluding unauthorized persons, for a specified number of years, from making commercial use" of it.[144] In the context of the U.S. control of assets during wartime, however, a difference was drawn in practice, because while only selected copyrights and trademarks were vested, "all patents of nationals of enemy and enemy-occupied countries" were vested.[145]

Copyrights. U.S. copyright protection was limited in scope for foreign holders, largely out of protectionist impulses. In the early 1940s, Congress had

> sought copyright monopoly for United States authors in other countries; but reciprocal protection in the United States could only be obtained on condition that for the most part copyrighted works should be manufactured in the United States. Thus, the text of a book published in another country would have to be re-set in type and wholly reproduced in this country or else be open to piracy by publishers here without any legal remedy by the holders of the violated copyright.[146]

As a result, even before APC began to vest copyrights, protection for non-U.S. authors was weak unless they had prewar agreements to produce their works in the United States. In any case, the freezing order had included copyrights, trademarks, and patents, and they had to be reported in the 1941 Census of Foreign-Owned Assets even if the value was less than $1,000.[147]

For the custodian, the operative principle in deciding to vest a copyright was whether a work had financial value or was of importance to the war effort. The latter reason justified taking copyright title not just from the nationals of enemy countries but also from nationals in enemy-occupied countries, which of course meant that the copyrights of victims might also be seized as no distinction was drawn at the time of vesting.[148] In a tally covering the wartime vesting period (March 11, 1942, to June 30, 1945), 120,690 of the nationally identifiable copyright interests vested were in fact for sheet music, 82 percent of which were in the hands of French and Italian music publishers. This is why almost all of the

$1 million in copyright royalties paid and collected by the custodian in this period were the result of prewar contracts, and why the lions' share went to French (49 percent) and Italian (17 percent) publishers and copyright holders.[149] Thus, Claude Debussy's Clair de Lune, used in the film Frenchman's Creek, brought royalties to the APC, as did performances of Puccini's La Boheme, Tosca, and Madame Butterfly. Even the German war song "Lili Marlene" brought in $10,000 in royalties by 1945 under the 23 licenses that were granted for its use in films, radio, on stage, and as sheet music.[150]

A more direct connection to the war effort was the licensing and republication of important German books and periodicals in metallurgy, physics, mathematics, medicine, and chemistry.[151] One of the most significant works was Friedrich Beilstein's *Handbuch der organischen Chemie,* originally published in 59 volumes at a cost of $2,000, but now made available in the United States in a photo-offset reprint for only $400, and a work on which the Custodian's Office collected nearly $41,000 in royalties.[152] By January 1, 1945, the Office had also "reprinted one or more volumes of approximately 100 different scientific periodicals, chiefly German," mostly for industrial concerns or research institutions and universities. The republication of articles from *Die Naturwissenschaften* and the *Zeitschrift für Physik* were regarded as "one of the factors which made the atomic bomb possible" by some of the American scientists involved in its development.[153]

However, the most surprising is the list of European authors whose works were vested, including Henri Bergson, Karl Capek, Madame Curie, Georges Clemenceau, André Gide, André Malraux, Guy de Maupassant, Baroness Orczy, Romain Rolland, Edmund Rostand, and Georges Simenon. "Among French books, the gay Babar elephant stories for children enjoy great popularity," one learns, and "the Seven Gothic Tales and Winter's Tales, by the Danish Baroness Blixen, earned substantial amounts in royalties collected by the Office."[154] However, Baroness Blixen's copyrights, including those to *Out of Africa*, were returned to her at the end of 1950, along with $33,558.67 in royalties.[155]

The number of victims whose copyright royalties were seized is unknown, but those who were victimized by the Nazis might have taken some satisfaction in knowing that one particular author did not see any of his royalties. Adolf Hitler's Mein Kampf, a work first published in the United States in 1933, had its copyright vested, and the royalties—totaling $20,580 by June 30, 1945—were held in an account in the name of Franz Eher, the publisher of Hitler and the Nazi Party. A dry note was added to the Custodian's 1944 Annual Report that "the ultimate disposition of Hitler's royalties, as of all other property in the hands of the Custodian, remains to be decided by the Congress."[156]

Trademarks. Trademarks, as devices that on the one hand imply a right to exclude others from using a name or symbol, and on the other hand try to provide assurances of goodwill (or an absence of deceptive practices) on the part of a business, are difficult to value in terms of dollars, let alone for war purposes. Dealing with trademarks nevertheless was part of a strategy to encourage a negative attitude towards the enemy:

> A trademark belonging to an Axis business enterprise represents an investment in good will, and is part of that enterprise's enduring roots in the country. Disposition of an enterprise should include the disposition of the trademark as well. Destruction of a trademark might be the best method of disposition.[157]

Anti-enemy sentiment was fanned by assertions such as "every time an American bought a box of headache remedy with a certain trademark a few cents were added to the German coffers,"[158] whether or not such statements were accurate.

Many trademarks went unused, as was true of the more than 7,000 trademarks in the names of nationals in enemy or enemy-occupied countries that were registered in the United States in 1944. By June 30, 1945, only 412 trademarks had been vested, 325 (79 percent) of which were owned by vested enterprises, and 357 (87 percent) of which were German.[159] An opinion of the General Counsel of the APC on July 22, 1943, stated bluntly that "unless the business and good will in connection with which a particular trademark is used are vested, a vesting of the trademark gives the Custodian nothing."[160] Furthermore, 47 percent of the vested trademarks were for cosmetic and soap products, and only 27 percent were for products, such as medicines, pharmaceuticals, chemicals, and scientific appliances, that were potentially useful for war purposes.[161] By June 30, 1945, only $568,000 had been collected by the APC in trademark contracts.[162]

Patents. Patents and their role in controlling the market through monopolies and cartels had been an issue long before the war. "The interchange of patents between American and foreign concerns," one journalist had argued,

> has been used as a means of cartelizing an industry to effectively displace competition. The production of...beryllium, magnesium, optical glass and chemicals has been restrained through international patent controls and cross-licensing which have divided the world market into closed areas.[163]

Indeed, the control or restraint of world trade through patent arrangements formed a prominent part of the Kilgore Committee hearings in the Senate in 1943 and 1944, with numerous antitrust cases subsequently filed against U.S. companies alleging "German control over our industry."[164] In light of prewar arrangements between I.G. Farben and Du Pont (1925) and between I.G. Farben and Standard Oil of New Jersey (1927), such concerns appeared warranted[165]— though the warnings of the danger sometimes verged on the hysterical.[166] Custodian Leo Crowley made clear the continuity between prewar cartels and wartime use of patents when he told the Senate that "the primary purpose of vesting and administering foreign-owned patents is to break any restrictive holds which these patents may have on American industry, particularly restrictions which may operate to impede war production."[167]

Soon after the Alien Property Custodian's office was established, it launched an investigation into patents, patent applications and patent contracts, in order to vest all that were "owned by persons in enemy and enemy-occupied countries," other than those in which a bona fide American interest existed. General Orders 2 and 3 (both June 15, 1942) of the Alien Property Custodian had already required the filing of a report by anyone claiming right, title, or interest to a patent granted to a "designated foreign national" since January 1, 1939, as well as a declaration that the patent holder was not at present residing in an enemy or enemy-occupied country. Armed with this information, the Office was able to exclude patents that needed more investigation to determine how much they were controlled by American interests. On December 7, 1942, the President sent a letter to the Custodian directing his Office "to seize all patents controlled by the enemy, regardless of nominal ownership, and make the patents freely available to

American industry, first for war purposes of the United Nations, and second for general use in the national interest."[168]

By the end of 1942, about 35,000 patents "presumed to be enemy owned or controlled" were vested.[169] A comprehensive list, organized into 110 different classifications, indicated a total of 36,675 patents vested by January 1, 1943, with the classifications ranging from a high of 1,998 patents vested in "radiant energy" and 1,607 in "chemistry, carbon compounds" down to two patents for fences and a single patent for needle and pin making.[170] By June 30, 1945, a total of 46,442 patents, patent applications, and unpatented inventions from nationals of enemy and enemy-occupied countries had been vested.[171] Of these 46,442, the vast majority (42,726) were patents, 64 percent of which were held by German owners. By June 30, 1945, about 6,000 of these 42,726 patents had expired, and patents held by Italian nationals as well as by Europeans in liberated countries were no longer vested after September 1944, so the effective number of "live patents" by 1945 was around 36,700, close to the number of patents vested by the end of 1942.[172] The Census of Foreign-Owned Assets in 1941 had indicated a total of around 65,000 foreign-held patents and agreements related to patents,[173] so only slightly more than half of all foreign-held patents were actually vested by the APC.

In making them "freely available," patents held by enemies were made royalty-free (so no profit went to the enemy), nonexclusive, and revocable (so no one using the patent could benefit from the value accruing to an exclusive right), and were licensed after the payment of a small fee. All of this was "tantamount to the destruction of the right."[174] For patents held by nationals of enemy-occupied countries, licensing was more complex. Initially, the Custodian issued royalty-free licenses for the duration of the war plus six months, but after several governments-in-exile protested, in 1944 this policy was changed to provide for licensing with "reasonable royalties" from the date of licensing, unless it was a license for war production. As countries were liberated, the policy changed again "because the nationals of the liberated countries now could carry on negotiations themselves" over patents.[175]

The total number of licenses actually granted under patents vested from nationals of enemy countries was very small, likely because of the complications that were feared once the patents were returned to their owners at the end of the war.[176] APC made considerable efforts to let potential users know about the technical information in the vested patents,[177] but the Office was hampered by the nature of patents themselves: many patents are taken out based on laboratory findings rather than commercial applicability, patents become obsolete, patents can be unworkable owing to lack of resources, and patents can be encumbered by prewar contracts and commitments. Thus in practice, only about two-thirds of the vested patents were licenseable, and of these 22,000, licenses were in fact granted under only 7,343 different patents—2,000 of them to a single firm.[178]

But if only about a third of the available patents were actually exploited in the United States, the following (selected) list of products manufactured under vested patent licenses by the end of 1944 gives a sense of which patents were of greatest interest: 42 million gallons of nitration-grade toluene (for explosives and aviation fuel), 66 million pounds of processed tin, 23 million pounds of polyvinyl chloride, 320,000 feet of steel cable, 500 propeller blades, 450,000 barrels of cement, and 110,000 dozen pairs of ladies hosiery.[179]

A different list from mid-1943 highlights those patents that in some manner were used to create products that contributed to the war effort:

> Typical licenses already issued are for high explosives, collapsible boats for the Navy, fire-fighting material, power transmission, intermediates for pharmaceuticals, a magnetic alloy composition, aluminum production, surgical bandages, electrical current amplifiers, synthetic resuscitants, machine tools, camera equipment, and die presses and machines for stretching and drawing metal.[180]

That not more than a third of the available vested patents were used was attributed to the revocability of the licensed patents, the absence of exclusivity and royalties, or the use by "big business" of these patents. In the view of the Custodian's Office, the "real explanation for the existence of unused vested patents is that they are not commercially valuable" even if they were helpful in certain aspects of war production.[181] But patents had to be put to work, as "our friends in the occupied countries would hardly have us do less than to turn their patent rights into active weapons of warfare for the defeat of their oppressors."[182] Thus, even if victims were seeing their patent rights seized, the APC wanted to reassure them that they were being put to good use.

By the end of June, 1945, $8.3 million in patent royalties had been collected under vested patents and patent contracts, two-thirds of them German. Half of the $8.3 million total had accrued prior to vesting,[183] indicating that the APC was merely continuing with freezing and immobilizing the financial assets represented by patents, while it tried to disseminate the information patents contained for use in manufacturing and in the war effort.

Businesses, Real and Personal Property, Estates and Trusts

Other property categories vested by the APC were easier to estimate in monetary terms than patents or copyrights. The following table highlights the major asset categories:

Table 7: Net Equity Vested by the Custodian, Ranked by Largest Type of Property[184] *(Domestic Assets Only, As of June 30, 1945)*

By Specific Type of Property	(in millions of dollars)
Vested businesses: stock	107.5
Vested businesses: equity	38.9
Cash: principal	38.1
Estates and trusts: trusts under wills	15.5
Cash: income	12.5
Estates and trusts: decedents' estates	7.4
Vested businesses: notes/accounts receivable	4.3
Estates and trusts: inter vivos trusts	3.8
Personal property: bonds	2.2
Real property: real estate	2.2
Personal property: notes, claims, credits	2.1
Estates and trusts: guardianship estates	1.2
Other	6.2
Total	235.7

By Category	Percent
Vested business enterprises	62.7
Cash	21.5
Estates and trusts	11.6
Other (real and personal property; royalties)	4.2

By Nationality of Former Ownership	
German	68.3
Japanese	22.4
Italian	6.7
Hungarian	1.0
Romanian	0.2
Bulgarian	0.2
Enemy-occupied	1.2

Businesses. Business enterprises in the United States were the single largest individual form of property in dollar terms controlled by nationals of enemy countries—$151 million of the $208 million vested in the Custodian.[185] A total of 408 enterprises, 71 percent of them corporations, with assets amounting to $390 million, had their interests vested from 1942 to 1945. Of these 408, 200 (49 percent) were German-owned, 169 (17 percent) were Japanese-owned, and 33 (8 percent) were Italian-owned.[186] Control was typically exerted through the acquisition of enough voting shares to exert dominant control, such that 61 percent of the 408 enterprises had 50 percent or more of their voting stock controlled by the Custodian.[187] In terms of categories of enterprises, those with the largest book value were chemical manufacturers (21 companies, most of them German, with total assets worth $162 million), but the largest single group was in wholesale trade (153 companies, mostly small, with total assets worth $45 million).[188] So though chemical manufacturers accounted for only 5 percent of the companies, they represented 41 percent of the assets vested, while wholesale trade accounted for 37 percent of the companies but only 11 percent of the assets vested.

If a business could be run profitably and perform useful functions, it was operated as a going concern. As of June 30, 1945, 117 of the 408 enterprises were operating with total assets of $257 million as of that date, the most important of which (in terms of total sales as well as sales of war products) were again the chemical manufacturers.[189] The remaining 291 enterprises were placed in liquidation, many of them having depended on trade with enemy countries (e.g., import/export firms, steamship companies). Relative to the amount realized, it can hardly be said that the United States profited much from the seizure of these businesses.[190]

Real Property and Tangible Personal Property. A small amount of real property ($4.3 million) was vested during the wartime operation of the Custodian's Office, of which German-owned properties were the largest ($2.3 million) by nationality. Most (worth $3.5 million) of this property was urban and consisted of either single dwellings or commercial buildings (319 and 96 of the 622 properties vested, respectively), though ten small hotels and rooming houses as well as two Japanese Shinto temples were also vested.[191] One-third of the properties were on the eastern seaboard, though there were properties scattered across the country.[192] Sales proceeds from properties, though 11 percent better than their appraised value, yielded only slightly more than $2 million.

As with the sale of vested businesses, there were difficulties in selling vested property, ranging from title insurance problems (affecting 81 real estate parcels) to political considerations (the sale of 98 real estate parcels vested from Italian and Austrian nationals, for example, was discontinued at the request of the State Department).[193] Vested tangible personal property was even more difficult to sell. The Custodian's annual report for 1943, for example, noted with some satisfaction that the Office had found "two carloads of steel bars owned by an Italian concern, which had stood on a siding in the New Jersey freight yards for almost 2 years," and that these were thereupon vested.[194] But though the Custodian "offered at public sale 77,161 pounds of steel bars vested from Alfa-Romeo" on April 3, 1944 (possibly these same bars), valued at $24,000, no buyers could be found at that price. In fact, the highest bid the Custodian received was $825. The warehouse where the bars were stored was urgently needed for other war purposes, and moving the bars would have cost $400, so the Custodian settled for the best price obtainable in September 1944: $1,375.[195] Of course, while this kind of property might end up being sold at steep discounts "or even at scrap value," personal property such as jewelry or art objects might sell for a third more than their appraised value. Total tangible personal property vested amounted to only $901,000 and sale proceeds by June 30, 1945 were only $452,000.[196]

Estates and Trusts. From March 11, 1942 until June 30, 1945, the Custodian vested a total of just under 2,997 estates and trusts, worth an estimated $41.1 million. Of that total, 77 percent (2,330) were formerly German-owned, constituting 82 percent ($33.6 million) of the total, the vast majority of which (1708) were decedents' estates and trusts under wills (541), valued at $11.7 and $17.1 million respectively[197]. Distribution to the Custodian from executors, trustees, and fiduciaries of estates reached $13 million by mid-1945, nearly all of which came from decedents' estates and trusts under wills.

Heirs and executors could find themselves brought up short by the fact that the Custodian's determinations as to property and survivorship were conclusive. That was despite the fact that survivorship was "often extremely difficult, and not infrequently insoluble" to determine when a legatee was an enemy national resident in an enemy country.[198] Complicating matters were contradictory legal rulings: some cases stated that lack of evidence of death created a presumption that heirs were still alive, while other cases declared the presumption did not exist owing to the ravages of war.[199]

Some securities from the distribution of estates and trusts or from the assets of vested enterprises were also vested, $1.8 million worth of stocks and $4.8 million worth of bonds, with more than three-fourths of the latter U.S. government bonds.[200] As of June 30, 1945, the Custodian still held $871,000 worth of stocks and $2.2 million worth of bonds, indicating that $3 million realized from these sales was less than half of their total value of $6.6 million.[201]

The Postwar Period

Postwar Vesting and Return of Assets

Though Germany capitulated on May 8, 1945, the official cessation of hostilities was only proclaimed on December 31, 1946, and the official declaration of the end of the state of war between the United States and Germany came only on October 25, 1951. Thus, at least in formal terms, the "end" of the war was protracted, and the same can be said for the end of vesting. To be sure, Italian assets were no longer vested after December 1943, and as European countries were successively liberated in 1945, the property of nationals from these formerly enemy-occupied countries ceased being vested, though by that date the only property still being vested by the United States was patents and copyrights.

Yet in the later years of the war, the fear grew that

> even though victorious, we shall still find large segments of our industry being controlled and manipulated from Berlin and we shall still be harboring within our borders a Nazi army ready to resume the task of boring from within in the hope of ultimately taking revenge for its previous defeat.[202]

Such an assessment may have lain behind the decision in the spring of 1945, when the Secretary of State, the Secretary of the Treasury, and the Alien Property Custodian agreed that all property in the United States of hostile German and Japanese nationals should be vested in the Alien Property Custodian and that neither the property nor its proceeds should be returned to the former owners. Accordingly, they recommended to the President that the Custodian be authorized to vest German and Japanese bank accounts, credits, securities, and other properties not seized under the original vesting program. This recommendation was approved, and the expansion of the vesting program was authorized by Executive Order No. 9567 on June 8, 1945.[203]

Postwar vesting of German and Japanese-owned property would not be terminated until April 17, 1953, by which time an additional $210 million was paid into the Treasury from these seizures.[204]

In October of 1946, the APC was transformed into the Office of Alien Property (OAP) in the Justice Department, and over the next seven years, the pace of vesting increased substantially.[205] In fact, 60 percent of all vesting orders issued from 1942 to 1953 were issued after 1946. The OAP relied on the FBI and the Treasury Department to investigate ownership before vesting, but with an important caveat.[206] All property of German and Japanese citizens "is vested unless available evidence indicates they were victims of persecution by their governments."[207] According to the Deputy Director of the OAP, the Office "took great pains to avoid vesting the property of such persons."[208]

Though postwar vesting was limited to property controlled by German and Japanese nationals, a reporting of assets similar to the wartime census was demanded of asset holders. Even among the first 12,000 reports received by October 1946, about one-third had to be set aside as they appeared to cover property that could not be vested.[209] On the other hand, the continued concern over cloaked ownership prompted intensive investigations to locate as yet undisclosed property still controlled by enemies.[210]

By 1947, the OAP began returning vested property of all kinds—including cash, patents, interests in estates and trusts, copyrights, shares, and real property—to claimant individuals and businesses. By 1958, approximately 3,700 return orders had been issued, as compared to the over 5,000 vesting orders issued during the war and the over 14,000 issued thereafter.[211] Thus, only about one in five of the properties seized were returned even by 1958, and of those 20 percent in turn, only about one in five were for properties vested during the war to judge by the related vesting order numbers. The names (and businesses) to whom property was returned give few clues as to identity or status, and even the precise nature of assets being returned is unclear: Return Order No. 4 gave back "certain patents" to "Arnold Janowitz and others" on February 24, and Return Order No. 2827 gave "securities" back to Leo Robinsohn on June 29, 1956, for example. A survey of the cash returned, some possibly from the sale of non-cash assets, shows a similar distribution as the 1941 Census of Foreign-Owned Assets, with quite small amounts (some as little as $3 or $10) returned to many individuals, and much larger amounts returned to a few companies and associations. Even the largest amounts were not that great. From 1947 to 1958, there were only 44 return orders, half of them to business enterprises, that were issued for amounts over $100,000. The largest single amount returned by the OAPC was the $4.7 million returned to "Wm. Kohler, Albert Arent, and Fidelity—Philadelphia

Trust Co., sub-trustees of Trust of Dr. Otto Rohm" on June 30, 1954; the next largest amount was the $1.5 million given back to the Banco di Napoli in 1949.[212]

War Claims

Initially during World War I, the Custodian thought of himself as a trustee; later, he saw himself as the confiscator of enemy property. Confiscated property was sold, and the proceeds were meant to be used to satisfy U.S. war claims.[213] The same line of thinking recurred during and after World War II with freezing (trusteeship) and vesting (confiscation) followed by the argument in Congress in 1946 that the proceeds from the sale of vested property should be used to pay for war damage claims of Americans. If foreign nationals had had their property seized abroad, then it was the responsibility of their governments to compensate them for those losses.[214]

In fact, the peace treaties signed with Italy, Bulgaria, Hungary, and Romania included explicit commitments by these countries to compensate their own nationals, but only Italy seems to have lived up to this obligation.[215] A similar commitment formed part of the Paris Reparation Agreement on Germany (as well as subsequently directly with Germany in 1952),[216] and was confirmed for the United States as well through passage by Congress of the U.S. War Claims Act in 1948.

The difficulty even for those working in the OAP was the "unrealistic bookkeeping" such commitments meant. Though U.S. war claims after World War II were greater than those made after World War I, less property was seized and the costs to the United States of occupying Germany were much greater than the war claims of Americans against Germany.[217] Thus it did make sense to use seized German-controlled property in the United States to settle American war claims against Germany while at the same time spending far larger dollar sums to occupy and rebuild Germany. It was a good deal more reasonable

> to recognize that the damages done by Germany will never be made whole; that valid war claims will never be paid; that compensation for war claims to the extent that it is allowed must come, if at all, from the American Treasury; and to devote all German assets in this country directly to the relief of Germany, which we have, in fact, undertaken.[218]

But the "theory that the interests of American claimants for damage suffered at the hands of the Nazi government should have precedence" evidently took priority.[219] Section 13 (a) of the 1948 War Claims Act created a War Claims Fund that was supervised by a Congressional War Claims Commission. That Commission saw its duty, according to an OAP critic, to "insure at all times the sufficiency of funds to provide for payment in full of every valid claim" possible under the Act.[220] But since claims greatly outstripped available funds, the War Claims Commission in effect became "a pressure group with official status seeking the enlargement of the Fund."[221] As the War Claims Act was financed through the Treasury Department, the argument in Congress was that proceeds from the sale of German and Japanese vested assets could be used to pay American war claims—an argument that drew objections from both the Justice Department and the Bureau of the Budget. For victims' heirs, the situation was even worse:

> when the question is presented whether property of Jewish families exterminated at Auschwitz and Buchenwald should continue to be held by the United States, the issue

should be determined in terms of the justification or lack of justification for the seizure and not in terms of the effect of a return on the [War Claims] fund.[222]

But in the end, by 1954, the War Claims Commission received $75 million in funding from seized German and Japanese assets, although evidently efforts had been made to insure that these would not, in fact, be assets of persecutees.

Summary

Though the category "victim" was not explicitly recognized as such until after the war, there was no evident intent to immobilize or seize assets from those who were clearly not enemies. Even in the midst of the war, John Foster Dulles could write that "nothing in the Congressional hearings or debates suggests any intention to confiscate the property of friendly aliens, neutrals, and the victims of German aggression" by the Alien Property Custodian.[223] In addition, assets vested after the war were limited to those controlled by Germans and Japanese.

In practice, both the Treasury and Justice Departments tried to distinguish a small, problematic group that was trying to exploit assets or their access to the United States from the large, unproblematic group of those with legitimate control over assets in the United States or legitimate reasons for being here. The focus was on potential saboteurs, smugglers and the businesses that acted as fronts for Nazi interests as well as on the assets of innocents abroad that had been, or were in danger of being, captured by Nazi invaders. The Alien Registration Act, the freezing and then licensing of financial transactions by FFC, and the work of Customs inspectors were all directed towards preventing the enemy from exploiting assets in or access to the United States. The very existence of error-correction or asset-protection mechanisms, whether in the form of Treasury regulations and policies or the APC claims process, lend weight to Dulles's assertion. Other practices, ranging from the wartime reassertion of the legal rights of aliens to the exclusion of certain nationality groups from enemy alien restrictions, also testify to a desire to draw distinctions that would benefit those who had been persecuted. The evolution in thinking about persecutees would lead to an explicit recognition of their special status reflected in the August 1946 revision of the Trading with the Enemy Act (TWEA); when they were excluded from postwar vesting.

Foreign Funds Control tried to protect European property owners from Nazi actions, though for assets already in the United States in 1940 and 1941 the effect was limited by the very nature of the asset pool. Not only was that pool comparatively small and skewed towards assets controlled by nationals of Allied rather than Axis powers, but according to the 1941 census, these assets were distributed between a small group of businesses with large holdings and a large group of individuals with small holdings. That same distribution was also evident in the claims honored by the OAP after the war, with a few large sums returned to a few companies and many small sums (and other assets) returned to many individuals.

In fact, other than the looted Dutch securities that were eventually restituted to the Netherlands, FFC controlled assets were not vested by the APC.[224] For individuals in the U.S. who needed funds during the war for living expenses, or for organizations working to help those trying to flee from Nazi-controlled territories, FFC tried to facilitate such access to assets. For bonafide refugees in the United States, FFC early on tried to ensure that their status not impinge upon access to their funds. After the war, the return of assets to the smallest property owners was eased by a unilateral decision to defrost accounts below a certain monetary threshold. Far less property was ever seized and sold than was temporarily frozen during the war, and even that freezing ensured oversight more than it absolutely prohibited transactions.

Assets vested by the APC during the war were explicitly to be used for the benefit of the United States, and when possible were converted into cash. While several hundred thousand individual assets were seized, in some of the largest categories such as patents and copyrights conversion into cash was impossible or impractical. Instead, their use was licensed, and the resulting revenues were paid to the custodian; in the postwar period, at least some of these copyrights and patents, along with the accumulated royalties, were returned to their former owners or their heirs, though with considerable delay. Claims could be and were filed for the return of vested assets, though the number of successful claims (under 4,000 by 1958) appears to have been much smaller than the number of properties seized (19,312 vesting orders).[225] Gold presented its own difficulties because of its liquidity, the manner in which the world gold trade functioned, and the difficulty of tracing ownership and a U.S. "unquestioned acceptance" policy. Some of the "flight capital" arriving in the United States before the war, including gold, undoubtedly came from victims, but available information permits no definitive conclusions about what proportion that might have been.

Endnotes for Chapter III

[1] Treas. Dept., FFC, "Administration of the Wartime Financial and Property Controls of the United States Government," June 1942, 1–3, NACP, RG 131, FFC Subj. Files, Box 367, Rpts TFR–300 [311908–963] (hereinafter "Administration of Wartime Controls"); "General Information on the Administration, Structure and Functions of Foreign Funds Control, 1940–1948," Ch. 1, 1 (hereinafter "History of FFC"), NACP, RG 56, Entry 66A816, Box 47 [331331–775].

[2] Exec. Order 8389 (Apr. 10, 1940), Sec. 2, in Martin Domke, *Trading with the Enemy in World War II* (New York: Central Book Co., 1943), 432–3.

[3] Domke, *Trading with the Enemy in World War II*, 391, 438. Congress amended Sec. 5 (b) on May 7, 1940, as did the First War Powers Act of Dec. 18, 1941.

[4] "History of FFC," Ch. 2, 3 fn. 6.

[5] Ibid., Ch. 2, 1–4. The memos were sent on Dec. 15 and 22, 1937; Oliphant drafted extensive regulations for such controls.

[6] Ibid., Ch. 2, 8.

[7] Ibid., Ch. 3, 2.

[8] 3 *Code of Federal Regulations* (CFR), 1938–1943 Compilation. Exec. Orders 8405 (657–659), E.O. 8446 (674), E.O. 8484 (687), and E.O. 8565 (796).

[9] CFR, 1938–1943 Compilation. E.O. 8701 (904), E.O. 8711 (910), E.O. 8721 (917), and E.O. 8746 (929).

[10] By October 1940, both agencies agreed to examine how German funds located in the Western Hemisphere were being used. Francis Biddle, Solicitor General of the Department of Justice, asked J. Edgar Hoover, the Director of the FBI, to provide whatever information he had on such funds "being used for propaganda in this country and South America." See Memo from Francis Biddle, Solicitor General, Dept. of Justice, to J. Edgar Hoover, Oct. 15, 1940, FBI Files [349171].

[11] Dean Acheson, *Present at the Creation* (New York: Norton, 1969), 23. The State Department was particularly concerned about the effect a communications freeze with enemy countries would have: "it was imperative that no action be taken by this government which might invite retaliatory measures against our [diplomatic] pouch." "History of FFC," Ch. 5, 101A [331331–775].

[12] Freezing orders were also extended to China and Japan (July 26), Thailand (Dec. 9), and Hong Kong (Dec. 26), retroactive to June 14, 1941. William Reeves, "The Control of Foreign Funds by the United States Treasury," *Law and Contemporary Problems* 11 (1945), 24; "Administration of Wartime Controls," 2 [331908–963]; Domke, *Trading with the Enemy in World War II*, 434.

[13] Starting on May 10, 1940, the Treas. Dept., had required that assets in the U.S. belonging to blocked countries or their nationals be reported (on Form TFR–100) as countries fell successively under the freezing order. Treas. Dept., *Annual Report* 1940, 543.

[14] "History of FFC," Ch. 4, 19–20.

[15] Memo from Elting Arnold, "Divulging Information from Form TFR–300 Reports to Foreign Countries and American Creditors of Nationals of Such Countries," Oct. 27, 1944, NACP, RG 131, FFC, Box 367, TFR–300 Release of Info [312003–009].

[16] U.S. Treas. Dept., *Census of Foreign-Owned Assets in the United States* (Washington: Government Printing Office, 1945), 8–9, 55–57 (hereinafter *Census of Foreign-Owned Assets*).

[17] See Judd Polk, "Freezing Dollars Against the Axis," *Foreign Affairs* 20 (1): Oct. 1941, 114. Polk's estimates differed significantly from the Census even thought his information came from Treasury Dept. compilations and other government sources.

[18] "History of FFC," Ch. 4, 22.

[19] *Census of Foreign-Owned Assets*, 14–15.

[20] It is worth noting in this context how comparatively small American investment in the neutral countries was. According to a 1942 American Economic Review article, American investment was largest in Spain ($86 million), followed by Sweden ($28 million), Portugal ($17 million) and Switzerland ($12 million). Cited in Edward Freutel, "Exchange Control, Freezing Orders and the Conflict of Laws," *Harvard Law Review* 56 (1942), 63.

[21] *Census of Foreign-Owned Assets*, 62.

[22] Ibid., 17–19.

[23] Ibid., 20, 66, 68.

[24] Ibid., 62, 75. The market value of foreign securities held in the U.S. by banks, brokers, and custodians for Danes and Norwegians was higher, at $23.5 million.

[25] This was from an unpublished Commerce Dept. estimate of 1940, reproduced as Table VI in the *Census of Foreign-Owned Assets*, 21.

[26] "Administration of Wartime Controls," 21 [311908–963].

[27] "History of FFC," Ch. 3, 28–29.

[28] "Administration of Wartime Controls," 21 [311908–963]; "History of FFC," Ch. 3, 29 [331331–775].

[29] Treas. Dept., *Annual Report* 1944, 215–16; Treas. Dept., *Annual Report* 1945, 200; Reeves, "Control of Foreign Funds," 42.

[30] "History of FFC," Ch. 3, 30; "Administration of Wartime Controls," 20 [311908–963]; Reeves, "Control of Foreign Funds," 42.

[31] "Administration of Wartime Controls," 22 [311908–963].

[32] Following Public Circular 6, as of September 13, 1941, such securities could not be redeemed unless a Form TFEL–2 was attached.

[33] Reeves, "Control of Foreign Funds," 43.

[34] Treas. Dept., *Annual Report* 1943, 126.

[35] Ruling 6A was revoked again in September 1943, and control of securities subsumed under General Ruling 5, with similar restrictions.

[36] "History of FFC," Ch. 5, 13–15. Reeves, "Control of Foreign Funds," 44. Reeves also asserts that the Treasury "did everything practical to depreciate the value of the American dollar bill in Europe and elsewhere."

[37] "History of FFC," Ch. 5, 14. Currency import controls were lifted in April 1947 since by that time most important European countries in Europe "had taken steps to detect and segregate any US currency within their borders in which there was an enemy interest." Ibid., Ch. 6, 47.

[38] Ibid., Ch. 5, 22.

[39] Ibid., Ch. 5, 22–23.

[40] Ibid., Ch. 5, 22–25. This ruling was revoked again on August 19, 1947. Ibid., Ch. 6, 47.

[41] Ibid., Ch. 5, 24–25.

[42] Barry Eichengreen, *Golden Fetters: The Gold Standard and the Great Depression, 1919–1939* (New York: Oxford Univ. Press, 1992), 194.

[43] "The 40 percent [gold cover] ratio was viewed as a critical threshold below which public confidence in convertibility would be threatened." Eichengreen, *Golden Fetters: The Gold Standard and the Great Depression, 1919–1939*, 116 n. 47. In the late 1920s, the gold cover ratios in other nations ranged from 33 percent in Albania to 75 percent in Belgium, Poland, and Germany. Barry Eichengreen, *Elusive Stability* (New York: Cambridge Univ. Press, 1990), 248.

[44] 48 Stat. 337, Sect. 8; the earlier wording comes from Sect. 2. See U.S. Statutes at Large, 73rd Congress, 2nd Session, Jan. 30, 1934, 337, 341. A license to take such actions with respect to gold was granted to the Federal Reserve Bank of New York by the Treasury Department on March 24, 1937. U.S. Treas. Dept., Spec. Form TGL–18, License No. NY–18–1, "License to Transport, Import, Melt and Treat, Export, Earmark and Hold in Cus-

tody for Foreign or Domestic Account," Mar. 24, 1937, Princeton Univ., Seely Mudd Lib. Harry Dexter White Collection, Box 3, File 82 [223773–774].

[45] Milton Friedman & Anna Schwartz, *A Monetary History of the United States 1867–1960* (Princeton: Princeton Univ. Press, 1963), 470–71.

[46] Though gold continued to come in under anti-hoarding provisions during the next 17 years, in no year was the amount greater than $240,000. U.S. Treas. Dept., "Material in Reply to Questions from Senator Knowland," no date [ca. April 1952], NACP, RG 56, Entry 69A7584, Box 4, Congressional and other Inquiries [204009].

[47] Friedman & Schwartz, *A Monetary History of the United States 1867–1960*, 473.

[48] G.A. Eddy, "The Gold Policy of the United States Treasury," 5th Draft, Jan. 7, 1949, NACP, RG 56, Entry 69A7584, Box 4, Congressional and other inquiries [204022]. The chief of the Balance of Payments Division of the Federal Reserve Bank of New York later argued that the transfer of foreign dollar assets worth $3.4 billion in the 1933 to 1940 era "reflected essentially 'autonomous' private transfers of 'hot money' from Europe and was accompanied, and in fact made possible, by large gold exports to this country." Fred Klopstock, "The International Status of the Dollar," *Essays in International Finance* 28 (May 1957), 7.

[49] Griffeth Johnson, *The Treasury and Monetary Policy 1933–1938* (Cambridge: Harvard University Press, 1939), 54. Friedman & Schwartz, *A Monetary History of the United States 1867–1960*, 509.

[50] Johnson, *The Treasury and Monetary Policy 1933–1938*, 154. $297 million of the $3 billion total came from the Netherlands, the next largest source. Memo from Mr. White to Secy. Morgenthau, "Gold Imports in the United States," May 9, 1939, NACP, RG 56, Entry 67A1804, Box 50, Divisional Memo #2, [202539, 545].

[51] Eddy, "The Gold Policy of the United States Treasury," Jan. 7, 1949, NACP, RG 56, Entry 69A7584, Box 4, Congressional and other inquiries [204022]. This 1949 total is of the same order of magnitude as the $14.47 billion noted in 1952 (see table). Likewise, though there are minor discrepancies in the figures for yearly gold imports, several sources agree that the yearly gold flows to the U.S. in the 1930s regularly amounted to between $1 and $2 billion worth. Eichengreen, *Golden Fetters: The Gold Standard and the Great Depression, 1919–1939*, 346, 353; Johnson, *The Treasury and Monetary Policy 1933–1938*, 56.

[52] This table is adapted from U.S. Treas. Dept., "Material in Reply to Questions from Senator Knowland," no date [ca. April 1952], NACP, RG 56, Entry 69A7584, Box 4, Congressional and other Inquiries [204009]. Senator Knowland sat on the Senate Appropriations Committee, and inquired of Treasury on April 14, 1952; this reply was prepared by early May [204010].

[53] From Table "Gold Movement Between the United States and the Axis Powers, 1934–1941," NACP, RG 56, Entry 67A1804, Box 50, Div. Memo #4 [202563], probably prepared by Mr. Bernstein for the Stabilization Fund Hearings in June 1941 [202561].

[54] Treas. Dept., Div. of Monetary Research, "Net Movement of Gold to the United States by Countries, 1940," NACP, RG 56, Entry 67A1804, Box 50, Div. Memo #4 [202562], probably prepared by Mr. Bernstein for the Stabilization Fund Hearings in June 1941 [202561].

[55] Memo from Mr. White to Secy. Morgenthau, "Gold Imports in the United States," May 9, 1939, NACP, RG 56, Entry 67A1804, Box 50, Divisional Memo #2, [202539, 545]. An earlier (March 17, 1938), unsigned, draft memo entitled "Merits of a Proposal to Place an Embargo on Gold Imports" exists in these files, and concludes that the disadvantages of an embargo greatly outweighed the advantages; gold inflows could be reduced by other means if so desired. NACP, RG 56, Entry 67A1804, Box 50, Division Memoranda #1[202515–520].

[56] H. D. White, "The Future of Gold," corrected copy, Dec. 12, 1940, Princeton Univ., Seely Mudd Manuscript Lib., Harry Dexter White Collection, Box 4, Future of Gold (Part I, Section III), Folder # 10 [223821–835].

[57] Memo from Mr. White to Secy. Morgenthau, "Gold Imports in the United States," May 9, 1939, NACP, RG 56, Entry 67A1804, Box 50, Divisional Memo #2, [202539, 545].

58 Note handed by Mr. Pinsent, Financial Counselor to Brit. Embassy, to Mr. Cochran in the Treasury at 7 P.M., May 27, 1940, NACP, RG 56, Entry 67A1804, Box 49, Discrimination (U.S.) [202514]. Pinsent estimated the worth of the gold at 50–100 million pounds.

59 Memo from Mr. White to Messrs. D.W. Bell, Cochran & Foley, June 4, 1940, NACP, RG 56, Entry 67A1804, Box 49, Discrimination (U.S.) [202512]. Though White does not explicitly say so, this assertion was most likely due to the practice among gold trading nations to resmelt, recast, and stamp bars of gold with national marks, thereby hindering the tracing of the previous origin.

60 Ibid. [202512–513].

61 H. D. White, "The Future of Gold," corrected copy, Dec. 12, 1940, Princeton Univ., Seely Mudd Manuscript Lib., Harry Dexter White Collection, Box 4, Future of Gold (Part I, Section III), Folder # 10 [223821–835].

62 Memo from Ms. Kistler to Mr. White, "Whose gold are we buying?" Feb. 13, 1941, NACP, RG 56, Entry 67A1804, Box 49, Acquisitions [202388–202389].

63 "History of FFC," Ch. 3, 14–17, under Gen. Licenses 32 (Aug. 1940) & 33 (Sept. 1940).

64 Reeves, "The Control of Foreign Funds by the United States Treasury," 38–41.

65 "Administration of Wartime Controls," 12 [311908–963].

66 The figures permitting this calculation may be found in Treas. Dept., *Annual Report* 1941, 219; 1942, 56; 1943, 125; 1944, 127; 1945, 206. In 1946, 112,000 applications were filed (1947: 54,000; 1948: 15,000), but no approval percentages are given. See Treas. Dept., *Annual Reports* 1946, 200; 1947, 123; 1948, 138.

67 Treas. Dept., *Annual Report* 1945, 423.

68 Reeves, "The Control of Foreign Funds by the United States Treasury," 52–53; "Administration of Wartime Controls," 19 [311908–963].

69 "History of FFC," Ch. 5, 82. This was "probably the most common device employed for large holdings."

70 "Administration of Wartime Controls," 4, 32, 37 [311908–963]; Reeves, "The Control of Foreign Funds by the United States Treasury," 54.

71 "Administration of Wartime Controls," 34–35 [311908–963]; "History of FFC," Ch. 5, 86. These sources do not make clear whether this is the number liquidated only by FFC, whether this represents liquidations by both FFC and the APC, or whether this included Japanese-controlled companies as well.

72 Mitchell Carroll, "Legislation on Treatment of Enemy Property," *American Journal of International Law* 37 (1943), 628.

73 Domke, *Trading with the Enemy in World War II*, 63.

74 Donald Perry, "Aliens in the United States," *The Annals*, v. 223 (September 1942), 5–7. The registration was mandated by the President on June 28, 1940. "Europe" in this list encompassed the Baltics, Russia, Eastern Europe and Turkey, as well as Austria-Hungary. No more than 1.5 million aliens (30 percent of 4.9 million) would have arrived after 1924, of whom no more than 1 million (30 percent of 3.57 million) came from "Europe."

75 That is, 25 percent of the Germans, 42 percent of the Italians, and 37 percent of the Japanese were aliens. Charles Gordon, "Status of Enemy Nationals in the United States," *Lawyers Guild Review* 2 (1942), 9, citing Att. Gen. Francis Biddle. See also "Alien Enemies and Japanese-Americans: A Problem of Wartime Controls," *Yale Law Journal* 51 (1942), 1317.

76 Maurice Davie, "Immigrants from Axis-Conquered Countries," *The Annals*, v. 223 (September 1942), 114. The countries were France, Belgium, Netherlands, Denmark, Norway, Greece, Poland, Czechoslovakia and Yugoslavia. Thus one reading is that most of the foreign-born had arrived long before 1940 and were already naturalized (though at least some may have never taken out U.S. citizenship); another reading is that for a given European immigrant group, around one-third in 1940 were registered aliens (among whom varying percentages would have been refugees).

[77] George Warren, "The Refugee and the War," *The Annals*, v. 223 (September 1942), 92. This figure was "based on Jewish immigration from Europe since 1933 and statistics of other admissions from European countries in which refugees have originated or through which they have passed."

[78] Domke, *Trading with the Enemy in World War II*, 39, 436. The freezing order definition of "national" extended to partnerships, associations, and corporation that had their principal place of business in such foreign country" or were controlled by such foreign country and/or one or more nationals. Also Reeves, "Control of Foreign Funds," 33–34; "New Administrative Definitions of 'Enemy' to Supersede the Trading with the Enemy Act," *Yale Law Journal* 51 (1942), 1392–93.

[79] According to the Treasury Department on May 8, 1943. Martin Domke, *The Control of Alien Property*, (New York: Central Book Company, 1947), 291. Thus, though "many refugees are stateless, statelessness is not the essential quality of a refugee." Jane Carey, "Some Aspects of Statelessness since World War I," *American Journal of International Law* 40 (1946), 113.

[80] Domke, *Trading with the Enemy in World War II*, 437.

[81] So persons *not* in designated enemy countries are not deemed nationals of a designated enemy country unless the Alien Property Custodian determined such a person is controlled by or acting for on behalf of a designated enemy country or person. Otto Sommerich, "Recent Innovations in Legal and Regulatory Concepts as to the Alien and his Property," *American Journal of International Law* 37 (1943), 65. See also Domke, *Trading with the Enemy in World War II*, 44. This Executive Order delimited the powers of the Alien Property Custodian.

[82] The stateless who were still resident in blocked countries were "nationals" as defined by the freezing order, while the stateless who were resident in the U.S. after June 17, 1940, were generally licensed nationals. The difficulties arose for refugees in transit, because though they might intend to never return, technically their domicile might still be in a blocked country. Arthur Bloch & Werner Rosenberg, "Current Problems of Freezing Control," *Fordham Law Review* 11 (1942), 75.

[83] "History of FFC," Chapter 4, 30–33. The New York law firm Topken & Farley, specializing in German business, was blocked in this "ad hoc" manner. Clearly ad hoc blocking also implied ad hoc mitigating circumstances for long-term U.S. residents who happened not to be U.S. citizens.

[84] Ibid., Chapter 5, 7–8.

[85] Rudolf Littauer, "Confiscation of the Property of Technical Enemies," *Yale Law Journal* 52 (1943), 741.

[86] Frank Sterck & Carl Schuck, "The Right of Resident Alien Enemies to Sue," *Georgetown Law Journal* 30 (1942), 433. The legal complications created by this Act are well summarized in Michael Brandon, "Legal Control over Resident Enemy Aliens in Time of War in the United States and in the United Kingdom," *American Journal of International Law* 44 (1950), 382–87.

[87] Domke, *Trading with the Enemy in World War II*, 63–64; Sterck & Schuck, "The Right of Resident Alien Enemies to Sue," 434.

[88] "New Administrative Definitions of 'Enemy' to Supersede the Trading with the Enemy Act," 1388. By the same token, "citizens domiciled in enemy territory are regarded as enemies." Leon Yudkin & Richard Caro, "New Concepts of 'Enemy' in the 'Trading with the Enemy Act'," *St. John's Law Review* 18 (1943), 58.

[89] The proclamations were issued on December 7, 1941, for Japanese (No. 2525, 6 F.R. 6321), and on December 8, 1941, for German (No. 2526, 6 F.R. 6323) and Italian (Proclamation No. 2527, 6 F.R. 6324) alien enemies. Travel and identification regulations were issued on February 5, 1942, and January 22, 1942, respectively. Gordon, "Status of Enemy Nationals in the United States," 12–13; Domke, *Trading with the Enemy in World War II*, 68; "Alien Enemies and Japanese-Americans: A Problem of Wartime Controls," 1319–1321.

[90] Earl Harrison, "Alien Enemies," 13 *Penn Bar Association Quarterly* 196, cited in Gordon, "Status of Enemy Nationals in the United States," 10–11.

[91] E.g., "many 'enemy aliens' are actually here because they are friendly," Clyde Eagleton, "Friendly Aliens," *American Journal of International Law* 36 (1942), 662.

92 "Alien Enemies and Japanese-Americans: A Problem of Wartime Controls," 1337; Domke, *Trading with the Enemy in World War II*, 29, 47.

93 Robert Wilson, "Treatment of Civilian Alien Enemies," *American Journal of International Law* 37 (1943), 41; "Alien Enemies and Japanese-Americans: A Problem of Wartime Controls," 1321; E. von Hofmannsthal, "Austro-Hungarians," *American Journal of International Law* 36 (1942), 292–294.

94 Sommerich, "Recent Innovations in Legal and Regulatory Concepts as to the Alien and his Property," 60; Domke, *The Control of Alien Property*, 47.

95 Gordon, "Status of Enemy Nationals in the United States," 11; "Civil Rights of Enemy Aliens During World War II," *Temple University Law Quarterly* 17 (1942), 87.

96 The quotes are from Department of Justice press releases on December 9 and December 14, 1941, respectively, cited in Sterck and Schuck, "The Right of Resident Alien Enemies to Sue," 421.

97 Ibid., 423.

98 32 N.Y.S. (2d) 450, 177 Misc. 939 (Jan. 21, 1942).

99 Sterck and Schuck, "The Right of Resident Alien Enemies to Sue," 431–432, 436. "Civil Rights of Enemy Aliens During World War II," 91 states that in this case "the alien enemy was considered an alien friend, rather than an enemy." Nonresident aliens did not have this right to sue.

100 As with citizens, the outcome was uncertain for aliens. "Even if he can prove that he is not an enemy," for example in pursuing a claim against the APC, he "need not necessarily succeed in obtaining possession of the property" if the court deemed otherwise. See Rudolf Littauer, "Confiscation of the Property of Technical Enemies," *Yale Law Journal* 52 (1943), 769; "Civil Rights of Enemy Aliens During World War II," 91.

101 Confiscation by the U.S. government was practiced on an unprecedented scale during World War II (in 1941 and 1942, the War Department took complete control of nearly ten million acres of land), and was legitimated by the legislative mandates provided by the Export Control Requisition Act of Oct. 10, 1940 and the Requisitioning Act of October 16, 1941, among other laws. For an extended discussion, see Paul Marcus, "The Taking and Destruction of Property Under a Defense and War Program," *Cornell Law Quarterly* 27 (1942), 317–346, 476–533.

102 *Russian Volunteer Fleet v. United States*, 282 U.S. 481, (1931) that "the petitioner was an alien friend and as such was entitled to the protection of the Fifth Amendment," and this ruling was subsequently upheld in *Becker Steel Co. v. Cummings* 296 U.S. 74 (1935). See Littauer, "Confiscation of the Property of Technical Enemies," 760; also "Former Enemies may sue in Court of Claims to Recover Value of Property Unlawfully Vested by Alien Property Custodian," *University of Pennsylvania Law Review* 106 (1958), 1059.

103 "Friendly Alien's Right to Sue for Return of Property Seized by Alien Property Custodian," *Yale Law Journal* 56 (1947), 1068–76; "Remedy Available to Alien Friend whose Property has been 'Vested' by Alien Property Custodian," *Columbia Law Review* 47 (1947), 1052–61.

104 "Return of Property Seized during World War II: Judicial and Administrative Proceedings under the Trading with the Enemy Act," *Yale Law Journal* 62 (1953), 1210–35.

105 In fact, licenses under the freezing order as well as the rights of the APC were "irrelevant," since the TWEA deals with "disabilities in respect of the privileges of trade" and they had "no connection with disabilities in respect of the ownership of lands." Lawrence Pratt, "Present Alienage Disabilities under New York State Law in Real Property," *Brooklyn Law Review* 12 (1942), 3.

106 Ibid., 3.

107 Sterck and Schuck, "The Right of Resident Alien Enemies to Sue," 422; for a discussion of this case, see Domke, *Trading with the Enemy in World War II*, 79–82.

108 Pratt, "Present Alienage Disabilities under New York State Law in Real Property," 2.

109 Ibid., 12–13. The catch was that aliens had no "heritable blood" in common law and therefore could not transmit by descent.

110 Ibid., 14; Sect. 60–70 of the Public Lands Law (N.Y. Laws 1909, c. 46).

[111] Pratt, "Present Alienage Disabilities under New York State Law in Real Property," 2; Domke, *Trading with the Enemy in World War II*, 96.

[112] Domke, *The Control of Alien Property*, 61–62. New Jersey had previously passed similar legislation (on April 8, 1943) removing the disabilities imposed upon resident aliens classified as "enemies."

[113] Doris Banta, "Alien enemies: Right to acquire, hold, and transmit real property: Recent change in New York Real Property Law abolishing all disabilities," *Cornell Law Quarterly* 30 (1944), 242.

[114] Ibid., 238. Banta further notes that even at the time, 19 states made no distinctions between aliens and citizens in their right to transfer property at death.

[115] William Butler, "Proving Foreign Documents in New York," *Fordham Law Review* 18 (1949), 49–71.

[116] "History of FFC," Ch. 5, 107.

[117] Ibid., 108.

[118] Ibid., 109.

[119] Ibid., 109–10. The President established the War Refugee Board by Executive Order at about the same time, a body dedicated to helping rescue persons in occupied territories who were in imminent danger of death. The Board's operations were mostly privately funded and required an FFC license: about $20 million in private funds was transferred abroad for private rescue and relief projects under this license, aided by a U.S. government appropriation of about $2 million for operations.

[120] John Foster Dulles, "The Vesting Powers of the Alien Property Custodian," *Cornell Law Quarterly* 28 (1943), 246.

[121] Kenneth Carlston, "Foreign Funds Control and the Alien Property Custodian," *Cornell Law Quarterly* 31 (1945), 5–6.

[122] Francis Fallon, "Enemy Business Enterprises and the Alien Property Custodian, I," *Fordham Law Review* 15 (1946), 223–24.

[123] Stuart Weiss, *The President's Man: Leo Crowley and Franklin Roosevelt in Peace and War* (Carbondale: Southern Illinois Univ. Press, 1996), 117, 127. Weiss implies the scandal involved patronage and a lack of transparency in the Custodian's actions.

[124] This Division was transferred, with all its property and personnel, to the APC on Apr. 21, 1942, by Exec. Order 9142. Office of Alien Property Custodian, *Annual Report*, [hereinafter APC Annual Report] 1944, 2 [322817]. See also Domke, *Trading with the Enemy in World War II*, 264.

[125] The best overview of the office and the assets under its control is Paul Myron, "The Work of the Alien Property Custodian," *Law and Contemporary Problems* 11 (1945), 76–91. Myron was Chief of the Estates and Trusts Sec. in the office during 1942 and 1943, then worked as Assistant to the Custodian in 1944 and 1945.

[126] APC *Annual Report*, 1942–43, 26–27 [322726–808].

[127] A. M. Werner, "The Alien Property Custodian," *Wisconsin State Bar Association Bulletin* 16 (1943), 15.

[128] APC *Annual Report*, 1943–43, 19–20 [322726–808].

[129] Werner, "The Alien Property Custodian," 15. This was meant as a means to protect due process. See Kenneth Woodward, "Meaning of 'Enemy' Under the Trading with the Enemy Act," *Texas Law Review* 20 (1942), 753.

[130] Dulles, "The Vesting Powers of the Alien Property Custodian," 259.

[131] APC *Annual Report*, 1944, V [322809–953].

[132] Sommerich, "Recent Innovations in Legal and Regulatory Concepts as to the Alien and his Property," 68.

[133] Carlston, "Foreign Funds Control and the Alien Property Custodian," 22.

134 Specimen copies of vesting orders from 1942 and 1943 can be found in Sommerich, "Recent Innovations in Legal and Regulatory Concepts as to the Alien and his Property," 67, and in Domke, *Trading with the Enemy in World War II*, 467–68.

135 Carlston, "Foreign Funds Control and the Alien Property Custodian," 7.

136 Dulles, "The Vesting Powers of the Alien Property Custodian," 257. The case referred to is *Swiss Insurance Company*.

137 Carlston, "Foreign Funds Control and the Alien Property Custodian," 8.

138 The following is from the discussions in APC *Annual Report*, 1942–43, 4, 68 [322726–808]; APC *Annual Report*, 1944, 4 [322809–953].

139 APC *Annual Report*, 1942–43, 69 [322726–808].

140 Ibid., 69–70 [322726–808].

141 APC *Annual Report*, 1944, 136 [322809–953].

142 APC *Annual Report*, 1945, 19 [322954–3090]. Assets were greater than equity because creditors other than the Custodian held interests in the companies, but also because total value included supervised property in which the Custodian had no equity.

143 Ibid., 1945, 17 [322954–3090].

144 Fritz Machlup, "Patents," *International Encyclopedia of the Social Sciences* (New York: Macmillan, 1968), v. 11, 461.

145 APC *Annual Report*, 1944, 109 [322809–953].

146 Wallace McClure, "Copyright in War and Peace," *American Journal of International Law* 36 (1942), 386.

147 Domke, *Trading with the Enemy in World War II*, 280.

148 APC *Annual Report*, 1944, 109–10 [322809–953].

149 APC *Annual Report*, 1945, 121 [322954–3090]; APC *Annual Report*, 1942–43, 39 [322726–808].

150 APC *Annual Report*, 1945, 132–33 [322954–3090].

151 For a sample list of titles, see the APC *Annual Report*, 1942–43, 64–65 [322726–808]. Given the fate of Jewish intellectuals employed in German universities before the war, it is likely that some of the royalties from such works belonged to victims.

152 APC *Annual Report*, 1945, 122 [322954–3090].

153 Ibid., 123–24 [322954–3090].

154 APC *Annual Report*, 1942–43, 64 [322726–808]; APC *Annual Report*, 1945, 126–27 [322954–3090].

155 Fed. Reg., Nov. 4, 1950, 7459–60.

156 APC *Annual Report*, 1945, 125 [322954–3090] for the royalty amount; the quote is from APC *Annual Report*, 1944, 113 [322809–953].

157 "Administration of Wartime Controls," 31 [311908–963]; Domke, *Trading with the Enemy in World War II*, 291–2.

158 Werner, "The Alien Property Custodian," 17.

159 ACP *Annual Report*, 1944, 115 [322809–953].

160 Domke, *The Control of Alien Property*, 190–191.

161 APC *Annual Report*, 1944, 116 [322809–953].

162 APC *Annual Report*, 1945, 137 [322954–3090].

163 Guenther Reimann, *Patents for Hitler* (London: Victor Gollancz, 1945), 137.

164 U.S. Senate, Committee on Military Affairs, Subcommittee on War Mobilization, Scientific & Technical Mobilization, Hearings, 78th Congress, 1st Session, 1943. A 1942 investigation by the Committee on Patents under Homer T. Bone had heard similar testimony. Mira Wilkins, *The Maturing of Multinational Enterprise: American Business Abroad from 1914 to 1970* (Cambridge: Harvard Univ. Press, 1974), 263.

[165] Wilkins, *The Maturing of Multinational Enterprise*, 79, 81. Wilkins (258) cites an April 18, 1941, cable from a Du Pont vice president to I.G. Farben, "suggesting that in view of government restrictions our two companies mutually agree discontinue exchange technical information patent applications etc on all existing contracts," which was a response to a Presidential proclamation of April 15, 1941, that required technical information exports to be licensed.

[166] E.g., "Few have appreciated until recently the extent to which enemy controlled patents had been used even before the war in a systematic conspiracy to throttle American war production." Werner, "The Alien Property Custodian," 17.

[167] Senate Committee on Patents, testimony given on Apr. 27, 1942, cited in Howland Sargeant & Henrietta Creamer, "Enemy Patents," *Law and Contemporary Problems* 11 (1945), 101.

[168] Cited in Carlston, "Foreign Funds Control and the Alien Property Custodian," 19.

[169] APC *Annual Report*, 1942–43, 27–28 [322726–808].

[170] Ibid., 40–45 [322726–808].

[171] Of the 44,796 vested patents (the number given in an article written by the Chief of the Division of Patent Administration in the Office of APC), half were for the machinery, chemical, automotive, electrical and radio industries. Sargeant & Creamer, "Enemy Patents," 107–08.

[172] APC *Annual Report*, 1945, 97, 99, 100 [322954–3090].

[173] Reeves, "The Control of Foreign Funds by the United States Treasury," 55.

[174] Carlston, "Foreign Funds Control and the Alien Property Custodian," 19–20; Sargeant & Creamer, "Enemy Patents," 96–105.

[175] APC *Annual Report*, 1945, 101 [322954–3090].

[176] Ibid., 102 [322954–3090].

[177] Edwin Borchard, "Nationalization of Enemy Patents," *American Journal of International Law* 37 (1943), 92–97.

[178] APC *Annual Report*, 1945, 105–108 [322954–3090].

[179] Ibid., 107–108 [322954–3090].

[180] APC *Annual Report*, 1942–43, 62–3 [322726–808]. Particular mention is also made of the patent for the synthetic antimalarial drug Atabrine, as "of vital importance to the successful prosecution of the war" after the Dutch East Indies—which produced 96 percent of the world supply of quinine—had fallen to the Japanese.

[181] APC *Annual Report*, 1945, 110 [322954–3090].

[182] The quote is from A. M. Werner, Gen. Counsel for the APC in early 1943. Werner, "The Alien Property Custodian," 17–18.

[183] APC *Annual Report*, 1945, 119 [322954–3090].

[184] Ibid., 21–22, 25 [322954–3090].

[185] Ibid., 31 [322954–3090]. For a very thorough survey of the control of enterprises by the APC, written by a former Assistant Gen. Counsel in the Office of APC, see Francis Fallon, "Enemy Business Enterprises and the Alien Property Custodian, I" *Fordham Law Review* 15 (1946), 222–247; Francis Fallon, "Enemy Business Enterprises and the Alien Property Custodian, II" *Fordham Law Review* 16 (1947), 55–85.

[186] APC *Annual Report*, 1945, 33, 36–37 [322954–3090]. The remaining six were owned by persons of "other" nationality.

[187] Ibid., 33 [322954–3090]. Types of enterprises included corporations (291), partnerships (27), proprietorships (23), nonprofit organizations (12), U.S. branches of foreign enterprises (52), and miscellaneous associations (3).

[188] Ibid., 36 [322954–3090]; APC *Annual Report*, 1942–43, 37 [322726–808]. Most of the banking firms that were vested were Japanese.

[189] APC *Annual Report*, 1945, 42–43 [322954–3090].

[190] Ibid., 49–54 [322954–3090]. There were high levels of insolvency (at least 81 companies), as well as uncertainties about liability in the case of sole proprietorships or unincorporated branches of foreign enterprises (77 companies), making it difficult to realize gain from their sale. Assets in foreign countries, and the difficulty of selling property for which there was no ready market provided further hindrances. Thus, of the vested enterprises on June 30, 1945, 30 were closed banks and insurance companies, 34 were in liquidation, 55 companies operated at a profit, but 172 operated at a loss: the net loss was thus $1.4 million (54). The sale of a few (largely Japanese) vested banks was marginally profitable.

[191] Ibid., 139 [322954–3090].

[192] Ibid., 140 [322954–3090]. That is, vested properties clustered along the New York (90), Pennsylvania (54), New Jersey (23), Maryland (16), and Washington D.C. (27) corridor, but Missouri (61) and Texas (34) were also well represented, likely owing to their relatively large German immigrant populations. California (98) and Hawaii (73) properties were largely Japanese-owned.

[193] APC *Annual Report*, 1945, 141 [322954–3090].

[194] APC *Annual Report*, 1942–43, 31 [322726–808].

[195] APC *Annual Report*, 1945, 145 [322954–3090].

[196] Ibid., 146 [322954–3090]. To judge by the disparities, the most difficult to sell were industrial machinery, equipment and materials.

[197] Ibid., 157 [322954–3090].

[198] Merlin Staring, "The Alien Property Custodian and Conclusive Determinations of Survivorship," *Georgetown Law Journal* 35 (1947), 264–265.

[199] APC *Annual Report*, 1945, 176 [322954–3090].

[200] APC *Annual Report*, 1944, 125 [322809–953]; APC *Annual Report*, 1945, 147 [322954–3090].

[201] APC *Annual Report*, 1945, 149 [322954–3090].

[202] John Dickinson, "Enemy-Owned Property: Restitution or Confiscation?" *Foreign Affairs* 22 (1943), 138–9. Leo Pasvolsky, an advisor in the State Department during the war, put it succinctly in 1942: "[w]e must make sure that the cessation of armed hostilities will not be followed by a continuation of economic warfare."

[203] Terminal Rpt., Office of APC, Oct. 1946, 3–4 [106992–7020].

[204] This sum represents mingled German and Japanese property, and claims were paid out of it to those who were neither German or Japanese, such as to Italian POWs. William Reeves, "Is Confiscation of Enemy Assets in the National Interest of the United States?" *Virginia Law Review* 40 (1954), 1046.

[205] In fact, by October of 1946, the APC vested four times as much as it had in the nine months preceding, and doubled the amount of cash it realized from sales and liquidation. However, the property of Hungarian, Romanian, and Bulgarian nationals was only still vested if the property had been acquired in the United States before December 7, 1945. Terminal Rpt., Office of APC, Oct. 1946 [106992–7020].

[206] Statement of Paul V. Myron, Dept. Dir. of the OAP, Feb. 20, 1953, U.S. Congress, Senate, Committee on the Judiciary, *Administration of the Trading with the Enemy Act*, 83rd Cong., 1st Sess., Hearings, Feb.–Apr., 1953, 106.

[207] Term. Rpt., Office of APC, Oct. 1946, 5 [106992–7020].

[208] Letter from Paul V. Myron to Congressman Arthur G. Klein, Aug. 10, 1956, AJA, WJC Papers, Box C294 [116923].

[209] Term. Rpt., Office of APC, Oct. 1946, 18 [106992–7020].

[210] Ibid., 19 [106992–7020].

[211] APC *Annual Report*, 1945, 9 [322954–3090] noted that by June 30, 1945, the APC had issued 5,226 vesting orders; the APC *Annual Report*, 1958, 82 [324619–718] noted a return order number 19,234 on Oct. 30, 1957. By the end of vesting on April 17, 1953, about 1,750 return orders had been issued. APC *Annual Report*, 1953, 147 [324089].

[212] All preceding information in this paragraph is from the OAP *Annual Reports,* 1948–1958.

[213] Malcolm Mason, "Relationship of Vested Assets to War Claims," *Law and Contemporary Problems* 16 (1951), 395.

[214] Term. Rpt., Office of APC, Oct. 1946, 14 [106992–7020].

[215] Mason, "Relationship of Vested Assets to War Claims," 398–399. Jessup, however, calls it a "dubious doctrine that there is no confiscation if the enemy state is required to assume an obligation to compensate its nationals whose property is held for the satisfaction of claims." Philip Jessup, "Enemy Property," *American Journal of International Law* 49 (1955), 62.

[216] Jessup, "Enemy Property," 58–59. See also the discussion of the Paris Agreement in Reeves, "Is Confiscation of Enemy Assets in the National Interest of the United States?" 1043.

[217] Malcolm Mason, "Relationship of Vested Assets to War Claims," *Law and Contemporary Problems* 16 (1951), 397. According to Philip Jessup, aid to Germany amounted to $1.47 billion from 1948 to 1954—see his "Enemy Property," *American Journal of International Law* 49 (1955), 58—but amounted to $3.3 billion from a 1952 HICOG report, "nearly all of this aid represents the cost of procuring and shipping food, industrial raw material and like commodities to Germany." Cited in Reeves, "Is Confiscation of Enemy Assets in the National Interest of the United States?," 1044.

[218] Mason, "Relationship of Vested Assets to War Claims," 398. Mason was chief of the legal branch in the Office of Alien Property in the Department of Justice.

[219] Jessup, "Enemy Property," 59.

[220] Mason, "Relationship of Vested Assets to War Claims," 403.

[221] Mason, "Relationship of Vested Assets to War Claims," 400–02.

[222] Mason, "Relationship of Vested Assets to War Claims," 404. Indeed, Mason states that the War Claims Commission "seriously delayed" a bill for the heirless property successor organization, and only withdrew later when it war argued that the sum involved would not be more than three million dollars.

[223] Dulles, "The Vesting Powers of the Alien Property Custodian," 252.

[224] The *Annual Reports* of the OAP list the dates and sometimes the amounts returned to the Netherlands.

[225] The total number of return orders was 4,475 by February 1965. OAP, Vesting Orders 1–19,312 and Return Orders 1–4,475, Recs. Office Civil Division, Dept. of Justice.

Chapter IV

Assets in Europe

Introduction

As American troops overran large areas of German-occupied Europe during the final phases of World War II, they discovered vast quantities of art, gold, and other valuables—looted and otherwise—left behind by a defeated Nazi regime. U.S. armed forces did not set out to become the guardians of property looted by the Nazis, but circumstances thrust this role upon them. American leaders recognized their responsibility to safeguard private property, to prevent its use by the enemy, and to lay the foundation for the eventual return of loot to its rightful owners. Field units could not distinguish victims' assets from war booty or legitimate German-owned property so emphasis was placed on the collection and control of all asset types. Later, once the military government was in full operation, officials made intermittent efforts to segregate obvious victims' assets from the general pool of assets under the control of the U.S. military government. Although policies and procedures surrounding collection and protection of assets evolved in response to the circumstances encountered by troops in Europe, U.S. officials did not always follow through in providing the resources necessary to deal adequately with this issue. As a result, policy implementation in the field often fell short of fully realizing the U.S. aim to protect property in its care from theft, deterioration, and general destruction.

Assets falling under the control of the United States came from a variety of sources. Initial collections of confiscated assets came primarily from the battlefields or deserted SS headquarters. As troops intensified their searches in the spring of 1945, they gathered assets from salt and potassium mines, castles, concentration camps, dredged rivers, intercepted trains, factories, sewers, private corporations, embassies, and various governmental agencies.[1] A large number of valuables, especially gold, currency, securities, precious metals and other financial assets, came from the vaults of Reichsbank branches found throughout the American-occupied sections of Germany and Austria. U.S. forces seized the currency reserves, bonds, mortgages, stocks, contents of safe-deposit boxes, and records of each bank branch, and forwarded these items to regional holding points for safekeeping. Initially, hundreds of makeshift depositories operated within the U.S. zones in Germany and Austria. During the last days of the war and the months that followed, officials consolidated seized assets and, as the process unfolded, segregated property obviously looted from persecutees.

The majority of recovered assets surfaced during and shortly after the final offensive into Germany and Austria in the spring of 1945, though valuables continued to come to light for many months following Germany's surrender. Operating under chaotic conditions and overwhelmed by the amount of valuables recovered and their geographical dispersal, units and individuals struggled to keep abreast of a steadily growing mass of materials. Even after Germany's surrender, efforts to accelerate the recovery process competed for manpower and resources with other military government functions. The massive movement of American troops out of Europe following the surrender adversely affected the collection process; assets were left vulnerable as guards were removed from their posts and shipped home. Nevertheless, U.S. forces made significant progress locating and consolidating scattered caches of valuables, and began to tackle the daunting task of inventorying the assets, determining their provenance, and preparing for their eventual restitution.

The inability of U.S. officials to guarantee the safety of assets in their hands stemmed from several factors. First, recovery and restitution of property seized by the Nazi regime held a lower priority than winning the war or preserving order in postwar Europe. Second, U.S. leaders were unprepared for the magnitude of problems they would face when their troops overran Germany and Austria. By the time U.S. and Allied forces launched their final offensive against the Third Reich, Allied leaders knew the Nazis had engaged in widespread looting of the Reich and its conquered territories, primarily directed against Jews and other victims of discrimination. U.S. officials recognized the need to identify and segregate Nazi loot from legitimately owned German property, but they realized that restitution of assets to rightful owners could commence only after assets had been secured, consolidated, and inventoried. They expected to find looted assets intermingled with property of German individuals and organizations, and anticipated that the new owners would attempt to hide these goods or move them beyond the reach of Allied authorities. Accordingly, the U.S. Army developed policies that aimed to recover as many assets as possible, prevent theft or damage, and gather information that could later be used to identify the assets' origins.

By 1946, U.S. officials' approach towards the recovered assets under their control had evolved. While they had placed their initial emphasis on keeping the assets out of enemy hands, once the war was over and assets had been transferred to more secure locations, they began to comprehend the extent of Nazi looting practices and took steps to segregate the assets in their care that had clearly been taken from those who had perished. This paradigm shift is exemplified by the establishment of the Offenbach Archival Depot in the spring of 1946—a facility specifically designed to protect and restitute, among other goods, the recovered Jewish ritual objects, books, manuscripts and other cultural property in the U.S. Zone. Whereas U.S. leaders initially focused on protecting Western civilization and depriving the Nazi faithful of resources needed to prolong the war, they eventually played a pivotal role in saving the remnants of the Jewish cultural heritage in Europe and restituting property confiscated by the Nazis to the rightful owners or heirs.

Organizations, Policies, and Operations to Protect Valuables in North Africa, Italy, and Western Europe, 1942–1945

Although most assets falling under U.S. control were recovered during and after the invasion and occupation of Germany and Austria, the campaigns in the Mediterranean and in Western Europe exposed Allied troops and leaders to the problems involved in locating and protecting valuables. These experiences helped shape the organizations, procedures, and policies that were in place in early 1945 for both combat troops and the specialized units responsible for locating and protecting valuables.

Protecting Art and Cultural Objects in North Africa & Sicily

The U.S. and British invasion of French North Africa in November 1942 offered American leaders their first experience in protecting valuables in the course of a military campaign. Interested primarily in the preserving the cultural heritage of Western civilization, General Dwight Eisenhower, commander of the Allied expeditionary force, instructed his Provost Marshal General to print and post "off-limits" signs on these historic and artistic monuments in an effort to keep damage to a minimum.[2]

The Allied experience in North Africa underscored the need for specialists to handle the protection of art and monuments and set a precedent for the later campaigns in southern and Western Europe. In late 1942 and early 1943, influential scholars and museum officials in the United States pressured the government to create an official body to help ensure the safety of works of art located in war zones.[3] With the planned invasion of Sicily just a few months away, the U.S. military agreed to assign knowledgeable officers to help protect art in Europe, and the President created a civilian advisory commission to operate in the United States (the Roberts Commission).[4] In May 1943, the War Department created the Office of the Advisor on Fine Arts and Monuments to the Chief Civil Affairs Officer of the Allied Military Government, and the first specialist personnel joined the military government section of General Eisenhower's staff.[5]

The Sicilian campaign served as a trial run for Allied military government and the office of the Advisor on Fine Arts and Monuments. The Advisor's staff was instructed to inspect all monuments, collections, libraries, and archives to determine what immediate repairs were needed to protect cultural assets from further damage.[6] Fine Arts and Monuments personnel determined that most of these objects had been well packed and adequately protected, and that art objects in most areas of Sicily had suffered relatively little battle damage or theft.[7]

Activities in Italy Relating to Art and Other Valuables

The Allied invasion in September 1943 quickly led to Italy's surrender. German forces, however, continued to occupy the Italian peninsula and the campaign there would drag on to the closing days of the war. Fine Arts and Monuments personnel followed the fighting units through Italy, hoping to minimize damage to the country's enormous wealth of art and architectural monuments. The Army's military government manual revised for use in Italy emphasized concern with preventing damage to art and cultural objects.[8] In December 1943,

General Eisenhower stressed the importance of preserving Italy's historic monuments: "Today we are fighting in a country which has contributed a great deal to our cultural inheritance, a country rich in monuments which by their creation helped and now in their old age illustrate the growth of the civilization which is ours. We are bound to respect those monuments so far as war allows."[9]

In the winter of 1943, the Fine Arts and Monuments office was reconstituted as the Monuments, Fine Arts, and Archives (MFA&A) Subcommission of the Allied Control Commission.[10] In March 1944, the MFA&A Director issued a statement setting out MFA&A missions and functions in Italy; these included preventing damage to historical monuments, buildings, works of art and historical records in Italy, and assisting in the recovery and restitution to their rightful owners of any works of art that had been looted or otherwise misappropriated. He instructed MFA&A officers to investigate "reports of alleged looting or other unlawful appropriation of art or historical objects" and recommend appropriate action for restitution.[11] Noting that advancing troops would probably uncover repositories of art treasures, in December 1944 Allied headquarters in Italy instructed tactical units to report such collections to MFA&A officials and to place the repositories under guard.[12]

MFA&A resources in Italy proved inadequate to carry out the assigned tasks, and headquarters failed to efficiently employ the few resources available. A fact-finding mission in late 1943 revealed that only five of the 15 MFA&A officers in the Mediterranean area had actually reached Italy, and that none of those officers were operating in areas near the front lines.[13] Major Norman T. Newton of the MFA&A reported in December 1943 that available MFA&A personnel and transport were grossly inadequate for the size of the territory covered.[14] The following summer, Major Newton reported that the MFA&A staff for Italy was comprised of only 12 officers, a number he considered insufficient to accomplish the assigned mission.[15]

As the Allies overran northern Italy in early 1945, intelligence units interrogated German *Kunstschutz* (art and monument protection) officials to elicit information about the location of moved or missing works of art or cultural treasures. MFA&A personnel pursued intelligence reports that the SS had transported looted Italian paintings and sculptures northward. These included items from the museums of Florence, as well as works confiscated from Jewish-owned collections.[16] The Germans had reportedly hidden these looted works in two repositories: a former jail in San Leonardo in Passiria, north of Merano, and Neumelans Castle at Campo Tures near Bolzano.[17] As the final Allied drive to the north got underway in April, American troops searched in earnest for the two repositories. By early May 1945, they had successfully recovered the contents of these stashes and captured the principal German personnel of the *Kunstschutz* staff in northern Italy. Information provided by these prisoners eventually led to the recovery of, what one officer described as, all but an "infinitesimally small number of the works" in Italy which had been moved by German forces.[18]

The scope of Nazi looting in Italy extended beyond art and cultural property. In the spring of 1945, American troops of the 88th Infantry Division discovered a large cache of gold at Fortezza, which contained approximately $25 million of gold removed from the Bank of Italy at Rome, as well as items originating in the Bank of Italy at Milan.[19] Troops returned this cache to Rome and placed it in the custody of the Allied Financial Agency.[20] Details regarding the gold's rightful owner, however, remained unclear; the Yugoslav government appealed to Allied leaders, claiming that Italian occupation forces had confiscated Yugoslavian gold and transported it to Italy.[21] The Italians, on the other hand, wished to maintain custody of the Fortezza gold cache because it represented a significant portion of Italy's gold reserves.[22] The thorny custody issue was not easily resolved. The United States and Great Britain finally agreed in 1947 to turn over the disputed Fortezza gold to Italy.[23]

MFA&A in France and the Benelux Countries

In November 1943, an MFA&A element joined the Chief of Staff of the Supreme Allied Command (COSSAC), the headquarters assigned to plan the invasion of France. When Supreme Headquarters, Allied Expeditionary Force (SHAEF) absorbed COSSAC in January 1944, MFA&A joined that organization. Under the command of General Eisenhower, SHAEF controlled almost all Allied ground forces in Western Europe from the landings in France in June 1944 through the German surrender in May 1945. The Operations Branch of SHAEF Civil Affairs Division (G-5) directed the operation and planning of MFA&A activities for France, Belgium, Luxembourg, and the Netherlands.

To prepare for the campaign, SHAEF attempted to clarify policies regarding the treatment of art and other valuables. The SHAEF "Civil Affairs Directive for France" released on May 25, 1944, further clarified the role of U.S. forces in the preservation of art and monuments in liberated France. It called upon commanders to take all measures consistent with military necessity to avoid damage to all structures, objects, or documents of cultural, artistic, archaeological, or historical value. The directive authorized commanders to place buildings off-limits to troops in order to prevent vandalism or theft.[24] On May 26, 1944, General Eisenhower directed his subordinate commanders "through the exercise of restraint and discipline" to preserve centers and objects of historical and cultural significance.[25] SHAEF Civil Affairs Instruction No. 15, revised in June 1944, reaffirmed Allied policy of protecting works of art from misappropriation or damage, and stressed the duty of MFA&A officers to care for moveable art. This instruction gave senior civil affairs officers the responsibility for keeping tactical units informed of monuments and artworks in their areas of operations, and for facilitating the activities of MFA&A field officers.[26]

SHAEF instructed MFA&A field officers to report immediately any cases of looting, wanton damage, or culpable negligence on the part of Allied troops or of the indigenous population. They were to leave artworks in place unless absolutely necessary to prevent further damage, and to prepare an exact inventory and provide the location of the new storage space. Any moveable art objects found outside a place belonging to the person or institution bearing title to the works were to be impounded and, if necessary, turned over to the Comptroller of Property. Obvious museum repositories were to be left intact and guarded.[27] On August 20, 1944, General Eisenhower issued a letter that stressed the importance of archives as intelligence sources and for reconstituting civilian life, and required all archives not destroyed or damaged to be placed "off limits" to all troops.[28]

In preparation for the invasion of France, SHAEF distributed maps of monuments in northwestern Europe and lists of European museum personnel, archivists, and librarians to tactical units and commanders of civil affairs detachments. Using lists compiled by the American Defense-Harvard Group, cultural atlases and handbooks, MFA&A personnel created a register of monuments and collections for France and the Benelux countries, detailing those monuments not to be used by troops. As the list grew, the overwhelming task facing MFA&A officers quickly became evident.

After the Allied landings in Normandy in June 1944, the area of Western Europe under Allied control increased rapidly. MFA&A personnel found it practically impossible to keep pace with the advance in order to inspect and report on all the officially protected monuments. Between D-Day to December 1, 1944, each MFA&A field officer visited an average of 125 sites in 60 towns each month.[29]

In France, depositories of art collections removed from their normal locations and dispersed for protection presented few problems; Allied forces generally left the locations undisturbed until claimed by French civilian authorities.[30] The greatest single problem MFA&A officers encountered was the billeting of troops in historic buildings and the constant struggle to protect those buildings from spoliation and damage. However, MFA&A officers in the European Theater of Operations (ETO) faced many of the same problems that hampered the efforts of their counterparts with MTO forces in Italy. Plagued by the lack of available personnel, MFA&A staff never exceeded 35: the average before the German campaign was 12.[31] Allied commanders did take steps to improve the efficiency of MF&A activities. In Italy, where each MFA&A officer had been assigned to an individual unit, officers had been restricted to covering particular areas, while some areas had no officers at all. To avoid this problem in France and the Benelux countries, MFA&A officers rotated between various headquarters in order to operate where they were most needed.[32] A chronic lack of assigned or adequate transportation, which had plagued the MFA&A subdivision since 1943, compounded the problem of insufficient specialized personnel.[33] These shortcomings had serious repercussions, since many of the repositories had been strategically located well off the beaten path in remote rural enclaves.

Preparations for the Final Offensive into Germany and Austria

MFA&A Roles and Responsibilities

As Allied forces crossed into German territory, MFA&A responsibilities changed to reflect intelligence reports that Nazi officials had moved massive quantities of looted artworks and other valuables from occupied territories into the Reich. In the autumn of 1944, Eisenhower's Chief MFA&A Advisor, Lieutenant Colonel Geoffrey Webb, joined SHAEF headquarters at Versailles, where he orchestrated the activities of MFA&A officers attached to the 12th and 21st Army Groups. While MFA&A officers had operated on a regional basis in liberated territories, this arrangement seemed ill-suited for the invasion of Germany, which would proceed along a broad front. As an alternative, Webb proposed attaching two MFA&A officers to each field army during the German campaign.[34]

In September 1944, the U.S. Group Control Council for Germany described the MFA&A duties in the proposed military government scheme for Germany. These included locating and securing for restitution "works of art and other materials of cultural importance or value looted from the governments or nationals of the several United Nations." [35] MFA&A officers were expected to take control of all publicly and privately owned art and cultural property within Germany until such objects could be restituted. MFA&A field officers would remain attached to Army Groups and their subordinate formations during active operations and then transfer to military government organizations once Germany surrendered.

The SHAEF MFA&A Advisor foresaw problems if MFA&A officers were made responsible for isolated caches of valuable artworks. He believed that finding suitable civilian custodians for such caches would prove difficult, since many German museum curators had participated in the Nazi art-looting program as recipients of stolen goods. He noted that because most MFA&A field specialists were assigned to particular armies, the task of protecting caches would be complicated when army boundaries shifted during military operations.[36]

MFA&A officers entering Germany in early 1945 drew guidance from technical notes published by SHAEF in October 1944. These notes instructed them to communicate with Provost Marshals of military units and with military government public safety officers to help locate and protect valuables vulnerable to damage and theft. Although the small cadre of MFA&A officers necessarily relied upon reports from field units and military government detachments for information on the location of certain caches, they were instructed to conduct personal reconnaissance trips at the earliest opportunity. The purpose of these trips was to inspect these sites and determine whether local units were enforcing orders and ordinances designed to protect valuables. To identify potentially looted valuables, MFA&A officers were directed to collect all records from museums and private collections that dealt with accessions made after January 1938. Officers were told to assess the risks to the property and to leave the valuables as found, post a guard, and pack the valuables to prevent further damage, or move them to a safer place. No matter what action was taken, they were instructed to create a record of the inspection with details about the site and its contents, and to place the repository in the custody of local civilian officials.[37]

As American forces advanced deeper into Germany in the spring of 1945, SHAEF issued a memorandum reminding MFA&A officers of their responsibility to investigate "all information which might contribute to the eventual restitution of works of art and objects of scientific or historical importance which might have been looted from United Nations governments or nationals."[38] To carry out this assignment, MFA&A personnel had to inspect and inventory all repositories of looted or dispersed collections and to arrange for their protection, care, and disposition.

In April 1945, to facilitate the process of inventorying and restituting artworks, MFA&A branches of the U.S. and British Group Command Councils agreed, in principle, to establish an information file of all artworks taken into custody in Germany. The system required a standard procedure for documenting information about objects, employing standard forms in both armies. MFA&A leaders were still reviewing the system in May 1945, but evidence suggests that the system was never put into effect.[39]

Other Organizations Participating in the Recovery of Assets

Military Government Detachments

MFA&A personnel operated as part of SHAEF Civil Affairs Division (G-5), which had general authority for military government operations.[40] SHAEF G-5 assigned the vast bulk of responsibility for military government activities to specially organized detachments attached to U.S. armies involved in the German campaign. These military government detachments, following on the heels of advancing combat troops, established government infrastructure in German towns, cities, and rural areas as they fell under Allied control.[41] Detachments varied in size depending upon the scope of their governing responsibilities, but all had the primary objective of maintaining order to facilitate the further progress of Allied fighting units.

In areas of Germany under military government control, detachment public safety officers were responsible for coordinating efforts to enforce military government laws and maintain civic order. Their duties included arranging for a police force, either military or civilian, to curb the practice of looting by troops and civilians, and the protection of emergency repositories of art and cultural objects. The U.S. Army's "Manual for Military Government in Germany" instructed public safety officers to safeguard records relating to art and cultural property in order to thwart any attempts to conceal looted artworks from the occupying forces.[42]

OSS Art Looting Investigation Unit

The Office of Strategic Services Art Looting Investigation Unit (ALIU) was authorized in a November 21, 1944 interagency directive "to collect and disseminate such information bearing on the looting, confiscation and transfer by the enemy of art properties in Europe, and on individuals or organizations involved in such operations and transactions."[43] The ALIU remained a small operation comprised of ten field representatives and analysts, three of whom were civilians. The ALIU main headquarters was in Washington and a field headquarters was established in London in January 1945. In its London office the ALIU worked closely with Allied Commissions concerned with art looting and became the clearinghouse for "all Allied information on enemy looting gained through intelligence channels."[44]

By V-E Day, the ALIU had amassed records on several thousand individuals concerned directly or indirectly with art acquisition by the enemy, and much detailed information on German art repositories had been passed on to G-5, SHAEF, for action. It had also prepared a "target list" of key enemy personnel concerned with art looting to be captured and held for interrogation in Germany.[45]

Unit investigators issued four consolidated reports including a final report documenting Nazi looting of European art. These reports covered the activities of *Einsatzstab Reichsleiter Rosenberg* (ERR)—the Nazi task force responsible for the confiscation and removal to Germany of Jewish-owned art collections in occupied regions; the fate of Hermann Goering's extensive looted art collections; the Nazis' "Möbel Aktion"—the wholesale confiscation of household goods and furnishings of French Jewish families in 1943 and 1944; and plans for Hitler's art museum at Linz. The ALIU investigations revealed that German art dealers had engaged in extensive private purchasing in occupied and neutral countries as well as in Great Britain, the United States, and South America. The reports also raised suspicions of widespread disposal of artworks throughout Brazil and Argentina, suggesting that a considerable volume of victims' loot may have reached South America.[46] ALIU personnel proved to be a valuable source of information on looted art in postwar Europe.[47]

Target Forces

Allied leaders believed that the capture of large town and cities in Germany and occupied territories would yield a rich harvest of intelligence items including documents, equipment, and persons with specialized technical knowledge. Allied Target or "T Forces" were special ad hoc military units created to search for and secure items of scientific or technical value.[48] These "T Forces" were modeled after similar and successful "S Forces" employed in Italy.[49] General Eisenhower ordered the creation of "T Forces" in July 1944; each "T Force" was to be staffed with personnel appropriate to the target intelligence asset.[50] In late 1944 the SHAEF Financial Branch attempted to expand the mission of the "T Forces" to include financial targets, but the "T" subdivision of the intelligence division (G-2) resisted this change.[51] Nevertheless, by March 1945 the main office of the Berlin Reichsbank appeared on a list of targets for that city.[52]

"T Force" personnel discovered caches of assets during their operations and served as temporary guards for collections of valuables.[53] In at least one instance, intelligence officers in the 7th U.S. Army utilized "T Force" personnel to track down hidden valuables identified during interrogation of German prisoners of war. The "T Force" utilized information from a nearby Counter Intelligence Corps (CIC) unit to locate a significant hoard of gold.[54] Throughout the invasion of Germany and the first weeks following Germany's surrender, "T Force" personnel examined some 3,000 planned targets and uncovered approximately 2,000 others.[55]

Directives on the Control of Assets in Germany and Austria

American policy on valuables in the Third Reich stemmed from decisions reached at the highest levels of government. On April 28, 1945, the Joint Chiefs of Staff directed General Eisenhower to "impound or block all gold, silver, currencies, securities, accounts in financial institutions, credits, valuable papers and all other assets" including property which had been "subject to transfer under duress or wrongful acts of confiscation, disposition, or spoliation, whether pursuant to legislation or by procedure to follow forms of laws or otherwise."[56] This confiscation served a dual purpose by keeping assets out of enemy hands and giving the U.S. authorities control over the economy and the disposition of any property found to be looted.

Prior to receiving this directive, SHAEF had established policies to handle the gold, financial assets, art, and cultural objects uncovered by troops in Germany. SHAEF policies reflected the fact that the Army did not have the time, manpower, or resources to perform detailed inspections of caches recovered during active military operations. Allied intelligence sources suggested that the Germans had integrated looted artworks into German museum collections. Regarding art caches in Germany, SHAEF G-5 noted in December 1944:

> Yet it is among such collections of objects that much of the loot from Allied
> countries has been dispersed, for it is known that apart from the actual bulk
> seizure and shipment of objects, (e.g., from France), much was acquired for

museums all over Germany, either by buying in a rigged market or by exchange for looted objects or works seized from Jewish collectors within the Reich. Such objects are therefore to be given all the protection possible, not only in accordance with policy of preserving objects of cultural interest and historical value in general, but as an essential preliminary stage of the process of securing and preserving looted objects for eventual restitution.[57]

Thus, Allied forces would have to treat all stashes of art as potential Nazi loot. SHAEF acknowledged that MFA&A officers could not possibly inspect and protect large numbers of small repositories in forward areas, and that, at least initially, the Army lacked sufficient transportation resources to move the art to safer locations. Protection of art caches therefore had to be arranged by nearby military units in all but the most exceptional cases, a task made more difficult by the frequent transfer and relief of military police units that were the primary source of guards.[58]

The recovery of artworks and cultural property, although essential to the effort to preserve European cultural heritage, represented only one element of the overall collection of moveable assets. Asset categories such as gold, silver, personal effects, securities, and currencies also bore extreme significance for U.S. authorities. The planned shift from military to civilian government depended on controlling these assets and, given their liquidity, preventing them from falling into enemy hands. SHAEF elected to segregate the recovered assets, creating separate facilities to house each group. Toward this end occupational and military government forces located and renovated existing structures to manage the diverse influx of assets falling under their control.

In September 1944 SHAEF created the Currency Section in its Finance Division to receive, supply, and store occupation currency for Allied armed forces and for military government operations. In addition, the Currency Section was to "act as required as a depository for and/or to exercise control over assets seized or impounded by Allied Military authorities."[59] It did not exercise the latter function until April 1945, when it began operations in the Frankfurt Reichsbank building and was renamed the Foreign Exchange Depository (FED).[60]

SHAEF officials soon realized that all asset types could not be handled in the same fashion. In March 1945, the Assistant Adjutant General of SHAEF, N. H. Newman, drafted specific procedures for handling currency and securities seized in enemy-occupied territories.[61] If the seized currency was still legal tender in the country of issue, troops were to turn it over to a finance officer so that it could be used to meet military requirements within the issuing territory. They were to hand over out-of-circulation currencies to the G-5 Controller of Finance and Accounts or to the appropriate Army group.[62] This directive made no attempt to distinguish possible looted currencies from the general pool, meaning that the Army may have inadvertently used looted currencies, or currencies obtained through the sale of victims' assets, to support the final American advance.

Securities, on the other hand, required special handling. Since many securities were bearer securities, tracing the ownership of a specific security and determining whether it had been taken under duress proved nearly an impossible task. The origin and circumstances surrounding its seizure were therefore extremely important. Newman instructed troops to hand over all securities found in enemy territory against receipt, with full particulars of the circumstances surrounding their capture, to the nearest Military Government officer to be treated as enemy property and used later to fulfill Axis reparations obligations. However, securities seized from enemy forces in liberated territories were to be handed over against receipt to the nearest Civil Affairs officer, who would then deposit them in the nearest Reichsbank branch and furnish full particulars to the Controller of Property of the SHAEF Mission to the government in whose territory the articles had been found. Officials hoped that this procedure of putting confiscated securities, with a description of the circumstances surrounding their seizure, in the hands of military officers would help determine which securities had in fact been looted and whether or not they were subject to restitution.[63]

These rules also applied to assets seized from prisoners of war, whenever circumstances indicated that the prisoner did not appear to be the legitimate owner of the valuables. Troops were given the latitude to leave in place any currency and financial assets found in public or private premises adequately safeguarded against theft; they merely had to report their location to the nearest military government officer.[64]

In March 1945, the 12th Army Group issued Operational Instruction No. 9, which covered the types of property falling under military government control. The instruction was intended to complement the policies contained in the SHAEF "Handbook for Military Government in Germany." Troops were directed to take control of property and records of Nazi party organizations, as well as abandoned property of sufficient value to the military government to warrant its control. Troops were also to seize *prima facie* loot obtained from outside Germany, but where evidence of duress was not immediately available, they did not have to treat questionable items as loot.[65]

Intelligence on German Looting and the Location of Valuables

The Allied liberation of southern Italy and northwestern Europe revealed the vast scope of Nazi looting in occupied countries. Recovery of looted valuables and other Nazi assets was a prerequisite for any attempts at restitution to lawful owners and other victims. American leaders were therefore anxious to prevent any cloaking of these assets within Germany or their transfer abroad. Although Allied nations had acted quickly to establish laws to prevent such activities, General Eisenhower ascertained that his command lacked the specialists needed to examine captured business and financial records to detect concealed Nazi assets. In March 1945, he requested the assignment of specialists from the U.S. Treasury and Justice Departments and from similar British organizations to perform such investigations.[66]

During the fall of 1944, MFA&A personnel at SHAEF worked to establish a system of intelligence gathering that would collect data on Nazi art looting in Western Europe.[67] By early 1945, investigators had assembled a wealth of information regarding the methods and aims of Nazi art looting during the occupation. They had confirmed that the Germans had systematically stolen and removed to Germany a significant number of Jewish-owned art collections (including the large Rothschild, Wassermann, and Goudstikker collections) thereby increasing German holdings of artworks at the expense of occupied territories.[68] Based on information gathered from a myriad of sources including captured documents, OSS reports, and prisoner interrogations, SHAEF published a preliminary list of repositories containing works of art to be taken into custody by Allied troops as they moved through Germany.[69]

Allied intelligence officers interrogated enemy prisoners in an effort to learn the likely locations of caches that had been used for safekeeping by the Nazi regime. These interrogation reports were forwarded to tactical units in raw form in order to make the information available as quickly as possible. Allied interrogators were particularly interested in plans for the evacuation of art and library collections from German cities vulnerable to destruction from Allied bombing, and their storage in out-of-the-way areas for safekeeping.[70]

Interrogations of Nazi officials continued after Germany's surrender. Some enemy officials responsible for hiding the artworks cooperated with Allied authorities in locating dispersed caches of art. One such individual provided military intelligence sources with detailed information regarding the repositories of art in the area around Salzburg, Austria.[71] U.S. officials interrogated prisoners ranging from the lowest to the highest ranks of the Nazi hierarchy; even Hermann Goering was interrogated in mid-May 1945 regarding possible repositories of French artworks that he had obtained through looting, pilferage, or purchase.[72]

In some cases, German officials cooperated with U.S. efforts to uncover loot, providing complete lists of the "official" art repositories in their area of control. Military Government detachments then forwarded these lists of repository locations with instructions to military personnel to place the caches off-limits. In late April, SHAEF reported that German officials had "noted the existence of over 100 depositories" of art and archives in western Germany, and that this information would soon be forwarded to tactical units.[73]

Detailed records from banks, museums, and other institutions provided another source of information on the location of valuables. American forces used bank records found among the enormous stash of valuables in the mineshafts at Merkers in April 1945 to locate other caches of valuables; by May 6, 1945, General Eisenhower could report that troops exploiting intelligence gathered at Merkers had discovered at least a dozen additional caches of gold, other precious metals, and currency.[74] German banks were obvious targets for investigation regarding hoards of valuables. Even ruined banks yielded finds; in one instance tactical troops blasted their way into the debris of a Reichsbank branch to discover a cache of gold coins belonging to Heinrich Himmler.[75]

Although informants, interrogations, and captured documents provided valuable leads in efforts to track down hidden valuables, only actual visits to the sites could confirm evidence gathered through second-hand sources. In some cases information regarding the location of caches of loot could not be confirmed because the area in question remained under enemy control. As late as the first week in May 1945, American forces were unable to follow up a report that 41 bags of gold had been transferred to the town of Aue because the town was still heavily defended by German troops.[76] Though initially hostile to Allied forces, German civilians proved more forthcoming once the fighting had ended and a semblance of order had been imposed by military government units. In early June 1945, for example, Army engineers used mine detectors to search an area near Wallgau, Bavaria, where local civilians claimed had been the sites of "suspicious activity" during the previous April. Using their detection equipment, engineers found hundreds of gold bars buried beneath the ground.[77]

Many leads detailing the existence and location of caches of valuables, however, proved to be of little value. Troops had to verify each rumor—a process often leading to fruitless hunts for the alleged hidden treasure troves. The 12th

Army Group reported in late March 1945 that it had received information regarding 103 repositories in western and southern Germany, although it doubted the veracity of these reports. One party of MFA&A officers braved mine-fields to inspect a castle alleged to contain a cache of artworks. The officers found no signs of the cache, and were therefore unable to determine whether they had been misled or the cache had been moved.[78]

A similarly futile mission evolved out of an April 1945 message from the Secretary of War to SHAEF detailing an alleged German attempt to move 6,000 kilograms of Reichsbank gold across the border into Switzerland.[79] SHAEF immediately ordered the 6th Army Group to seize the suspected gold shipment said to be located in the town of Lorrach in the province of Baden.[80] At the cutting edge of this endeavor, the 6th Army Group dispatched a Counter Intelligence Corps (CIC) agent to investigate the existence of a gold cache. After interviewing sources in the area and inspecting potential repositories, the agent could not confirm the existence of the reported gold cache.[81]

Many captured documents containing information on caches of valuables were not immediately available to frontline units and MFA&A officers. For example, in March 1945 the 12th Army Group reported that a civilian in OSS employ had noted, unofficially, that a checklist of the repositories for the city of Baden had been discovered in Strasbourg, France, and placed in an envelope marked "very important." The source forwarded no further information.[82] In another case, the G-5 section of the 6th Army Group reported in May 1945 that documents captured in Munich contained a list of places where German officials had hidden art and archival materials. The report noted that the list failed to specify "whether there is some looted material among these collections or whether it consists exclusively of German possessions," and suggested that the addresses be investigated.[83] Months after the fighting ended, masses of documents and other leads remained in disarray. In August 1945, U.S. forces were still compiling lists of possible caches of cultural objects based on the information provided by captured documents.[84]

Discovery of Caches During the Final Offensive

Nazi officials and individual private owners used castles, private homes, air raid bunkers, and underground mines to shield public and private collections of art, cultural property, gold, jewelry and other valuables, many of which were later found to contain the property of Holocaust victims. In their final offensive against the Reich, U.S. forces found enormous quantities of valuables scattered across southwestern Germany and Austria in large numbers of emergency repositories. The majority of these caches, which held anywhere from one to thousands of objects, had been created in response to the Allied bombing campaign that concentrated on German and Austrian urban areas. The threat of damage from aerial attacks had led Nazi officials to remove valuable assets from cities and store them in remote areas less likely to be targeted by Allied bombs. Although the exact number of caches falling under U.S. control remains unknown, in September 1948, OMGUS estimated that U.S. forces had found approximately 1,500 repositories of art and cultural objects in Germany. These repositories contained approximately 10.7 million objects worth an estimated $5 billion.[85]

The discovery of loot and other valuables began almost immediately as the U.S. 9th, 1st, 3rd, and 7th Armies moved into Germany in the spring of 1945. On April 8, 1945, American forces discovered a massive stash of valuables hidden in a complex of interconnected potassium mines near Merkers, Germany. Deep within the mine, in a secret cavern behind a well-fortified masonry wall, the Americans unearthed a treasure trove containing tons of artworks and large quantities of gold, silver, and currency.[86] At the time, they estimated that the gold found in the Merkers mine represented approximately 80 percent of the total gold held by the Reichsbank.[87]

By far the richest single stash uncovered, the Merkers mine yielded an immense quantity of assets, including an estimated 2.76 billion Reichsmark notes and containers brimming with foreign currency.[88] The most gruesome find, however, was a section of the cavern devoted to SS loot containing 207 bags and suitcases filled with jewelry, silverware, teeth, watches, cigarette cases, and razors clearly taken from persecutees, including murdered inmates of concentration camps.[89]

Although Reichsbank accounting books revealed that much of the Merkers gold and currency had been seized from banks in occupied countries, the suitcases bearing loot were unmistakably taken from victims under duress. U.S. forces quickly secured the stash, and, on April 15, 1945, escorted the contraband deep into the American zone, where experts could organize, inventory, and appraise the assets in the new Foreign Exchange Depository in Frankfurt.[90] The financial assets found in the Merkers mine stash included 3,682 bags and cartons of German currency, 80 bags of foreign currency, 63 bags of silver bars, 6 platinum bars, 8 bags of gold rings, 190 parcels containing engraving plates and dies, and 207 containers containing SS loot of jewelry, silverware, coins, stamps, dental fillings and miscellany. The combined weight of the precious and semi-precious stones and novelty jewelry alone was an estimated 2,527 pounds. U.S. Treasury experts, sent to evaluate the Merkers stash in June 1945, estimated that its value exceeded $500 million. Of this amount, they determined, gold and precious metals (mainly gold bullion and gold coins) alone comprised $300 million.[91]

On April 29, 1945, Major Howard M. McBee, an officer on the 1st U.S. Army Judge Advocate General staff, made a similar discovery in a quarry on the outskirts of the Buchenwald concentration camp. Buried deep beneath a bunker, McBee uncovered 313 suitcases, wooden boxes and barrels, filled with gold bars, U.S. currency, gold coins, diamonds, various precious stones, boxes of silver spoons, watches, clocks, and other items weighing an estimated twenty-one tons. A random sampling of the loot determined that the stash contained more than 600 pounds of fountain pens, watchstraps, and novelty jewelry, more than 17,000 pounds of silver tableware, and hundreds of wedding bands and thousands of gold teeth. Using nine two-ton trucks, the 12th Army Group shipped seven truckloads under tight security to Frankfurt on May 16, 1945, retaining two truckloads for War Crimes Section of the 12th Army Group pending further war crimes investigations.[92]

Although the Merkers and Buchenwald caches were unique because of their size and the prevalence of obvious loot, they exemplified a general pattern repeated throughout Germany, as private owners, branch banks, and local museums took drastic steps to protect their accumulated valuables. Reichsbank branch offices proved to be a major source of gold and currency caches, with finds at Halle (gold allegedly from France), Nuremberg (gold bars allegedly from the Netherlands), Plauen (gold currency from Himmler's account), Eschwege (82 gold bars), Magdeburg (silver bars allegedly from Hungary, bank records, and foreign securities), and others.[93] By September 1945, General Eisenhower reported that his forces had recovered 300 pounds of precious and semi-precious stones, 700 pounds of rings, 3,000 pounds of novelty jewelry, 3,500 pounds of watches, 650 pounds of gold and silver tooth fillings, 4,500 pounds of scrap metal, and 18,000 pounds of tableware and eyeglass frames—items clearly looted from Holocaust victims.[94]

The wide dispersal of caches prevented U.S. forces from fully implementing policy directives, especially those regarding works of art and cultural property, which tended to be more widely dispersed than other assets. The limited number of MFA&A specialists available to the Army forced these personnel to cover a large amount of territory with few resources. As a result, MFA&A staff had to put off inspections of many reported caches, and often could perform only cursory inspections of others. Thus, much of the raw information regarding suspected caches often went unverified, and collections remained unprotected. For example, by midsummer 1945, two months after the fighting ended, the six MFA&A officers assigned to the 12th Army Group had inspected only 200 of the 850 emergency repositories of art and archival materials that were located in the Army Group's zone.[95]

Time, distance, and resources were the chief determinants of how quickly uncovered hoards of valuables were inspected, moved, or placed under guard. The 12th Army Group reported that during April 1945 its forces had discovered or reported 232 repositories of art and archives. The actual number of repositories known to U.S. forces frequently exceeded those listed in published reports because of the scarcity of clerical staff to keep reports up to date.[96] The capture of large areas of western Germany gave U.S. forces access to numerous curators, archivists, and officials of cultural institutions, who provided considerable information regarding depositories of art and cultural objects. Unfortunately, the rapidity of the advance combined with the paucity of MFA&A personnel (one officer for the entire 1st U.S. Army area) prevented any action being taken in time to avoid serious losses to the contents of the depositories.

The experiences of Captain Walker Hancock, the MFA&A officer attached to the 1st U.S. Army, illustrate conditions during this fluid period. In late April, Hancock reported that he had learned the locations of 109 repositories over the course of just a few days. Between March 24 and April 24, he had been able to inspect just 31 of 230 known sites in the 1st Army's area of operations. Of these sites, over one-third showed signs of damage from troops, displaced persons (DPs), and/or bombing.[97]

To a great extent, the 1st Army relied on tactical units to report on and secure depositories discovered during the advance, although "securing" was usually limited to simply posting signs putting the area off-limits. Damage by troops and DPs occurred despite such signs, and Hancock reported that it was "manifestly impossible" to post guards at every repository. He also noted that "in the absence of guards almost all [sites] are in danger of damage or looting under the prevailing conditions in this country." He cited the example of a repository containing materials from the State Archives (*Staatsarchiv*) in Marburg, where records had been thrown outdoors to make way for occupying troops.[98]

Hancock noted that the posting of "off limits" signs did little to protect against looters, although it did prevent units from billeting troops directly in the repositories. He reported his conviction that the only solution was to physically secure the artworks in a limited number of central depositories that could be guarded. Yet, because MFA&A officers lacked the transportation and personnel necessary to move threatened art, Hancock doubted that any action could be taken in time to avoid "widespread and irreparable damage."[99]

Captain Hancock's experiences were typical of all MFA&A officers involved in the German campaign. As the number of discovered valuables skyrocketed in spring of 1945, the U.S. Army's attempts to safeguard and inventory these assets met with less and less success. MFA&A resources were stretched to the breaking point as U.S. forces rapidly overran large sections of western Germany. In April 1945, for example, the 1st and 3rd U.S. Armies operating under 12th Army Group's control had only two fulltime MFA&A officers to cover an area of approximately 47,000 square miles.[100] Tactical units and local military government detachments were forced to take up the slack, relying on whatever information was available from MFA&A or local sources. As a report from the 12th Army Group noted in February 1945, "[i]n a rapidly moving situation, initial measures for protection have to be taken by Mil. Gov. officers of tactical commands and by those of detachments as soon as these are deployed."[101]

As tactical units moved on, they handed control of towns and villages over to specially organized military government detachments. These detachments with their assigned specialists had the task of controlling occupied areas and restoring a modicum of government, but their numbers proved insufficient to meet requirements. To fill the need for military government units, the 1st U.S. Army created 52 provisional military government detachments during the campaign.[102] Thus, security for caches of valuables often depended on military government units whose personnel had little or no specialized training.

After mid-April, German resistance began to collapse, and discoveries of new repositories increased as the pace of the advance quickened. In late April 1945, SHAEF G-5 reported that U.S. forces had made numerous finds of gold, silver, and currency in the preceding week, including approximately 80 tons of silver.[103] The 9th Army MFA&A officer noted that the rapidly increasing number of reported repositories, chance finds, and logistical problems necessitated a constant vigil by MFA&A officers and military government detachments.[104] During May 1945, units of the 12th Army Group uncovered nearly 400 new repositories; the Army Group reported that its MFA&A officers were "short-handed" and "harassed by continual calls to inspect new discoveries reported from one end to the other of their respective vast areas."[105]

The physical condition of discovered caches of valuables varied considerably. Several locations reported loss of items to U.S. forces hunting for keepsakes.[106] The 12th Army Group reported in mid-May 1945 that most of the inspected repositories were "poorly housed, and in some cases, commander(s) have ordered their evacuation to establish adequate security and the physical conditions suitable for preservation."[107]

U.S. forces entering Austria encountered conditions and problems similar to those found in Germany, though on a smaller scale. The contents of the museums at Klagenfurt, Austria, for example, had been dispersed across the countryside. By late May 1945, 21 of these repositories had been identified, although

MFA&A personnel had been able to visit only 13.[108] As in Germany, the largest caches were discovered hidden deep within mines. The salt mine at Alt Aussee, for example, contained art and furnishings from throughout Nazi-occupied Europe, much of it looted from Jewish families. The collection had been destined for Hitler's planned art museum in the city of Linz.[109]

The plethora of art caches found during the German campaign made it difficult for SHAEF headquarters to keep its records up to date. In early April 1945, SHAEF G-5 issued the third edition of its list of art and cultural property repositories in Germany.[110] Just eight days later SHAEF published an addendum to this list containing 46 new entries.[111] Before the end of the month, a second addendum added more than 140 new locations to the tally.[112] In May, a third addendum added even more.[113]

Initial Activities Following the German Surrender

Although the unconditional surrender of all German military forces on May 7, 1945 ended the fighting in Germany and Austria, conditions in those countries remained chaotic. U.S. forces quickly shifted from military operations to occupation duties, with the goal of imposing order in their zones of occupation. The U.S. Zone in Germany was divided into two military districts, each under control of an individual army headquarters. The 3rd U.S. Army controlled the Eastern Military District, comprised of Bavaria; the 7th U.S. Army was responsible for the Western Military District, which included the regions of Baden-Württemberg and Hesse. District commanders were responsible for the primary missions of the occupation and, when possible, for service functions within their districts.[114]

In Austria, the transition from military operations to military government proceeded less smoothly than in Germany. In January 1945, military government organizations for Austria had been established in the Mediterranean Theater of Operations (MTO) with the assumption that MTO forces would occupy Austria from the south. However, events in April and May 1945 changed these plans. The first U.S. troops to enter Austria were from the 6th Army Group under SHAEF; these forces overran large portions of Austria from the north while MTO units remained busy clearing northern Italy. The Allied command therefore transferred control of the region from MTO to European Theater of Operations (ETO) units, except for military government personnel who joined the staff of the occupying forces.[115] Tactical military government continued in Austria for several weeks into May 1945 until the military government detachments were in position. Military government detachments found themselves in a confused situation. The chain of command was obscured because U.S. forces in Austria included all or parts of two army groups, two field armies, four army corps, and 12 divisions.[116] The situation improved in July 1945 when the 15th Army Group was reorganized and designated as the U.S. Occupational Forces Austria, under the command of General Mark Clark.

With the end of combat operations and the re-disposition of Allied forces into national zones of occupation, the multinational military mission led by SHAEF ended. Accordingly, in early July 1945, SHAEF disbanded; control over U.S. forces in Europe and responsibility for occupation of the American zones in Germany and Austria then passed to U.S. Forces, European Theater (USFET).[117] Day-to-day government operations in American-occupied areas were in the hands of about 450 military government detachments, almost half of which were ad hoc units hastily assembled from combat formations.[118]

Conditions in Austria at the end of war were abysmal. Business and industry were at a complete standstill: postal, telephone, and telegraph services had been cut off, train lines were inoperable, food and fuel were scarce, and the water supply was contaminated. Housing was in short supply. U.S. troops were responsible for providing food and shelter for 250,000 German prisoners and 700,000 DPs and refugees. Once hostilities ended, however, the situation improved greatly.[119]

During the first few weeks of the occupation, U.S. officials took steps to gain control over valuables, looted and otherwise, within the territories under their control. As U.S. forces entered Germany, they issued Military Government Law No. 52. This law made certain properties subject to seizure by the military government, including those belonging to the German State, the Nazi Party and its adherents, and non-German absentee owners. This law also blocked transactions in property transferred under duress or through wrongful acts of confiscation during the Nazi regime, as well as all art or cultural property of value or importance, regardless of ownership.[120]

On May 31, 1945, the U.S. Military Government passed MG Law No. 53, requiring all persons in Germany owning or controlling any foreign currency to deposit those funds in the nearest Reichsbank branch.[121] Stateless and displaced persons still living in Germany fell under MG Law No. 53; they, too, were required to turn over their foreign exchange assets, against receipt, to the military government for safekeeping. In return, the military government promised that their assets would be returned once they left German soil.[122]

After the surrender, MFA&A officers continued to work to locate and protect widely scattered caches of art and cultural objects. The basic plan for control of postwar Germany gave the MFA&A Branch responsibility for providing information and preparing directives that covered a number of areas including the protection of art and cultural property, selection of German civilian MFA&A employees, freezing and control of artworks subject to restitution, and the process of restitution itself.[123] Soon after the surrender, the MFA&A established a headquarters in Frankfurt to serve as the central administrative and intelligence unit for operations of specialist officers in the field. It passed field reports on to higher military government echelons and transmitted policies and procedures down to field officers.

American forces continued to discover additional repositories of valuables following the German surrender. In late May 1945, SHAEF issued the fourth edition of its list of repositories of art and archives in Germany, Austria, and Tyrol. The information had been derived from every available source, and much of it had yet to be evaluated. Entries such as "reported to contain part of Rothschild collection" or "looted works of art reported sent to house of (E.Z.)" underscored SHAEF's admission that many of the entries could prove to be obsolete or inaccurate.[124] The following month, SHAEF published an addendum to the fourth edition list of art repositories containing more than 200 additional entries.[125] Reports of newly discovered repositories reached headquarters on a daily basis throughout the early summer; by the end of June 1945, the total number reported to the 12th Army Group alone reached 849.[126]

When the fighting ended, MFA&A officers faced many of the same problems that had hindered their activities during the advance into Germany. In early June

1945, the MFA&A officer for the U.S. 7th Army reported that the Army's territory stretched approximately 280 miles from Bad Ischl in Austria to Darmstadt, Germany, and was roughly 80 miles wide. Approximately 175 repositories had been reported in the 7th Army area; captured documents, including some of the records of *Einsatzstab Reichsleiter Rosenberg* (ERR), indicated many others remained undiscovered. The small number of MFA&A personnel on hand could do little more than protect the larger repositories and those containing mostly looted assets from outside Germany. In cooperation with 7th Army intelligence officers, MFA&A officers had begun collecting and collating captured documents that they hoped would help them locate and restitute looted art.[127]

Despite directives to the contrary, local military government officers sometimes took it upon themselves to move artworks from the places where they had been discovered. Problems arose in part because the smaller military government detachments assigned to control districts and less important cities usually had no personnel with expertise in MFA&A work and lacked the specialized knowledge required to handle artworks safely.[128] In May 1945, the MFA&A Advisor for SHAEF complained about such activities, noting that unauthorized movements of art increased the difficulty of keeping adequate records and jeopardized the physical condition of delicate artworks.[129] In July 1945, SHAEF notified the 12th Army Group that only MFA&A officers who had been approved by SHAEF or the U.S. Group Control Council had the necessary qualifications to oversee movement of fine art.[130] Although this restriction protected art from unauthorized transfers, it undoubtedly decreased the number of repositories cleared by U.S. forces over the following months.

In July 1945, the MFA&A Operations Director working out of the United States Forces European Theater (USFET) headquarters estimated that the work of evacuating repositories might have to continue for three or four months, an estimate that proved extremely optimistic. One MFA&A officer, familiar with such operations, suggested forming a "T Force" like unit comprised of specialists that would move about the U.S. Zone visiting and evacuating repositories.[131] This advice went unheeded, resulting in continued headaches for MFA&A officers through the summer and fall of 1945 and into 1946.

In January 1946, for example, the MFA&A officer for the area around Frankfurt reported that a major task for his office consisted of collecting art and cultural objects from dispersed repositories, and screening the materials to determine what might have been illegitimately acquired from governments or individuals of the United Nations. He noted, however, that the 12 most important local art collections had been dispersed into 118 repositories scattered across his area of responsibility, and that the actual contents and relative value of these repositories remained unknown.[132]

The erosion of relations with the Soviet Union affected the recovery of valuables in the field. U.S. troops had overrun several areas of Germany and Austria that fell outside the occupation zones designated by agreements between the Allied powers. Though these areas were slated to be turned over to the Soviets, the Allied command decided to retain responsibility for the valuables located there. In June 1945, the War Department ordered SHAEF to have U.S. and British troops remove art and cultural property from areas they currently occupied that were outside their designated zones of occupation. The art in question included works believed to have been looted by the Nazis from countries within the ETO and MTO (Italy and Western Europe) as well as art that MFA&A experts felt originated from within the U.S. and British zones in Germany.[133]

The confusion and uncertainty at local levels caused some concern within the high command. In early August 1945, General Eisenhower, who had taken command of U.S. Forces, European Theater (USFET) after SHAEF disbanded, noted that nearly 500 repositories of art and cultural materials had been reported in the U.S. Zone in Germany and directed his subordinate commanders to prepare accurate information lists about the repositories' contents and location to expedite the evacuation of those that contained inadequately housed or looted artworks.[134]

U.S. forces continued to discover more repositories throughout the summer of 1945; in September of that year they found 98 new repositories in the U.S. Zone in Germany, bringing the total to 736. The burden of protecting repositories fell squarely on the shoulders of local Military Government detachments, whose personnel were already stretched thin. A progress report from one unit summed up the problem it faced only a few months after the surrender:

> The responsibility of the local, and often small, Military Government Detachment is not a little nor an idle one. It is just one more responsibility among a great many, and one which every MG detachment wishes to be rid of at the earliest practicable moment—especially the Property Control officer, whose personal "headache" some particular repository often is.... With the redeployment and removal of American troops accelerated, the problem of maintaining adequate military guards at repositories becomes a serious one. Already many military installations have withdrawn guard details from repositories and made necessary the procurement by MG detachments of civilian guards.[135]

The pressure to reduce the number of repositories became more evident as the availability of military guards decreased. Unable to adequately screen or guard the valuables in their care, U.S. forces began turning repositories directly over to German civilian control if the contents did not include looted works or works of great cultural or monetary value. As a result, the military government in the U.S. Zone was able to clear 72 repositories from its responsibility during September 1945.[136] This procedure was broadly applied. In July 1946, for example, the Office of Military Government for Bavaria granted German civilian owners title to paintings and furniture in a church repository upon proof of ownership. In each case the only protocol was that the owner sign a sworn statement averring that none of the objects had been obtained outside Germany after January 1, 1938.[137] The primary goal of this turnover was to absolve the military government of any further responsibility for the valuables.

Despite such risky practices the closing of repositories proceeded slowly. To transfer these repositories to Germany, military government officials had to rely extensively on German personnel to help in the process of identifying and moving the contents of art caches. In Baden-Württemberg, for example, the military government allowed German authorities to handle the job of reassembling public art collections from repositories scattered around the countryside. U.S. officials deemed this expedient necessary to safeguard against looting and further deterioration.[138] The clearing of repositories continued well into 1946. In March of that year the Property Disposition Board of the Office of Military Government, U.S. Zone reported that "vast quantities" of cultural objects remained in the now 923 repositories uncovered in the U.S. Zone in Germany.[139]

Efforts to recover looted valuables not under military government control continued throughout 1945, often by individuals with no "official" responsibility for such activities. In one example, a Netherlands liaison officer posed as a Swiss buyer to help recover a Dutch painting that was being sold illegally by the wife of a former high-ranking Nazi official. During his undercover work, this officer was told that he could purchase the service of someone who could paint over a valuable artwork so that it could be smuggled across the border.[140]

Consolidation of Assets—Establishing Collecting Points

The next stage in the evolution of U.S. control of assets involved the immense task of consolidating these assets in secure facilities. As long as art, gold, and other valuables remained housed in depositories lacking adequate security, they remained vulnerable to thieves and vandals. Allied commanders and art specialists had been surprised at the extent to which art collections and other valuables had been scattered and by the number of small emergency repositories. Realizing the scope of the problem, leaders took steps to establish collecting points where they could safely store gold, jewelry, art, and cultural property stashed around the country.

In early May 1945, as fighting still raged across Germany, General Eisenhower's MFA&A Advisor Lt. Colonel Geoffrey Webb determined that scattered artworks could be protected and catalogued only if U.S. forces could assemble them in a manageable number of collecting points. He therefore urged SHAEF to speed repairs to selected buildings, mostly museums, so that large-scale movement of artworks from vulnerable caches could begin as soon as transportation became available.[141] He proposed that Eisenhower order his subordinate commanders to set aside museums or other suitable buildings for use as collecting points, to allot transportation and manpower for use by MFA&A officers, to maintain the security of caches and collecting points to the extent consistent with military requirements, and to advise SHAEF if the subordinate command needed additional MFA&A specialists.[142]

In addition to their concerns about security, Allied leaders learned that in many cases artworks and cultural property were in danger of deterioration if left in the repositories in which they had been discovered. In April 1945, art experts informed SHAEF that salt mines like the Kaiseroda mine at Merkers were poor choices for storing art because the salt dust in the mines could damage paintings and books.[143] American officials were forced to move artworks found in the Siegen copper mine to save them from further deterioration caused by the extreme humidity in the mine.[144] These kinds of problems increased the urgency of finding suitable collecting points for seized valuables.

In May 1945, Eisenhower directed the Army Groups to take responsibility for the storage and safeguarding of art treasures discovered in areas occupied by their forces. The Army Groups were to take immediate steps to concentrate and safeguard the art in suitable accommodations within their assigned zones in Germany, taking care to have the art handled only by MFA&A officers and skilled labor. SHAEF ordered the Army Groups to report by June 1, 1945 the buildings they had selected to serve as central repositories and the dates that concentration and inventories would be completed.[145]

The process of selecting collecting points proceeded in an ad hoc fashion. The initial MFA&A plan for collecting art and cultural assets envisioned the establishment of two major collecting points in Frankfurt and Munich.[146] The obvious requirements for collecting points were security against theft and vandalism, protection against natural deterioration, and reasonable proximity to transportation and to caches in the field. In practice, U.S. forces established several minor collecting points in addition to the major facilities. For example, the 15th Army opened an art repository in Bonn. The building was a three-story bunker with working air conditioning and steel doors that could be guarded with minimal effort.[147]

The U.S. 3rd Army established a collecting point at its Frankfurt headquarters. By the end of June 1945, two trucking teams operated out of the collecting point with the aim of collecting, securing, and preserving all cultural treasures found in temporary repositories in the 3rd Army's area of responsibility.[148]

Shortages of qualified personnel and inadequate transportation slowed the movement of art and cultural objects from repositories to the central collecting points. There were only about 35 personnel in the U.S. Zone qualified to supervise the movement of fragile artworks. These experts were forced to rely on a random assortment of organizations to evacuate repositories. They often employed Displaced Persons (DPs) for manual labor and moved fragile valuables without the benefit of proper packing materials. To speed the process of evacuation and avoid unnecessary damage to artworks, the MFA&A Branch of the United States Group Control Council (USGCC) recommended the establishment of a semi-permanent, well-equipped unit to handle the task of art movement within the U.S. Zone.[149] U.S. officials failed to implement this recommendation, and art movement remained an ad hoc endeavor.

The 3rd and 7th U.S. Armies established a collecting point at Munich at the request of MFA&A officers who needed a secure storage area for numerous art repositories discovered in Austria. The Army requisitioned two monumental former Nazi party buildings for this purpose, and an MFA&A officer reported in July 1945 that truckloads of art objects were arriving daily at the collecting point.[150]

By July 1945, U.S. forces had established the two chief central collecting points at Munich and Wiesbaden—one in each of the two military government districts in the U.S. Zone in Germany[151]—and several subordinate sub-collecting points in Bad Wildungen, Heilbronn, Kochendorf, Marburg, Nuremberg, Oberammergau, and Offenbach.[152] In Austria, the Property Control Warehouse in Salzburg was designated the gathering point for all assets recovered in the U.S. Zone.

By mid-August 1945 the Munich collecting point was staffed by nearly 200 personnel. By September 1945, it had become the primary site for looted artworks found within the U.S. zones of Austria and Germany awaiting eventual restitution. Among the art treasures brought to Munich were the contents of the Alt Aussee cache not belonging to Austria.[153] The Munich collecting point also housed a large portion of the records of the *Einsatzstab Reichsleiter Rosenberg* (ERR), and the U.S. command proposed that all documents pertaining to art looting in Europe be concentrated there in order to facilitate identification and restitution operations.[154]

Troops occupying the city of Marburg, Germany found the *Kunsthistorisches Museum* (Art History Museum) and *Staatsarchiv* (State Archives) buildings still intact and ideal for storage. MFA&A officers brought works of art from a major cache at Siegen to the Marburg museum after deciding that the drive over damaged roads to Bonn might damage the fragile valuables. Works from other nearby repositories were also shipped, and Marburg became one of the first art collecting points in Germany. By October 1945, the Marburg collecting point held 3,511 art objects from 15 repositories, over 12,000 books and over 17,000 linear meters of archives; at that point the inventory process of the collection was nearly half-completed.[155] By November 1945, the staff (mostly German civilians) had produced an estimated inventory of 60 percent of the collection, and a nearby U.S. military unit had established a 24-hour guard for the facility.[156] Marburg never became a major collecting point for artworks, and during the summer of 1946, officials prepared to close the facility moving most of the remaining art holdings to a new collecting point in Wiesbaden.[157]

American forces in Austria made similar efforts to consolidate valuables in secure collecting points. By August 1945, the Military Government's Property Control Office for Land Salzburg had established "a large two-story, fire-resistant, well guarded warehouse, as a repository for *prima facie* loot and art collections."[158] By the end of the month, the Salzburg Military Government warehouse had received several shipments of valuables, including paintings, books, jewelry, while the Property Control Office had taken control over 17 caches of currency, coins, and precious metals.[159]

In November 1945, the American Military Government for Austria reported that 41 deposits of art and cultural objects had been found in the U.S. Zone in Austria; of these 41, however, only 13 held non-Austrian art. The U.S. Military Government intended to return Austrian assets directly to the Austrian government, and encouraged Austrian museums to clear repositories containing only Austrian art. Three collecting points handled the receipt of materials from emergency repositories in Austria: Munich took non-Austrian assets from Alt Aussee; the Property Control Warehouse in Salzburg handled non-Austrian assets from other repositories; and the abbey at Kremsmunster stored Austrian assets. The military government gave priority to clearing Alt Aussee because of its valuable contents and because its mountain location was inaccessible during the winter months.[160]

Procedures established to control MFA&A activities included specific rules for movement of art and other cultural objects from caches to collecting points. Military government officials set up intermediate collection points and depots as needed to handle valuables en route from repositories to major collecting points. Art was not to be moved to collecting points unless such movement was necessary for security, cataloging, or restitution and then only under expert supervision and in a manner that would preserve the integrity of the collections. However, only the military government for the German state concerned could authorize such a movement.[161] Although an obvious attempt to limit the destruction of cultural treasures, this order placed additional pressure on the dwindling number of MFA&A officers still in the field.

Unlike fragile art objects, caches of gold and other nonperishable valuables were moved to safer locations at the earliest opportunity. Tactical troops turned over currency, jewels, and precious metals to local military government units, which in turn forwarded them to headquarters. In some cases, only the most cursory inventory of the contents of caches was performed before the materials were forwarded, and at interim stops units had to make security arrangements on an ad hoc basis. In one case, a military government detachment recovered five bags of miscellaneous valuables from the Reichsbank in Holzminden and turned the contents over to the 9th Army's G-5 Financial Branch without an adequate inventory. Officers from the 9th Army inventoried the contents, packed fragile items more securely, and passed on all of the materials to SHAEF control.[162]

Some materials arrived at higher headquarters with only the most perfunctory information regarding their value. For example, in June 1945, the U.S. Currency Section for Germany received a shipment from the Reichsbank branch in Regensburg via a military government unit. The shipment's record offered only a general description of the contents, referring to "9 suitcases said to contain securities and jewelry" and "one cardboard carton said to contain jewelry."[163] Descriptions of other shipments demonstrate that the inventory process was anything but uniform.

As American troops prepared to evacuate the Merkers stash of gold and financial assets, Colonel Bernard Bernstein, Deputy Chief of SHAEF Financial Branch, toured several facilities in the U.S. Zone in search of a suitable depository. He eventually selected the Reichsbank Building in Frankfurt to serve as the collecting point for the Merkers treasure.[164] The Frankfurt Reichsbank received shipments from the Merkers mine hoard and the mine at Ranbach, consisting of gold, currency, and artworks of inestimable value. A team of U.S. Army engineers was called in to renovate the facility, providing larger vault space and greater security for incoming shipments.[165]

After Germany's surrender, Bernstein determined that the collecting points for currency and financial assets established under the wartime directives were inadequate to handle the large volume of items being seized by Allied forces. He decided that SHAEF should establish one large central collecting point for currency and other financial assets, and instructed Chief of the Currency Section Lt. Col. H.D. Cragon to obtain more space, if necessary, to expand his section's Frankfurt operations.[166] The Frankfurt collecting point thus began to accept gold and other financial assets from repositories and from other collecting points, and with the name changed to Foreign Exchange Depository, it eventually became the central collecting point for all gold, precious metals, and financial assets collected in the U.S. Zone in Germany, Austria, and Czechoslovakia.

Operation of Collecting Points

Once U.S. forces had safely transported valuables from repositories to central collecting points, they could begin the process of identifying and inventorying their finds. In order to provide the organizations responsible for restitution with adequate information regarding the contents of the collecting points, U.S. officials developed a uniform system of numbering which would classify cultural property by type, collecting point, condition, cache where discovered, and likely provenance.[167]

During the first few months of occupation, military government officials addressed the shortcomings of the collecting points. Higher headquarters took interest in this work, although the responsibility chiefly fell to the individual military districts. Having determined that restitution of looted artworks to their rightful owners had become a "high priority as a military necessity," the high command pushed each of the Military Districts to accelerate repairs to buildings selected as collecting points.[168] General Eisenhower specifically instructed his subordinates to provide collecting points with sufficient fuel and personnel to allow them to continue operations throughout the harsh winter of 1945-1946.[169] The high command split responsibility for operation of collecting points for art and cultural objects. Local military government agencies were responsible for transportation, security, accommodation, and building repair, while collecting point "directors" (i.e., MFA&A officers appointed by Military District commanders) handled the technical and functional administration.[170]

The Foreign Exchange Depository (FED) in Frankfurt was deluged with gold and other financial assets from it inception. In its first month of operations, the new FED received nine separate shipments of valuables, currencies and records. In May 1945, an additional 15 convoys reached Frankfurt, bearing securities, currencies, and hundreds of boxes of miscellaneous valuables, many looted from inmates at the Buchenwald and Belsen concentration camps.[171]

Financial assets continued to pour into the FED from a wide variety of sources. FED Shipment 21, received from the 7th Army in mid-May 1945, reveals the diverse origins of the collected assets. It contained four boxes of coins and jewelry found by a Counter Intelligence Corps (CIC) officer of the 36th Infantry Division in a sewer of a cement factory at Eiberg, a silver ingot left on the desk of a 7th Army quartermaster by an unknown person, two bags of coins from the 36th Division Finance Officer, who had received them from a sergeant while in combat near Bad Tolz, three boxes of currency taken from prisoners captured by the 20th Armored Division, and eight bags of coins found in a Nazi Party office in Salzburg, Austria.[172]

On May 8, 1945, the day the war ended in Europe, FED Chief Col. William Brey admitted that his staff was completely overwhelmed by the sheer volume of assets arriving in the depository. Since April 10, 1945, the FED had committed the entire personnel of the Currency Section to receive, hold, verify, and inventory the tremendous stocks of gold, foreign currency, and looted property captured by U.S. forces. As a result, the facility fell behind in its other duties, such as issuing Allied military currency and filing mandatory reports.[173]

The Currency Section reported in June 1945 that the FED had received 40 shipments of valuables from various locations in the U.S. Zone, many of which had yet to be examined or inventoried.[174] Staff divided incoming shipments into three categories: valuables looted by the Germans from occupied Europe; valuables belonging to German state and banking institutions; and property turned in by the Germans in compliance with Military Government Law No. 53. Although no additional category was established for confiscated assets, officials anticipated victims' assets would be present in each category.

The majority of non-monetary gold assets collected in Europe between 1945 and 1950 eventually found their way to the FED. However, it was not the sole depository in the U.S. occupied regions. In the U.S. Zone in Germany, German State Central Banks and the State Military Government Headquarters also served as depositories and overflow facilities for the FED. Several asset collection points and warehouses also dotted the U.S. Zone of Austria, mainly regional banks and the storage facilities of the U.S. Property Control Division.

Each shipment arriving at the FED contained a brief description of the circumstances surrounding the collection of assets in its holdings. Although the bulk of shipments received after July 1945 consisted of foreign exchange assets acquired under Military Government Law No. 53,[175] several clearly contained valuables taken under duress from victims of Nazi persecution. FED Shipment No. 53, for example, containing the vault contents of the Reichsbank branch in Eschwege, bore a suitcase filled with currency, jewelry, watches, and teeth—items easily identifiable as property once belonging to Holocaust victims.[176]

Table 8: Itemized Victims' Assets found in the Shipments received by the Foreign Exchange Depository (FED) in 1945[177]

FED Shipment Number	Origin	Contents
1	Merkers Mine	207 containers holding several tons of loot: 2,270 pounds of novelty jewelry, 3,219 pounds of scrap metal; 1,842 pounds of tableware, etc.
3	Lublin concentration camp	2 chests containing gold table service; 2 boxes in the Sparkasse contained valuables including gold-plated porcelain, tableware and several crucifixes obviously looted from churches.
4	Reichsbank-Plauen	35 of 57 bags containing coins and currency deposited by German Army Security forces for Heinrich Himmler.
16	Buchenwald Concentration Camp	313 boxes containing a large variety of items such as coins, clocks, razors, tools, tableware, dishes, teeth fillings, etc.
18	Reichsbank-Munich	SS bags containing 17 kinds of currency. 4 boxes and 3 valises of loot. Random sampling revealed boxes contained personal valuables and foreign currencies.
20	National Bank of Hungary Train	Jewelry and rings said to belong to the Hungarian Military Police. A sack containing one case of sealed envelopes regarding Jewish properties and a box containing valuables.
21	U.S. Seventh Army Group	Four boxes of currency coin and jewelry found in a sewer of a cement factory; 3 boxes of currency seized from German prisoners said to be loot, owner unknown. Also, 8 bags of coins taken from NSDAP Office in Salzburg.
22	Friedrichshall Salt Mine-Stassfurt	58 containers and 14 bags of precious metals found in the Friedrichshall Salt Mine, Stassfurt, Germany. Included 2 resmelted from Melmer (SS) gold.
23	Reichsbank-Holzminden	5 bags, sealed with the Nazi emblem, of jewelry, currency, bonds and coins from the Reichsbank in Holzminden. Gold coins, foreign notes and gold bars belonging to the Schwerin Gestapo.
26	Reichsbank-Regensburg	9 suitcases of jewelry and securities, 4 wooden boxes containing securities and jewelry, 1 carbon carton containing jewelry, 1 sack containing a Russian Orthodox tabernacle and 43 bars of silver bullion at 25 kilos each confiscated from the Gestapo Property Office in Prague.
27	Organisation Todt-Igls German Foreign Office Nazi Party, Waffen SS	Two bags found on a farm containing currencies, securities belonging to the government of Netherlands and might constitute part of requisitioned Jewish property in Holland.

31	Town of Rauris in the Alps— Reichsbank Berlin	shipments not reaching the Merkers Mine 1 sack and 3 boxes of currency, 3 bags of jewelry and silverware (watches, chains, rings, tableware, misc. jewelry; 2 boxes and 10 bags of silver coins and bullion; and 1 envelope containing gold coin, currency and jewelry.
52	Dachau Concentration Camp	4 packages said to contain misc. gold and silver items, such as wedding rings, fillings, etc., and one box of miscellaneous valuables. Item E of this shipment contained approximately 1,300 envelopes, each bearing the name and number of a prisoner containing jewelry, currency, and other valuables.
53	Eschwege Reichsbank	Suitcase containing 6 paper bags of loose paper money, and 5 envelopes containing jewelry, rings, teeth, pearls and gold watches.
70	Turned in to the Division of Investigation of Cartels and External Assets, Individuals Investigation Branch	Sack of assorted "Goering" jewels valued at 15,437, 750 francs.
79	Uncovered at Rittmanschausen and Kreis-Eschwege	Silver objects, tableware, jewelry, and miscellaneous items

In the summer of 1945 the FED staff consisted of 16 officers and 130 enlisted men, few of whom had any background in the rigors of inventorying, sorting, cataloging, and storing the mix of valuables in FED vaults.[178] The massive redeployment of soldiers out of Europe in the summer of 1945 created critical shortages of experienced personnel, hampering operations at all the collecting points. General Eisenhower regretted the problems in establishing an inventory of the holdings of the Foreign Exchange Depository caused by the rapid departure of military personnel. Eisenhower stressed his belief that the task required additional forces, noting that the FED collection of foreign securities alone weighed over five tons. Unfortunately, temporary replacements only exacerbated the situation due to the strict standards and the amount of specialist training the work required.[179] In October 1945, when the FED became part of the Finance Division of OMG (U.S. Zone) under USFET, personnel deficiencies caused its operations to slow considerably. Deliveries of Law 53 assets were discontinued, and never resumed.[180]

A routine general staff inspection conducted between October 3 and November 6, 1945, gave the FED a failing grade. The inspecting officer criticized the staff's obvious lack of training and experience, identifying the personnel as "not technically qualified to completely inventory, classify and account for the vast and varied assortment of valuable foreign exchange assets."[181] He criticized poor record keeping procedures that prevented the staff from compiling complete a inventory of the assets; inadequate security procedures and failure to properly account for keys compounded this problem and created the risk of undetected theft.

The chronic manpower shortage led the FED to suspend all efforts to inventory its vast collection of valuables. Although eight additional shipments arrived at the depository between October and December 1945, the skeletal crew made no attempt to document their contents. USFET responded to the crisis by requesting additional personnel from the Army, while kindly reminding the Army that the absence of a precise inventory only further delayed the restitution process and prevented the depository from discovering any thefts from its holdings.[182] The calls for experts apparently fell on deaf ears since no additional personnel were assigned to the facility. By the end of 1945, however, despite its difficulties, the FED had 77 shipments stored in its vaults, originating from locations scattered throughout Germany, Austria, and Czechoslovakia.

The U.S. Treasury's preliminary survey of the FED shipments conducted in the summer of 1945 hinted at the immense wealth contained within the depository, but an exact valuation of assets remained unattainable until experts had the opportunity to conduct a detailed inventory of its holdings. A preliminary inventory of the shipments received between April and August 1945 estimated the FED holdings included gold and silver worth more than $241 million, more than $275 million in currency, and hundreds of yet-to-be-inventoried parcels, boxes, and suitcases filled with personal property such as jewelry and silverware.[183]

The use of the Frankfurt Reichsbank as the central collecting point for gold and financial assets compromised its suitability as a storage center for artworks and other cultural assets. In late April 1945, it contained more than 3,000 items of art and cultural property, although space within the building was already in short supply. Given the fragility of the artworks and the fact that they had already been moved twice within a few months, MFA&A officers determined that, for the time being, overcrowded conditions in the building posed less of a threat to these assets than the rigors of another road march.[184]

To remedy the overcrowding at the Reichsbank, in June 1945 the military government detachment assigned to Frankfurt asked SHAEF to requisition nearby buildings at the University of Frankfurt and undertake essential repairs so that the artworks could be transferred to those buildings.[185] An inspection of the Reichsbank building later that month revealed that the growing hoard of gold bullion and similar items at the FED had begun to crowd out the artworks already stored there. Necessary repairs to potential art storage buildings at the University of Frankfurt would take several weeks, so the relatively undamaged Wiesbaden Museum was proposed as a suitable alternative.[186]

The rehabilitation of the Provincial Museum (*Landesmuseum*) in Wiesbaden commenced shortly after the German surrender, with the goal of starting operations in August 1945.[187] Shipments of art began to arrive that summer; in February 1946 the Wiesbaden Central Collecting Point received two truckloads of Jewish religious objects and other artworks from the Rothschild collection.[188] That same month, MFA&A officers shipped more than 1,000 paintings from the depositories at Rossbach to Wiesbaden for screening and safekeeping.[189]

The collecting point at Offenbach was unique in U.S. collection efforts because it was transformed from being a collecting point for various asset types into an archives-specific depot where victims' assets, as a matter of policy, were segregated from other collections and given priority for restitution. The collecting point was established in July 1945 in the I.G. Farben structure on the Main River just outside Frankfurt. A five-story concrete building, the collecting point served as one of several sub-collecting points subordinate to the Munich and Wiesbaden facilities. I.G. Farben police and U.S. military guards provided security for the facility, which joined the Oberammagau sub-collecting point as one of the two principal archive depositories in the U.S. Zone.[190]

In March 1946, a memo circulated requesting that OMGUS rename the Offenbach facility the Offenbach Archival Depot (OAD), making it the "sole archival depot in the U.S. Zone" and a "first-priority restitution project."[191] On May 1, 1946, Lt. Col. G.H. Garde complied with this request, creating the OAD. He requested the OAD director maintain contact with MFA&A officers at headquarters in each state to make arrangements for the transfer of materials to the OAD.[192] In early 1946, for example, the Offenbach Collecting Point received the entire holdings of the Rothschild Library in Frankfurt, which included Jewish and Masonic cultural and ritual objects looted by the ERR from individuals and institutions in Germany and Nazi-occupied territories. The removal of Jewish property from sub-collecting points commenced in May and continued into autumn.[193] By the end of July 1946, the 140 members of the OAD staff reportedly worked fifteen-hour days, six days a week to effect restitution of looted books, archives and cultural property. OAD personnel located and segregated books believed to have been taken from Holocaust victims and initiated the return of identifiable museum and library collections to Western Europe and within Germany.[194]

In addition to the contents of many German state and private libraries, the OAD housed the largest collection of Jewish cultural property in the world[195] and was the only known repository of Jewish cultural property in postwar Europe.[196] It contained a large number of volumes in Hebrew and Yiddish, requiring the hiring of additional personnel who were both "competent in the recognition of rarities" and "acquainted with the Hebrew and Yiddish languages and literatures."[197] In July 1946 the OAD reported having 137,809 unidentifiable Hebrew-language books, 49,000 Jewish religious and historical books written in the German language, and 405,688 identifiable books taken from Jewish libraries in Germany, Austria, Eastern Europe, and the Baltic countries.[198] Of the unidentifiable property on hand in July 1946, the OAD reported that nearly 70 percent were either "books in the Hebrew language" or "Jewish cultural and historical books in the German language."[199] The OAD continued to gather, sort, inventory its collections, and effect the restitution of items until the facility closed in 1948 and its remaining items were transferred to the collecting point in Wiesbaden.[200] Although central collecting points proved superior to scattered caches as locations for protecting artworks and other valuables, they still suffered serious shortcomings. The evacuation of emergency repositories undoubtedly saved many irreplaceable artworks, but the transport of items only added to the backlog at understaffed and often overcrowded collecting points.

In the end, as seen in the case of the OAD, the consolidation of assets into central collecting points proved to be an essential step on the road to restitution. With the security and space the collecting points provided, staff could begin the arduous process of inventorying and identifying the assets on hand.

The Case of the Hungarian Gold Train

The case of the Hungarian Gold Train illustrates several of the problems U.S. forces faced as they gradually came to understand the volume and complexity of the assets under their control. In May 1945, forces of the U.S. Army seized a train near the town of Werfen, Austria containing valuables spirited out of Hungary by members of the pro-Nazi Hungarian government. This train, referred to by U.S. authorities as the "Gold Train" or "Werfen Train," consisted of 24 rail cars containing gold, jewelry, works of art, household items, and other property, much of which had been confiscated from the Jewish population of Greater Hungary.[201] U.S. authorities classified these assets as "enemy government" property despite ample evidence linking the property to the Hungarian Jewish community.[202] As a result of this classification, materials on the train were subject to requisition by American officials, and in some cases, the property was not returned.

The background of the train highlights the difficulties inherent in establishing origin of the assets found on board. In April 1944, the Hungarian government issued a decree requiring Hungary's 800,000 Jews to surrender their valuables to the state.[203] To prevent these assets from falling into the hands of Soviet troops, the Hungarians and their Nazi allies loaded them on a train heading west in December 1944. Over the next five months the guarded train traveled a slow and circuitous route through Hungary and Austria in the general direction of Switzerland. During this interval the assets on board were frequently rearranged and repacked, divided and subdivided, loaded and unloaded, and repeatedly looted by German soldiers, Hungarian guards, and Austrian civilians. The contents of the train were divided. One section was loaded onto trucks and later intercepted by the French Army in its zone of occupation.[204] The other section remained aboard the train seized by the 3rd U.S. Infantry Division near Werfen, Austria in mid-May 1945.[205] The section recovered by the U.S., which contained rail cars laden with state and personal property removed from Hungary, remained under Hungarian armed guard until it arrived in July 1945 at the Military Government Warehouse in Salzburg.[206]

On July 8, 1945, the USFA Property Control Division in Salzburg was notified that "a railroad train known as the 'Hungarian Train' alleged to contain valuable property belonging to the Hungarian State" would arrive at the Military Government Warehouse the following day.[207] A detail of Hungarian guards agreed to cooperate with U.S. soldiers from the 101st Airborne Division to protect the train during transport.[208] However, the train did not leave Werfen for Salzburg until mid-month, and it was not scheduled for unloading until July 23, 1945.[209] The property register prepared by the U.S. military government in Austria, which provided a general inventory of the assets removed from the train, noted August 29, 1945 as the date when the Property Control officers took the assets into custody.[210]

American Property Control officers completed a general inventory of the train's contents that had been unloaded on the ground floor of the Salzburg Military Government Warehouse. Included in their inventory was a box said to contain "lists of names of people from whom some of the items on the train were taken."[211] The interrogation of Dr. László Avar—the train's Hungarian custodian—yielded information that "the train contained items which had been taken mostly from Jewish people and from banks in Hungary."[212] Property Control officials listed in their inventory the words "enemy government" as the reason for control and offered the following description:

> The train was said to be loaded with money, gold and jewelry taken from small town Hungarian treasuries, personal property belonging to Hungarian Jews and personal property belonging to Hungarian gentiles who voluntarily loaded their belongings on the train in order to escape the advancing Russians.[213]

Despite official awareness of the property's Hungarian Jewish origins, once assets from the Gold Train were designated as enemy property, they became available for requisition by high-ranking U.S. officials.[214] For example, in July 1945 Major General Harry J. Collins, Commander of the 42nd Division in western Austria, requisitioned for his headquarters "furniture and furnishing" from the Office of Property Control for Land Salzburg, including "objects made of onyx, 5 rugs and 8 paintings" clearly designated as Gold Train property.[215] Collins issued further requests for Gold Train valuables "of the very best quality and workmanship available in the Land of Salzburg" for his home and office, including enough china, silverware, glasses, and linens (sheets, towels, pillow cases, tablecloths, and napkins) to entertain anywhere from forty-five to ninety guests.[216] Subsequent requisitions for silver candlesticks and carpets were also filled.[217]

Collins was not alone in his desires. A list maintained by the Office of Property Control detailed the loaned materials and indicated that several ranking U.S. Army officers had requisitioned rugs, tableware, silverware, and silver plates from the Gold Train materials to decorate their residences.[218]

In October 1945, a Property Control Warehouse preliminary report detailed the variety of items unloaded from the Gold Train, including:

> Alarm clocks, cheap and expensive wristwatches, cheap and expensive cameras many of which have been spoiled by the weather, and cheap and expensive jewelry. Consumer goods such as bolts of cloth, large quantities of new and used clothing ranging from underwear to overcoats, typewriters in poor condition, chinaware of superior quality and workmanship, table linen and glassware, flat silverware of superior quality and workmanship, approximately 5,000 rugs many of which are hand-woven Persian and all are valuable, stamp collections, old coin collections and currency.[219]

As American forces settled in for what they expected to be an extended stay in Austria, the arrival of more American military families led to greater demand for household furnishings in the Property Control Warehouse in Salzburg. Anticipating the influx of families, USFA Property Control Officer Major O.R. Agnew was notified in March 1946 that "General Collins was interested in providing proper quarters and house furnishing for families of the military, and quite probably demands might be made upon property in the warehouse."[220] Collins' requisitions alone amounted to 22 shipments of property totaling "a substantial sum of money . . . [all] drawn from the so called Hungarian 'Werfen Train.'"[221]

The redeployment of troops from Europe affected the workings of the Property Control Division. In many cases, officers left for home without returning the requisitioned items. The warehouse staff also changed frequently due to troop redeployments, making the task of tracking requisitioned materials more difficult. On February 28, 1946, Property Control Officer Lt. Homer Heller was redeployed and replaced by Major C. R. Agnew Jr., who "strongly recommended" that new requisitioning rules be drawn up by a Purchasing and Construction Officer to ensure "accountability."[222] Nevertheless, he maintained that "if certain of the Werfen Train property is required for the usual needs of the Occupation Forces, it could be requisitioned. . . ."[223] One month later Agnew was redeployed and replaced by Capt. Howard A. Mackenzie as Property Control Officer.

Following his predecessor's call for greater accountability, Mackenzie began to catalogue numerous, systemic failures inherent in the requisitioning procedure.

With reference to the fact that USFA personnel had "establish[ed] that the [Gold Train] property was taken from Jewish people by order of the last Hungarian Nazi Government," Mackenzie described in great detail the handling and requisition of this property and the responsibilities of the Property Control Officer for its safekeeping.[224]

On March 14, 1946, the Chief of the Property Control Branch reported having "considerable doubt as to the present location of the furnishings on loan." [225] Mackenzie informed the Chief of the USFA Property Control Branch that this was indeed the case.[226] USACA then instructed Mackenzie to make certain that "no further items of the Werfen Train . . . be assigned for the use of family billets or for any other purpose."[227] Further, in August 1946, officials agreed that:

> Werfen train properties could not be requisitioned since that would make them property of the US Army and they were at that time the subject[s] of diplomatic negotiations with Hungary.[228]

Mackenzie received no further instructions regarding the Gold Train property until February 24, 1947, when he was instructed that the Gold Train property would be released to the Intergovernmental Committee on Refugees (IGCR). Mackenzie and his assistants attempted to compare receipts with the expectation that items would be "found to be missing" and admitted that his office had "never had any means of keeping track of items located in or missing from Vienna Area Command."[229] He further expressed his frustration that:

> A large number of officers were being redeployed, units were being reorganized and headquarters being relocated and this office in spite of diligent efforts could not keep track of all the property in Land Salzburg and could, of course, exercise no control of properties located outside of Land Salzburg.[230]

Security problems persisted in the Property Control Warehouse in Salzburg, and concern over the warehouse's lax security practices soon extended beyond the Army. In July 1946, a State Department official warned:

> Property is now located in large warehouse at Salzburg which is not and probably cannot be adequately guarded. Strongly recommend that unless property can be promptly placed in well-guarded bank vaults it be transferred to Frankfurt. I have been informed that a certain amount of looting from warehouse has already taken place and do not see how further dissipation of property can be prevented under present conditions. Fact that no inventory exists makes almost impossible for control officers to know whether looting taking place.[231]

Although measures were taken to tighten security at the facility, several thefts of Gold Train property nevertheless occurred. In one case, an American civilian employee was "suspected of pilfering jewelry, watches and miscellaneous supplies" clearly designated as "properties of the Werfen Train."[232] In another, someone had placed a bag of gold and silver dust into a hole dug in the warehouse floor where Gold Train properties were kept.[233] It is possible that this case was related to an October 1946 report that indicated that two small suitcases of gold dust had disappeared from the Military Government warehouse.[234] In response to this case, Mackenzie explained "every apparent possibility for tracing the gold dust has been exhausted" and concluded that:

Some months ago [the] Property Control Warehouse was burglarized by military guards. It is possible that the subject gold dust was stolen at that time. However, the inventory of the warehouse is still being checked.[235]

The Werfen train case highlights some of the practical problems involved in safeguarding victim's assets under American control. The Property Control Division in Austria proved to be an imperfect guardian of victim's assets, with lax security, high personnel turnover, and poor record keeping. Although its warehouse in Salzburg did successfully protect a substantial number of assets in storage, the example of the Hungarian Gold Train shows how the property under its control—regardless to whom it belonged—remained vulnerable to loss, theft, and unaccountable requisition.

Security Issues

Problems in the Field

As Allied forces liberated large areas of Europe and began to close in on Germany itself, leaders received disturbing reports regarding acts of theft and vandalism perpetrated by U.S. and British troops. In late March 1945, the MFA&A branch at SHAEF noted that reports of thefts by troops of the 9th U.S. Army might be a symptom of a growing problem. The MFA&A report stated that Allied troops seemed to have less regard for property in Germany than in occupied countries and argued that this attitude, combined with the wide dispersion of art caches, presented a major danger to looted art.[236]

MFA&A officers were alert to the possibility that Allied troops might pose a significant threat to works of art and other cultural property stored in small isolated caches. They also realized that with the collapse of German civil government in occupied territories and the inadequate resources available to MFA&A officers and other military government personnel, the safety of scattered art repositories depended on the good discipline of military personnel. In March 1945, Eisenhower instructed his field commanders to give the matter their "urgent and immediate attention," and reminded them of the pressing need to prevent theft and vandalism by Allied forces.[237] Such behavior, he pointed out, would not only alienate citizens in liberated Allied nations, but also interfere with the restitution of valuables from Germany to their rightful owners. In order for the latter task to be accomplished, Eisenhower emphasized that the importance of carefully preserving possibly looted treasures should be impressed upon all troops.[238]

The problem of troop misbehavior was exacerbated by the presence of millions of liberated Displaced Persons (DPs) who roamed freely about the countryside behind Allied lines. High-level officers were fully aware of the problems of theft by both DPs and U.S. troops, and Eisenhower's deputy theater commander brought them to his chief's attention in late April 1945.[239] Eisenhower's staff concluded that U.S. forces simply lacked the resources to suppress looting by DPs, noting that by late April DP camps housed over a million people. The staff determined that subordinate commanders were taking reasonable steps to stop looting, and that no further action from SHAEF headquarters was required.[240]

The growing number of DPs seeking to return to their native countries posed a further potential security problem. Allied planners were concerned that some DPs might agree, for financial or political reasons, to aid Nazi officials by smuggling looted gold, currency, and other valuables through Allied lines and out of Germany. In December 1944, the SHAEF Foreign Exchange Control and Blocking Section proposed that Allied forces screen all DPs leaving Germany at the border and force them to declare all precious metals, currency, securities, and deeds in holding accounts run by the Allied military government.[241] The immense number of people in transit, however, made any thorough screening process nearly impossible.

U.S. authorities failed to adequately screen packages shipped home by American soldiers, thereby creating additional opportunities to hide valuables obtained through theft and misappropriation. In April 1945, a representative of the Roberts Commission reported that such shipments by Allied soldiers included boxes large enough to contain important paintings.[242] In late May 1945, Eisenhower's Adjutant General reported that a random examination of parcel post packages sent by U.S. military personnel to friends and family back home had uncovered evidence of widespread theft by U.S. troops. Numerous packages examined were found to contain "various items of prohibited 'loot,' including U.S. small arms and other Government property."[243]

This problem persisted well into the period of American occupation in Europe, and undoubtedly contributed to the thriving black market in postwar Germany. In January 1948, the Secretary of the Army wrote senior U.S. commanders in Europe regarding allegations that military personnel had been bringing loot and black market items into the United States. He noted that "information already received does indicate a laxity in the inspection of personal and household effects being shipped back to the US and also that certificates are sometimes signed in blank without the required inspection" and urged that commanders take action to curb such practices.[244]

Despite the establishment of the military government following the surrender, certain elements among the DPs and the civilian population continued to pose a threat to valuables in postwar Germany. In June 1945, SHAEF G-5 reported that the "otherwise generally satisfactory" public safety situation in occupied Germany did not obtain in areas having large concentrations of DPs and prisoners of war. G-5 noted that it received daily reports of looting, rape, and murder from those areas, and warned that local, unarmed police were completely incapable of dealing with the "dangerous elements" among the DPs.[245]

The problem of lawless DPs continued to plague the American military government in Germany for many months. As late as May 1946, a year after the German surrender, the military government issued a directive noting that "the Theater Commander views with alarm the state of lawlessness existing in the U.S. Zone and is determined to prevent crimes committed by DPs. He has directed the deportation of displaced persons guilty of illegal possession of firearms."[246]

DPs were only one of the threats to unprotected valuables. In September 1945, Lt. General Lucius Clay made no effort to hide his disappointment in a memo issued to all USGCC personnel, in which he condemned "incidents of theft carried out by GIs in the Berlin area," noting that the "unlawful acquisition of private property by U.S. personnel in the Berlin area has assumed such proportions as to embarrass this Command."[247] He pointed out how the personal antics of Army personnel had the potential to escalate, creating problems for the military government by eroding public confidence in their ability to govern:

To condemn and put others to trial for looting, while at the same time recognizing no law ourselves, exposes the U.S. Forces to the accusation of hypocrisy and undermines the position of respect and confidence necessary for effective Military Government administration.[248]

It is clear that theft by U.S. personnel in the months following the war was prevalent enough to concern military officials.

Repositories of art and other valuables undoubtedly made tempting targets for larcenous individuals, both civilian and military. As units redeployed and troops demobilized after the German surrender, even those repositories that had originally been assigned guards were sometimes left unprotected. For example, the American unit assigned to protect the art collection in Schwarzburg Castle departed in early July 1945, and the cache was broken into shortly thereafter. The Director of the State Art Collection in Weimar alleged that several valuable paintings were stolen from the castle, and that physical evidence suggested that the perpetrators were almost certainly American soldiers.[249]

A castle located in the Hessian town of Hochstadt contained a large number of artworks apparently looted by the Nazis from areas within the Soviet Union. The castle had been occupied as quarters by elements of an engineer unit in June 1945 despite having been posted "off-limits" and despite protests from local military government officers. This unit was followed by another tactical unit, which had left by the time that military government officers inspected the repository in early August 1945. They found that many packing cases had been broken open and that their contents had been scattered about, with many articles broken or damaged.[250]

Unprotected repositories in Germany and Austria were especially vulnerable because there often was no single unit responsible for protecting the valuables stored in them. In late April 1945, for instance, SHAEF G-5 reported that Rimberg Castle near the Westphalian town of Merkstein had been under the successive jurisdiction of a number of military government units and had been occupied by various tactical units. An inspection of the castle revealed that the main building had been thoroughly ransacked. Deeming it impractical to guard the castle with civilians because of the presence of troops, remote location, and proximity to the Dutch border, Allied authorities posted it as a historic monument and planned to remove the few remaining items of value.[251]

Under the circumstances, Allied authorities had difficulty ascertaining how many items, including the property of Holocaust victims, had been stolen while under American control. In March 1947, nearly two years after the surrender, the Adjutant General's office in Berlin issued a list of the artistic and historic objects that it presumed to have been stolen from Germany by American troops. The report listed nearly 150 artworks, giving the place and approximate date of the theft.[252] The lack of information regarding possible perpetrators reflected the confused situation on the ground during and just after the period of active military operations, as well as the limited resources that were available to investigate alleged thefts. As the final report on MFA&A activities in northern Bavaria stated:

> In the early stages of the occupation, several historic castles and palaces were occupied by U.S. troops or DP's. During their occupation, considerable material disappeared. As in most cases no information was available as to the identity of the looters, beyond gathering information no positive action could be initiated.[253]

Given these limitations, U.S. officials could only distribute lists of stolen works to dealers and museums in the United States in the hope of recovering a portion of the items listed.

Problems at Collecting Points

Even after valuables were sequestered in centralized collecting points, security remained a major concern. The end of fighting in Europe resulted in a rapid demobilization and transfer of troops to the Pacific Theater, prior to August 1945, and to the United States. These troop reductions created security problems for collecting points when the troops assigned as guards received orders to redeploy.

For example, the central art collecting point in Wiesbaden relied on U.S. troops for security and, by December 1945, reductions in Army manpower threatened to reduce the guard on the collecting point below the minimum necessary to protect the thousands of paintings estimated to be worth over half a billion dollars.[254] American leaders had learned from experience that civilian guards were no substitute for military units, because they were unable to exercise any authority over armed soldiers seeking to gain entry into prohibited areas.[255] Consequently, orders were given to maintain the military guard at the Wiesbaden collecting point.

Despite this precaution, problems persisted and in January 1947 personnel at Wiesbaden discovered that a number of artworks were missing.[256] In February of that year, the director of the collecting point complained "no security worth mentioning has been provided by the Military Guard during the month of January."[257]

The Munich collecting point suffered from similar security problems. In September 1945, 3rd Army headquarters blamed the theft of four paintings on workers repairing the building, and warned that personnel turnover among military guards increased the difficulty of preventing such thefts.[258] In February 1946, a senior MFA&A officer in Bavaria expressed alarm at the drastic cuts in military personnel serving as guards for art repositories. He noted that personnel shortages had caused the military government to remove guards from various important art caches, and to reduce the guard at the collecting point from 25 soldiers to six. The director of the collecting point had concluded "that to reduce the military guard further is to make this military installation dangerously insecure."[259]

Despite security precautions, the Munich Central Collecting Point (CCP) suffered from a number of thefts between 1946 and 1948. In 1946 thieves stole a number of items from the collecting point, including silver, a valuable picture, and rugs.[260] The most famous case involved a German guard who stole almost 100 artworks and art objects during this period. U.S. officials eventually caught the guard, but not all of the stolen art was recovered.[261]

The Munich CCP fell victim to another type of theft in 1949, when it mistakenly transferred 166 cultural objects into the custody of Mr. Mate Topič who first arrived at the Munich collecting point in December 1948, claiming to be the director of the Yugoslav National Museum.[262] His accomplice, Dr. Wiltrud Mersmann—a German civilian who worked as a junior curator at the collecting point from 1946 to 1949—provided Topič detailed descriptions of valuable items stored in the collecting point, allowing him to develop lists of items to be claimed on the behalf of the Yugoslav government.[263]

On March 31, 1949, Topič submitted his claims to Stefan Munsing, the facility's chief MFA&A officer.[264] OMGUS Chief of Reparations and Restitution Officer, M. H. McCord, approved the Topič claims three weeks later, [265] ordering the release of four shipments in June 1949.[266] These shipments contained a significant number of cultural objects, including paintings and oriental rugs.[267]

OMGUS Property Control authorities later realized their mistake when they received duplicate claims for items released to Topič. Further investigation revealed that all but two of the 166 items transferred to Topič should not have been restituted to Yugoslavia.[268] At least some of these objects were found to have been looted by the ERR from Holocaust victims in Western Europe.[269] As a result, OMGUS launched efforts to reclaim the objects. On June 1, 1950, the Office of Economic Affairs of the Property Division explained the situation to the chief of the Yugoslav Military Mission in Berlin, stating that the "the U.S. High Commission [of Germany] is obliged to take advantage of the provision of paragraph 3 of the Receipt of Cultural Objects which requires a receiving Government to return any objects which have been delivered to it by mistake."[270]

On June 13, 1950, one full year after Topič disappeared with the objects, OMGUS Property Division notified the State Department of the erroneous restitution,[271] claiming that the shipments had taken place "during a period of confusion" and that the "episode clearly shows folly of attempting hasty disposition of cultural properties still undergoing screening at Munich and Wiesbaden."[272] The State Department revisited the issue in February 1954 when the French and Italian governments raised questions about the paintings. The State Department then cabled its embassies in Rome, Belgrade, and Bonn instructing that:

> No public statement [is] possible [at] this time but interested inquirers should be reminded (1) all cultural restitutions effected by agencies [of the] US government subject [to] review whenever counter claims [are] presented and (2) in receipting for cultural objects recipient government has been required [to] assume [the] obligation [to] restore any objects subsequently shown to have been delivered [to] it in error.[273]

Despite its informal inquiries, the State Department was unable to determine whether or not the artwork restituted to Topič ever reached the Yugoslav government.[274] Under pressure from claimant countries, the Office of the Legal Advisor for the State Department issued a memorandum on September 12, 1956 explaining that the State Department refused to admit the circumstances of the case to claimant governments and would take no further action "beyond notifying Belgrade claimant governments" of the disputed claims."[275] On December 5, 1956, the Legal Advisor released his final decision on the case:

> After weighing the legal considerations referred to, Mr. Reinstein, Director of the Office of German Affairs, decided on policy grounds that the Department should not notify the countries concerned. The basis of his decision was that we were acting at the time in question as the occupying power in Germany, that we voluntarily undertook to return a great deal of property to various countries, that we did the best we could to carry out this program, that we acted in good faith and that we cannot go on indefinitely trying to remedy or assume responsibility for possible errors in carrying out occupation programs of this sort.

> Accordingly it was agreed that action of the case should by suspended unless some of the foreign countries concerned initiated action anew. Since it is greatly to our interest not to stimulate any such interest or inquiries on the part of those countries it is desirable the matter not be raised in any communications or discussions with representatives of those governments on this subject.[276]

Apparently, the Legal Advisor feared that renewed claims for the property in question would be filed against the U.S. government. The case was effectively closed.

The Topič episode highlights several difficulties U.S. authorities faced in the implementation of their restitution policy: 1) the inability of Property Control officers to conduct thorough background checks on individuals claiming to represent foreign governments; 2) the State Department decision not to disclose to claimant governments or heirs the facts of the erroneous restitution; and 3) the failure by U.S. authorities to hold recipient nations to the terms of the transfer agreement. As a result of this incident, the artworks errantly restituted to Topič were never recovered, barring persecutees (or their heirs) from recovering their property.

Laying the Groundwork for Restitution

In mid-September 1945, SHAEF informed subordinate commanders about the policy for returning looted artworks to the countries of origin. Artworks were divided into three categories; those readily identifiable as looted works that had been publicly owned or seized from private owners without compensation, those for which some compensation was alleged to have been paid, and those which were bona fide German property. The first two categories were to be returned to the nation of origin; and a representative from each "western" nation was to be attached to the occupation district headquarters to identify and claim artworks.[277]

No definitive policy was set by September 1945, but interim policy allowed restitution of artworks and cultural objects to Allied governments upon application and if the property was identifiable and was removed from occupied territory by the Nazis by whatever means. All questions of restitution were to be handled on behalf of property owners by the government of which they were citizens, unless other arrangements were made with the nation from which the property was removed. Allied governments were to submit lists of items and quantities claimed for restitution, along with preliminary evidence supporting the claim.[278]

The U.S. Group Control Council, Germany developed a form for the "Receipt and Agreement for Delivery of Cultural Objects" for use in turning over such objects to claimant governments. Collecting points were to attach this form to shipments each time objects were transferred. The form included a clause in which the receiving government agreed to hold the items as a custodian, pending the determination of lawful owners. Items were to be returned to the lawful owners unless the owner was a former enemy government or national, in which case they were to be returned to USFET. Claimant governments also agreed to provide USFET with an estimate of the object's value, as well as any information regarding possession of the object since September 1, 1939, and the compensation paid for the object by the German government or its agents.[279]

Summary

During the final, chaotic act of the most destructive war in history, the United States government, through its armed forces and interested civilian organizations, recovered considerable quantities of assets believed to be the property of victims and other persecutees of Nazism. Based on the experience of their earlier campaigns, American leaders prescribed methods for identifying and protecting assets and created special units to carry out these tasks. These mechanisms proved insufficient to handle the widespread dispersal of assets that troops encountered upon entering Germany and Austria. The immense scope of the problem soon undermined attempts to establish a firm collection policy and maintain the chain of custody. Amid the confusion, hampered by inadequate resources and uncertain lines of authority, a relatively small number of officers and civilians nevertheless secured what recovered valuables they could, in the hope that eventually they could identify assets looted by the Nazis and restitute these items to the countries from which they had been looted or their rightful owners. Under the prevailing conditions in Austria and Germany in 1945, such efforts fell short of perfection, as the protection and consolidation of valuables were subordinated to the urgent military requirements of winning the war, preventing a total collapse of government in the occupied zones, restoring a semblance of normal civilian life, and sending home American troops.

In the months following the German surrender, U.S. forces made significant progress in consolidating widely scattered caches of valuables. During this phase, protection of repositories remained imperfect; undoubtedly some moveable assets, including assets possibly looted from Holocaust victims, fell prey to thieves or were damaged by the elements. Because U.S. officials had only limited knowledge regarding the contents of many caches and the individuals who had access to them, they often were unable to detect thefts or identify those responsible. At the same time, U.S. armed forces failed to establish tight controls over packages mailed or carried home by Americans in Europe. These conditions, combined with the existence of a thriving black market in postwar Germany, created an opportunity for individuals to move stolen assets out of Europe without detection. Nevertheless, the evacuation of temporary deposits and the creation of collecting points added immeasurably to the security of the assets involved.

By the spring of 1946, the U.S. military governments in Germany and Austria had established a network of collecting points where assets could be safely stored while awaiting final disposition. These collecting points had their own shortcomings, but they provided a reasonably secure haven for valuables that otherwise may have been pilfered by military and civilian criminals or destroyed by the elements. Though faced with other more pressing concerns, U.S. policymakers nonetheless made the seizure and identification of assets an important element of the Allied campaign to defeat the Nazi regime and stabilize Europe. Without the concerted efforts expended by U.S. forces to protect the gold, financial assets, and art and cultural property in former Nazi-occupied territory, restitution of Holocaust victims' assets could never have been realized. When OMGUS became operational in April 1946, the process of asset collection and protection was well underway and a detailed inventory and appraisal of assets had begun. Newly appointed experts devoted their time to determining the provenance and value of individual assets, to facilitate the eventual disposal of the assets in accordance with international law. Their efforts, and the work of those who had protected the assets in their care, laid the foundation for restitution efforts to come.

Endnotes for Chapter IV

[1] Fred C. Mehner, "Report on the FED, Military Government Training Program," NACP, RG 260, FED, Box 394 [312827].

[2] *Report of the American Commission for the Protection and Salvage of Artistic and Historic Monuments in War Areas* (Washington, DC: U.S. Government Printing Office, 1946), 47 (hereafter "Roberts Commission Report").

[3] Lynn Nicholas, *The Rape of Europa: The Fate of Europe's Treasures in the Third Reich and the Second World War* (New York: Alfred A. Knopf, 1994), 210–214.

[4] Ibid., 218–222.

[5] Harry L. Coles & Albert K. Weinberg, *Civil Affairs: Soldiers Become Governors* (Washington, DC: Office of the Chief of Military History, Dept. of the Army, 1964), 87.

[6] Roberts Commission Report, 51–53.

[7] Nicholas, *Rape of Europa*, 224–226.

[8] Coles & Weinberg, *Civil Affairs: Soldiers Become Governors*, 89.

[9] Roberts Commission Report, 48.

[10] Ibid.

[11] Coles & Weinberg, *Civil Affairs: Soldiers Become Governors*, 419.

[12] Ibid., 420–21.

[13] Report from Lt. Colonel Sir Leonard Woolley, Archaeological Advisor to War Office, "Report on a Mission to Tripolitania, Sicily and Italy affecting the M.F.A.A. (Monuments, Fine Arts and Archives) subcommission," [circa 1944], NACP, RG 331, 130 G-5 Fine Arts, Box 272 [117220–224].

[14] Roberts Commission Report, 61.

[15] Coles & Weinberg, *Civil Affairs: Soldiers Become Governors*, 423.

[16] Nicholas, *Rape of Europa*, 256–57.

[17] Roberts Commission Report, 79.

[18] Ibid., 80.

[19] Telegram to Secy. of State, May 29, 1945, NACP, RG 59, Decimal File 1945–49, Entry 865.51, Box 6947 [220967].

[20] Telegram to Secy. of State, May 23, 1945, NACP, RG 59, Decimal File 1945–49, Entry 865.51, Box 6947 [220964].

[21] Dispatch No. 74 from the American Embassy, Belgrade, Yugoslavia to the Dept. of State, July 6, 1945, "Yugoslav Foreign Office Note Concerning Gold and Silver of the National Bank of Yugoslavia Confiscated by the Italian Occupation Authorities," NACP, RG 59, Decimal File 1945–49, Entry 865.51, Box 6947 [220971–972].

[22] Governor of the Bank of Italy to Allied Commission in Rome, Jan. 22, 1946, NACP, RG 59, Entry 2780, Box 21, 851 Italy-Miscellaneous [221022–023].

[23] Telegram From Secretary of State No. 1908, Oct. 1, 1947, NACP, RG 59, Entry 2780, Box 21, 851 Italy Miscellaneous [221031].

[24] Roberts Commission Report, 102.

[25] Coles & Weinberg, *Civil Affairs: Soldiers Become Governors*, 864–865.

[26] Ibid., 866.

[27] Roberts Commission Report, 103.

[28] Coles & Weinberg, *Civil Affairs: Soldiers Become Governors*, 867.

[29] Roberts Commission Report, 105.

[30] Ibid., 109.

[31] Ibid., 121.

[32] Ibid., 122.

[33] Ibid., 106.

[34] MFA&A Adv. to ACOS SHAEF G-5, Dec. 1944, "Report on Monuments, Fine Arts and Archives to 1 Nov. 1944," NACP, RG 331, Entry 55B, SHAEF G-5 MFA&A, Box 333 [113151–153].

[35] MFA&A Br., U.S. Group Control Council to Col. H. Newton, War Dept. Rep. at SHAEF for Monuments, Fine Art and Archives, Sept. 12, 1944, "Monuments, Fine Arts and Archives Operations in Germany," NACP, RG 331, Entry 55B, MFA&A, Box 329 [319758–760].

[36] Lt. Col. Geoffrey Webb, MFA&A Adv. to SHAEF G-5 Ops. Br., Dec. 6, 1944, "Note on MFA&A Problems in Germany," NACP, RG 331, Entry 55B, SHAEF G-5 MFA&A, Box 331 [319785–786].

[37] SHAEF G-5, "Technical Notes for the use of Monuments Fine Arts and Archives Specialist Officers in Germany," Oct. 1944, NACP, RG 331, Entry 55B, SHAEF G-5 MFA&A, Box 333 [113256–283].

[38] Memo, SHAEF G-5 to Army Groups and Communications Zone, Mar. 27, 1945, "Memorandum, Duties and Projected Operations, MFA&A Officer, Fifteenth U.S. Army," NACP, RG 331, Entry 55B, SHAEF G-5 MFA&A, Box 323 [319553].

[39] Memo from Lt. C. Hathaway, MFA&A to A/Director, RD&R Division, May 1, 1945, "Establishment of Uniform Practice in Recording Works of Art," NACP, RG 331, Entry 55B, SHAEF G-5 MFA&A, Box 324 [319746–747].

[40] Harold Zink, *American Military Government in Germany* (New York: Macmillan, 1947), 46–48.

[41] Earl F. Ziemke, *The U.S. Army in the Occupation of Germany, 1944–1946* (Washington, DC: Center of Military History, 1975), 187–94.

[42] "Technical Manual on Military Government in Germany," Public Safety, [circa May 1945], 18–19, NACP, RG 331, Entry 23, Box 41 [314054].

[43] Art Looting Investigation Unit, Strategic Services Unit. Office of the Asst. Secy. of War, War Dept., "Art Looting Investigation Unit Final Report," May 1, 1946.

[44] Charles Sawyer, "Report on the Activities of the Office of Strategic Services as they have related to the Roberts Commission," Dec. 27, 1945, NACP, RG59, Entry: Lot 62D–4, Box 24 [114005].

[45] Ibid. [114003].

[46] Ibid. [114003].

[47] The entire collection of the OSS interrogation reports (4 consolidated and 15 detailed) is found in the National Archives, College Park, MD. NACP, RG 38, Entry 98A, Strategic Services Unit, ALIU, Box 421; NACP, RG 239, Entry 73, Strategic Services Unit, ALIU, Box 83; and NACP, RG 239, Entry 74, Strategic Services Unit, ALIU, Box 84.

[48] Charles B. MacDonald, *The Last Offensive* (Washington, DC: Office of the Chief of Military History, Dept. of the Army, 1973), 332.

[49] Col. George S. Smith to Commanding General, Rome Area Command, "Final Report of 'S' Force Operations," June 17, 1944, NACP, RG 331, Entry 18, Box 150, File: Final Report on S Ops in Rome [220905–908]. "S forces" had been formed "with the mission of exploiting the city of Rome and its environs for intelligence, including the seizure of documents, records and archives to prevent their dissipation and destruction, the apprehension and proper disposition of enemy agents and sympathizers, and the arranging for a more detailed long range exploitation."

[50] SHAEF Chief of Staff to ACOS G-2 SHAEF, "Intelligence Directive Number 17, T Force," July 27, 1944, NACP, RG 331, Entry 11, Box 1 [313907–908].

[51] SHAEF G-5 Coordinating Route Slip, "Financial Targets," Nov. 18–22, 1944, NACP, RG 331, Entry 18A, Box 161 [313700].

[52] Berlin Second Priority Targets List, Revision No. 3, Mar. 31, 1945, NACP, RG 331, Entry 18, Box 137 [348958–959].

[53] G-5 Section, 6th Army Group to ACOS G-5, SHAEF, "Report on Monuments, Fine Arts and Archives," May 19, 1945, NACP, RG 331, Entry 55B, SHAEF G-5 MFA&A, Box 335 [320197].

[54] Lt. E. Perez to Commanding Officer, T-Force, 7th Army, "Chronological Report on the Mittenwald Mission," June 9, 1945, NACP, RG 338, G-2 Dec. 1944–Nov. 1945, Box 4 [221054–057].

[55] Ziemke, *The U.S. Army in the Occupation of Germany, 1944–1946*, 314.

[56] JCS 1067: Directive to Commander in Chief of the U.S. Forces of Occupation regarding Military Government in Germany, Apr. 28, 1945, Cited in Hajo Holborn, *American Military Government: Its Organization and Policies* (Washington, DC: Infantry Journal Press, 1947), 157–172.

[57] Memo from SHAEF G-5 Operations Br., "The Problem of Moveable Art in Germany," Dec. 16, 1944, NACP, RG 331, Entry 55B, SHAEF G-5 MFA&A, Box 322 [319509–511].

[58] Ibid.

[59] Rpt. from FED, "History from V-E Day, 8 May 1945 to 30 June 1946," NACP, RG 260, FED Central Files, Box 394, File 900.10 [310197–203]. The Currency Branch/Depository remained under the control, supervision and direction of the Finance Division of the following successive Headquarters: SHAEF G-5 to July 14, 1945; USFET G-5 to October 1, 1945; OMG (US Zone) to April 1, 1946; and OMGUS thereafter.

[60] Rpt. from FED "History from V-E Day, 8 May 1945 to 30 June 1946" NACP, RG 260, FED Central Files, Box 394, File 900.10 [310197].

[61] SHAEF Administrative Memo No. 49, "Disposition of Currency and other Financial Assets Seized from Enemy Forces or Found Abandoned," Mar. 7, 1945, NACP, RG 260, FED Records, Box 394, File 900.10 [312784–785].

[62] Ibid.

[63] Ibid. Enemy territory includes the territory of the German Reich and Austria prior to December 31, 1937.

[64] Ibid.

[65] G-5 Operational Instruction No. 9, "Property Control," Mar. 1, 1945, NACP, RG 331, Entry 54, Box 163 [319003–006].

[66] Memo from Eisenhower to AGWAR for Combined Chiefs of Staff, Mar. 21, 1945, NACP, RG 331, Entry 47, Box 1 [319493–494].

[67] MFA&A Adv. to ACOS SHAEF G-5, "Report on Monuments, Fine Arts and Archives to 1 Nov. 1944," Dec. 1944, NACP, RG 331, Entry 55B, Box 333 [113151–153].

[68] Report, "Appreciation of Enemy Methods of Looting Works of Art in Occupied Territory," Mar. 1945, NACP, RG 331, Entry 58, Box 55 [328817–826].

[69] SHAEF G-5 Internal Affairs Br., Monuments, Fine Arts and Archives Report, "Repositories of Works of Art in Germany," Mar. 11, 1945, NACP, RG 331, Entry 58, Box 55 [328827–835].

[70] Fourth compilation of Interrogations of Prisoners of War, [circa 1945], NACP, RG 331, Entry 18A, Box 161 [314037–041].

[71] Memo from 7th Army Interrogation Ctr. to ACOS G-2, 7th Army, "Location of Art Treasures," Aug.16, 1945, NACP, RG 338, USFET Adjutant General Classified File, Box 326 [108314–108315].

[72] Report by 7th Army Interrogation Ctr., "French Works of Art Obtained by Former Reichsmarschall Hermann Goering," May 19, 1945, NACP, RG 331, Entry 55B, Box 323 [319530–531].

[73] SHAEF G-5 to listed Addressees, "Field Reports Received During April 1945," June 1945, Annex III, CG 9th U.S. Army to CG, 12th Army Group, no date, "MFA&A,

Semi-Monthly Report, 1–15 April 1945," NACP, RG 338, USFET G-5 Decimal File 1942–1945, Box 1 [313949–314006].

[74] SHAEF signed Eisenhower to AGWAR for Combined Chiefs of Staff, May 6, 1945, NACP, RG 338, USFET G-5 Decimal File, Box 13 [313868–871].

[75] Commanding General, 87th Infantry Div. to SHAEF, Apr. 26, 1945, NACP, RG 331, Entry 47, Box 1 [319444–445].

[76] Deputy ACOS G-5 SHAEF to Supreme Commander, SHAEF, "Report of gold, silver, etc. located in Germany during the past week," May 5, 1945, NACP, RG 338, USFET Secy. Gen. Staff Decimal File, Box 13 [313863–864].

[77] Memo from 1st Lt. Jack H. Stipe, HQ 7th Army, re: Amounts and Locations of Found Gold, June 9, 1945, NACP, RG 260, FED, Box 432 [219762].

[78] HQ 12th Army Group to SHAEF, "Monthly Report on Monuments, Fine Arts and Archives," Mar. 31, 1945, NACP, RG 331, Entry 55B, Box 323 [319549–551].

[79] AGWAR from Marshall to SHAEF, Apr. 17, 1945, NACP, RG 331, Entry 47, Box 1 [319418].

[80] SHAEF to CG, 6th Army Group, Apr. 18, 1945, NACP, RG 331, Entry 47, Box 1 [319419].

[81] Memo from Special Agent Friebolin to CIC Section "LL," 6th Army Group, "Mission to Lorrach, Germany, RE: Possible German Gold Cache," May 3, 1945, NACP, RG 331, Entry 47, Box 1 [319449–452].

[82] HQ 12th Army Group to SHAEF, "Monthly Report on Monuments, Fine Art and Archives," Mar. 10, 1945, NACP, RG 331, Entry 55B, SHAEF G-5 MFA&A, Box 323 [319543–544].

[83] G-5 Sec., HQ, 6th Army Group to ACOS G-5, SHAEF, "Report on Monuments, Fine Arts and Archives," May 19, 1945, NACP, RG 331, Entry 55B, Box 335 [320197–198].

[84] Letter to Commanding General, 7th Army, "Recently Received Information on Repositories in U.S. Zone," Aug. 15, 1945, NACP, RG 338, USFET G-5 decimal file 1945–1946, Box 37 [313923].

[85] Staff Study by OMGUS, "Transfer of Functions and Personnel dealing with Monuments, Fine Arts, Archives & Libraries from Property Division to Education and Cultural Relations Division," Sept. 10, 1948, NACP, RG 260, Entry AG 1948, Box 344, Arts and Museums [118997].

[86] Col. Bernstein to Brig. Gen. McSherry, "Report of Developments in Removal of Treasure from Kaiseroda Mine at Merkers, Germany," Apr. 18, 1945, NACP, RG 260, FED, Box 424 [314007–022].

[87] Brig. Gen. Frank McSherry to Commanding Gen., ETO, "Gold bullion, currency and other property discovered by 3rd Army near Merkers," Apr. 19, 1945, NACP, RG 338, Recs. of Secy., Box 13, 123.2 [314025–027].

[88] "Shipment 1 Inventory" Apr. 8, 1945, NACP, RG 260, Fin. Div., Gold & Silver, Box 50 [312199–286].

[89] Greg Bradsher, "Nazi Gold: The Merkers Mine Treasure," *Quarterly of the National Archives and Records Administration 31,* (1999): 9. Bradsher notes that the SS made seventy-six deliveries to the Reichsbank of property seized from concentration camp victims between August 26, 1942 and January 27, 1945. As Allied troops approached Berlin, SS leaders demanded that shipments to the Merkers mine include their loot as well.

[90] Ibid., 2; "Register of Valuables in the Custody of the Foreign Exchange Depository, Frankfurt A/M Germany," Feb. 9, 1948, NACP, RG 260, FED, Box 161 [300012–025].

[91] Rpt. from FED, "History from V-E Day, 8 May 1945 to 30 June 1946," no date, NACP, RG 260, Recs. of the FED, Box 394, 900.10 [310200].

[92] Carolsue Holland & Thomas Rothbart, "The Merkers and Buchenwald Treasure Troves," *After the Battle* 93 (1996): 1–28.

[93] Eisenhower to Secy. of War, May 6, 1945, NACP, RG 338, USFET Secy. Gen. Staff File, Box 13, 123/2, [313868–871].

94 Telegram S–21742 from USFET Gen. Eisenhower to USGCC, Sept. 6, 1945, NACP, RG 338, USFET G–5 Decimal File, Box 13 [313877].

95 Rpt. of Ops (After Action Rpt.) 12th Army Group, Vol. VII, G-5 Sec., 122, [circa July 1945], NACP, RG 331, Entry 54, Box 163, Civil Affairs and MG [318903].

96 Rpt. by HQ 12th Army Group, Annex V, "Monthly Report on Monuments, Fine Arts and Archives," May 17, 1945, NACP, RG 338, USFET G-5 Dec. File 1942–1945, Box 1 [313994].

97 SHAEF G-5 to listed Addressees, June 1945, "Field Reports Received During April 1945," Annex I, "Monuments, Fine Arts, and Archives, Area of the First United States Army, Interim Report," Apr. 24, 1945, NACP, RG 338, USFET G-5 Decimal File 1942–1945, Box 1 [313949–963].

98 Ibid.

99 Ibid.

100 Roberts Commission Report, 128.

101 Rpt. by HQ 12th Army Group, "Civil Affairs and Military Government Summary No. 260," Feb. 21, 1945, NACP, RG 260, OMGUS Monthly Field Reports, Box 137 [335625–627].

102 Ziemke, *The U.S. Army in the Occupation of Germany, 1944–1946,* 236.

103 SHAEF G-5 to SCAEF, "Report of gold, silver, etc., located in Germany during the past week," Apr. 29, 1945, NACP, RG 338, USFET Secretary of General Staff Decimal File 1944–1945, Box 13 [213664–665].

104 MFA&A Semi-Monthly rpt. of the 9th Army, Apr. 16–30, 1945, NACP, RG338, USFET G-5, Decimal File 1942–1945, Box 1 [313981].

105 12th Army Group to SHAEF, "Monthly Report on Monuments, Fine Arts and Archives," July 10, 1945, NACP, RG 260, OMGUS MFA&A Reports, Box 369 [335630–631].

106 Lt. Jack Stipe, MFA&A Officer, 7th Army, Monthly Rpt., Apr. 10, 1945, NACP, RG338, USFET G-5, Decimal File 1942–1945, Box 1 [313998].

107 Lt. Col. J.H. Bloss 12th Army Group, Monthly MFA&A Rpt., May 17, 1945, NACP, RG338, USFET G-5, Decimal File 1942–1945, Box 1 [313995].

108 Allied Force HQ G-5, AFHQ Civil Affairs Rpt. (Austria) No. 2, Period 10 May to 21 May 1945, NACP, RG 331, Entry 34, Box 126 [316896].

109 History of the R&R Br. (Austria), no date, NACP, RG 260, USFA General Records, Box 167 [106372–412].

110 SHAEF G-5 to listed addressees, "Third Edition of Repositories of Works of Art and Archives in Germany," Apr. 2, 1945, NACP, RG 331, Entry 55B, Box 325 [319658–707].

111 SHAEF G-5 to listed addressees, "Addendum I to Third Edition of Repositories of Works of Art and Archives in Germany," Apr. 10, 1945, NACP, RG 331, Entry 55B, SHAEF G-5 MFA&A, Box 325 [319708–713].

112 SHAEF G-5 to listed addressees, "Addendum II to Third Edition of Repositories of Works of Art and Archives in Germany," April 1945, NACP, RG 331, Entry 55B, SHAEF G-5 MFA&A, Box 325 [319715].

113 SHAEF G-5 to listed addressees, "Addendum III to Third Edition of Repositories of Works of Art and Archives in Germany," May 1945, NACP, RG 331, Entry 55B, SHAEF G-5 MFA&A, Box 325 [319728–734].

114 *The First Year of the Occupation,* Occupation Forces in Europe Series, 1945–1946, Vol. 1 (Frankfurt: Office of the Chief Hist. EUCOM, 1947), 53 [122880].

115 Ibid., 85.

116 Ibid., 86.

117 Ziemke, *The U.S. Army in the Occupation of Germany, 1944–1946,* 317–318.

118 Ibid., 269.

[119] "History of the US Element, Allied Commission Austria," no date, 75, NACP, RG 260, USACA Recs., Files of the Dir. 1946–1951, Box 45 [212861–953].

[120] Special Rpt. of the Mil. Governor Germany, "Property Control in the U.S.-Occupied Area of Germany, 1945–1949", July 1949, Hoover Lib., Stanford Univ., CA, (Territory Under U.S. Occupation, 1945—U.S. Zone) [106833–836].

[121] MG-Germany, Supreme Commander's Area of Control, "Law No. 53: Foreign Exchange Control," no date, NACP, RG84, IARA/TGC, Entry 2113M, Box 5, File XG13 [106887–890].

[122] Notice No.2 under MG Law No. 53, "Foreign Exchange Assets of Displaced Persons and Stateless Persons" [106891–892].

[123] Annex XX (MFA&A) to Basic Preliminary Plan, Allied Control and Occupation of Germany (Allied Control Authority period), May 29, 1945, NACP, RG 331, Entry 55B, Box 324 [319628–633].

[124] SHAEF G-5 to listed addressees, "Fourth Edition of Repositories of Works of Art and Archives in Germany," May 1945, NACP, RG 331, Entry 55B, SHAEF G-5 MFA&A, Box 325 [319562–609].

[125] SHAEF G-5 to listed addressees, "Addendum I to Fourth Edition of Repositories of Works of Art and Archives in Germany," June 1945, NACP, RG 331, Entry 55B, SHAEF G-5 MFA&A, Box 323 [319610–623].

[126] Ziemke, *The U.S. Army in the Occupation of Germany, 1944–1946*, 271.

[127] Lt. James Rorimer, MFA&A to ACOS G-5, 7th Army, "Seventeenth Report (First for Germany), Monuments, Fine Arts and Archives (Period: 15 April—31 May 1945)," June 3, 1945, NACP, RG 331, Entry 55B, Box 335 [320199].

[128] Zink, *American Military Government in Germany,* 59.

[129] MFA&A Adv. to ACOS, G-5, May 21, 1945, NACP, RG 331, Entry 55B, Box 331, Policy and Procedure [319798].

[130] SHAEF G-5 to 12th Army Group G-5, "Unauthorized Moving of Works of Art," July 2, 1945, NACP, RG 331, Entry 55B, Box 324 [319657].

[131] Ops. Office, MFA&A, USFET G-5 to A/Chief, MFA&A, RD&D Div., U.S. Group C.C., "Special Personnel for Evacuating Repositories," July 17, 1945, NACP, RG 331, Entry 55B, Box 330 [319767–770].

[132] MFA&A Office to Dir., OMG, Stadtkreis Frankfurt am Main, "Duties and Projected Operations, Monuments, Fine Arts, and Archives Branch, Detachment E-6, 2nd Mil. Govt. Branch," Jan. 23, 1946, NACP, RG 260, SHAEF G-5 MFA&A, Box 136 [335728–736].

[133] Telegram WX-17918, AGWAR to SHAEF, "Re: Removal of Art Treasures from Areas now Occupied by Allied Troops," June 16, 1945, NACP, RG 338, USFET G-5 Decimal File 123/2, Box 13 [313886]. "[T]o the fullest extent practicable before withdrawing from areas now occupied you should seek to effect removal into United States and United Kingdom zones of occupation of art treasures believed to have been looted by Nazis from liberated countries within ETO and MTO as well as such treasures as MFA&A officers feel should be removed because of originating from US or UK zones."

[134] HQ USFET to Commanding Gen., Eastern and Western Military Districts, "Inspection and Report of Art Repositories," Aug. 8, 1945, NACP, RG 338, USFET G-5 Decimal file, Box 13 [313617–618].

[135] Maj. William G. Wiles to RMGO, Det. E-201, Co. F, 3rd Mil. Govt. Regt., "Monuments, Fines Arts & Archives Report for August, 1945," Aug. 29, 1945, NACP, RG 260, OMGUS Detachment Rpts., Box 370 [335507–510].

[136] Monthly Rpt. of the MG, U.S. Zone, Reparations and Restitutions, Oct. 20, 1945, NACP, RG 239, Box 70 [319403–409].

[137] OMG Bavaria, Status of Cultural Objects Rpt., July, 1946, NACP RG 260, Ardelia Hall Collection, Status Cultural Objects, Box 135 [335562–575].

[138] Lt. Robert Koch to Office of Military Government for Baden-Württemberg, "Monthly Consolidated Field Report, October 1945," Oct. 31, 1945, NACP, RG 260, OMGUS Consolidated Monthly Report, Box 136 [335747–758].

[139] Memo from the Chairman, Property Disposition Board to Deputy Military Governor, OMGUS, "Report of Property Disposition Board," Mar. 26, 1946, NACP, RG 260, Entry 1, Box 81 [100110].

[140] Chief, Restitution Control Br., USFET to Dir. Economics Division, OMGUS, "Report on the Painting of the Dutch Painter Willem van der Velde called 'The Four-day Seabattle,'" Dec. 3, 1945, NACP, RG 338, USFET G-5 Decimal File 1943–1945 [313938–941].

[141] MFA&A Adv., SHAEF G-5 to Chief, Internal Affairs, "Accommodation for Works of Art Uncovered in Germany," May 3, 1945, NACP, RG 331, Entry 55B, Box 324 [319736].

[142] Memo from SHAEF, Adj. Gen., "Protection of Repositories of Works of Art and Archives in Germany," no date, NACP, RG 331, Entry 55B, Box 324 [319737–738].

[143] SHAEF G-5 to ACOS G-5, 12th Army Group, "German Repositories of Works of Art," Apr. 17, 1945, NACP, RG 331, Entry 55B, Box 323 [319560–561].

[144] SHAEF G-5, Military Government-Civil Affairs Weekly Field Report No. 47, May 5, 1945, NACP, RG 331, Entry 34, Box 126, Decimal File 1945 [316927].

[145] SHAEF to CG, 12th Army Group, May 21, 1945, NACP, RG 338, USFET Decimal File 123/2, Box 13 [313885].

[146] HQ U.S. Group CC, RD&R Div., MFA& A Br. to Dir., RD&R Div., "Organization Necessary for Movement of Works of Art," June 19, 1945, NACP, RG 331, Entry 55B, Box 324 [319640–319643].

[147] HQ 15th U.S. Army to CG, 12th Army Group, "Safeguard and Collection of Art Treasures," May 28, 1945, NACP, RG 331, Entry 55B, Box 323 [319558–559].

[148] Rpt., 3rd U.S. Army to Commanding General, 12th Army Group, "Monuments, Fines Arts and Archives Monthly Report for Period Ending 30 June 1945," July 7, 1945, NACP, RG 331, Entry 55B, SHAEF G-5, MFA&A, Box 334 [320158–163].

[149] MFA&A Br., U.S. Group CC to Dir., RD&R Div., "Organization Necessary for Movement of Works of Art," June 19, 1945, NACP, RG 331, Entry 55B, Box 324 [319640–645].

[150] Lt. J. Hamilton Coulter to CG, USFET, "Semi-Monthly Report on Monuments, Fine Arts and Archives for Period Ending 2 July 1945," July 24, 1945, NACP, RG 260, OMGUS Army Detachment Reports, Box 370 [335498–499].

[151] Report "Art Objects in the US Zone," July 29, 1945, NACP, RG 338, USGCC HQ, ROUS Army Command, Box 37, File: Fine Art [313574–575].

[152] Roberts Commission Report, 135.

[153] Lt. Col. E. De Wald, MFA&A, USACA to CO, Regional Military Government Team—(Austria), "Removal of Art Objects," Aug. 11, 1945, NACP, RG 260, USACA–USFA, Reparations and Restitution, Box 1 [106015–016].

[154] ACOS G-5 Internal Route Slip, "Evacuation of Documents," Sept. 14, 1945, NACP, RG 338, USFET G-5 Decimal File 1945–46, Box 37 [318928].

[155] Roberts Commission Report, 130.

[156] HQ MG Landkreis-Stadtkreis Marburg to CG, 7th U.S. Army, "Status of Collecting Point Report," Nov. 3, 1945, NACP, RG 260, Ardelia Hall Collection, Box 234 [119116–117].

[157] Liaison and Security Office, Stadtkreis-Landtkreis Marburg to OMG for Greater Hesse, "Status of Collecting Point Report," Aug. 5, 1946, NACP, RG 260, Ardelia Hall Collection, Box 234 [119135–119136].

[158] Prop. Cont. Officer, Land Salzburg to Regional Group, "Initial General Survey of the Property Control situation in Land Salzburg," Aug. 6, 1945, NACP, RG 260, Prop. Cont. Br. Gen. Corresp. 1945–1950, Box 5 [110322–110324].

[159] Prop. Cont. Officer, Land Salzburg to RD&R Div., Property Control Br., USACA, "Report of Properties under Control by Land Salzburg," Aug. 25, 1945, NACP, RG 260, Property Control Br. Gen. Corresp. 1945–1950, Box 5 [110320–110321].

[160] *Report of the U.S. Commissioner for Military Government in Austria*, No. 1, Nov. 1945, 150, CMH.

[161] Military Govt. Handbook, Chapter XVIII, MFA&A, no date, NACP, RG 260, File 18 (MFA) Archives Lib., Box 720 [110526–530].

[162] 9th U.S. Army G-5 Fin. Br., "Memorandum Regarding Five Bags from Holzminden Reichsbank, Germany," May 29, 1945, NACP, RG 260, FED, Box 432 [220412].

[163] Chief, Currency Sec.—Germany, U.S. Br., June 9, 1945, NACP, RG 260, FED, Box 432 [220419].

[164] Rpt., SHAEF G-4 Representative to ACOS G-4, "G-4 Functions in ETOUSA Operations Merkers-Herringen-Frankfurt Areas in Germany, 9 April to 22 April 1945," Apr. 26 1945, NACP, RG 260, Box 167 [313710–313714].

[165] Bradsher, "Nazi Gold,"12.

[166] Memo, Currency Section for Germany, SHAEF, "Application of Administrative Memo No. 49," May 19, 1945, NACP, RG 260, FED, Box 394 [312789].

[167] Notes on Procedure of Inventory of Works of Art, no date, NACP, RG 260, Ardelia Hall Collection, Box 56 [109023–026].

[168] Asst. Adj. Gen., USFET to Commanding Gen., Eastern Mil.District, "Restitution of Looted Works of Art," Aug. 23, 1945, NACP, RG 338, USFET Adj. Gen. Decimal File 1945, Box 326 [317859].

[169] Asst. Adj. Gen., USFET to Commanding Gen., Western Mil. District, "Repair of Art Collecting Point Buildings," Sept. 25, 1945, NACP, RG 338, USFET Adj. Gen. Decimal File 1945, Box 326 [317845].

[170] Acting Adj. Gen., USFET to Commanding Gen., Eastern and Western Military Districts, "Art Collecting Points," Aug. 24, 1945, NACP, RG 328, USFET Adj. Gen. Decimal File 1945, Box 326 [317855–856].

[171] Rpt. from FED, "History from V-E Day, 8 May 1945 to 30 June 1946," no date, NACP, RG 260, FED, Box 394, File 900.10 [310916–203]. U.S. troops discovered 319 boxes hidden near the camps containing currency, jewelry, coins, alarm clocks, toys, razors, scrap leather, and dental gold.

[172] Rpt., "Shipment 21 (Items A.B.C.D)," no date, NACP, RG 260, FED, Box 424, File 940.40 [220299].

[173] Lt. Col. H.D. Cragon, Chief, SHAEF Currency Sec., "Report on Section to Commanding Officer of European Civil Affairs Division," May 8, 1945, NACP, RG 260, FED Records, Box 420.

[174] Rpt. of Currency Sec. for Germany, U.S. Army Br., to Fin. Div., U.S. Group CC, re: "Report on Treasures Held at Frankfurt," June 27, 1945, NACP, RG 56, Entry 69A4707, Box 82 [204762].

[175] Rpt. from FED, "History from V.E. Day, 8 May 1945 to 30 June 1946" NACP, RG 260, FED, Box 394, File 900.10 [310201].

[176] NACP, RG 260, FED, Shipment Summaries, Box 470. [312199–286].

[177] Ibid.

[178] Rpt. from FED, "History from V.E. Day, 8 May 1945 to 30 June 1946," NACP, RG 260, FED, Box 394, File 900.10 [310201].

[179] Message from USFET signed Eisenhower to AGWAR, Sept. 30, 1945, NACP, RG 260, FED, Box 397, File 910.13 [217878].

[180] Rpt. from FED, "History from V-E Day, 8 May 1945 to 30 June 1946" NACP, RG 260, FED, Box 394, File: 900.10 [310201].

[181] Memo from Col. William R. Watson, Chief Inspections Section to the Commanding Gen., USFET, "Report of Investigation," Nov. 10, 1945, NACP, RG 260, FED, Box 395 [312891–900].

[182] USFET signed McNarney to Secretary of War, Nov. 29, 1945, NACP, RG 260, FED, Box 397 [217886].

[183] "Summary Inventory of Currency and Financial Assets stored in Reichsbank Frankfurt am Main," Apr. 20, 1945, NACP, RG 218, Entry 2, Box 72, File: Control of German

Property and Assets 3–21–45 [226614]. It is important to note that these figures, although detailed down to the currency's denomination, were reached "without weighing or counting gold bars, coins, currency, etc."

[184] MFA&A Col. Webb to DACOS G-5 SHAEF, "Storage of Works of Art at Frankfurt," Apr. 23, 1945, NACP, RG 331, Entry 55B, Box 324 [319654–655].

[185] MG Detachment E1D2 to HQ, Commandant, SHAEF Forward, "Repository for Works of Art," June 4, 1945, NACP, RG 331, Entry 55B, Box 324 [319656].

[186] MFA&A Br., Capt. Rae, to Dir., RD&R Division, US Group CC, "Proposed Repository for Works of Art at Present Stored in the Reichsbank, Frankfurt a/M," June 27, 1945, NACP, RG 331, Entry 55B, Box 324 [319646–647].

[187] Nicholas, *The Rape of Europa*, 376–377.

[188] Rpt. by Capt. E.P. Lesley, MFA&A Special Officer, Feb. 26, 1946, NACP, RG 260, Ardelia Hall Collection, Box 136 [100888].

[189] Rpt. by Capt. E.P. Lesley, MFA&A Special Officer, Feb. 17, 1946, NACP, RG 260, Ardelia Hall Collection, Box 136 [100889].

[190] Memo from Capt. Ralph E. Brant to OMG-Hesse, Feb. 14, 1946. NACP, RG 260, Ardelia Hall Collection, Box 250 [100890–891].

[191] Capt. Robert Wallach to Commanding Officer, Detachment F-13, "Re: Establishment of the OAD," Mar. 2, 1946, NACP, RG 260, OMGUS, Activity Rpts., Box 259, File: OAP Reports, March 1946 [100886–887]. A historical synopsis of the Offenbach Archival Depot can be found on the website of the U.S. Holocaust Memorial Museum [http://www.ushmm.org/oad/main2.htm]. In a section entitled "Offenbach Archival Depot: Antithesis to Nazi Plunder" links are provided to explore the historical background, photos, and archival documents pertaining to the OAD procedures for the collection and restitution of assets under its control.

[192] Memo from Lt. Col. G.H. Garde, AGD to Directors of OMG Bavaria, Hesse, Württemberg-Baden, "Re: Removal to Central Archival Depot of Archives, Books, other Library Materials and Jewish Religious Objects," Sept. 10, 1946, NACP, RG 260, OMGUS, Box 722, File: Restitution Germany, Feb. 1946—Aug. 1947 [101389–390].

[193] From Edwin Rae, Chief MFA&A, Rest. Br. to OMG-Nuremberg, Oct. 18, 1946, NACP, RG 260, Ardelia Hall Collection, Box 252 [100794].

[194] OAD Monthly Report, July 31, 1946, NACP, RG 260, Ardelia Hall Collection, Box 259, OAD Reports—July 1946 [101401–411].

[195] MFA&A document, Mar. 5, 1946, NACP, RG 260, OMGUS, Entry: MFA&A Sec. Chief, Box 720, File: MFA&A Library—OAD [100877].

[196] Cable CC–6925 from OMGUS Gen. L. Clay to AGWAR. June 15, 1946. NACP, RG 260, OMGUS, Ardelia Hall Collection, Box 254, File: AJDC/OAD [101200].

[197] Memo from Capt. Ralph E. Brant to OMG–Hesse, Feb. 14, 1946. NACP, RG 260, OMGUS, Ardelia Hall Collection, Box 250 [100890–891].

[198] OAD Monthly Report, July 31, 1946, NACP, RG 260, Ardelia Hall Collection, Box 259, OAD Reports—July 1946 [101410]. The OAD also identified 1,225 items belonging to German Free Mason lodges.

[199] Ibid.

[200] Letter from William G. Daniels, Chief, OMGUS Prop. Div. to Mr. Hermann, NACP, RG 260, Ardelia Hall Collection, Box 76. [100448].

[201] The Hungarian Gold Train was one of many trains intercepted by U.S. Forces in spring 1945. Others contained the property of banks and museums that oftentimes included assets looted from Nazi-occupied nations and victims of the Holocaust.

[202] Italics added. Memo, "Military Government—Austria, Property Register, 'Hungarian (Werfen) Train,'" Aug. 29, 1945, NACP, RG 260, USACA, Entry 113, Box 20, File S4.8007 [119282]; "Report on the 'Werfen Train'," Sept. 17, 1945, NACP, RG 260, USACA, Entry 113, Box 20, File S4.8007 [119285–286].

[203] Letter from the Central Bd. of Jews in Hungary to the State Dept., July 28, 1947, 3, NACP, RG 84, Entry 2692, Box 4 [103312–317].

[204] Rpt. of Béla Zolnai, István Jeszenöy, István Horváth, & László Avar, Sept. 20, 1945, Hungarian National Archives, RG 29, L–2–r73/36–40–12 [122900–903].

[205] Memo from 1st Lt. J. A. Mercer to HQ, 3rd Infantry Div., "Hungarian Train Bearing Civilians," May 16, 1945, NACP, RG 260, USACA, Entry 113, Box 20, File S4.8007 [119272]; "Report on the 'Werfen Train," Sept. 17, 1945, NACP, RG 260, USACA, Entry 113, Box 20, File S4.8007 [119285–286].

[206] Rpt. of László Avar & István Mingovits, Aug. 2, 1945, Hungarian National Archives, RG 29, L–2–r73/36–40–12 [122882–899].

[207] Memo from Col. Harry L. Bennett, HQ, MG, to Commanding Officer., XV Corps Arty, Plans to Unload & Store Contents of "Hungarian Train" in the MG Warehouse, Salzburg, July 8, 1945, NACP, RG 260, USACA, Entry 113, Box 20, File S4.8007 [119277–278].

[208] Ibid.

[209] Memo from Lt. Col. Homer K. Heller, Prop. Control Officer, to Commanding Officer., E2 K3, "Property Control Section Report, 19 July thru 23 July 1945," July 23, 1945, NACP, RG 260, USACA, Entry 113, Box 20, File S4.8007 [119280]; Memo from Col. Harry L. Bennett, HQ, MG, to Commanding Gen., II Corps, "Movement Hungarian Property from Werfen," July 17, 1945, NACP, RG 260, USACA, Entry 113, Box 20, File S4.8007 [119279].

[210] "Military Government—Austria, Property Register, 'Hungarian (Werfen) Train,' " Aug. 29, 1945, NACP, RG 260, USACA, Entry 113, Box 20, File S4.8007 [119282].

[211] Memo from Capt. John F. Back to G-2, USFA, "Inventory of 'Werfen Train,' " Sept. 1945, NACP, RG 260, USACA, Entry 113, Box 20, File S4.8007 [119283–284].

[212] Memo from Capt. John F. Back to G-2, "Report on the 'Werfen Train,' " Sept. 17, 1945, NACP, RG 260, USACA, Entry 113, Box 20, File S4.8007 [119285–286].

[213] "Military Government—Austria, Property Register, 'Hungarian (Werfen) Train,' " Aug. 29, 1945, NACP, RG 260, USACA, Entry 113, Box 20, File S4.8007 [119282].

[214] Ibid.

[215] Memo from Lt. Col. Homer K. Heller, Property Control Officer, to Commanding Officer, "Inventory of furniture and furnishing," July 31, 1945, NACP, RG 260, USACA, Entry 102, Box 77 [111585–587].

[216] Memo from Maj. R.W. Cutler, Jr. to Lt. Col. Homer K. Heller, Aug. 28, 1945, NACP, RG 260, USACA, Entry 102, Box 77 [111589].

[217] "Rugs removed from Military Government Warehouse Maxglan, Salzburg by order of Major General Harry J. Collins for use in his villa Maria Theresien Schlossl," no date, NACP, RG 260, USACA, Entry 102, Box 77 [111591].

[218] "List of Material Loaned from Property Control Warehouse," no date, NACP, RG 260, USACA, Entry 102, Box 77 [111609–610].

[219] Memo from Lt. Col. Homer K. Heller, Prop. Control Officer, to Chief, Prop. Control Br., "Status of the Hungarian Train, referred to as the 'WERFEN TRAIN,' " Oct. 21, 1945, NACP, RG 260, USACA, Entry 113, Box 20, File S4.8007 [119287].

[220] Memo from Maj. O.R. Agnew Jr., Prop. Control Officer, to Maj. Kontz, Chief, Prop. Control Br., "Property of Werfen-Train in Military Government Warehouse, Serial No. S 4.8007 Sa.," Mar. 8, 1946, NACP, RG 260, USACA, Entry 102, Box 77 [111627–628].

[221] Memo from Capt. Howard A. Mackenzie, Prop. Control Officer, to Maj. Cullus M. Mayes, Investigating Officer, "Orders & Actions taken by Prop. Control Sec., MG, re: household furnishings loaned," July 17, 1947, NACP, RG 260, USACA, Entry 113, Box 20, File S4.8007 [119299–306].

[222] Ibid.

[223] Ibid.

[224] Ibid.

[225] Ibid.

[226] Ibid.

[227] Ibid.

[228] Ibid.

[229] Ibid.

[230] Ibid.

[231] Memo from Caffery, U.S. Embassy Paris, to Secy. of State, July 3, 1946, NACP, RG 260, USACA, Entry 113, Box 20, File S4.8007 [117440–442].

[232] Rpt. from James A. Barr, Acting Chief, RD&R Div., "Report of Incidents," July 15, 1947, NACP, RG 260, USACA, Entry 113, Box 21, Gold Found in Austria [119361].

[233] Memo from William W. Schwartzmann, Chief, Bus. Enterprise Subsec. to Prop. Control Officer, "Alleged Theft or Diversion of Werfen Train Property," July 15, 1947, NACP, RG 260, USACA, Entry 113, Box 20, File S4.8007 [119297–298]; Memo from Capt. Howard A. Mackenzie, Prop. Control Officer, to Lt. Col. Gun, "Alleged theft or diversion of Werfen train property," July 17, 1947, NACP, RG 260, USACA, Entry 113, Box 20, File S4.8007 [119307].

[234] Memo from Cpt. Howard A. Mackenzie, Prop. Control Officer, to Chief, Movable Prop. Dept., "Missing Property," Oct. 2, 1946, NACP, RG 260, USACA, Entry 102, Box 77 [111619].

[235] Ibid.

[236] MFA&A, G-5 Internal Affairs Br., SHAEF to ACOS G-5 SHAEF, "Report on Monuments, Fine Arts and Archives for Month of Feb 1945," March 1945, NACP, RG 260, Ardelia Hall Collection, Box 369 [106070–071].

[237] Chief Internal Affairs Div. SHAEF G-5 to G-1 Div., "Pillage and Wanton Damage by Allied Troops," Mar. 22, 1945, NACP, RG 331, Entry 55B, Box 324 [319739–741].

[238] SHAEF Chief of Staff to Commanding Gen., Communications Zone, "Looting by Allied Troops," Mar. 28, 1945, NACP, RG 338, USFET Secretary of General Staff Classified File, 1944–1945, Box 19 [313843–845].

[239] Deputy Theater Commander, ETO to Gen. Eisenhower, Apr. 22, 1945, NACP, RG 338, USFET Secretary of Gen. Staff Classified File, 1944–1945, Box 19 [313842].

[240] ACOS G-1 to COS, "Looting by U.S. Troops in Germany," May 5, 1945, NACP, RG 338, USFET Secretary of General Staff Classified File, 1944–1945, Box 19 [313840–841].

[241] Chief, Foreign Exchange Control and Blocking Sec. to Dir., Fin. Div., USGCC, "Treatment of Property of Displaced Persons," Dec. 25, 1944, NACP, RG 56, Entry 69A4707, Box 82, Legal Staff—Special Subjects [108588–591].

[242] Sumner M. Crosby, Special Adv. to the American Commission for the Protection & Salvage of Artistic and Historic Monuments in War Areas, "Interim Report, April 6—April 17, 1945," Apr. 18, 1945, NACP, RG 239, Entry 13, Box 39 [111128–130].

[243] Adj. Gen., ETOUSA to listed addressees, "Theft of Government Property and Looting," May 23, 1945, NACP, RG 338, USFET Secretary of General Staff Classified File, 1944–1945, Box 19 [313838–839].

[244] Secy. of the Army to CINCFE, [circa January 1948], NACP, RG 84, Entry 2056, Box 24, File 822–1948 [119565–566].

[245] SHAEF G-5, "MG—Civil Affairs Weekly Field Report No. 55," June 30, 1945, NACP, RG 331, Entry 18A, Box 161 [314061–067].

[246] OMGUS Public Safety to listed addressees, May 15, 1946, NACP, RG 338, USFET G-5 History file, Box 1 [313664].

[247] Memo from Lt. Gen. Lucius Clay to all Personnel, USGCC, "Re: Looting and Removal of Private Property," Sept. 9, 1945, NACP, RG 260, Entry: Adjutant General Decimal Files, Box 43, File: 250.1 [112005].

[248] Ibid.

249 Statement (translated) of the Dir. of the State Collection of Art in Weimar, "Lootings from the Property of the State Collections of Art in Weimar," Oct. 12, 1945, NACP, RG 260, Econ. Div., Box 46 [106046–051].

250 MG Detachment E–206 to RMGO, Det. E–201, Co. F, 3rd MG Regiment, Aug. 13, 1945, NACP, RG 260, Ardelia Hall Collection, Box 410 [110832–835].

251 SHAEF, G-5 Division, "Military Government-Civil Affairs Weekly Field Report No. 46," Apr. 28, 1945, NACP, RG 331, Entry 34, Box 126, G-4 Decimal File 1945 [316922–925].

252 Lt. Col. G. H. Garde to Dir., CAD, "Art Looting by American Personnel," Mar. 1, 1947, NACP, RG 260, OMGUS File 1946, Box 129 [119450–462].

253 Report by MFA&A Officer for Northern Bavaria, [circa December 1948], "Re: Final Report on MFA/A Activities in Northern Bavaria, April 1945—December 1948," NACP, RG 260, Ardelia Hall Collection, Box 375 [119545–554].

254 OMG of Greater Hessen to Commanding Gen., USFET, Dec. 7, 1945, "Security Guard for Central Collecting Point, Wiesbaden," NACP, RG 338, USFET G-5 Decimal file 1945–1946, Box 37 [313579–580].

255 Econ. Division, OMG (U.S. Zone) memo, Dec. 29, 1945, NACP, RG 338, USFET G-5 Decimal file 1945–1946, Box 37 [313577–578].

256 Statement of Francis Bilodeau, Dir. of Weisbaden Central Collecting Point, Feb. 18, 1947, NACP, RG 260, Ardelia Hall Collection, Box 56 [119527–528].

257 Wiesbaden Collecting Point to Director, OMG for Greater Hesse, "Status of Collecting Point Report," Feb. 4, 1947, NACP, RG 260, Ardelia Hall Collection, Box 128 [111042a–043].

258 Office Memorandum, HQ 3rd United States Army, G-5 Section, "Permanent Guard for the Central Collecting Point Munich," Sept. 13, 1945, NACP, RG 260, Ardelia Hall Collection, Box 268 [117739–117740].

259 Chief, MFA&A Sec., Rest. Br. to OMG (U.S. Zone), Econ. Div., Rest. Control Br., "Military Guards at Repositories and Collecting Points for Works of Art in Bavaria," Feb. 6, 1946, NACP, RG 260, Ardelia Hall Collection, Box 268 [117741–117742].

260 Dir., Munich Central Collecting Point to Criminal Investigations Department, Sept. 19, 1946, NACP, RG 260, OMGUS Ardelia Hall Collection, Box 268 [177747–748].

261 List of items stolen from Central Collecting Point, Munich, [circa 1948], NACP, RG 260, OMGUS Ardelia Hall Collection, Recs. of the Prop. Div., Box 485 [117601–605].

262 Memo from Stefan P. Munsing, Chief, MFA&A Sec., Rest. Br. of MG for Bavaria, to Otto F. Yanisch, Chief, Rest. Br., OMG for Bavaria, "Visit of Yugoslav Mission at the Munich Central Collecting Point," Dec. 22, 1948, NACP, RG 260, Ardelia Hall Collection, Box 316, Prop. Div. [112198].

263 Biographic sketch of Wiltrud Mersmann, no date, NACP, RG 260, Ardelia Hall Collection, Box 316, Prop. Div. [112192]; Anonymous note, "Yugoslav Situation," no date, NACP, RG 260, Ardelia Hall Collection, Box 316, Prop. Div. [112194].

264 Letter from Mate A. Topič, Yugoslav Representative for Rest. Fine Arts & Monuments, to Stefan P. Munsing, Chief, MFA&A Sec., Rest. Br. of MG for Bavaria, Mar. 31, 1949, NACP, RG 260, Ardelia Hall Collection, Box 316, Prop. Div. [112201–112210].

265 Letter from M. H. McCord, Chief, R&R Liaison Officer., R&R Br., Prop. Div., OMGUS to Otto Yanisch, Officer of MG for Bavaria, Rest. Br., Apr. 20, 1949, NACP, RG 260, Ardelia Hall Collection, Box 316, Prop. Div. [112211–212].

266 Memo from Allied Control Authority, RD&R Directorate, "Yugoslavian Receipt No. 4, Receipt for Cultural Objects," June 2, 1949, NACP, RG 260, Ardelia Hall Collection, Box 316, Prop. Div. [112221–229]; Allied Control Authority, RD&R Directorate, "Yugoslavian Receipt No. 5, Receipt for Cultural Objects," June 2, 1949, NACP, RG 260, Ardelia Hall Collection, Box 316, Prop. Div. [112230–232]; Allied Control Authority, RD&R Directorate, "6th Yugoslavian Shipment, Receipt for Cultural Objects," June 10, 1949, NACP, RG 260, Ardelia Hall Collection, Box 316, Prop. Div. [112233–235]; Allied Control Authority, RD&R Directorate, "7th Yugoslavian Shipment, Receipt for Cultural Objects," June 10, 1949, NACP, RG 260, Ardelia Hall Collection, Box 316, Prop. Div. [112236–241].

[267] Ibid.

[268] Letter from Wiesbaden Central Collecting Point, "Cultural Restitution to Yugoslavia," Jan. 5, 1951, NACP, RG 260, Ardelia Hall Collection, Box 316 [112282].

[269] Letter from Conrad Snow to Mr. Raymond, "Mistaken Restitution of Cultural Objects to Mr. Mate Topic for the Yugoslav Government," Feb. 27, 1956, NACP, RG 260, Ardelia Hall Collection, Box 316 [112319–323].

[270] Letter from Frank J. Miller, Chief, Prop. Div., to Chief, Yugoslav Mil. Mission, Berlin, June 1, 1950, RG 260, Ardelia Hall Collection, Box 316, Prop. Div. [112272].

[271] Letter from William G. Daniels, Chief, Prop. Div., Office of Econ. Affairs, HICOG, to State Dept., June 13, 1950, NACP, RG 260, Ardelia Hall Collection, Box 316, Prop. Div. [112273].

[272] Ibid.

[273] Telegram from State Dept. to U.S. Embassies, Rome, Belgrade, Bonn, no date, NACP, RG 260, Ardelia Hall Collection, Box 316, Prop. Div. [112293].

[274] State Dept. to the Am. Embassy, Belgrade, "Erroneous restitution to Yugoslavia," Mar. 15, 1954, NACP, RG 260, Ardelia Hall Collection, Box 316, Prop. Div. [112297–298]; Memo from Edwin M. J. Kretzmann, First Secy. of Embassy, Am. Embassy, Belgrade, to State Dept., May 6, 1954, NACP, RG 260, Ardelia Hall Collection, Box 316, Prop. Div. [112300]; Am. Legation, Tangier, to the Secy. of State, Mar. 27, 1956, NACP, RG 260, Ardelia Hall Collection, Box 316 [112344]; Deputy Dir., CIA, to Secy. of State, "Mate A. Topič, with aliases," Dec. 12, 1955, NACP, RG 260, Ardelia Hall Collection, Box 316, Prop. Div. [112305–308]; Am. Legation, Tangier, Morocco, to the State Dept., "Activities of Topič Matutin, Ante Mimara, Yugoslav National," Dec. 19, 1955, NACP, RG 260, Ardelia Hall Collection, Box 316, Prop. Div. [112309–312]; U.S. State Dept. to Am. Embassies in Bonn & Belgrade, & the Am. Legation, Tangier, Morocco, Mar. 5, 1956, NACP, RG 260, Ardelia Hall Collection, Box 316, Prop. Div. [112329]; Am. Embassy, Belgrade, to the U.S. State Dept., Mar. 15, 1956, NACP, RG 260, Ardelia Hall Collection, Box 316, Prop. Div. [112335]; Am. Legation, Tangier, Morocco, to the Secy. of State, Mar. 18, 1956, NACP, RG 260, Ardelia Hall Collection, Box 316, Prop. Div. [112336]; U.S. State Dept. to the Am. Legation, Tangier, Morocco, & the Am. Embassies in Belgrade & Bonn, Mar. 21, 1956, NACP, RG 260, Ardelia Hall Collection, Box 316, Prop. Div. [112340].

[275] U.S. State Dept., Memo of Telephone Conversation, Participants: Wehmeyer & Ardelia Hall, "Yugoslav Case," Sept. 12, 1956, NACP, RG 260, Ardelia Hall Collection, Box 316, Prop. Div. [112355].

[276] Donald A. Wehmeyer to Ardelia Hall, "Mistaken Restitution of Cultural Objects to Matutin (Mate) Topič," Dec. 5, 1956, NACP, RG 260, Ardelia Hall Collection, Box 316, Prop. Div. [112359].

[277] USFET to CG, Western Military District, "Return of Looted Works of Art to Owner-Nations," Sept. 15, 1945, NACP, RG 338, USFET G-5 Decimal File 123/2, Box 13 [313878–879].

[278] USGCC to ACOS G-5, USFET, "Restitution Policy and Procedure," Sept. 24, 1945, NACP, RG 338, USFET G-5 Situation Reports, Box 1 [313683].

[279] ACOS G-5 Memo, "re: Receipt and Agreement for Delivery of Cultural Objects," Sept. 29, 1945, NACP, RG 338, USFET G-5 Decimal File 1945–1946, Box 37 [313929–932].

Chapter V

Restitution of Victims' Assets

Introduction

In 1944, policymakers in the State Department examined the means that would enable "German racial or religious minorities" to receive compensation for what had been inflicted on them. Once the war ended, U.S. officials consulted with their Allies, Jewish organizations, and German officials before implementing plans in Europe to allocate reparations to survivors and restitute looted property. Having secured control of innumerable pieces of real estate, cultural artifacts, and financial assets, the United States inaugurated its general restitution program in the summer of 1945. By that time, some U.S. officials already had begun to consider victims of Nazi persecution as representing a distinct category of property claimants. In 1946, Congress enacted legislation enabling persecutees to claim property frozen in the United States during the war. To further address the needs of Holocaust survivors, U.S. officials designated the Jewish Restitution Successor Organization (JRSO) to receive the assets of heirless victims and employ those funds for the rehabilitation of survivors worldwide.

Not all U.S. authorities recognized persecutees as a special category. Much of the documentation created in the immediate postwar era pertaining to restitution does not distinguish between victims' and nonvictims' assets, for instance. Consequently, property that was identifiable as to its country of origin would not be further categorized to designate an owner who had been persecuted by the Nazi regime. The measures envisioned for effecting restitution also shifted over time: while State Department officials initially favored only a modest indemnity payment for dispossessed persecutees, Military Government authorities promulgated a law in 1947 that promised full restitution of property. During the period between 1944 and 1947, neither a uniform nor a fixed conception of "victim" prevailed among U.S. authorities.

Sensitivity to survivors, heirs, and the successor organizations attempting to claim property fluctuated in the postwar era; other U.S. policies sometimes adversely affected the restitution program. For instance, the decision to return many governing tasks to the Germans in 1945, allowed some who benefited from Aryanizations to participate in the administration of the restitution program.[1] In the United States, the desire to compensate U.S. citizens for damages suffered overseas competed with the restitution of victims' assets, because both programs drew sums from the same fund of vested property.

The impulse to protect the assets falling under U.S. control delayed restitution to claimants and the successor organizations. This concern held certain advantages, however. The United States insisted that any law providing for restitution in Germany contain a presumption of duress—that is, it was assumed that persecutees who transferred property after 1935 did so unwillingly, and that current "owners" of such property could be sued for its return to the original owner. By holding out for this clause, the United States forced the creation of a much broader restitution program than initially envisioned by German authorities after the war. This also meant, however, that the promulgation of the restitution law in Germany did not occur until November 1947, more than two years after hostilities ceased.

In the United States, the Office of Alien Property (OAP) carefully examined individual claims to determine the legitimate ownership of assets. On average, this resulted in a delay of more than three years before a victim could recover property. The OAP also tracked down surviving owners and heirs in Germany before agreeing to release assets to the JRSO. After realizing the extensive time and resources necessary to fulfill this responsibility, the JRSO negotiated an agreement with the United States government in the early 1960s as a result of which the successor organization reluctantly accepted a lump-sum settlement of $500,000.

Even though officials frequently did not distinguish victims' property from other assets recovered, the United States nevertheless employed seven mechanisms that affected assets belonging to Nazi persecutees:

- External restitution policy—the return of "identifiable" property from Germany to its country of origin—applied to victims' assets.

- The United States agreed with its allies at the Paris Conference on Reparations to pool all the monetary gold discovered in Germany, some of which contained gold taken from victims, for restitution to countries.

- In Paris, the United States also agreed to distribute the "non-monetary gold" found in Germany and a sum of $25 million to a refugee relief organization for aiding "non-repatriable victims of German action."

- The Office of Military Government for Germany, United States (OMGUS) issued Law 59 in Germany that effected restitution ("internal restitution") for those who had been persecuted "for reasons of race, religion, nationality, ideology, or political opposition to National Socialism."

- OMGUS designated the JRSO to claim heirless Jewish property for Jewish communities worldwide.

- Congress authorized the release of assets seized in the United States that belonged to persecutees.

- President Eisenhower designated the JRSO to receive and distribute heirless vested assets in the United States.

U.S. government officials were aware of the special circumstances surrounding Nazi persecutees at war's end. Although other policy considerations impeded progress, agencies of the United States government demonstrated a significant commitment to return the property of Holocaust victims after the Second World War.

Restitution in Europe

Context and Planning

The United States had refused to sanction war plundering since it became a signatory to the Hague Convention in 1907, if not before.[2] After World War I, the victorious Allies, including the United States, enacted a reparations program to compensate countries for the property damages wrought by the Germans. The London Declaration of January 1943 reaffirmed the commitment to annul wrongful property dispossession under wartime conditions. Signed by the United States, the Soviet Union, and sixteen other nations, the London Declaration stated that the Allies:

> Reserve all their rights to declare invalid any transfers of, or dealings with, property, rights and interests of any description whatsoever which are, or have been, situated in the territories which have come under the occupation of control, direct or indirect, of the governments with which they are at war or which belong or have belonged, to persons, including juridical persons, resident in such territories. This warning applies whether such transfers or dealings have taken the form of open looting or plunder, or of transactions apparently legal in form, even when they purport to be voluntarily effected.[3]

Although scholars disagree about whether or not the London Declaration made an express commitment to restitution, at least to the country of origin, the Commission staff believes that it laid the foundation for postwar restitution policy.

As early as November 1943, the U.S. State Department created an Interdivisional Committee on Reparation, Restitution, and Property Rights to formulate the "general bases of departmental policy on the questions of reparation, restitution, and related matters."[4] It is noteworthy that this committee specifically endeavored to construct a "restitution" policy. Although there had been some discussion of restitution among the Allies after the First World War, reparations had emerged as the dominant means to address property losses. Given the incessant crises of the German reparations program during the 1920s and 1930s, however, the interest in exploring an alternate policy such as restitution is understandable.

From the outset, committee members subordinated restitution to other concerns by agreeing that "policy with respect to reparation and restitution should be formulated in such a way as to interfere as little as possible with the major economic objectives of this government."[5] Similarly, the principle of restitution to governments rather than individuals arose soon after deliberations began. On February 5, 1944, an unidentified participant declared that "individual claimants should look for satisfaction of their claims solely to their national governments" and that "no attempt can or should be made. . .to regulate or otherwise deal with the relations between individual claimants and their national governments."[6]

The same argument against restitution to individuals appeared on April 10, 1944. A memorandum entitled "Recommendations on Restitution" suggested that "no attempt should be made to make restitution to the original owners individually." Property looted from occupied countries should be returned to the legitimate governments of the liberated countries, and all property moved to Germany during the occupation "should be presumed to have been transferred under duress."[7] The committee members made clear their conviction that U.S. occupation officials should bear only initial responsibility for effecting restitution.

> The question of restoration to individual owners is a matter for these [legitimate] governments to handle in whatever way they see fit. The original owners may have received part payment for property taken from them under duress and the governments in question may wish to make adjustments for this circumstance in returning the property. In some cases it may be impossible to locate the original owners or their heirs and the governments involved will have to decide what should be done with the property or proceeds therefrom.[8]

Once assets had been delivered to representatives of claimant nations, no further U.S. involvement was deemed necessary or desirable.

The Committee acknowledged that "for political reasons the right to restitution should be recognized in all cases and for all classes of property," in part because a restitution program would be "a logical corollary to the inter-Allied Declaration of January 5, 1943." Nevertheless, the Committee believed that certain limitations should apply. "As a practical matter, restitution should be restricted to relatively few kinds of property such as archives and records of the occupied countries: gold; works of art, books and other cultural and educational treasures; securities, major means of transport, mostly rolling stock and ships; industrial equipment; registered livestock, and agricultural equipment."[9] Household items would be excluded from restitution efforts, since "practical considerations make it necessary to ignore the problem of restoring small items such as furniture and fixtures, rugs and hangings, and similar items." Any attempt to restitute these assets promised to be a "difficult" and "relatively unimportant" task.[10]

One member of the Interdivisional Committee, Eleanor Dulles, objected to the principle of returning assets to countries instead of individuals. Dulles thought that "securities, at any rate, should be returned on the basis of citizenship rather than residence." She described a hypothetical example of an American whose stock certificate had been looted from a safety deposit box in Paris; Dulles argued that such a certificate "should be returned to the American wherever he may be and not to the French government." For reasons of "administrative convenience and equity," however, the other committee members disagreed.[11]

The issue resurfaced a few days later. Jacques J. Reinstein and some of his colleagues remained convinced that goods had to be restored to governments. They thought that "no international commission could attempt to deal with the complicated questions of individual ownership," and "only the government of the territory could untangle the question of title." Evidently this argument proved persuasive; Dulles eventually endorsed the idea of restitution to governments instead of individuals.[12]

In April 1944, the committee issued recommendations on "Compensation for Injuries to Members of German Racial or Religious Minorities." Such compensation did not include absolute restitution of property seized. "The difficulties and questionable aspects of a program to restore all their former property to the Jews appear to dictate some compromise measure." Resentment toward the Jews "might well build up further" if a program were established to restore all lost property. The German government could not "be expected to administer such a program sympathetically," and, given the difficulties of converting assets into foreign denominations, Jewish owners would probably have to return to Germany to obtain settlements. "This raises the question of whether it is desirable to provide a stimulus for the return of Jews to Germany."[13]

The committee considered the possibility of a limited program of German indemnification instead of wholesale restitution. One idea required the German government to help finance the resettlement of former persecutees through an international organization responsible for receiving and distributing the funds. "The amount of the payments should be related not to the losses suffered by the members of these groups but to the requirements of the resettlement schemes." In addition, the German government would "provide an indemnity up to some moderate maximum per person, which maximum should be identical for all claimants regardless of loss," for all those dispossessed by the Nazis on racial or religious grounds. The committee recognized that under such a program wealthy claimants would fare worse than poor claimants, but "indemnification for all their losses would not be feasible in any event."[14]

On June 29, 1944, the Interdivisional Committee delivered the final report to the Executive Committee on Economic Foreign Policy (ECEFP). Assistant Secretary of State Dean Acheson presided at this meeting; officials from the Departments of Treasury, Agriculture, Commerce, and Labor attended, as did representatives from the United States Tariff Commission, Bureau of the Budget, and Foreign Economic Administration.[15] The ECEFP approved a slightly revised "Report on Reparation, Restitution, and Property Rights—Germany" on August 4, 1944,[16] and transmitted it to the Secretaries of War and the Navy.[17]

The sections most relevant to restitution clearly derived from the statements crafted earlier that spring. The report recognized that practical considerations might restrict a desired unlimited obligation on Germany to restore identifiable looted property. The right to restitution, moreover, should not be absolute. The Allied authorities should reserve the right to delay or deny restitution of certain objects if necessary. Only identifiable property in existence before the German occupation would be subject to restitution. Looted property should be returned in the condition found and restored to the existing governments of the territories where the property had its situs and not to the former owners individually. All property that the German occupiers removed to Germany (except for current output) would be presumed to have been transferred under duress and recognized as looted property. Apart from gold and works of art and other treasures, no claims for replacement should be allowed.[18]

The report also acknowledged the self-evident moral basis for compensation for injuries to persecutees. Practicalities and politics, however, would make compensation difficult. It was assumed that many who might have been in a position to seek restitution of property within Germany were dead. Others no longer lived in Germany, and many of these individuals "would not find it worthwhile to return in order to regain their property." Further, an enormous transfer of assets abroad might create "strong social tension" and was therefore "out of the question." Finally, such a large restitution program might impose an overwhelming administrative burden. The twofold plan of resettlement aid and limited indemnification for property losses thus emerged as the recommended solution to the restitution question.[19]

These initial ideas concerning restitution were directly linked to and must be interpreted in the context of how State Department officials envisioned the role of postwar Germany. They desired a speedy return of the German economy to "normal" conditions and advocated the reintegration of Germany into the community of European nations. They believed that by ensuring favorable conditions for recovery, rather than imposing draconian measures, the United States might best realize its goal of securing lasting peace with Germany. The fairly mild restitution proposals reflected this thinking, and for that reason the State Department recommendations drew sharp criticism from Treasury Secretary Henry Morgenthau. Believing that peace could only be obtained by stripping Germany of its industrial capacity and punishing the German people, Morgenthau and his staff in the Treasury Department crafted their own proposals for the postwar administration of Germany. [20]

The ensuing debate between the opposing visions meant that the ideas for limited restitution crafted in the State Department in the spring of 1944 did not translate directly into U.S. policy at war's end. Officials accepted the principle of restitution to countries rather than individuals. On the other hand, the State Department proposals envisioning a meager recompense for persecutees disappeared from policy discussions. An ambitious program to return victims' property emerged instead.

Restitution to Countries, Not Individuals (External Restitution)

Although no comprehensive policy for restitution had yet been transmitted to military authorities in Europe, President Truman had approved the return of "readily identifiable" works of art from U.S. Collecting Points in July 1945.[21] The following month, U.S. officials began restitution of art and cultural property from their zone of occupation in Germany. Belgium received the first delivery, accepting the Ghent altarpiece "The Adoration of the Mystic Lamb."[22] In the weeks thereafter, representatives from many nations presented claims for property held at the Collecting Points and "streams of art" began "flowing in both directions at the Munich Collecting Point."[23]

An interim restitution policy memorandum issued in September described the standard operating procedure for returning these artworks. Governments submitted consolidated lists of items taken by the Germans, providing information about the location and circumstances of their theft. U.S. authorities examined each list and permitted small missions to enter the U.S. Zone to identify the materials and undertake preparations for their return.[24]

At the end of November 1945, the Joint Chiefs of Staff instructed commanders in Germany and Austria to return to the government of issue all currency issued by member states of the United Nations that had been occupied by the Germans "without the necessity of proof that it was looted or otherwise acquired from that country during the period of German invasion or occupation." U.S. authorities were also directed to return heavy agricultural and industrial equipment, locomotives, rolling stock, barges, transportation equipment (except for seagoing vessels), and communication and power equipment which had been "identified as having been looted or acquired in any way by Germans from United

Nations during German occupation." Further, other goods, materials, equipment, livestock and other property "looted or acquired in any way by Germans" was subject to restitution. The Joint Chiefs also instructed commanders to return valuables excluding gold, securities, and foreign currencies other than those specified above. The procedure for restitution mirrored that already established for art and cultural property: upon submission of lists by governments, U.S. authorities allowed small missions to identify and retrieve property. Currencies that comprised part of the Melmer loot, however, were turned over to the International Refugee Organization (IRO) for the support of refugees and displaced persons.[25]

Initially, only certain governments—France, Belgium, Luxembourg, the Netherlands, Norway, Denmark, Poland, the Soviet Union, Czechoslovakia, Greece, and Yugoslavia—could present claims. In March 1946, ex-enemy nations, including Hungary, Romania, Finland, and Italy, obtained the privilege of submitting claims for items taken during the period when Germany occupied these countries.[26] The Soviet Union claimed and received some materials looted from the Baltic states (Latvia, Lithuania, and Estonia) in 1945,[27] but by 1946, the U.S. government had ceased restitution of items belonging to those countries because it did not "recognize [the] incorporation of these states into the Soviet Union."[28]

By 1947, additional policies for returning other currencies and securities to countries of origin were in place. Currencies were to be given back to nations that had experienced German occupation, and to countries that belonged to the Inter-Allied Reparation Agency.[29] An exception to this broad policy gave Hungarian, Romanian, Bulgarian, and Finnish currencies to the Soviet Union.[30] Moreover, identifiable securities were to return "in the normal way to the claimant nation." Securities issued or owned by German corporations or the German government were not, however, subject to release.[31]

U.S. authorities stopped accepting claims for external restitution in 1948.[32] Restitution missions could submit petitions for cultural items and securities until September 15 and December 31, respectively, but the deadline for all other materials was April 30, 1948. Meritorious claims would be considered thereafter "when it can be established that the delay in filing resulted from the fact that the German holder of the claimed property conspired to conceal its existence."[33] U.S. authorities justified the termination of external restitution by arguing that the United States "cannot agree to maintain such a considerable staff [to administer restitution] for an indeterminate period," and that by mid-1948, nations had three years since the end of the war to file claims. In August 1948, the United States announced that it intended to complete both investigations and shipments of claimed materials by December 31, 1948.[34]

In October 1948, a collective protest from the restitution missions of Austria, Belgium, Czechoslovakia, France, Italy, Yugoslavia, Poland, and Romania challenged these decisions. It argued that in certain situations, the restitution missions could not comply with the demands of the U.S. authorities "despite all [their] efforts" to do so.[35] Further, cessation of investigations would assuredly permit Germans to keep the items they had stolen, since it "is obvious that the German holder of looted properties" realized that the deadline for restitution was rapidly approaching and "is hiding this property or denies possession of goods without risk, that his case could be reinvestigated."[36] The restitution missions, therefore, asked that the United States reconsider its policy. The United States declined to review its decision.[37]

By returning looted, identifiable assets to countries, U.S. authorities certainly restituted assets belonging to Holocaust victims. By June 1946, the Offenbach Archival Depot, described by U.S. officials as the "only central repository of Jewish cultural property in [the] U.S. zone," [38] had delivered 523 cases of "readily identifiable Jewish property" to France, 544 cases to the Netherlands, and nine cases to Belgium. Restitution of similar material was pending for the Soviet Union, Czechoslovakia, Yugoslavia, Great Britain, Greece, Poland, Hungary, and Italy.[39] Approximately six months later, Offenbach had shipped a total of 1,909,383 items to 12 different countries.[40] This figure had increased by almost a million by January 28, 1949, when the Office for Military Government, Hesse reported a total disbursement of 2,837,821 items. At that time, 371,444 items remained at Offenbach awaiting final disposition.[41]

U.S. authorities restituted more than just victims' cultural materials to countries, however. At Dachau, U.S. troops recovered 2,826 envelopes containing items such as wedding rings, watches, and pins.[42] Appraisers at the FED valued these items at less than $10,000. The Nazis had listed the name and nationality of the owner on 23 percent of the envelopes; OMGUS approved the return of these packages to the respective countries on August 12, 1947.[43] Almost a year later, on July 2, 1948, the FED released the envelopes to representatives of Belgium, Czechoslovakia, the Netherlands, Poland, Italy, Norway, and Yugoslavia.[44]

In October 1947, the Department of the Army instructed OMGUS to restitute registered bonds acquired from concentration camps if the FED could identify the names of owners and their countries.[45] Consequently, the FED authorized the release of six securities to Poland in 1947.[46] OMGUS returned to Czechoslovakia a cache of jewelry, silver bullion, precious stones, securities, and wedding rings contained "in envelopes bearing names and addresses of Czech nationals from whom [they were] said to have been confiscated for political, racial, and religious reasons."[47] These valuables, found at the Reichsbank in Regensburg, were valued contemporaneously at $500,000. Although some of the items appeared unidentifiable, U.S. authorities defended the restitution of the entire cache by arguing that "there was not the slightest doubt. . .that all of these valuables had been removed from Czechoslovakia" and should therefore be returned to that nation.[48]

Unfortunately, most of the data recorded by the main repositories of assets in the U.S. Zone of occupation, the Collecting Points and the FED, do not distinguish between victims' and non-victims' property. For instance, the Deputy Chief for Industrial Restitution, K.A. de Keyserlingk, indicated that as of November 23, 1948, 300 million Reichsmarks (based on 1938 valuations) had been restituted from the U.S. Zone, excluding cultural items. Of that sum, RM 100 million represented Hungarian gold, and Dutch diamonds amounted to RM 7.5 million. Neither these nor the other figures, however, indicate the percentages or values of Holocaust victims' assets.[49] When MFA&A officers completed a final report in December 1948, they listed totals of cultural items restituted to various countries from Germany by that date (1.7 million objects) but failed to mention how many works of art or books may have belonged to persecutees.[50] Similarly, the U.S. High Commissioner for Austria reported that as of December 1948, an estimated $20 billion (based on 1948 dollars) had been restituted from the U.S. Zone of occupation in that country (including the Vienna area), but the officials who prepared this report did not calculate the percentage of victims' loot included in this total.[51] Calculating the precise quantity of Holocaust victims' assets restituted according to the basic principle of returning identifiable property to its country of origin remains, therefore, impossible. For the most part, U.S. authorities simply did not distinguish victims' assets from other property.

Victims' Assets and the Paris Reparations Agreement

The Gold Pot

From November 9 to December 21, 1945, representatives of 18 countries met in Paris to discuss how to distribute reparations from the western-occupied zones of Germany. The Soviet Union renounced claims from these zones and did not participate. One issue included in the negotiations was the return of monetary gold looted from occupied countries. The United States favored pooling all monetary gold found in Germany, along with any German monetary gold that had been transferred abroad. Nations that had suffered gold losses would receive portions of this pot. The idea gained acceptance at the conference, and the United States, Great Britain, and France accepted responsibility for distributing the monetary gold among claimant nations.[52] These nations established a Tripartite Gold Commission (TGC) to carry out the task.

On September 27, 1946, the TGC met in Brussels, Belgium; a commissioner and deputy commissioner represented each government. The TGC opened gold accounts at the Federal Reserve Bank, New York, the Bank of England, and the Bank of France and was responsible for the restitution of 10.8 million ounces (336.4 thousand kg) of fine gold, amounting to over $379 million ($35/ounce).[53]

Ten countries submitted claims totaling more than twice the amount in the gold pool. Even after the TGC discounted some claims, the total remained about 50 percent higher than the sum administered by the TGC. The Paris Agreement stipulated a prorated basis for the return of gold; by 1950, over 80 percent of the gold had been returned to claimant countries. The next and "quasi-final" distributions took place in 1958 and 1959, when all claimants except for the Netherlands, Poland, Czechoslovakia, and Albania received gold. The last of these countries (Albania) received its portion in 1996, and the TGC closed on September 9, 1998.

U.S. officials knew by 1945 that the Nazis had looted gold from persecutees, melted it down, and incorporated it into the German monetary gold supply.[54] Nevertheless, in 1947 the State-War-Navy Coordinating Committee decided to place all monetary gold in the gold pot, even though some bars and bullion contained victims' gold.[55]

A study on Nazi-looted gold and its restitution, coordinated in 1997 by Under Secretary of Commerce for International Trade, Stuart E. Eizenstat, helped lead to the creation of a humanitarian fund to benefit Holocaust survivors. The TGC notified potential recipients that it would be making a final distribution of the remaining gold (amounting to 5.5 tons in the fall of 1996) and also informed them of the report's findings. By December 1997, an international fund had been established to compensate victims of Nazi persecution.[56] In 1998, the United States pledged $25 million to this fund.[57]

"Non-Monetary Gold" and the "Non-Repatriable Victims of Nazism"

In 1945 and 1946, the United States, France, Great Britain, Czechoslovakia, and Yugoslavia agreed to provide swift relief to thousands of former persecutees by turning over all "non-monetary gold" found in Germany—consisting primarily of loot the Nazis had seized from concentration camp inmates—to an international relief organization. This agency, known successively as the Inter-Governmental Committee on Refugees (IGCR), the Preparatory Commission for the International Refugee Organization (PCIRO), and finally the International Refugee Organization (IRO), would also acquire up to $25 million from German assets and heirless victims' assets in neutral countries. The program was a part of the overall reparations agreements and therefore cannot be considered "restitution." It utilized victims' assets and government officials agreed that ninety percent of the funds should assist Jews.

Officials in the State Department endorsed the idea of providing funds to an international relief agency to support resettlement and rehabilitation. President Truman's representative to the Moscow Reparations Conference in the summer of 1945, Edwin Pauley, suggested that the United States, the Soviet Union, and Great Britain establish an "International Board of Trustees" to represent the thousands of individuals made stateless by the Nazi regime, noting that such people "have no government to represent them in making claims either for restitution or reparations."[58] He advised the Allies to set aside a fixed percentage of reparation sums for the International Board of Trustees, to have it operate as a quasi-government to determine which claims would be recognized or dismissed and apportion monies accordingly. "Particular effort should be directed to secure equipment helpful in resettlement for groups of stateless persons in Palestine, or in other parts of the world where there is opportunity for resettlement."[59]

It was certainly in the best interests of Great Britain and the United States to accept these recommendations, Pauley argued, because establishing a reparations fund for stateless individuals would ease the financial burden borne by those two countries. Through large contributions to the Red Cross and UNRRA, private philanthropy, and Army food provisioning, U.S. and British citizens already were paying for the care of refugees and displaced persons. Pauley noted optimistically that, "with the moral and social conscience of the average U.S. and British citizen being what it is, one can rest assured that they will continue to bear this burden as long as they have anything to contribute." Nevertheless, Germany should assume full responsibility for providing the necessary assistance. This could be accomplished by "treating the problem of people who are robbed and made stateless by Hitler as a problem of reparations and restitution."[60] Although Pauley never had an opportunity to present his ideas to other Allied representatives, he did send it to Secretary of State James Byrnes in August 1945 with hopes that "the matter might be raised by you at the Council of Foreign Ministers in London."[61]

It is unknown whether Byrnes agreed to this request, but the idea of establishing an organization to represent stateless claimants—particularly Jews—gained momentum in the autumn of 1945. Chaim Weizmann, on behalf of a newly founded Jewish umbrella committee whose members included the World Jewish Congress, the American Jewish Conference, and the Jewish Agency for Palestine, contacted representatives of the United States, Great Britain, France, and the Soviet Union to demand that the Allies consider the claims of the Jewish people when assessing reparations. Weizmann advocated that if funds were allocated, a portion would go to the Jewish Agency for Palestine, which would use the funds to establish communities in Palestine.[62] A delegation from the committee met with Dean Acheson in October to reiterate these arguments, and American Jewish Committee official Jacob Blaustein visited Byrnes for the same reason.[63]

By late autumn 1945, U.S. officials had decided to raise with the Allies the issue of reparations for persecutees. The leader of the U.S. delegation to the Paris Conference, James W. Angell, provided his French and British counterparts with a summary of the U.S. position on delivering assets to an international organization. "During the negotiations aimed at achieving American aims, U.S. officials consulted with the representatives of Jewish philanthropic organizations and pressured other delegations to make concessions on behalf of Nazi victims."[64] The U.S. representatives managed to achieve a consensus agreement before the conference ended.[65]

Article 8 of the Reparations Agreement provided for an "Allocation of a Reparation Share to Non-Repatriable Victims of German Action." The delegates recognized that "large numbers of persons have suffered heavily at the hands of the Nazis." Although these individuals stood "in dire need of aid to promote their rehabilitation," they would be unable to obtain assistance from any government receiving reparations claims. Therefore, all the non-monetary gold found by the Allies in Germany, up to $25 million from German assets located in neutral countries, and heirless assets "of victims of Nazi action" held in neutral countries would be allocated for "non-repatriable victims." Assistance would be limited to "nationals or former nationals of previously occupied countries who were victims of Nazi concentration camps"; those incarcerated in camps erected by regimes sympathetic to the National Socialists would also be eligible for aid. Furthermore, "refugees from Nazi Germany or Austria" could obtain support if they "cannot be returned to their countries within a reasonable time because of prevailing conditions," while Germans and Austrians still living in those countries might receive assistance "in exceptional cases in which it is reasonable on grounds of humanity to assist such persons to emigrate and providing they emigrate to other countries within a reasonable period." This aid, which would be administered by the Inter-Governmental Committee on Refugees (IGCR), would not be used for individual compensation but instead to "further the rehabilitation or resettlement of persons in the eligible classes."[66]

The Allies postponed discussion of a timetable and procedure for turning the assets over to the IGCR. On June 14, 1946, the United States, Great Britain, France, Czechoslovakia, and Yugoslavia signed an implementation agreement.[67] Significantly, it designated 90 percent of all sums made available for "non-repatriable victims" for Jewish resettlement and rehabilitation. The American Joint Distribution Committee (AJDC) and the Jewish Agency for Palestine would administer these funds, while the IGCR would control the remaining ten percent. Further, neutral countries would transfer 95 percent of heirless victim assets located in their countries to the AJDC and the Jewish Agency for Palestine.[68]

During the summer of 1946, State Department officials constructed a definition of "non-monetary gold" that included many items not containing the precious metal. The Adjutant General of the War Department (AGWAR) informed OMGUS in August that the State Department favored the "broadest possible interpretation" so that the "general financing burden of [the] U.S. will be decreased."[69]

In November 1946, a directive from the Joint Chiefs of Staff to USFET Commanding General McNarney and USFA Commanding General Clark spelled out the definition of "non-monetary gold." The commanders were authorized to release to the IGCR "all valuable personal property which represents loot seized or obtained under duress from political, racial, or religious victims of Nazi

Germany or its satellite governments," so long as the material could not be identified as to its nation of origin and restituted according to general restitution policy.[70] The instructions advised flexibility when determining whether property was eligible for delivery to the relief agency. Items could be released when the "determination of national origin is impractical;" in determining "impracticality," U.S. military authorities were to assess the "extent of commingling with other property and difficulty and expense of determination of ownership in comparison with [the] value of [the] property."[71] In other words, officials in Europe were expected to judge how long it might take to obtain positive identification of items and weigh that against the possible worth of the assets in question. If the investigation seemed to cost more than the value of the asset, they designated the property as "unidentifiable" (thereby not subject to external restitution) and consigned it to the IGCR.

In March 1947, the Council of Foreign Ministers approved the new U.S. definition of "non-monetary gold." In addition, the definition also applied to property seized in the western occupation zones of Austria. [72]

Generals McNarney and Clark received additional instructions for designating the types of materials eligible for release. In cases where assets had become heirless, or where the identification of the owner was deemed "impractical," the IGCR would take possession of the property. This category included items of furniture, clothing, and other personal effects "of uncommon value," but excluded property with only "small intrinsic value." Real property interests located in Germany, German currency, instruments of exchange payable in German currency, and "Jewish books, manuscripts, and literature of cultural or religious importance were to remain under American control pending further instructions."[73]

In this context, the decision to release the contents of the Hungarian "Gold Train" to the relief organization sparked controversy. As Secretary of State George Marshall explained to the U.S. legation in Budapest in 1948, the materials found on the train were "unidentifiable as to owners and, in view of the territorial changes in Hungary, as to national origin." Hungary, an Axis partner of Nazi Germany, had annexed areas of Slovakia, Romania, and Yugoslavia before and during the Second World War. Marshall added that, as a consequence of the territorial changes, "restitution to Hungary [was] therefore not feasible."[74]

As early as December 20, 1945, however, the Temporary Managing Committee of the Central Bureau of Hungarian Jews argued that the United States should return the property to Hungary. The Central Bureau offered a powerful emotional appeal:

> The Jews having been robbed also of everything else they possessed, such as clothes, underwear, furniture, etc. It is not only their undoubted right to claim that the objects stored in the railway-cars under American Control, should be rendered to them, but their demand is justified from humane standpoint too. By recovering a part of the valuables lost, many of them could begin to rebuild their homes and their existence.[75]

The Central Bureau maintained that, except for a relative handful of items, the contents of the Gold Train were confiscated from Jews living under Hungarian jurisdiction, most of them in territories belonging to Hungary as defined by the peace treaty following the First World War. According to Hungarian claims made at the time, the treasures included 10 cases of gold jewelry (45 kg each), 32 cases of gold watches (30–60 kg each), 18 cases of gold jewelry containing gems and semi-precious stones (35 kg each), 1 case of gold coins (100 kg), 1 suitcase containing currency, 1,560 cases filled with silver, 1 case of silver bricks, 3,000 Oriental (Persian) carpets, 100 paintings, and large quantities of furs, porcelain, cameras, and other luxury objects.[76]

Repeated and persistent requests from Hungarian Jewish representatives and the government[77] did not sway U.S. officials, who continued to insist that the property from the train was "unidentifiable." On May 19, 1947, the U.S. Legation to Hungary defended the decision to release the property from the Gold Train to the relief organization:

> With the approval of the United States Government, the Commanding General, U.S. Forces, Austria, determined, that the property should be turned over to the Intergovernmental Committee on Refugees for relief and rehabilitation of non repatriable victims of German action. This means in practice that ninety per cent of proceeds will be disposed of by the American Jewish Joint Distribution Committee and the Jewish Agency for Palestine. This decision was based on the fact that it was impracticable to return individual items to the original owners or heirs and is believed to have been made in [the] best interest of the class which was despoiled.[78]

The Hungarian effort to recover the contents of the Gold Train got nowhere. While there was no policy that allowed for an inspection by a Hungarian Jewish delegation, U.S. authorities appeared insensitive to the pleas of the Hungarian Jews that they be permitted to visit the property warehouse and attempt to identify the assets.

It took two years for the items to appear at auctions in the United States. The IRO opened an office in New York and established a Merchandising Advisory Committee of prominent American businessmen to handle the disposal of assets from the Gold Train along with other property turned over to the relief organization. Crates of Jewish property labeled "unidentifiable as to ownership" started to arrive at Staten Island in mid-December 1947, with initial sales scheduled at the Parke-Bernet Galleries in New York in June 1948. The *New York Times* reported: "In the first [auction], June 16 to 18, jewelry and diamonds will be offered, while in the second, June 20 to 25, silver, glass, china, and gold objects will be put up for bids."[79] The Parke-Bernet staff divided the jewelry into 400 catalogue lots, with three to four pieces in each lot. Items in the jewelry sale included a large miscellaneous collection of unset diamonds along with other precious stones, pearls, gold and jeweled watches, and numerous pieces of Victorian jewelry.[80]

The exact content of the boxes shipped from Europe "were unknown until opened" at the warehouse in New York.[81] The *New York Times* described the scene at the warehouse:

> Laid out on tables were dozens of tinted and cut glass goblets and liqueur glasses, decorative porcelain vases, Bohemian cut sapphire blue and ruby glassware, Meissen, Dresden, Herend, Rosenthal, and Vienna porcelain statuettes and figure groups, eighteenth and nineteenth century Continental pewter flagons and tureens....An estimated 22 tons is on hand, marked and unmarked, used and unused, plain and ornate, consisting of every conceivable shape of platter, tureen, tray and dish, and great quantity of candlesticks, vases and dishes, single and sets.[82]

The warehouse also contained thousands of oriental rugs, as well as cameras, microscopes, tapestries, and thousands of other items.[83] The *New York Times* reported that the sale on June 22, 1948, exceeded expected revenues by 40 percent [84] and the week's receipts totaled $152,850.[85] This and subsequent auctions netted almost $500,000 in sales.[86]

Even today, there is no consensus either on the identifiability of Gold Train property or whether it should have been restituted to Hungary. Some Hungarian scholars assert that it would have been possible to identify the owners of a great number of objects. They argue that although the Hungarian train commander burned the original inventory complete with names and addresses of the owners, various lists and envelopes survived, which might have provided similar information.[87] This contention is based on the records of American Property Control officers who wrote that "lists of names of people from whom some of the items on the train were taken" were found on the Gold Train.[88] Nevertheless, the property was turned over to the IRO for auction.

The IRO did not accept all the assets offered to it. The organization rejected items of "low intrinsic value," such as currency that was no longer valid and considered worthless by the issuing country.[89] The IRO also refused imitation pearls, bracelets in poor condition, pocketknives, fountain pens, and flashlights.[90]

By October 1947, the FED in Germany had delivered $747,367 worth of assets to the Preparatory Commission of the International Refugee Organization (PCIRO, the successor to the IGCR). How much came from Austria is unknown; this valuation must be considered a rough estimate only. Representatives from both the FED and the PCIRO endeavored to assess the items set for release to the IRO, but whereas the U.S. officials relied on French appraisals in francs and current French market values, PCIRO evaluators made their calculations in U.S. dollars and current U.S. market values. The two agencies therefore only came to "tentative agreed valuation."[91] The items obtained included wedding rings, precious metal bars made from melted-down jewelry, precious jewelry, dental gold and platinum, cigarette cases, cameras, china and crystal ware, medallions, clocks and watches, and silverware.[92] U.S. authorities released other assets to the PCIRO and its successor, the IRO, up to 1950. In December 1950, the final balance sheet for the FED showed that the IRO, had obtained 1,197,416 units of undefined content valued at $808,369.[93]

Thus, U.S. military authorities delivered to the relief organization finally known as the International Refugee Organization approximately $800,000 worth of property recovered in Germany and an undetermined amount found in Austria. Most of these assets belonged to Holocaust victims, for they came largely from property discovered at concentration camps. U.S. officials encouraged a quick characterization of property as "unidentifiable" regarding former owner or nationality so that the IRO might more rapidly acquire these assets. The Allies turned property over to the IRO to assist in the resettlement and rehabilitation of former persecutees, so the desire to proceed quickly is certainly understandable.

The Restitution of Identifiable Property in Germany: Law 59

Restitution to victims within Germany, known as "internal restitution," began in late 1947 with the promulgation of Military Government Law 59, entitled the "Restitution of Identifiable Property." Despite the limited measures envisioned by State Department officials in 1944, U.S. planners and military authorities decided to apply a comprehensive legal framework for persons deprived of property "for reasons of race, religion, nationality, ideology or political opposition to National Socialism."[94] The United States imposed this law on its zone of occupation, but the drafting of the legislation as well as its implementation involved cooperation with German authorities as well as Jewish representatives.

Beginning in the summer of 1945, German state officials independently prepared drafts of restitution laws in Bavaria, Baden-Württemberg, and Greater Hesse. U.S. authorities had not requested such proposals and subsequently paid little attention to them.[95] Only after the Property Disposition Board, an agency within OMGUS, recommended in March 1946 that the Stuttgart *Länderrat* (legislature) develop a comprehensive restitution law did U.S. officials begin working extensively with German representatives on this issue.[96]

U.S. policy aimed to return governmental responsibilities to German hands as soon as possible, not only to relieve U.S. forces of many administrative burdens, but also to begin teaching German politicians the precepts of democracy.[97] The American delegation present at the initial meetings concerning restitution clearly stated what it expected the law to entail but allowed the German representatives to craft the proposals. The United States wanted immediate relief measures for individual persecutees, followed by suggestions for returning property to organizations. U.S. officials told their German counterparts that the financing of the restitution program would probably have to come from property confiscated from individual Nazis and party agencies. OMGUS expected a draft law by mid-May 1946, and hoped the legislation might take effect by July.[98]

The United States Military Government found the subsequent *Länderrat* proposals unacceptable because there was no provision for the return of property Aryanized by private citizens. Instead, the *Länderrat* limited restitution to assets the Nazi state had seized and which were then held publicly.[99] Thus began an extended debate in which German officials, American military government authorities, and representatives from five Jewish groups discussed the legislation.[100] The protracted negotiations, slowed by U.S. attempts to gain quadripartite approval, dashed hopes for the speedy enactment of restitution laws in Germany. German representatives still tried to avoid including property held by private citizens, while U.S. and Jewish officials maintained that a presumption of duress had to be assumed for property transfers from Jewish to non-Jewish hands following the promulgation of the discriminatory Nuremberg Laws on September 15, 1935.[101]

Other issues also engendered dispute. No unanimous opinion existed about how to supervise the restitution process. In a draft law of July 25, 1946, Nehemiah Robinson, Director of the Office of Indemnification for the World Jewish Congress, proposed establishing indemnification agencies in each German *Land*. Minister presidents would appoint two officials to oversee each agency, a Jewish representative organization would appoint two individuals, representatives of another category of victims would name one member, and the U.S. Military Governor would designate two other officials from among his personnel. Only two German citizens, moreover, would sit on a five-member review panel.[102] The German *Länderrat* representatives, on the other hand, argued that only Germans should administer the restitution program.[103]

Another point of contention emerged over the disposition of heirless assets. Here significant differences of opinion separated U.S. officials and Jewish representatives. OMGUS authorities initially favored using the assets to help surviving persecutees in Germany, an idea shared by some German Jewish communities.

OMGUS also feared that a large property transfer out of the country might upset the overall economic recovery of Germany. Jewish groups outside Germany believed that a successor organization would make the best use of these funds which could support rehabilitation for and resettlement of Jews in other parts of the world. By late autumn 1946, General Clay subscribed to this latter point of view and agreed with the president of the American Jewish Committee, Joseph M. Proskauer, that OMGUS choose the successor organization. Given the close involvement of U.S. Jewish leaders with the formulation of the restitution law, this agreement increased the likelihood that military authorities would designate a U.S.-led successor organization, as opposed to a German-based agency.[104]

The German legislators never fully agreed with any of the restitution provisions worked out in conjunction with U.S. military authorities and Jewish representatives. The *Länderrat* refused to take political responsibility for enacting such a law, objecting to "certain of its more rigorous aspects" and its possible implementation in only one zone of Germany.[105] Some U.S. officials, too, questioned the desirability of establishing restitution legislation solely in the U.S. Zone of occupation. The promulgation of a military law would raise doubts about how effectively German courts might enforce that law and therefore require the creation of U.S. tribunals.[106] In addition, overall policy still dictated that U.S. officials in Germany seek to obtain agreement among the Allies on such broad issues. In this instance, however, officials in Washington would have been satisfied even if only the British agreed to enact the draft restitution law ready by the summer of 1947.[107]

Such agreement proved elusive. The United States, Great Britain, and France did concur on several important facets of restitution, including the ideas that zone commanders should decide how to dispose of heirless assets, that a presumption of duress transference of property should exist, and that all persecutees should receive equal treatment under the law. The Soviets, alternatively, argued that heirless assets should escheat to the state, that claimants should prove duress, and that the restitution law should exclude former Germans who had accepted a new nationality.[108]

Another major issue dividing all of the powers was the successor organization. The Soviets believed heirless assets should become state property, while the French argued for establishing an agency that would assist all Nazi victims, not merely Jews.[109] Middle East interests helped define the British position. Fearing that assets transferred to an outside Jewish successor organization might be used for augmenting Jewish settlements in British-controlled Palestine, the British urged that heirless property revert to a German relief agency.[110] By the autumn of 1947, the United States, France, and Great Britain came to a compromise: each zone commander could choose the successor organization he wanted. Other issues remained outstanding, including the question of whether claimants or another agency should receive the profits accrued during the period of expropriation.[111] By October 1947, General Clay finally decided to promulgate the restitution law as a military law in the U.S. Zone.[112]

U.S. military authorities insisted on maximum publicity for this legislation, which took effect November 10, 1947. When Clay informed his superiors in Washington that he had chosen to announce the law without waiting any longer for a quadripartite agreement, he stated,

It is important that publicity be given to this law and implementing regulations in all countries of the world. We will make them available to all [military missions] accredited to [the] Allied Control Authority and Consulates accredited to [the military government]. Please request [the State Department] to transmit pertinent documents to every nation and request that each duly publicize them to its own nationals and residents.

Clay requested that the State Department or Department of the Army draw attention to this law within the United States by distributing it to the Federal Register and private publications.[113] By the end of the month, the State Department instructed its overseas missions to convey the substance of the law to foreign governments.[114]

The urgency of General Clay's request stemmed from the realization that many claimants no longer lived in Germany and otherwise would not find out about the new restitution law. Perhaps the primary motivation for the wide and speedy announcement of Military Law 59 had to do with the short deadline for filing claims. According to Article 56, all petitions for restitution had to be submitted by December 31, 1948.[115] The military authorities extended the deadline to June 30, 1949, for "meritorious" claims.[116]

Law 59 aimed to "effect to the largest extent possible the speedy restitution of identifiable property... to persons who were wrongfully deprived of such property within the period from 30 January 1933 to 8 May 1945 for reasons of race, religion, nationality, ideology, or political opposition to National Socialism."[117] Several provisions of this legislation merit attention. First, the law applied only to the U.S. Zone of occupation, including Bremen but not the U.S. sector of Berlin.[118] A presumption of duress existed for properties that had been transferred from persecutees since September 15, 1935 (the promulgation of the first Nuremberg Laws).[119] Anyone found to have obtained property under duress would be liable to the original owner for damages and the profits generated since Aryanization.[120] The law even went so far as to require individuals who even suspected that assets in their possession had been confiscated to report them to the Central Filing Agency by May 15, 1948.[121]

The Central Filing Agency, located in Bad Nauheim, also processed victims' claims for restitution. Significantly, the petitions did not initially require documented proof of former ownership. Claimants submitted a description of the confiscated property along with an accounting of the time, place, and circumstances of its confiscation. Further, petitioners offered the name and address, if either were known, of the potential restitutor.[122]

The filing agency then transferred the petition to a Restitution Agency (or Agencies) in the German state in which the property was located. By mid-April 1948, Bremen, Hesse, Bavaria, and Baden-Württemberg had established such agencies.[123] These offices were responsible for notifying the potential restitutor, or the State Minister of Finance, if the assets had fallen into the custody of the state, and for attempting to reach an amicable settlement. If the parties could not agree to such a settlement, the case would be referred to the Restitution Chamber of the District Court. Three judges—one of whom belonged to the class of persecutees identified by the law—heard the cases referred to this chamber. Claimants or restitutors who disagreed with initial judgments could appeal to the Civil Division of the Court of Appeals (*Oberlandesgerichte*) or, finally, a supreme Board of Review.[124] Only U.S. judges were included on this board.[125]

Finally, the legislation stipulated that the U.S. military authorities designate a successor organization to administer heirless assets and also to obtain title to victims' property unclaimed as of the December 31, 1948 deadline. The U.S.-based Jewish Restitution Successor Organization (JRSO) became the agency empowered to submit such claims.[126]

The Jewish Restitution Successor Organization

The need for a Jewish successor organization to handle heirless assets surfaced before the war's end. In his book, *Indemnification and Reparations—Jewish Aspects*, Nehemiah Robinson of the World Jewish Congress argued that the property of murdered Jews should not escheat to the German state.[127] Instead, these assets ought to be utilized to ameliorate the physical and economic hardships of survivors. He expected most of the survivors to scatter throughout the world and he believed that only an international organization could obtain and distribute the material assistance necessary to support them. His idea gained recognition and acceptance when the conference of the World Jewish Congress decided at its November 1944 meeting to establish a successor organization[128] to assist in the rehabilitation of European Jewry and to help develop Palestine as a Jewish state.[129]

The foundation for what became the Jewish Restitution Successor Organization (JRSO) appeared in the summer of 1945, when five American-based Jewish groups formed a committee to represent Jewish interests in reparations and restitution negotiations. An additional component emerged later that year, when U.S. Jewish religious leaders, scholars, and teachers created the Commission on European Jewish Reconstruction.[130]

In late autumn 1946, General Clay met with representatives of both agencies and agreed to support the designation of a Jewish successor organization to obtain Jewish heirless assets and cultural treasures.[131] On May 15, 1947, "The Jewish Restitution Commission" was incorporated as a charitable organization in New York. The new commission served initially as an umbrella for seven organizations: the Jewish Agency for Palestine, the American Jewish Joint Distribution Committee, the American Jewish Conference, the American Jewish Committee, the World Jewish Congress, the Board of Deputies of British Jews, and the Commission on European Jewish Cultural Reconstruction. In order to achieve full legitimacy as an organization representing the world Jewish community, the Jewish Restitution Commission widened its constituent membership to include agencies such as the Central Committee of Liberated Jews in Germany and the Agudat Israel World Organization.[132] It eventually changed its name to the Jewish Restitution Successor Organization, evidently at the request of American military authorities.[133]

The JRSO was designed to "acquire, receive, hold, maintain and distribute for purposes of Jewish relief, rehabilitation, reconstruction, resettlement, and immigration, the property of Jews, Jewish organizations, cultural and charitable funds and foundations, and communities which were victims of Nazi or Fascist persecution or discrimination."[134] State Department officials quickly accepted the JRSO request for appointment in November 1947, but Major General Daniel Noce, the Chief of Civil Administration of the War Department, objected. He argued that the successor organization must be German and that the assets it acquired had to be used within Germany—precisely the contention raised by American allies and ultimately rejected in the autumn of 1947.[135] His objection extended the delay until June 23, 1948, when OMGUS appointed the JRSO.[136]

The Director General of the JRSO in Germany, Benjamin B. Ferencz, initially believed that the December 31, 1948 deadline for filing claims would be impossible to meet. General Clay refused to grant the JRSO an extension, but he did permit Ferencz to borrow one million Occupation Marks to finance the JRSO operations in the autumn of 1948.[137]

The JRSO employed more than 300 clerks, typists, investigators, and lawyers to work around the clock during the summer and autumn of 1948. Military authorities permitted the JRSO to examine Nazi documents and property control files in the American zone to locate information about confiscated Jewish property. Such evidence included real estate registries, commercial registries, tax returns, bank files, pawnbroker records, and notary records.[138] Ferencz and his team copied all entries containing "Jewish-sounding names."[139] JRSO officials also examined reports filed by Germans in possession of duress properties.[140] Of course, the JRSO did not have access to the records or recollections of families that had been scattered or even worse, killed.

According to the JRSO, its employees managed to produce eight copies of each claim at a rate of 2,000 per day. By December 1948, it had lodged over 163,000 claims at the Central Filing Office in Bad Nauheim. The organization later recognized that it had no time initially to determine whether heirs still existed for some properties. Instead, its policy had been to "claim everything and later sort the wheat from the chaff."[141] Despite the few months with which it had to operate, the JRSO observed in 1953 that "nothing has appeared in the past five years to indicate that substantial assets were overlooked in [its] desperate rush to safeguard Jewish interests."[142]

Having amassed the claims, the JRSO next worked to determine how many duplicates existed. The JRSO discovered that not only did it "compete" with petitions completed by previous owners before the 1948 deadline, but also it received demands from individuals months and even years later for assets the JRSO had claimed as "heirless."

"We were not out to enrich the JRSO," Ferencz explained. Rather, the organization's aim was to provide assistance to Jews worldwide as quickly as possible. "We were under great pressure to liquidate our holdings; we couldn't wait with these properties to see if someone would eventually claim them." The idea was to "get [the assets] to where they were needed as soon as possible."[143] By mid-1954, the JRSO had released assets amounting to $3.5 million to claimants.[144]

Another imposing obstacle remained before the distribution of material relief could begin. Many German restitutors balked at making amicable settlements because they expected a new, less severe restitution law. Because of the delay, more cases had to be adjudicated in court and took time to resolve. In February 1950, JRSO officials suggested to the American High Commissioner for Germany, John J. McCloy, that the organization approach the *Länder* and negotiate lump-sum settlements. McCloy reacted enthusiastically to this idea and arranged meetings between JRSO representatives and German state officials.[145]

Negotiations between the two groups encountered many problems, and over a year passed before Hesse became the first *Land* to settle with the JRSO. It offered almost $6 million to the successor organization, whittled down by "various deductions and deletions" to about $4 million.[146] In 1951, Bremen agreed to transfer almost $500,000 to the JRSO, while Württemberg-Baden conceded approximately $2.5 million. Bavaria followed in 1952 by promising about $4.8 million.[147] Although the settlements transferred assets to the JRSO rapidly, the director of the organization in Germany remained dissatisfied with the entire process. Benjamin B. Ferencz told the *New York Times*, "we are selling under duress because we are afraid of what will happen when the Germans take over." He continued, "at best, we can only wind up with a poor amelioration of the desperate plight in which the Jews find themselves in tents in Israel, while the Germans will retain the Jews' former homes and properties."[148]

Problems with Restitution

Restitution under Law 59 did not proceed smoothly. The Military Government's strict adherence to the December 31, 1948, deadline meant that some victims failed to file claims in time. Individuals sometimes discovered that the JRSO had submitted a claim for their property and they then turned to the successor organization for restitution; the JRSO handled over 4,800 such claims by 1955.[149] After internal discussion,[150] the JRSO agreed to restitute property to such claimants even though it had obtained title to such assets under Military Law 59.[151] It did, however, assess a service charge to the late petitioners to cover its costs. The fees depended on the relationship of the claimant to the former owner and the appraisal of the property. If the JRSO had actually recovered a property, a surcharge of ten percent augmented these costs (although the organization reduced this to five percent if a claimant was indigent).[152]

One claimant sharply criticized U.S. authorities for "awarding" her property to the JRSO. She argued that she had not heard about the filing deadline until after it had passed, and instead discovered that, "I shall be punished because the Occupation Army, for whom my husband and I pay plenty, deems it right to take my property and gives it to who knows whom."[153] The frustration and anger expressed in this letter likely mirrored the sentiments of other claimants who missed the deadline; individuals hurled "demands" and "protests" at the JRSO for the immediate return of their property.[154]

In 1948, the introduction of currency reform—the Deutschmark replaced the Reichsmark—in the western German zones of occupation caused the "greatest difficulties" for restitution progress, according to a HICOG official.[155] Different conversion rates covered different debts:

> The exchange ratio was graded according to the nature of the debt: wages, salaries and rents were transposed at the ratio of 1–1, mortgages and other private debts at the rate of 1:10. Holders of bank deposits and cash had to be satisfied with an exchange ratio of DM 6.5 : RM 100. Altogether 93.5 percent of the former stock of Reichsmark was withdrawn from circulation.[156]

The variation produced tension between claimants and restitutors; disagreements about the real worth of a given asset reduced the willingness of disputants to settle claims amicably and forced court proceedings.[157] In Baden-Württemberg, "The arbitrators frequently practice agreements on the ground 10:5 that are accepted both by the restitutors and the claimants,"[158] but for those unwilling to agree to such a formula, court action delayed the return of property, or an equivalent sum, to claimants.

Another problem afflicting restitution concerned the size of the endeavor itself. Given the magnitude of the program, potential for fraud existed. The Property Control Division of OMGUS held ultimate authority for supervising the return of so-called "duress property," but it also possessed responsibility for seizing, holding, and disposing of several other categories of assets, including those belonging to National Socialists and their organizations. Between 1945 and 1949, Property Control took custody of 153,759 properties, estimated to be worth RM 13,745 million.[159] Significantly, German citizens performed many of the daily operations as American military government authorities in 1946 swiftly began transferring administrative responsibilities to German Property Control offices in the various *Länder*.[160] Between two and three thousand German civilians worked for the *Land* Civilian Agencies and their supporting county agencies. The approximately 80,000 property custodians who were "responsible for operating and preserving the assets of the property,"[161] greatly augmented the number of German personnel involved in property control administration.[162]

Although the American Counter Intelligence Corps (CIC) checked their backgrounds,[163] not all custodians proved themselves honest and reliable. During the first three months of 1948, *Land* property control officials conducted about 3,500 formal inspections of properties in custody and subsequently recommended the removal of 54 custodians due to a variety of abuses including black market activities, political unreliability, embezzlement, failure to comply with military government directives, illegal sale of assets, and gross negligence. Many of the custodians were fined or jailed.[164] U.S. officials also charged that in Bavaria, restitution agencies did not consider claims in numerical order, "but rather act only where it is more likely that the claim will be partially, or totally, rejected."[165]

Questions of personal impropriety also surfaced within the higher levels of the restitution administration. Dr. Sebastian Endres, the Head of the Bavarian *Land* Central Office for Restitution, retained that position even after the Office of Military Government (OMG) for Bavaria obtained information that he had employed slave labor during the Third Reich. According to a report filed in October 1948, Endres had managed an Aryanized machine factory, becoming a "fanatic war sympathizer" and doing "everything possible to include the firm in the war effort." By 1941 the firm had employed slave laborers, and "as early as 19 May 1941 [Endres] requested radical treatment for these prisoners." The report continued, "with the coming of steady defeats in Russia and the realization that the war was probably lost, Endres began having the slave laborers in the firm beaten, starved, and brutally over-worked punishing them not only for minor mistakes but also for exhaustion."[166] Despite this information and subsequent complaints levied against him, Endres remained in his position at least through April 1951.[167]

Along with Endres, other Germans administering restitution in Bavaria raised suspicions. OMG Bavaria surveyed the professional and personal histories of officials involved with restitution and provided a list of those whose backgrounds appeared most dubious. Several had been members of the Nazi party, though one had been "exonerated" by denazification courts and one had filed a restitution claim himself. The Chief of Field Operations for Property Control, Werner Loewenthal, queried: did American supervision of the restitution program include "the responsibility to assure the political reliability of personnel" or allow the employment of persecutees who sought assets?[168] Loewenthal's question indicates uneasiness within the Property Control Division that German officials with suspect sympathies might impede restitution efforts.

Not surprisingly, many German restitutors hesitated before relinquishing "their" property. As early as 1946, the first *Land* representatives charged with constructing restitution legislation knew that such a law would prove unpopular and refused to enact restitution measures once the Americans insisted on the presumption of duress. By 1949, however, German restitutors sought to delay proceedings, evidently because they believed the severity of the law would ease. The Property Division for OMG Bavaria noted in January 1949 that "there are indications of passive resistance to [Law 59]. Influential German citizens affected by the law believe that Military Government will make modifications if the program does not run smoothly," so they undertook efforts to delay any restitution action.[169] A later report provided details of the delaying tactics: individuals waited until the last possible moment to respond to restitution notices and then requested a postponement of hearings.[170]

In February 1949, the Property Division Branch in Bavaria claimed that "cases involving influential people are being postponed and apprehension exists that, unless Military Government maintains an active interest in these courts, the program will take a similar trend to that of the denazification law"—meaning that its current prosecution would weaken or even become more favorable to the "Aryanizer."[171]

The Restitution Section of the Ministry of Justice in Baden-Württemberg shared this assessment. Officials there contended that Germans affected by claims "take the standpoint that in the restitution case [it] will be the same as in the denazification, i.e. the more the procedure is prolonged the more favorable will be [the] decision for the restitutor." Further, many believed that the new Federal Republic, established May 23, 1949, would promulgate a single restitution law to replace the four existing statutes present in each of the three Allied territories and Berlin. Restitutors hoped that the new legislation would be "modeled after the mildest" law then in place.[172]

Such notions gained political currency when, in November 1949, a political party (the *Freie Demokratische Partei*) submitted a motion for uniform restitution legislation to the German Parliament (*Bundestag*).[173] This act received "wide publicity by the German press and radio," according to an official with the Internal Restitution Supervision Branch.[174] The Acting Advisor on Jewish Affairs to the U.S. Commands in Germany and Austria, Major Abraham S. Hyman, quickly responded to this political maneuvering. He countered that to ignore the motion "would encourage other parties to consolidate their strength in a drive to dilute the restitution laws" and that without swift opposition, restitutors might gain false expectations that a new, milder law would soon emerge and thus continue to reject amicable settlements. Major Hyman presented his concerns to American High Commissioner John J. McCloy, who in turn declared publicly that the Americans would tolerate no weakening of Military Law 59.[175]

In addition to the delaying tactics adopted by restitutors, the lack of speed with which German authorities settled claims concerned U.S. supervisors. OMGUS informed the Military Governments in the *Länder* in January 1949 that "deficiencies" in "administrative requirements and adequate financial allowances" had begun to hinder restitution efforts. Military authorities in these states were directed to ensure that "responsibility for administration and supervision should be vested in a competent administrative official," that "sufficient qualified personnel should be authorized to cope with present and future work-load[s]," that "adequacy of facilities" for all restitution offices "must be assured," and "adequate budgetary allowances to meet requirements in personnel, facilities and supplies must be assured through specific financial appropriations and allocations."[176]

Later that month, Fred Hartzsch, the Chief of the Property Control and External Assets Branch, Property Division, OMGUS, along with the Chief of the Claims Section, John Porter, toured the *Länder* to review property control and restitution issues. In Bremen they found that "on the basis of the number of petitions received and the processing of such petitions, the record . . . is on the whole good."[177] In Hesse, on the other hand, Porter noted that German "restrictions presently existing on employment of personnel, the reductions in personnel, and the reclassification of personnel [were] seriously impairing the proper functioning of the [restitution] Agencies and Courts." Porter suggested that the Deputy Director for Military Government in Hesse, Sheehan, discuss this problem with appropriate German officials "to secure sufficient budgetary appropriations and allocations for the expansion of organization and personnel required for the execution of the restitution program."[178]

In Baden-Württemberg, similar personnel and financial difficulties existed. Here, however, resistance from German officials evidently posed the greatest hindrance. Porter revealed that "the Ministry of Justice [in Württemberg-Baden] had made a direct appeal for intervention to secure sufficient financial allowances in order effectively to do what is necessary in connection with the restitution program which had thus far been met with outright refusal on the part of the German governmental officials." Another U.S. official, Zinn Garret, confirmed Porter's allegation and mentioned that he had already drafted a letter to the Minister President of the *Land* "designed to correct this situation."[179] In Bavaria, too, Porter advised that a letter should be sent to the Minister President to secure additional resources for speeding up the restitution program.[180]

A U.S. official in Bavaria, Harold S. Kidder, provided an example in April 1949 of how the German restitution bureaucracy tended to move very slowly. He surmised that his district held the largest number of duress properties—almost 4,000—in Bavaria. "One should expect the [restitution] agencies would be very busy. To date, to my knowledge there has been no meeting of the Restitution Chambers," even though at least seventeen cases had been sent to them. The committee designed to effect amicable settlements held only four to six meetings per month. Although Kidder prodded the restitution officials to speed matters along, "nothing has been done."[181]

Despite the efforts of U.S. officials to pressure German restitution authorities, by the end of November 1949, restitution agencies throughout the American zone had disposed of only 12 percent of the cases received. The Chief of the Internal Restitution Supervision Branch, W. M. Loewenthal, estimated that at this rate the agencies would require about four years to settle all claims. He calculated that about 23 percent of cases would require adjudication in restitution chambers; at the 1949 rate, litigation of these cases would not end until almost 1958.[182] Loewenthal proposed an almost four-fold increase in settlements per month in each *Land*.[183]

Nevertheless, by October 1950, as many as two-thirds of individual claims remained unresolved.[184] In an attempt to expedite the process, the Office of the

High Commissioner for Germany amended Law 59. The first amendment reduced stays of proceedings that the restitution agencies and chambers could grant claimants from six to three months. Second, losing parties in restitution cases would bear court fees and costs. This measure meant to dissuade those who filed appeals primarily to delay final settlement.[185] Years continued to pass before restitution in Germany concluded, but the pace of efforts certainly increased. By the end of 1953, almost 93 percent of individual claims had been settled.[186]

Berlin

Military Law 59 did not apply to Berlin. The city nevertheless contained much property once belonging to victims; the Deputy Chief of the OMGUS Property Division, W.J. Dickmann, revealed that over 1,500 duress properties had been seized by April 1948.[187] The negotiations among the Allies in Berlin about restitution policy remain unclear, but on July 26, 1949, the United States, Great Britain, and France issued the Berlin Kommandatura Order (49) 180. As in the U.S. Zone, restitution agencies and chambers administered claims for victims' property, and litigants could appeal claims to the Board of Review, consisting of judges from the United States.[188] By December 1973 over DM 463 million had been restituted to individual claimants in West Berlin.[189]

Restitution Efforts in Austria

Restitution efforts in Austria differed somewhat from those in Germany. As in Germany, U.S. Reparations, Deliveries, and Restitution Division (RD&R) authorities administered external restitution. But unlike Germany, where American officials administered internal restitution, in Austria a new democratically elected government was responsible for enacting and implementing internal restitution policy. Although they maintained a supervisory role, the Allied powers entrusted Austrian authorities with the task of restituting victims' assets that had been Aryanized while Austria was part of the Reich (1938–1945). This peculiar arrangement resulted from the Allies' declaration in Moscow on November 1, 1943 that their governments regarded the German annexation (*Anschluss*) of Austria on March 15, 1938, as "null and void," that Austria was the "first free country to fall a victim to Hitlerite aggression," and that they wished to "see re-established a free and independent Austria."[190] They added, however, that Austria, despite its status as a "liberated" nation, still had "a responsibility, which she cannot evade, for participation in the war" at the side of Nazi Germany.[191]

At the Yalta Conference in February 1945, the Allies decided that Austria, like Germany, would be divided into four zones of occupation. United States Forces in Austria (USFA) was created from the Supreme Allied Command Mediterranean Theater and placed under the command of General Mark Clark. When Allied armies divided Austria into four separate zones of occupation, they permitted, if not encouraged, Austria to reestablish first a provisional, then an elected, federal government soon after hostilities ceased. Furthermore, they reserved the right to ensure the "protection, care, and restitution of property belonging to the Governments [sic] of any of the United Nations or their nationals."[192] U.S. officials thus became responsible for locating and returning those assets located in their zone of occupation.

U.S. Army units discovered several large repositories of looted assets in Austria. These assets had accumulated in the Austrian "redoubt" because of the presence of safe storage facilities and also because the German Army maintained control of that area until the end of the war.[193] In order to locate and identify stolen assets, other than those found in the large repositories, within Austria generally and in their zone in particular, U.S. authorities released with the other occupying powers a "Decree on the Declaration and Registration of Property Belonging to the United Nations."[194] This regulation took effect on May 25, 1946, and it required all institutions and private individuals to declare within thirty days all the looted movable property and assets valued at more than 500 Schillings in their possession.[195]

External Restitution

The evidence documenting American external restitution from both Germany and Austria did not distinguish between assets belonging to Holocaust victims and non-victims. It is nevertheless clear that American troops discovered property belonging to victims of the Holocaust in Austria, especially at the Alt-Aussee salt mine. Several caves there contained paintings, furniture, and other items owned by "important Jewish families such as Rothschild, Bondi, Pollak, Gutmann" and others.[196]

American restitution officials accepted claims up to January 19, 1949.[197] A report issued by the American High Commissioner for Austria on October 1, 1950, revealed that U.S. forces had received a total of 3,989 claims, of which they disallowed 2,940.[198] Total restitution amounted to over 3,000 freight cars worth of assets valued at $198 million.[199] A document published about a year earlier, with approximately 88 percent of the restitution program completed, offered a more detailed analysis of the types of materials returned to countries. For instance, as of July 31, 1949, RD&R had restituted over $155 million of art, more than 90 percent of it to the government of Austria. Industrial equipment amounted to about $21 million, transport equipment approximately $11 million, and "other properties" restituted totaled close to $10 million.[200]

Internal Restitution

The Austrian government enacted legislation concerning internal restitution soon after the end of the war. These laws, which the American Property Control Branch widely publicized in the United States, dealt with looted property held by the state and individuals, as well as the restitution of pensions, wages, and so forth for those whom the Nazis forced out of work.[201] As of September 30, 1952, a total of 43,475 claims had been filed under the main restitution laws, including 30,398 pertaining to cases of individuals holding Aryanized property.[202] This document, unfortunately, failed to list a total value for these claims.

Before the Allies signed the State Treaty with Austria in 1955, they could by unanimous consent annul legislation passed by the Austrian parliament.[203] Not all of the restitution laws received unanimous approval from the occupying powers, but all took effect. In the early 1950s, however, when the Austrian parliament attempted to weaken certain aspects of the restitution legislation (allowing Aryanizers to reclaim enterprises already restituted, for instance), the Allied Commission objected. The parliament never enacted this "Reacquisition Law," as it was known.[204]

As the occupation ended, the Allies sought to ensure that Austria fulfilled its obligation to return property looted from victims. The treaty of 1955 specifically provided that Austria was responsible for disposing of assets confiscated from those persecuted because of race or religion. As far as possible, Austrian authorities were to return property to former owners, or grant compensation when restitution was "impossible." Heirless or assets unclaimed after six months would be transferred to the control of the Austrian government. The Austrians would then deliver "such property, rights, and interests to appropriate agencies or organizations" that the Allies would designate. These assets would then be used "for the relief and rehabilitation of victims of persecution by the Axis Powers."[205]

Recovery of Property in the United States

American officials imposed strict controls on assets belonging to foreign nationals during the war years. On August 8, 1946, Congress passed legislation amending the Trading with the Enemy Act so that former persecutees or their heirs could reclaim their property. Congress defined the persecutees as individuals "deprived of life or substantially deprived of liberty pursuant to any law, decree, or regulation [or who were victims of] discrimination against political, racial, or religious groups...in an enemy country."[206] As a later report issued by the Senate Committee on the Judiciary characterized this legislation, "by this amendment a necessary and clear-cut distinction was effected between the property of those individuals who were in fact our enemies in the last war, and those who by their extreme persecution at the hands of their governments were the 'enemies of our enemies' and our own allies."[207]

Unblocking Assets at the FFC

Just as the Treasury Department initiated control of foreign assets well before the United States entered the Second World War, so it started to consider the issue of how to end those controls in January 1944, well before hostilities ended.[208] The end of controls involved efforts on two tracks for Foreign Funds Control. The agency developed an extensive "defrosting" program designed to end wartime controls of "frozen" assets while ensuring the exposure of enemy interests in such accounts; it additionally sought to end restrictions on trade and imports, while preventing looted assets from reaching the market. The defrosting program relied heavily on cooperation with the governments of liberated and neutral nations. Faced with declining resources, and pressed to terminate the wartime controls with all due speed, the FFC decentralized the procedure, devolving responsibility for the certification of assets to foreign governments. The overall program was generally successful, since the majority of all frozen assets were eventually certified and unblocked. FFC's efforts with respect to looted property are more difficult to judge. While the wartime restrictions on trade and imports were quickly removed, the issue of looted property lingered and responsibility for U.S. efforts eventually passed from the FFC, which ceased operations in September 1948, to the Office of Alien Property.

Defrosting

The Treasury Department did not intend to maintain controls on foreign funds beyond the point where they were essential.[209] "It is the intention of the Treasury Department," Acting Foreign Funds Control (FFC) Director Orvis

Schmidt said in a speech on October 9, 1944, "to relax and eliminate them as rapidly as can be done consistent with the protection of American financial interests and the completion of Foreign Funds Control's wartime objectives."[210] These objectives included:

- protection of American creditors deprived during the war period of their normal recourse against foreign debtors;

- protection of American financial institutions against adverse claims resulting from conflicts over ownership or control of foreign companies, doubtful validity of transfers of property under enemy occupation, payment orders executed under duress, and other consequences of the confused commercial and financial situation emerging from the war;

- insuring against concealment or release of enemy assets held through non-enemy financial institutions; and

- prevention of the completion of transactions effected under duress or for the benefit of the enemy.[211]

Such objectives could not, however, be met unless there was an "orderly transition" and a "gradual removal of controls" in a defrosting program,[212] at the very least because the situations in enemy-occupied (France, Norway, Belgium, Holland), enemy (Germany, Japan), and neutral countries (Switzerland, Sweden, Spain, Portugal) differed.[213] "A lack of safeguards at the time of the lifting of freezing restrictions," a contemporary analysis noted, "would cause harm to many legitimate interests."[214]

The issue of cloaked or looted assets, and of financial transactions carried out under duress, loomed large. The United States—at least in the view of the Chief Counsel and Associate Chief Counsel of the FFC—"was committed to supporting an international program for 'preventing the liquidation of property looted by the enemy'," as Resolution VI at Bretton Woods had stated.[215] A simple lifting of controls might allow "frozen" transactions that had been made under duress to be completed, cloaked assets in neutral countries would enter the marketplace, and the lifting of wartime import restrictions might turn the United States into a major market for looted securities. Worse, "the unqualified release of frozen funds...might easily result in the surrender of frozen funds to the enemy" or "to those adherents of the enemy's cause who will seek to continue their warfare into the postwar period."[216] The parallels with the beginning of the war were not lost on the FFC: "We find that considerations very similar to those which led to the original application of the freezing controls make it strongly undesirable to completely wipe out the controls immediately after the liberation of the country by Allied armed might," acting FFC Director Orvis Schmidt put it in October of 1944.[217] This view suggested that similar policy solutions were in order, in this case adopting a "certification" program (like the wartime "licensing") that permitted legitimate transactions but tried to control undesirable transactions.[218] The gradual, successive "freezing" of assets before and during the war suggested a gradual, successive "defrosting" of assets after the war. There was also a sense that if the United States had acted as a trustee in freezing foreign property, "it would be anomalous to permit such a trust relation to serve as a medium for putting owners in a worse position than that which they enjoyed at the time when the relationship was created."[219]

Process

Defrosting was a three-step process. First, the United States reopened communication with liberated areas between November 1944 and May 1945. Each liberated area was declared to be no longer "enemy territory," and hence its residents were no longer "enemy nationals" and thus no longer subjected to General Ruling 11 that had prohibited trade and communication with the enemy unless authorized by license.[220] Adequate machinery, according to the FFC, had to be established in the liberated area to prohibit certain transactions, such as:

a) the completion of payments, transfers, withdrawals, or other transactions effected under duress, compulsion, or other unlawful means during the period of occupation;

b) the recognition of changes of ownership, powers of attorney, changes in signing authority, or the consummation or validation of other transactions effected under duress and compulsion even though ostensibly legalized by enemy decrees; and

c) the dissipation or hiding of funds owned by or cloaked for enemy interests or persons collaborating with them, or by the completion of any other transactions benefiting such persons.

Initially, these assurances were obtained from the Allied military authorities operating within the liberated area.[221]

By May 1945, all formerly occupied European countries were no longer "enemy territory." The ban on communication with Bulgaria, Hungary, Romania, and the Allied-occupied parts of Italy was lifted in October 1944, but for Germany and Japan this ban was not lifted until March 1947.[222]

The second step, carried out from October to December 1945, started business and financial transactions with European countries anew. As a matter of policy, the United States wanted the post-liberation governments to take over the responsibility for meeting the objectives of freezing control, and ensure that "no transactions effected under duress were permitted to be consummated contrary to the wishes of the rightful owners of the funds."[223] Yet foreign-controlled property remained blocked in the United States, and transactions in such property still required licenses.

Thus, only new, postwar financial transactions were defrosted in this second stage. The United States permitted trade and commerce, with the dollars consequently generated considered "free" rather than "frozen." To start this process, FFC removed existing controls on financial transactions country by country. This was a rather inefficient way to relax controls, and so on December 7, 1945, General License 94 unblocked all current transactions and all new dollar assets in all blocked countries (excepting Germany, Japan, the four European neutrals, Liechtenstein, and Tangier).[224]

Two of the provisions of General License 94 were particularly relevant to individuals. Nationals of specified blocked countries who were not in a blocked country had their property immediately unblocked, and newly created "free" foreign-owned assets did not need to be reported in the United States.[225] Securities still needed certification, however, and had to be surrendered (under General Ruling 5) if imported into the United States.[226] Suspicion remained that property ostensibly owned by the nationals of friendly countries was in fact secretly owned by enemies. Neutral nations were also excluded from General Ruling 94 "until they have taken effective action to search out, immobilize, and control all enemy assets within their jurisdiction,"[227] with the result that Switzerland and Liechtenstein remained blocked until late November 1946. Germany, Japan, and Sweden were unblocked in March of 1947; Spain and Portugal followed in 1948.[228]

The third step was the certification process. The United States demanded that foreign governments investigate and ascertain the true ownership of blocked property. Certification would be supplied by an official government agency that would verify the ownership of the property, thereby placing the responsibility for determining ownership on the foreign government. To "give the liberated countries free scope in dealing with wartime transfers according to their own laws, a simple test was applied: What was the ownership of the property on the effective date of the [U.S.] Freezing Order?"[229] General License 95 (December 29, 1945) initiated this certification procedure, and agreements were negotiated with France, Belgium, Norway, and Finland by that date, as well as subsequently with the Netherlands (February 13, 1946), Czechoslovakia and Luxembourg (April 26, 1946), Denmark (June 14, 1946), Greece (October 15, 1946), Switzerland and Liechtenstein (November 20, 1946), Poland (January 7, 1947), Austria (January 16, 1947), and Sweden (March 28, 1947).[230] Once property was certified, it was no longer regarded as blocked.[231]

Victims and Certification

Demanding certification from foreign governments relieved the FFC of certain practical problems, such as that it lacked the manpower or appropriate knowledge about local situations abroad to be able to ascertain true ownership. But there were larger political problems as well. Only the country where a blocked national resided exercised the legal and political jurisdiction to conduct the appropriate investigation. While many asset owners would have preferred independent action by U.S. authorities so as to prevent the disclosure of their assets to fiscal authorities in their home countries, the U.S. Treasury Department had no authority to investigate, meaning it was "virtually impossible for the Treasury Department to attempt to ascertain the real ownership of property held by residents of foreign countries."[232] A certification program restricted to U.S.-led investigations might have allowed enemy assets to escape detection. The FFC "did not countenance schemes which would have required a sacrifice of our objectives—to discover enemy assets held in the United States in the names of nationals of the liberated countries—in order to assist these foreign nationals to avoid the regulations of their own governments."[233]

The first law allowing the return of property seized under the Trading With the Enemy Act (TWEA) failed to incorporate all the legislative needs of victims seeking return of their property in the United States. Subsection 32(a), added to the TWEA on March 8, 1946, when Congress amended the First War Powers Act of 1941, allowed the return of property to non-enemy aliens. It specifically prevented individuals from seeking the return of their property under 32 (a)(2) if they had voluntarily resided in, or were citizens of, nations with which the United States had been at war at any time since December 7, 1941.[234] Although the inclusion of terms such as "voluntarily" and "citizenship" seemingly would have granted Jews and other victims the authority to make claims, ambiguities as to the exact status of victim claimants remained.

Congress amended Section 32(a), on August 8, 1946, so that "technical" enemies could regain their property under this Section. The new provisos, added to subsections (c) and (d) by this amendment created an exception for individuals who had been "deprived of life or substantively deprived of liberty pursuant to any law, decree or regulation of such nation discriminating against political, racial, or religious groups." Such individuals were not "deemed to have voluntarily resided in such territory" or to have "enjoyed the full rights of citizenship...of such nation." [235] This amendment gave persecutees the same status as nationals of formerly occupied countries.

Transfer of Responsibility to the OAP

By January 1947, a little over a year after the defrosting process began, it was clear to Treasury that the pace of decontrol was too slow to allow the operations of FFC to end by mid-1947 as planned. Although FFC reckoned that in early 1947 three-quarters of all certifiable assets had been put under license, "substantial amounts" nevertheless remained uncertified.[236] French and Swiss certifications, especially, appeared to be lagging.[237] Officials at FFC believed that owners of blocked assets were reluctant to come forward because that property had escaped taxes or exchange restriction. Such assets might also fall under an immediate conversion requirement into domestic currency at a time when exchange rates were unstable. The main reason for holding dollar-denominated assets had been preservation of capital values in real terms. The fact that some assets would remain uncertified because whole families had been exterminated and there simply were no owners or heirs to apply for certification never entered the policy discussion.[238]

The Departments of Treasury and Justice, in consultation with the Department of State, decided in April 1947 to put all uncertified property under threat of vesting as of a specified date. Officials in these departments believed that this could be accomplished without sacrificing the anonymity of the owners of blocked assets, even though OAP had some doubts that this could be achieved under current legal authority.[239] The program finally adopted was embodied in a letter, dated February 2, 1948, from Treasury Secretary Snyder to the Chairman of the Senate Foreign Affairs Committee, Arthur H. Vandenberg. Secretary Snyder stated that information on dollar holdings belonging to nationals of countries receiving aid under the European Recovery Program (ERP)—the Marshall Plan— would be shared with those countries so that they could exert better control over such holdings and, moreover, lessen the burden of ERP on U.S. taxpayers. Furthermore, the plan gave notice that, as a last step, consideration would be given to the vesting of assets that remained blocked on the presumption of enemy interests therein.[240]

On March 1, 1948, Secretary of Treasury Snyder announced that as of June 1, 1948, Treasury would cease to have jurisdiction over blocked foreign funds. On that date, responsibility for any funds remaining would be transferred to OAP.[241] Attorney General Clark joined Secretary Snyder in urging that those who could avail themselves of the certification procedure do so promptly because the licensing system would cease after June 1. A census, to be taken immediately after that date, would disclose the value and the beneficial ownership of assets still blocked and such disclosure would be shared with the governments of the relevant countries. Assets for which ownership could not be ascertained would be vested, as would those held in Swiss and Liechtenstein accounts. Assets proven to contain no enemy interest would be released whether vested or not.[242]

The 1948 census of blocked assets revealed that a surprisingly large amount— $956.9 million—still remained uncertified as of June 1948. Assets of individuals from countries benefiting from the ERP accounted for $491.3 million of this sum.

OAP – Divesting and Unblocking

Two years after assuming the frozen asset program, OAP took a census of property still blocked as of October 2, 1950, belonging to nations participating in the ERP. This yielded 6,900 reports covering approximately $140 million worth of assets. By mid-1951, OAP had issued 231 vesting orders covering approximately $7.5 million, on the basis of the program laid out in the February 2, 1948, letter sent by Treasury Secretary Snyder to Senator Vandenberg.[243] Victims' heirless assets might have been commingled with these assets.

With the termination of the vesting program in April 1953, OAP also took the final step to end blocked property controls as they applied to Western Europe and Japan. OAP considered that with the Snyder–Vandenberg program virtually completed—only an estimated $15 million remained blocked—final release of the blocked property of these countries was appropriate. This was accomplished on June 27, 1953, by the issuance of General License No. 101 and the revocation of other restrictive rulings. Only some looted securities and property belonging to countries located in the Soviet sphere remained blocked.[244]

The release of the last $15 million in blocked assets for which no application had been received over the seven years since defrosting had begun raises the question of whether this amount contained victims' property; some of these assets might not have been claimed because the previous owners and their heirs had been murdered.

OAP and Other Victim Assets

In 1953, a Senate Judiciary Subcommittee delving into the activities of the OAP sharply criticized the agency for lack of good business practices in the way it handled its own affairs and the assets under its control. The report particularly singled out the "inefficient and dilatory" manner in which claims were being handled. Of approximately 15,000 title claims, only about 6,000 had been processed. The average length for processing a claim in 1952 was 46.6 months, while the overall average (including other years) was 31.7 months.[245]

The Commission staff draw a sample of 90 vesting orders, covering 150 claims, drawn from a known set of JRSO claims with the presumption that this set would include a large number of victims' assets. The sample revealed that the average claim indeed took more than three years. These cases represent instances where the JRSO interest conflicted with that of living beneficial owners. The sample helps illuminate how the OAP handled both victims' and non-victims' claims.[246]

The set of 150 claims analyzed included 35 victim cases.[247] These were compared with 35 non-victim cases drawn from the same set and a sample of 35 stateless cases, drawn separately and not analyzed in detail.[248] The average time from claim through disposition for all 150 claims was 44 months. Victims' claims on average took somewhat less time than those of non-victims. These nevertheless still lasted more than three years—38 months—as compared with 51 months for non-victims. Claims filed by stateless individuals took an average of 42 months to process. The Commission staff presumed that this included a fairly significant percentage of victim cases. Of the non-victim and stateless cases, more than 40 percent took over four years as compared with over one-third for the victim group. Values of assets returned, after exclusion of a few claims whose worth placed them at the extreme edges of the sample, averaged $1,701 for victim claims and $2,919 for non-victim ones.[249]

No noticeable relaxation of the rules or procedures facilitated victims' claims. The relative speed with which the OAP concluded these cases likely reflects the fact that the agency did not need to explore a claimant's background once victim status had been proven.

Heirs faced more challenges than named account holders. Many case histories demonstrated that the initial claimant died during the claim process. In those circumstances, OAP conducted further investigations, which delayed cases that might have been at the brink of conclusion. In one case involving patents, a Norwegian filed a notice on January 31, 1944. The claimant died in 1947, leaving seven beneficiaries: two Norwegians, four British residents and one Austrian national. OAP investigated each beneficiary, all of whom were found to have been subject to the Nuremberg laws. Two had been trapped on enemy territory while in the process of emigration while two had been recognized in England for their intelligence service work after the war. It still took until September 1955 to complete the case.

The JRSO and Recovery of Heirless Assets in the United States

The legislation adopted in the United States in August 1946 allowing the release of property to former persecutees did not include consideration of heirless property. By 1949, however, the Senate passed a measure to remedy this shortcoming; in 1954, the Congress approved a law permitting a successor organization to claim heirless assets. In 1955, President Eisenhower appointed the JRSO as this agency. In the next few years, the JRSO submitted thousands of claims. The process extended over many years, because the Office of Alien Property examined these petitions carefully to ensure that the JRSO did not receive title to anything belonging either to a legitimate, living claimant or to an ex-enemy. In the late 1950s, the JRSO negotiated a bulk settlement with the United States government for $500,000, an amount the Congress believed to be the maximum figure the JRSO would have ultimately obtained had it pursued each case. The JRSO received the $500,000 in 1963.

In 1946, Congress amended the Trading with the Enemy Act to allow former persecutees the right to recover vested property, but the Senate Judiciary Committee only proposed legislation addressing the problem of heirless assets in 1949.[250] During the elapsed time, it had become "abundantly and tragically clear" that some of the property eligible for release would never be claimed, because the formers owners and heirs had perished. In order to support the relief and rehabilitation of Holocaust survivors in the United States, a successor organization would be appointed to obtain and distribute heirless property, very roughly estimated at a value between $500,000 and $2,000,000.[251]

Several months later the JRSO employed a "group of fairly recent German-Jewish émigrés" to the United States to survey the 14,400 vesting orders issued by the Office of Alien Property "with a view to picking out those names which appeared to be Jewish."[252] Executive Secretary of the World Jewish Congress Abraham S. Hyman later admitted that this method did not provide "an infallible guide," but argued that "it does provide a measure of proof which an administrative agency, adjudicating these claims, may, with a minimum of risk, respect." Hyman also noted that when the Congress enacted the National Origin Immigration Law in 1924, it had relied on the surnames of individuals reported in the 1790 census to determine those persons of "colonial stock."[253]

The German-Jewish émigrés sought to assess the value of unclaimed accounts and determine more precisely the overall worth of heirless Jewish property then in American custody.[254] Although 1,200 vesting orders carried "names which were clearly Jewish,"[255] this group excluded some individuals for various reasons (low value accounts, the name identified a trustee rather than owner, and so forth).[256] Calculations of the remaining orders yielded an estimate of $1.5 million.[257]

Heirless assets legislation passed the Senate on August 9, 1949. Some opposition to the bill arose from the War Claims Commission. The War Claims Commission, using funds acquired from the liquidation of vested enemy assets, paid Americans for damages suffered at the hands of the enemy during the Second World War.[258] Because heirless assets paid to the JRSO would come from the funds available to this agency, its chairman raised objections. Seymour J. Rubin, then foreign affairs counsel to the American Jewish Committee, suggested that "it might be possible to persuade the War Claims Commission to change its views if there were a top limit put on the recovery of heirless property," observing that little work would be necessary to effect that change in the legislation. Rubin "did not expect recovery to go beyond an outside figure of two million dollars."[259]

Chairman of the War Claims Commission Daniel Cleary accepted the suggestion of Judge Robert Patterson, former Secretary of War, for a $3 million limit to claims provided for in heirless assets legislation.[260] Another obstacle rapidly appeared, though. Harold Baynton, Acting Director of the Office of Alien Property, informed Rubin that "he saw no objection to the legislation but that if asked, he would have to say that the Department of Justice wished to examine the costs of administering the legislation if and when it became law." As Rubin pointed out, such an investigation would likely take a significant amount of time and reduce the chances that the legislation would pass. Rubin believed that "this attitude on the part of the Department of Justice is very likely to kill whatever chance [this law] now has for passage."[261]

It is unknown whether Baynton undertook an examination of the costs. Later that year, the House Interstate and Foreign Commerce Committee added amendments to the legislation approved by the Senate, including a $3 million cap for claims, and subsequently referred it to the entire House in the summer of 1950. That body took no action.[262]

In 1954 the Senate Judiciary Committee made a fresh attempt. By the committee meeting of July 30, the $3 million figure had become part of the proposed Senate legislation. It remained somewhat unclear to members of this committee, however, how the amount had been ascertained. Senator Everett Dirksen observed that he "could find no tangible evidence with respect to that estimate." The chief of the Claims Section in the Office of Alien Property, Thomas Creighton, believed that it was "purely an arbitrary figure based upon the investigations probably made by the various organizations that are interested in the bill."[263] In contrast, in testimony before the Subcommittee on the Trading with the Enemy Act of the Senate Committee on the Judiciary, Seymour Rubin stated that, "[t]he $3 million total limitation which is present in Public Law 626 provides a ceiling which was inserted with due regard for financial availabilities presented by the Office of Alien Property in connection with the legislative consideration of that law."[264]

On August 23, 1954, Congress passed Public Law 626 amending Section 32 of the Trading with the Enemy Act. This legislation permitted the President to designate one or more organizations as successors in interest to obtain victims' heirless assets. The successor organization had one year to file claims, and it was to receive no more than $3 million. Further, the law required the agency to use the funds for "rehabilitation and settlement of persons in the United States" who had been subject to Nazi persecution, to return property to rightful owners should they appear within two years, to provide detailed reports on how the assets were used, and finally to guarantee that no proceeds from the heirless property paid for the organization's administrative expenses.[265]

The JRSO applied immediately for recognition as the successor organization, but President Eisenhower did not appoint it until January 13, 1955.[266] Once again this agency found itself confronted with a rapidly approaching deadline for filing claims; the JRSO nevertheless managed to obtain information swiftly and submitted over 8,000 petitions for property.[267] Much as had been the case in Germany, the JRSO filed some duplicate or otherwise invalid claims. It "had to establish whether an individual claim was [already] filed and, if not, to submit evidence that the former owner had been a Nazi victim."[268]

During this period, the JRSO also identified the problems of "omnibus accounts" in the OAP. These were pooled accounts held in the names of Swiss, Dutch, or French banks where the names of the individual depositors were not known. The JRSO logically deduced that there was a "substantial possibility that some portion of these accounts may be the funds of persecutees who were seeking to avoid the foreign exchange restrictions of Germany."[269] The JRSO staff identified 325 vesting orders in this category. Analysis by the Commission staff reveals that in more than half the cases no return orders were issued for the return of the property to claimants. This unreturned amount was then transferred to the War Claims Fund, suggesting that victims' assets may have been used to pay war claims of American citizens.

In some instances, the Office of Alien Property attempted to trace assets and former owners in Europe. At least 200 former owners or heirs were discovered in this manner.[270] By 1956, the JRSO pursued only about half of its original claims,[271] and by 1960 it had withdrawn all but 1,800 claims.[272] Moreover, the U.S. government had made no payments by this date "primarily because of the difficulties attendant upon proof of ownership of specific assets."[273] The significant amounts of time and money necessary to pursue these claims led the JRSO to advocate a bulk settlement with the U.S. government.

Already by March 1956, a representative of the successor organization proposed that Congress authorize $865,000 to resolve all of the JRSO petitions. Seymour J. Rubin, Washington counsel for the JRSO, explained that this figure represented the maximum amount that "would appear to be valid claims of the JRSO."[274] In another statement submitted for this hearing, however, Deputy Director of the Office of Alien Property Paul V. Myron argued that only about half that sum might prove to be heirless. Myron dismissed any amendment to the law offering a bulk settlement between $2 and $3 million (something the JRSO had initially proposed) as "wholly unrealistic. The amendment would result in the JRSO's acquisition of assets which were not owned by persecutees of the Nazi government, and thus would be contrary to the intention of Congress in enacting Public Law 626."[275]

Although the negotiations remain obscure, the JRSO and Congressional leaders arrived at a compromise sum of $500,000 by 1960. During House proceedings on March 1, 1960, Arkansas Representative Oren Harris explained that this figure emerged from a report filed by the Department of Justice. This agency believed that the total number of valid claims submitted by the JRSO totaled 500, representing a value of approximately $500,000.[276] Representative Peter Mack (Illinois) offered testimony supporting legislation designating this amount while observing that "it is clear that heirless property exists in amounts substantially larger than the amount stated in this bill." Given the burden of proof, however, it was likely that only claims approximating $500,000 would be accepted by the Office of Alien Property. The Bureau of the Budget advocated a limit of $250,000, but Representative Mack and his colleagues on the Subcommittee on Commerce and Finance, which had held hearings on the proposed legislation, recommended the $500,000 figure.[277] The legislation had "the enthusiastic support of all interested organizations," according to Representative Mack.[278]

"Enthusiastic" is assuredly too strong a characterization, for the JRSO had hoped since the late 1940s for a much larger sum. Seymour J. Rubin observed in 1959 that the JRSO believed the figure for $500,000 to be "very low." The successor organization only agreed to the proposal "in the knowledge that time is running out for these people whom the Congress has said it wished these funds to benefit." Rubin continued, "There is no point in getting a little more for a former persecutee who is now living on a meager pension than would be available now if the amount which is so obtained is made available after his death."[279] Saul Kagan, Executive Secretary of the JRSO, similarly expressed disappointment with the law. "The settlement of 1962 was take it or leave it," Kagan explained. The JRSO "settled to salvage what was salvageable."[280]

The law, eventually passed by Congress on October 22, 1962, authorized the President to pay $500,000 out of the War Claims Fund to a successor organization. The legislation further stipulated that the "acceptance of payment . . . shall constitute a full and complete discharge of all claims" brought by such an organization.[281] By executive order, President Kennedy granted payment of $500,000 to the JRSO on February 26, 1963.[282] The entire sum was then used in the United States for "the rehabilitation and resettlement of persons in need who had suffered the loss of liberty at Nazi hands." The JRSO allocated $350,000 to help establish housing projects in New York City and environs for former victims, while $100,000 established a scholarship fund for the children and grandchildren of victims of the Holocaust in memory of Dr. Nehemiah Robinson and $50,000 went to the Catholic Relief Service–National Catholic Welfare Conference in New York to provide disabled Nazi victims with rehabilitation grants.[283]

Although it appears as though both the JRSO and the Congress agreed on the settlement amount, the successor organization expressed interest during the 1950s in pursuing many more claims that might have resulted in larger sums. In its annual report for 1955–1956, the JRSO noted that so-called "omnibus claims" could yield further assets. The claims were "collective accounts in the names of various European banks which. . .concealed the identity of the actual owners." Many Jews hid assets in such accounts to protect them from Nazi seizure; the JRSO sought to examine the accounts to determine whether some funds there belonged to murdered, heirless Jews and could be claimed by the JRSO.[284] The extent to which the successor organization pursued these claims, or whether they ever entered into negotiations with the Congress officials remains unclear.

Summary

The United States government provided the major impetus for a restitution program unparalleled in history. Although initial proposals to aid Nazi persecutees envisioned only limited compensation for expropriation, the United States developed measures to ease material suffering and effect the return of stolen property as sensitivity to the plight of victims grew after the war. The United States and its allies apportioned reparation monies for stateless victims, insisted on a strict restitution law in Germany, allowed a successor organization to recover heirless assets, and passed laws releasing to victims, their heirs, or the JRSO the assets that had been frozen or vested during the war.

U.S. officials never explicitly stated where restitution stood among other policy priorities. The goal of rebuilding Germany's governing apparatus soon after war's end clearly took precedence over restitution, however. By encouraging German authorities to regain extensive administrative duties, U.S. officials involved Aryanizers in the restitution process and failed to address an obvious conflict of interest.

The bureaucratic process associated with restitution, and the release of assets to the JRSO in the United States, proved time-consuming. The Office of Alien Property strove to ensure that assets in its possession would be returned to rightful owners or heirs; it did not possess the resources necessary to process cases quickly. Individual claims on average took over three years to process. After realizing how long it would take the OAP to investigate each of its claims for heirless property, the JRSO eventually settled for the lump sum payment of $500,000.[285]

In sum, U.S. authorities developed a restitution program through which victims could recover their looted property, but did not fully ensure that this program met its goals. Whether negotiating settlements with Aryanizers, pursuing litigation in Germany, or awaiting judgment from the Office of Alien Property, claimants had to clear many bureaucratic hurdles before they could regain their assets.

Endnotes for Chapter V

[1] That is, the process of transferring property under duress from persecutees to non-persecutees.

[2] Several articles of the 1907 Hague Convention prohibit wartime looting. See the relevant passages in Elizabeth Simpson, ed., *The Spoils of War. World War II and its Aftermath: The Loss, Reappearance and Recovery of Cultural Property* (New York: Harry N. Abrams, 1997), 278–79.

[3] The text of the London Declaration may be found in Monroe Karasik, "Problems of Compensation and Restitution in Germany and Austria," *Law and Contemporary Problems* 16, 5 (Summer, 1951), 449, n. 1.

[4] Mtg. Mins., Interdivisional Comm. on Rep., Rest., & Prop. Rights, Nov. 30, 1943, NACP, RG 59, Lot 62D–4, Box 50, State/Notter, 1 [320617–619].

[5] Ibid., 3 [320617–619].

[6] Memo from Interdivisional Comm. on Rep., Rest., & Prop. Rights, Subcomm. 2, "Draft Memo on II B, 1, of Agenda (Reparation 1)," Feb. 5, 1944, NACP, RG 59, Lot 62D–4, Box 49, State/Notter, 1 [320630–632].

[7] Memo from Interdivisional Comm. on Rep., Rest., & Prop. Rights, Subcomm. 6, "Recommendations on Restitution," Apr. 10, 1944, 1, NACP, RG 59, Lot 62D–4, Box 49, State/Notter, [320633–644].

[8] Ibid., 2 [320623–644].

[9] Ibid., 4 [320633–644].

[10] Ibid., 5 [320633–644].

[11] Mtg. Mins., Interdivisional Comm. on Rep., Rest., & Prop. Rights, Apr. 11, 1944, 3, NACP, RG 59, Lot 62D–4, Box 50, State/Notter [320650–652].

[12] Mtg. Mins., Interdivisional Comm. on Rep., Rest., & Prop. Rights, Apr. 14, 1944, 1–3, NACP, RG 59, Lot 62D–4, Box 50, State/Notter [320653–659].

[13] Memo from Interdivisional Comm. on Rep., Rest., & Prop. Rights, Subcomm. 6, "Recommendations on Property of Racial or Religious Minorities Seized by the Germans or Otherwise Transferred under Duress," Apr. 10, 1944, 2–3, NACP, RG 59, Lot 62D–4, Box 49, State/Notter [320660–662].

[14] Memo from Interdivisional Comm. on Rep., Rest., & Prop. Rights, Subcomm. 6, "Recommendations on Compensation for Injuries to Members of German Racial or Religious Minorities," Apr. 22, 1944, NACP, RG 59, Lot 62D–4, Box 49, State/Notter [320669–673].

[15] Mtg. Mins., ECEFP, June 29, 1944, NACP, RG 353, Entry 190, Box 56, ECEFP Mins. 1/44–20/44 [204346–352].

[16] "Summary: Report of Reparation, Restitution, and Property Rights—Germany," NACP, RG 353, Entry 192, Box 45, File 5.19B ECEFP Meetings, 3. Documents 11/44–20/44 [204362–377].

[17] See the memo to this effect at NACP, RG 353, Entry 192, Box 45, File 5.19B ECEFP Meeting, 3. Documents 11/44–20/44 [204358].

[18] "Summary: Report of Reparation, Restitution, and Property Rights—Germany," NACP, RG 353, Entry 192, Box 45, File 5.19B ECEFP Meetings, 3. Documents 11/44–20/44 [204373].

[19] Ibid., 14–15 [204362–377].

[20] Constantin Goschler, *Wiedergutmachung: Westdeutschland und die Verfolgten der Nationalsozialismus 1945–1954* (Munich: Oldenbourg, 1992), 57–60.

[21] *Report of the American Commission for the Protection and Salvage of Artistic and Historic Monuments in War Areas.* (Washington, DC: U.S. Government Printing Office, 1946), 47 (hereafter "Roberts Commission Report"), 148. See also "Art Objects in US Zone [sic]," NACP, RG 330, U.S. Army Command, Box 37, Fine Art [313574–576].

[22] Lynn Nicholas, *The Rape of Europa: The Fate of Europe's Treasures in the Third Reich and the Second World War,* (New York: Alfred A. Knopf, 1994), 408.

[23] Nicholas, *The Rape of Europa,* 409.

[24] Memo from HQ, USGCC to ACOS, G–5, USFET, "Restitution Policy and Procedure," Sept. 15, 1945, NACP, RG 338, USFET G–5 Sitreps, Box 1 [313683].

[25] Message from JCS to Commanding Gen. Clark, U.S. Forces of Occupation, Austria, & Commanding Gen. McNarney, USFET, Germany, Nov. 29, 1945, NACP, RG 56, Entry 69A4707, Box 84, Germany-Reps., Vol. 2 [215765–768]; From HICOG to the State Dept., July 14, 1950, NACP, RG 59, Lot 53D 307, Box 14, Rep. May–Dec. 1950 [337588].

[26] Memo from James F. Byrnes to Certain Am. Diplomatic & Consular Ofcs., "Current Statement of U.S. Restitution Policy," July 17, 1946, NACP, RG 84, Entry 2113/0, Box 1, File XI E. Rest. Policy [204251–253]. Although Finland had never been occupied, it was nevertheless included in this memorandum.

[27] See Memo from HQ, USFET, to Commanding Gen., Eastern Mil. Dist., on the release of Latvian materials to Soviet Mil. authorities, Sept. 25, 1945, NACP, RG 260, Prop. Div., Box 723 [105668].

[28] Message from AGWAR to OMGUS, May 2, 1946, NACP, RG 84, Entry 2531B, Box 53, File 400B [114559]. The Baltic nations, established as independent countries after the First World War, had been annexed by the Soviet Union in the summer of 1940. This memo only referred to Lithuania and Latvia, but in a memo from 1947, Estonia was also listed as a Baltic state to which restitution was denied. See OMGUS, "Restitution in the Four Zones," Nov. 1947, NACP, RG 56, Entry 69A4707, Box 84, German-Rest. [106277].

[29] Established at the Paris Conference on Reparations, the Inter-Allied Reparation Agency allocated German reparations to the eighteen signatory nations. See "Paris Conference on Reparation November 9th—December 21st, 1945, Final Act," no date, 15, NACP, RG 84, Entry 2113T, Box 3, IARA [204193–217].

[30] Cable from AGWAR to USFET, Jan. 21, 1947, NACP, RG 260, FED, Box 167 [219720–721]. Currencies not belonging to any of those groups mentioned above were to be held pending further instructions.

[31] Memo from OMGUS Econ. Div. to Rest. Control Br., "Restitution of Securities," Oct. 3, 1947, NACP, RG 260, Prop. Div., Box 14 [311563–564].

[32] Memo, "A Short History of External Restitution (Non-Cultural)," Mar. 24, 1949, RG 260, R&R Br., Box 13 [306185].

[33] Rept. From Keifer, "CFM REPARATORY PAPER: Restitution from Germany," May 18, 1949, 5, NACP, RG 59, Lot 62D–4, Box 26 [106638–651].

[34]Memo, "A Short History of External Restitution (Non-Cultural)," Mar. 24, 1949, RG 260, R&R Br., Box 13 [306185].

[35] Memo from Am. Embassy, Warsaw to the Secy. of State, Nov. 23, 1948, NACP, RG 84, Entry 2531B, Box 211, File 400B [320996]. This memo contains a summary of the protest.

[36] Foreign Missions for Restitutions, "Protest on Restitution Program," Oct. 27, 1948, NACP, RG 260, Prop. Div., Box 15 [302073].

[37] "A Short History of External Restitution (Non-Cultural)," Mar. 24, 1949, 9, NACP, RG 260, R&R Br., Box 13 [306186]. The discussion of the termination of the restitution program provided does not indicate that the military authorities granted any extension of the Dec. 31, 1948, deadline.

[38] Message from OMGUS to AGWAR, June 15, 1946, NACP, RG 260, Ardelia Hall Collection, Box 283 [131119].

[39] Ibid. [131119].

[40] OAD, Monthly Rpt., Jan. 1947, 6, NACP, RG 260, Activity Rpts., Box 261, OAD Rpts. [100650].

[41] Memo from Office of MG for Hesse, "Materials on Hand, 25 Jan 1949 [sic]," Jan. 28, 1949, NACP, RG 260, Ardelia Hall Collection, Box 63 [112443].

[42] Cable from AGWAR to OMGUS, Sept. 30, 1947, NACP, RG 84, Entry 2531B, Box 130, File 400B [328990–992].

[43] Memo from Fin. Div., OMGUS, to FED, OMGUS, Aug. 12, 1947, NACP, RG 260, Recs. of Shipments, Box 435 [216940].

[44] Edwin P. Keller, Head, Depository Sec., to Mr. Gabell, "Weekly Progress Report for Week Ending 3 July 1948," July 6, 1948, NACP, RG 260, Entry FED, Box 400 [217754–755].

[45] Cable from the Dept. of the Army to OMGUS, Oct. 21, 1947, NACP, RG 84, Entry 2531B, Box 130, File 400B [321708].

[46] Memo from Albert F. Bender, Jr. to Theodore H. Ball, "Securities Authorized for Release to PCIRO [sic]," Nov. 21, 1947, NACP, RG 260, Fin. Adv., Box 165, International Bank for Reconstruction & Development [220123].

[47] Memo, "Status as of August 31, 1948, of Assets held by FED," NACP, RG 260, Fin. Div., Box 93, FED [308118–122].

[48] Memo, "Draft of Particulars," no date, NACP, RG 260, Fin. Div., Box 93, FED [308125].

[49] Memo from K.A. de Keyserlingk to N. H. Collison, Nov. 23, 1948, NACP, RG 260, Prop. Div., Box 28, Semi-Monthly Rpts. [308238].

[50] OMGUS, Prop. Div., "Final Report, MFA&A," Dec. 30, 1948, NACP, RG 260, Ardelia Hall Collection, Box 712, Final Rpts. [119200]. This document does contain numbers of items released from Offenbach (almost three million items, including materials released in Germany), but remains silent on the issue of potential victims' property restituted from the Munich and Wiesbaden Collecting Points.

[51] Rpt. of the U.S. High Commissioner, ACA, 4 Q 1948, Vol. 36, 37, 38, NACP, RG 84, Entry 2082, Box 4, Rpts. of U.S. High Commissioner [101770].

[52] U.S. Department of State, *Preliminary Study on U.S. and Allied Efforts To Recover and Restore Gold and Other Assets Stolen or Hidden by Germany During World War II*, coordinated by Stuart E. Eizenstat and prepared by William Z. Slany (Washington, DC: US Government Printing Office, May 1997), 56–57.

[53] For this and the following, see "The Final Report of the Tripartite Commission for the Restitution of Monetary Gold," Sept. 3, 1998, NACP, RG 59, Entry 5382, Box 4 [201538–546].

[54] Dept. of State, Eizenstat/Slany, *Preliminary Study*, 177.

[55] Ibid., 171.

[56] Amb. Louis Amigues, "The Closing of the Tripartite Gold Commission for the Restitution of Monetary Gold," *Proceedings of the Washington Conference on Holocaust-Era Assets* (Washington, DC: U.S. Government Printing Office, 1998), 64–65.

[57] Stuart E. Eizenstat, "Review of Gold issues, Research and Resolution," *Proceedings of the Washington Conference on Holocaust-Era Assets*, 62.

[58] Memo from Edwin Pauley, "Reparations and Restitution for Stateless Persons," July 18, 1945, NACP, RG 59, European Mission Subj. Files '45–'47, Box 20, Stateless Persons [320972].

[59] Ibid., 3 [320972–975].

[60] Ibid., 3–4 [320972–975].

[61] Letter from Edwin Pauley to Secy. of State James F. Byrnes, Aug. 29, 1945, NACP, RG 59, European Mission Subj. Files '45–'47, Box 20, Stateless Persons [320977].

[62] Goschler, *Wiedergutmachung: Westdeutschland und die Verfolgten der Nationalsozialismus*, 64.

[63] Ibid., 64–65. Blaustein, however, did not insist on the formation of a wholly Jewish agency to administer assets. Instead, he called for a "United Nations Trusteeship of Indemnification."

[64] Dept. of State, Eizenstat/Slany, *Preliminary Study*, 59.

[65] Goschler, *Wiedergutmachung: Westdeutschland und die Verfolgten der Nationalsozialismus,* notes on 66–67 that the British especially wished that refugees and displaced persons would return to their homelands—thus reducing tensions in Palestine.

[66] "Paris Conference on Reparation November 9th – December 21st, 1945 Final Act," no date, 14, NACP, RG 84, Entry 2113T, Box 3, IARA [204193–217].

[67] For discussion of the negotiations between the Allies leading up to the implementation agreement, see Dept. of State, Eizenstat/Slany, *Preliminary Study,* 89–94.

[68] Nana Sagi, *German Reparations. A History of the Negotiations* (New York: St. Martin's Press, 1986), 36.

[69] AGWAR to OMGUS, Aug. 23, 1946, NACP, RG 260, Dec. File, Box 111, File 602.3 [300851–854].

[70] Cable from AGWAR to USFET & USFA, Nov. 16, 1946, NACP, RG 260, Ardelia Hall Collection, Box 283 [101129–130].

[71] Ibid. [101129–130].

[72] Ibid. [101129–130].

[73] Telegram from Secy. of State George Marshall, May 8, 1947, NACP, RG 260, Fin. Adv., Box 167 [219690–691].

[74] Airgram No. A–142 from Secy. of State G. Marshall to the U.S. Legation to Budapest, July 27, 1948, NACP, RG 84, POLAD–USCOA, Entry 2054, Box 106 [111328–329].

[75] Letter from the Temp. Managing Comm. of Central Bureau of Hungarian Jews to A. Schoenfeld, Dec. 20, 1945, NACP, RG 84, Entry 2691, Box 65, File 840.1[103364–365].

[76] Letter from the Central Board of Jews in Hungary to the Department of State, July 28, 1947, 3–4, NACP, RG 84, Papers of the U.S. Legation to Budapest, Classified General Records, Box 4 [103312–317].

[77] The Hungarian Minister of Finance, Nikolaus Nyaradi, informed U.S. authorities in July 1946 that the Hungarian government and Jewish groups in the country had formed the Jewish Rehabilitation Agency; Nyaradi believed that the "Gold Train" assets should benefit the agency. U.S. officials disagreed. See Telegram No. 43 from Heath, "AGWAR's telegrams WX 93185 of July 2 to USFET and USFA," July 7, 1946, NACP, RG 84, Entry 2691, Box 103, File 840.1 [111529].

[78] Letter from Robert S. Folson, U.S. Legation in Budapest, to the Central Bd. of Jews in Hungary, May 19, 1947, NACP, RG 84, Entry 2692, Box 4, File 840.1 [103481].

[79] "Vast Loot of Nazis Will Be Sold Here," *New York Times,* May 22, 1948.

[80] "Sale of Loot Tops All Expectations," *New York Times,* June 23, 1948.

[81] Ibid.

[82] Ibid.

[83] Ibid.

[84] Ibid..

[85] "Nazi Loot Brings $31,520," *New York Times,* June 25, 1948.

[86] IRO White Paper, June 7, 1949, NACP, RG 59, Lot File 53D307, Box 20, [329015–017].

[87] See Gábor Kádár and Zoltán Vági, "The Economic Destruction of Hungarian Jewry," (forthcoming).

[88] Memo from Capt. John F. Back to G–2, USFA, "Inventory of 'Werfen Train,'" Sept. 1945, NACP, RG 260, USACA, Entry 113, Box 20, File S4.8007 [119283–284].

[89] Letter from Abba P. Schwartz, PCIRO Rep. Dir., to Col. William G. Brey, FED Chief, "Contemplated Transfer of Additional Non-Monetary Gold to PCIRO under JCS Non-Monetary Gold Directive," July 27, 1948, NACP, RG 260, Fin. Adv., Box 162, FED–IRO [304780].

[90] Note with Attachment from George Wenzel, IRO Reparations Officer, to FED, [circa Oct., 1948], NACP, RG 260, FED, Box 421, File 900.154 [328997–9003].

[91] Internal Route Slip with Proposed Cable from Col. William G. Brey to OMGUS, Fin. Div., July 23, 1947, NACP, RG 260, FED, Box 424, File 940.38 [329007–009].

[92] Letter from Theodore H. Ball to P. Lercy-Beaulieu, Oct. 14, 1947, NACP, RG 260, FED, Box 167 [219695–696]. The actual delivery was made on September 5, 1947. See the letter from W. Hallam Tuck to Rear Admiral Lewis L. Strauss, Sept. 15, 1947, NACP, RG 59, Lot 53D307, Box 19, IRO Preparatory Comm. (June–Sept. 1947) [337427].

[93] Memo from FED, "Status as at C/B December 15, 1950," RG 260, FED, Box 400 [219601].

[94] MG Law 59, 1, found in Military Government Gazette, Germany, United States Area of Control, Issue G, Nov. 10, 1947, NACP, RG 260, German External Assets, Box 167, OMGUS—Contacts With [106777–819].

[95] Goschler, *Wiedergutmachung: Westdeutschland und die Verfolgten der Nationalsozialismus*, 91–95.

[96] The first meeting to discuss restitution proposals took place on April 24, 1946. See Goschler, *Wiedergutmachung: Westdeutschland und die Verfolgten der Nationalsozialismus*, 103. For the recommendations of the Property Disposition Board, see its report from Mar. 26, 1946 at NACP, RG 260, Ardelia Hall Collection, Box 81 [100109–133].

[97] See Clay, *Decision in Germany*, 84–103, for an examination of this political philosophy.

[98] Goschler, *Wiedergutmachung: Westdeutschland und die Verfolgten der Nationalsozialismus*, 103–04.

[99] Ibid., 105.

[100] Of particular importance in maintaining direct contact with officials in Washington as well as OMGUS was a collective of five American-based Jewish organizations, the WJC, the AJDC, the Jewish Agency for Palestine, the American Jewish Committee, and the American Jewish Conference. See Goschler, *Wiedergutmachung: Westdeutschland und die Verfolgten der Nationalsozialismus*, 107.

[101] Ibid., 108. Goschler explains that disagreement existed even within OMGUS concerning this date. Members of the Finance Division and the Property Control Br. sided with German opinion that November 9, 1938—the *Kristallnacht*—should be regarded as the date after which Jewish persecution began in earnest. The Legal Division, however, sided with Jewish representatives.

[102] Nehemiah Robinson, "Draft of an Indemnification Law for Germany," July 25, 1946, NACP, RG 260, R&R Br., Box 713 [303332].

[103] The Jewish Community of Berlin protested to OMGUS against a draft it had seen from August 1946, in part because "the enactment of this law is especially put into the hands of exclusively German authorities" with no "participation of Jewish authorities" in the restitution procedure. See the letter from the Juedische Gemeinde zu Berlin to OMGUS, Prop. Control Br., Sept. 16, 1946, NACP, RG 260, R&R Br., Box 713 [303392–394]; Goschler, *Wiedergutmachung: Westdeutschland und die Verfolgten der Nationalsozialismus*, 108.

[104] Goschler, *Wiedergutmachung: Westdeutschland und die Verfolgten der Nationalsozialismus*, 108–111. Already by October, Washington officials had informed OMGUS that it believed "that in loss of Jewish property successor organizations should be designated or approved by [the Military Government] and that appearance of designation by [German Authorities] will meet strong objection." See the cable from AGWAR to OMGUS, Oct. 14, 1946, NACP, RG 84, Entry 2531, Box 53, Rest.– Gen. [320890].

[105] CINCEUR Berlin to War Dept., Apr. 8, 1947, NACP, RG 56, Entry 69A4707, Box 84, Rest. [220641]. For a further discussion of German opposition to the restitution law, see Goschler, *Wiedergutmachung: Westdeutschland und die Verfolgten der Nationalsozialismus*, 112–113.

[106] Cable from CINCEUR Berlin to War Dept., Apr. 8, 1947, NACP, RG 56, Entry 69A4707, Box 84, Rest. [220641].

[107] Cable from AGWAR to EUCOM, July 9, 1947, NACP, RG 84, Entry 2531B, Box 130, File 400B [321003].

[108] Cable from OMGUS to AGWAR, Sept. 13, 1947, NACP, RG 56, Entry 69A4707, Box 84, Rest. [220628–630].

[109] Goschler, *Wiedergutmachung: Westdeutschland und die Verfolgten der Nationalsozialismus*, 119.

[110] Memo from Irwin S. Mason, Adv. on Internal Rest., to Gen. Lucius Clay, Feb. 7, 1948, NACP, RG 260, Dec. File, Box 510 [315696]. In this memo, Mason quotes from a cable dated July 30, 1947, in which Gen. Clay explained the British position to AGWAR.

[111] Goschler, *Wiedergutmachung: Westdeutschland und die Verfolgten der Nationalsozialismus*, 120–21.

[112] Cable from CINCEUR to Chief of Staff, U.S. Army, Oct. 29, 1947, NACP, RG 84, Entry 2531B, Box 130, File 400B Rest. Gen. [320955–957].

[113] Ibid., 1 [320955–958].

[114] Circular Airgram to All Am. Diplomatic Ofcrs., Nov. 25, 1947, NACP, RG 84, Entry 2108, Box 113, File 7116 [320931–932].

[115] MG Law 59, 16, found in "Military Government Gazette, Germany, US Area of Control," Issue G, Nov. 10, 1947, NACP, RG 260, USACA, Entry 108, Box 167, OMGUS—Contacts with [106777–819]. According to Regulation No. 5 of Law 59, issued on Jan. 5, 1949, initial petitions would be considered valid so long as they were postmarked by Dec. 31, 1948, and were received by the Central Filing Agency by Mar. 31, 1949. See Office of MG for Bavaria, Monthly Rpt., Feb. 4, 1949, NACP, RG 466, Entry 160A, Box 4 [303039–040].

[116] US Courts of the Allied High Commission for Germany, Court of Restitution Appeals, Vol. I, 1950, 490 [106730]. This document cites an Order of the Military Governor, Subject: Petition by Public Prosecutor, Feb. 28, 1949.

[117] MG Law 59, 1, found in "Military Government Gazette, Germany, US Area of Control," Issue G, Nov. 10, 1947, NACP, RG 260, USACA, Entry 108, Box 167, OMGUS—Contacts with [106777–819].

[118] Press Release, OMGUS, Nov. 10, 1947, NACP, RG 260, Ardelia Hall Collection, Box 67 [106823].

[119] MG Law 59, 2, found in "Military Government Gazette, Germany, US Area of Control," Issue G, Nov. 10, 1947, NACP, RG 260, USACA, Entry 108, Box 167, OMGUS—Contacts with [106777–819].

[120] Ibid., 9 [106777–819].

[121] Ibid., 20 [106777–819].

[122] Ibid., 16 [106777–819].

[123] W.J. Dickmann, Deputy Chief, Prop. Control & External Assets Br., "Report on the Administration of Military Government Law No. 59, 'Restitution of Identifiable Property' for the 10 Months Period Beginning 10 November 1947 until 30 August 1948," no date, 4, NACP, RG 260, Prop. Div., Box 4, File 17 [308401–411].

[124] MG Law 59, 17–19, found in "Military Government Gazette, Germany, US Area of Control," Issue G, Nov. 10, 1947, NACP, RG 260, USACA, Entry 108, Box 167, OMGUS—Contacts with [106777–819]. Claimants could also skip the intermediary appeals court and place a case before the Board of Review. See J. H. Lennon, Land Prop. Control Chief, "Minutes of Meeting Held in OMGB, Munich, on 18 March 1949 Regarding Law No. 59," Apr. 15, 1949, NACP, RG 466, Entry 160A, Box 4, File 254.1 [327058].

[125] Karasik, "Problems of Compensation and Restitution in Germany and Austria," 456.

[126] Composition of this organization included international components. The thirteen groups represented were the Jewish Agency for Palestine, the AJDC, the American Jewish Committee, the WJC, the Agudat Israel World Organization, the Board of Deputies of British Jews, the Central British Fund, the Council for the Protection of the Rights and Interests of the Jews from Germany, the Central Committee of Liberated Jews in Germany, the Conseil Représentatif des Juifs de France, the Jewish Cultural Reconstruction, Inc., the Anglo-Jewish Association, and the Interessenvertretung israelitischer Kultusgemeinden in the U.S. Zone in Germany. This list is provided in Sagi, *German Reparations. A History of the Negotiations*, 41.

[127] See Nehemiah Robinson, *Indemnification and Reparations, Jewish Aspects* (New York: Institute of Jewish Affairs of the American Jewish Congress and World Jewish Congress, 1944).

[128] Sagi, *German Reparations. A History of the Negotiations,* 23–25.

[129] Goschler, *Wiedergutmachung: Westdeutschland und die Verfolgten der Nationalsozialismus,* 47.

[130] See the following chapter on this Commission and its successor, the Jewish Cultural Reconstruction, Inc.

[131] See Goschler, *Wiedergutmachung: Westdeutschland und die Verfolgten der Nationalsozialismus,* 111, for Clay's meeting with committee delegates under the leadership of Judge Joseph M. Proskauer, and the letter describing the General's meeting with Commission representatives from Rabbi Philip S. Bernstein, Advisor on Jewish Affairs to the Commander in Chief, European Command to Dr. Salo W. Baron, NACP, RG 260, Ardelia Hall Collection, Box 129 [101115].

[132] Goschler, *Wiedergutmachung: Westdeutschland und die Verfolgten der Nationalsozialismus,* 172. A full list of JRSO members is provided above.

[133] Ibid., 173.

[134] Cert. of Inc. of the Jewish Rest. Commission, May 15, 1947, AJA, WJC Papers, Box C289 [115847–880].

[135] Goschler, *Wiedergutmachung: Westdeutschland und die Verfolgten der Nationalsozialismus,* 173.

[136] MG—Germany, U.S. Area of Control, Reg. No. 3 Under MG Law No. 59 & Appointment Thereunder; Designation of Successor Orgs. Pursuant to MG Law No. 59 & Appointment of a Successor Org. to Claim Jewish Prop., June 23, 1948, NACP, RG 260, Dec. File, Box 510 [315639–641].

[137] PCHA Interview with Benjamin B. Ferencz, Washington, DC, Oct. 5, 2000 [124721–724].

[138] Memo from Lt. Col. G. H. Garde, Adjutant Gen., to the Dir., JRSO, "JRSO Authorization No. 1," Aug. 18, 1948, NACP, RG 260, Dec. File, Box 510 [315659–663].

[139] PCHA Interview with Benjamin B. Ferencz, Washington, DC, Oct. 5, 2000 [124721–724].

[140] Jewish Restitution Successor Organization, *After Five Years: A Report of the Jewish Restitution Successor Organization on the Restitution of Identifiable Property in the U.S. Zone of Germany* (Nuremberg: JRSO, 1953), 4.

[141] PCHA Interview with Benjamin B. Ferencz, Washington, DC, Oct. 5, 2000 [124721–724].

[142] JRSO, *After Five Years,* 4–5.

[143] PCHA Interview with Benjamin B. Ferencz, Washington, DC, Oct. 5, 2000 [124721–724].

[144] Memo from the JRSO to the United Service for New Americans, June 23, 1954, NACP, RG 466, Entry 160A, Box 6, File 257.1 (JRSO) [124425–426].

[145] Goschler, *Wiedergutmachung: Westdeutschland und die Verfolgten der Nationalsozialismus,* 175–176.

[146] JRSO, *After Five Years,* 6.

[147] JRSO, *After Five Years,* 6–7. Dates for these agreements are provided in Goschler, *Wiedergutmachung: Westdeutschland und die Verfolgten der Nationalsozialismus,* 176–180.

[148] "Jews' Claims Cut to Aid Restitution," *New York Times,* Feb. 13, 1951. See the clipping in USHMM, Ferencz Papers, 12.008, Correspondence and Related Records Regarding the Jewish Restitution Successor Organization (JRSO), Box 1, Folder 10 ("Clippings: JRSO and Reparations, Early 1950s").

[149] Saul Kagan & Ernest H. Weisman, *Report on the Operations of the Jewish Restitution Successor Organization 1947–1972* (New York: JRSO, [1972]), 30.

[150] See the Corresp. between Benjamin Ferencz, Dir. Gen. of the JRSO, & Eli Rock, Am. Jewish Joint Distribution Comm., June 10 & June 14, 1949, Stanford Univ., Salo Baron Papers, Box 234, Files 2–3 [326603–606].

[151] JRSO, *After Five Years*, 9–10.

[152] Memo from JRSO, "Criteria for Equitable Determination of Claims by Persons Who Lost their Legal Rights by Failing to File their Petitions for Restitution Within the Time Limit Prescribed by U.S. Military Government Law No. 59," Central Archives for the History of the Jewish People, Jerusalem, File JRSO, NY, 906 [343030–031].

[153] Letter from Thea Cerf to unknown recipient, May 16, 1949, NACP, RG 260, Prop. Div., Box 11, Gen. Recs. of the Dir. '44–'50 [120682].

[154] Kagan & Weisman, *Report on the Operations of the Jewish Restitution Successor Organization*, 29.

[155] "Monthly Report on Analysis of Court Decisions," HICOG, Internal Rest. Supervision Br., Nov. 22, 1949, NACP, RG 466, Prop. Office, Recs. Relating to Rest. of Prop. under MG Law 59, Box 3, Court Decisions File [225580].

[156] Hans–Joachim Braun, *The German Economy in the Twentieth Century* (New York: Routledge, 1990), 154–55.

[157] "Monthly Report on Analysis of Court Decisions," HICOG, Internal Rest. Supervision Br., Nov. 22, 1949, NACP, RG 466, Prop. Office, Recs. Relating to Rest. of Prop. under MG Law 59, Box 3, Court Decisions File [225580].

[158] Memo from Ministry of Justice, Württemberg-Baden to Internal Rest. Supervision Br., Nov. 9, 1949, NACP, RG 466, Entry 160A, Box 5 [303087].

[159] OMGUS, "Property Control in the U.S.-Occupied Area of Germany 1945–1949. Special Report of the Military Governor," July 1949, 1, Stanford Univ. Hoover Lib., Govt. Docs.—Germany [106833–870].

[160] Ibid., 14 [106833–870].

[161] Ibid., 10 [106833–870].

[162] Ibid., 1 & 10 [106833–870].

[163] Ibid., 10 [106833–870].

[164] Ibid., 11–12 [106833–870].

[165] Office of MG for Bavaria, Prop. Div., Monthly Rpt., Jan. 5, 1949, NACP, RG 466, Entry 160A, Box 4, File 254.1 [327102].

[166] Office of MG for Bavaria, Prop. Control & External Assets Br., Dist.Unterfranken, "Information Concerning Dr. Sebastian Endres," Oct. 28, 1948, NACP RG 260, Prop. Div., Box 17, Gen. Recs. 1944–50, Endres File [327497–500].

[167] See letter from William G. Daniels, Chief, Prop. Div., Apr. 23, 1951, NACP, RG 466, USHCG, Class. Gen. Recs., 1949–52, Box 9, File Endres [327532].

[168] Memo from Werner M. Loewenthal, Chief, Field Operations to John A. Porter, Chief, Claims Sec., "Problems Concerning the Political Reliability of Restitution Personnel," Jan. 3, 1949, NACP, RG 466, Entry 160A, Box 4, File 254.1 [327104–105].

[169] Monthly Rpt., Office of MG for Bavaria, Prop. Div., Jan. 5, 1949, NACP, RG 466, Entry 160A, Box 4, File 254.1 [327101–102].

[170] Memo from Werner Loewenthal, Internal Rest. Supervision Br. to Mr. Miller, Prop. Div., "Conditions Impeding Restitution Progress," Dec. 1, 1949, NACP, RG 260, Prop. Div., Box 9, Law 59 [308366].

[171] Monthly Rpt., Office of MG for Bavaria, Prop. Div., Feb. 4, 1949, NACP, RG 466, Entry 160A, Box 4, File 254.1 [327103]. For a recent volume on denazification, see Wilfried Loth and Bernd A. Rusinek, eds., *Verwandlungspolitik: NS-Eliten in der westdeutschland Nachkriegsgesellschaft* (New York: Campus, 1998).

[172] Memo from the Rest. Sec., Ministry of Justice, Württemberg-Baden to Mr. Yager, Internal Rest. Supervision Br., "Restitution Procedure under Law No. 59," Nov. 9, 1949, NACP, RG 466, Entry 160A, Box 5, File 254.3 [303087].

173 Maj. Abraham S. Hyman, Acting Adv. on Jewish Affairs to U.S. Commands in Germany & Austria, "Final Report," Jan. 30, 1950, 6, Hoover Inst., Grossman Collection, Box 49, Jews in Germany [328138].

174 Memo from Werner Loewenthal, Internal Rest. Supervision Br. to Mr. Miller, Prop. Div., "Conditions Impeding Restitution Progress," Dec. 1, 1949, NACP, RG 260, Prop. Div., Box 9, Law 59 [308366].

175 Maj. Abraham S. Hyman, Acting Adv. on Jewish Affairs to U.S. Commands in Germany & Austria, "Final Report," Jan. 30, 1950, 6, Hoover Inst., Grossman Collection, Box 49, Jews in Germany [328138].

176 Memo from OMGUS to the Directors of the OMG for Bavaria, Hesse, Württemberg-Baden, & Bremen, Jan. 12, 1949, NACP, RG 466, Entry 160A, Box 1, File 213 AG Letters [124308–309].

177 OMGUS, Prop. Div., "Report of Field Trip by Mr. Hartzsch and Mr. Porter to the Various *Laender* in the U.S. Zone," Feb. 8, 1949, NACP, RG 260, Prop. Div., Box 11 [313442 of 313441–458].

178 Ibid. [313450 of 313441–458].

179 Ibid. [313452 of 313441–458].

180 Ibid. [313455 of 313441–458].

181 OMG for Bavaria, Prop. Div., "Minutes of Meeting Held in OMGB, Munich, on 18 March 1949 Regarding Law No. 59," Apr. 15, 1949, NACP, RG 466, Entry 160A, Box 4, File 254.1 [327088].

182 USHCG, Office of Econ. Affairs, Prop. Div., Internal Rest. Supervision Br., "Conference held at Bad Nauheim on December 14, 1949," Jan. 31, 1950, 2–3, NACP, RG 260, Box 10, File 44 [308387–400].

183 Ibid. 9 [308395].

184 USHCG, Press Release, Oct. 27, 1950, Stanford University, Salo Baron Papers, Box 44, Folder 2 [326575]; also see USHCG, Press Release, Oct. 27, 1950, NACP, RG 466, McCloy Papers, Box 22, File D (50) 2636–2679 [315716].

185 Ibid. [315716].

186 Goschler, *Wiedergutmachung: Westdeutschland und die Verfolgten der Nationalsozialismus*, 181.

187 Memo from W.J. Dickmann, Deputy Chief, OMGUS Prop. Div., to Phillips Hawkins, June 8, 1948, NACP, RG 260, Box 10, File 57 [300472].

188 USHCG, "Conference held at Bad Nauheim on December 14, 1949," Jan. 31, 1950, 10–11, NACP, RG 260, Prop. Div., Box 10, File 44 [308387–400].

189 Walter Schwarz, *Rueckerstattung nach den Gesetzen der Allierten Maechte* (Munich: Verlag C. H. Beck, 1974), 392.

190 *A Decade of American Foreign Policy: Basic Documents, 1941–1949* (Washington, DC: Government Printing Office, 1950).

191 Ibid.

192 Control Agreement for Austria, Article V, Para. III, cited in the History of R&R Br., External Restitution, no date, NACP, RG 260, Entry 103, Box 167, History of R&R Br. [320065].

193 The Rehabilitation of Austria, 1945–47, no date, NACP, RG 407, Entry 368b, Box 1451, Rehabilitation of Austria [319358].

194 Ibid.

195 History of R&R Br., External Rest., no date, NACP, RG 260, USACA, Entry 103, Box 167, History of R&R Br. [320067].

196 Ibid. [320073].

197 HQ, USFA, USACA Sec., Summary Rpt. on Claims & Rest. as of 31 Dec. 1948, no date, NACP, RG 407, Entry 368B, Box 1432, Reps. & Rest.-Austria [312636].

[198] Final Rpt. of U.S. High Commissioner for Austria, Vol. 1, Oct. 1, 1950, NACP, RG 260, USACA, Files of the Dir. 1946–51, Box 23, Dec. Files 1945–51 [212752]. American authorities dropped claims, for instance, when the property could not be located within the U.S. Zone, or when a claim duplicated another petition. See the History of R&R Br., External Rest., no date, NACP, RG 260, USACA, Entry 103, Box 167, History of R&R Br. [320076–077].

[199] Final Rpt. of the U.S. High Commissioner for Austria, Vol. 1, Oct. 1, 1950, NACP, RG 260, USACA, Files of the Dir. 1946–51, Box 23, Dec. Files 1945–51 [212752].

[200] Rpt. of the U.S. High Commissioner for Austria, Vol. 45, 46, 47, 3 Q 1949, NACP, RG 84, Entry 2082, Box 5 [119041].

[201] "Introduction to First Phase of Property Control History," no date, NACP, RG 260, Entry 119, Box 2 [104846]. Property Control evidently prepared a general information letter along with other claimant forms for distribution in the United States.

[202] *Austrian Information*, Jan. 3, 1953, NACP, RG 59, Lot 62D4, Box 18, Austria Rest. Policies [311703].

[203] "A Review of Austria," Am. Legation, Vienna, Sept. 1, 1947, NACP, RG 260, USACA, Files of the Dir. 1946–51, Box 16, File Dec. Files 1945–51 [311731].

[204] Resume of the Austrian Internal Rest. Problem, Jan. 1, 1954, NACP, RG 84, Entry 2057, Box 6 [113626–633].

[205] Dept. of State, "Multilateral Austrian State Treaty," *United States Treaties and Other International Agreements*, Vol. 6, Part 2, 1955, 2435–2436 [320418–419].

[206] Cited in Amending the TWEA, rpt. (No. 784) to accompany S. 603, Comm. on the Judiciary, U.S. Senate, 81st Congress, 1st Session, July 25, 1949, 1 [332740–743].

[207] Ibid., 1–2 [332740–743].

[208] "History of FFC," Ch. 6, 1 [331331–775].

[209] Ibid., Ch. 6, 1 [331331–775].

[210] Speech to be delivered by Orvis Schmidt, "Lifting Foreign Funds Control," at 31st National For. Trade Convention, NY, Oct. 9, 1944, NACP, RG 131, FFC, Box 95, Defrosting [200366–376].

[211] "History of FFC," Ch. 6, 1 [331331–775].

[212] Ibid. [200366–376]; also cited in Rudolf Littauer, "The Unfreezing of Foreign Funds," *Columbia Law Review* 45 (1945): 134.

[213] Speech to be delivered by Orvis Schmidt, "Lifting Foreign Funds Control," at 31st National For. Trade Convention, NY, Oct. 9, 1944, NACP, RG 131, FFC, Box 95, Defrosting [200366–376].

[214] Littauer, "The Unfreezing of Foreign Funds," 146.

[215] Isadore Alk & Irving Moskowitz, "Removal of United States Controls over Foreign-owned Property," *Federal Bar Journal* 10 (1948), 10.

[216] Littauer, "The Unfreezing of Foreign Funds," 147, paraphrasing Orvis Schmidt's Oct. 9, 1944 speech.

[217] Speech to be delivered by Orvis Schmidt, "Lifting Foreign Funds Control," at 31st National For. Trade Convention, NY, Oct. 9, 1944, NACP, RG 131, FFC, Box 95, Defrosting [200366–376].

[218] Alk & Moskowitz, "Removal of United States Controls over Foreign-owned Property," 5; Memo for the Files, Jul 13, 1944, NACP, RG 131, FFC, Box 95 [310700–701].

[219] Littauer, "The Unfreezing of Foreign Funds," 156.

[220] Alk & Moskowitz, "Removal of United States Controls over Foreign-owned Property," 5–6.

[221] "History of FFC," Ch. 6, 2–3 [331331–774].

[222] Alk & Moskowitz, "Removal of United States Controls over Foreign-owned Property," 6.

[223] Treas. Dept. *Annual Report,* 1945, 107.

[224] "History of FFC," Ch. 6, 12 [331331–775].

[225] Press Release accompanying Gen. Ruling 94, reprinted in Docs Pertaining to FFC, Sept. 1946, 82.

[226] "History of FFC," Ch. 6, 13 & 16 [331331–775].

[227] Press Release accompanying Gen. Ruling 94, reprinted in Docs Pertaining to FFC, Sept. 1946, 82.

[228] Alk & Moskowitz, "Removal of United States Controls over Foreign-owned Property," 8; "History of FFC," Ch. 6, 14 [331331–775].

[229] Alk & Moskowitz, "Removal of United States Controls over Foreign-owned Property," 18.

[230] "History of FFC," Ch. 6, 24 [331331–775].

[231] Press Release accompanying Gen. Ruling 94, reprinted in Docs Pertaining to FFC, Sept. 1946, 83.

[232] "History of FFC," Ch. 6, 31 [331331–775]. This formulation is repeated verbatim in testimony given to Congress in 1947 by John Richards, then Director of FFC. Hearings before the Subcommittee of the Committee on Appropriations on the Supplemental Appropriations Bill for 1948, House of Representatives, Eightieth Congress, 1st Session , June 2, 1947, 184.

[233] "History of FFC," Ch. 6, 31 [331331–775].

[234] P.L. No. 322, 60 Stat. 50., hearings on the legislation, H.R. 3750 *Return of Vested Property to Persons not Hostile to the United States*, September 12, 1945, Senate report No. 920, 79th Congress, 2nd Session, 11.

[235] P.L. No. 79–671, c. 878, Sec. 2, 60 Stat. 925, 930.

[236] Memo from John S. Richards, Dir., FFC, to A.N. Overby, "Resolution of Problem of Uncertified Accounts," Jan. 16, 1947, NACP, RG 131, FFC, Box 457, Switz. Defrosting, Vol. II [349188–194]; U.S. Treasury Dept., *Annual Report*, 1947, 53–54.

[237] In testimony on FFC appropriations Deputy Director Richards noted that the French Government sent periodic reports and on May 2, 1947 reported that they had certified $193 million out of total of French assets of $1 billion; these assets were then unblocked. Switzerland had certified $130 million out of $1.2 billion in April 1947. *Supplemental Appropriations Bill for 1948*, 80th Congress, 1st Sess., Hearings, 1947, p.189.

[238] Memo from John S. Richards, Dir., FFC, to A.N. Overby, "Resolution of Problem of Uncertified Accounts," Jan. 16, 1947, NACP, RG 131, FFC, Box 457, Switz. Defrosting, Vol. II [349188–194]. This memo mentioned the census option as one means of determining the size of the heirless assets issue.

[239] Memo for the Files: Uncertified Accounts, Apr. 2, 1947, NACP, RG 131, FFC Corresp. 1942–60, Box 459, Switz. Defrosting [314437–438]. OAP vesting authority required public notice being given of any intent to vest.

[240] OAP, *Annual Report*, Fiscal Year ended June 30, 1949, Dept. of Justice, 1949, [323618–689].

[241] The actual transfer was made effective midnight Sept. 30, 1948 by Executive Order No. 9989 and the licensing system remained in effect, under OAP purview, up to Jan. 1, 1949, OAP, *Annual Report*, Fiscal Year ended June 30, 1949, Dept. of Justice, 1949 [323618–689].

[242] Treasury release as reprinted in an official notification by the Netherlands Bank, which urged, in comment, immediate application for certification of still uncertified blocked accounts; Archives of the Dutch Ministry of Foreign Affairs, code 3, Deel III, 47–49, [326939–940].

[243] OAP, *Annual Report*, Fiscal Year ended June 30, 1951, Dept. of Justice, 1951 [323764–860].

[244] OAP, *Annual Report*, Fiscal Year ended June 30, 1953, Dept. of Justice, 1953 [323936–4098].

[245] "Senators Attack Alien Claim Job," *The New York Times*, Feb. 1, 1953 [336631].

[246] The designation "victim," "non–victim," and "stateless" describes the original owner, rather than the beneficiary.

[247] Persecutees would claim their status as such in their correspondence with OAP.

[248] The OAP specifically identified such claims as involving "stateless" individuals in their records.

[249] Neither the number of victims' claims nor the total amounts of assets they recovered can be ascertained without two systematic investigations that fell beyond the capacities of the PCHA. First, it would be necessary to examine the petitions lodged with foreign national governments as part of the certification process necessary before "frozen" assets could be "thawed" (see explanation below). These petitions, if still extant, would be located in foreign repositories. Second, the individual claims lodged with the Office of Alien Property—amounting to 67,025—need careful review to identify those filed by victims. Whereas such a thorough investigation has not been undertaken, PCHA researchers did sample 150 cases to obtain estimates of the length of time necessary to process a claim fully (38 months) and the average amount returned to victims ($1,701). Greater specificity is currently impossible.

[250] The American Jewish Committee employed Judge Robert Patterson, ex-Secretary of War, to work "on and for this bill" already by 1948. Seymour J. Rubin, "Report to Executive Committee of Jewish Restitution Successor Organization re: Heirless Assets in the United States," Sept. 1955, 1, YIVO, RG 347.17, Am. Jewish Committee (Gen-10), Box 295, File 9 [345138–145].

[251] Amending the TWEA, rpt. (No. 784) to accompany S. 603, Comm. on the Judiciary, U.S. Senate, 81st Congress, 1st Session, July 25, 1949 [332740–743].

[252] "Survey of OAP Vesting Orders to Obtain Estimate of Heirless Jewish Accounts," Mar. 6., 1950, Central Archives for the History of the Jewish People, Jerusalem, TWEA-916a [336611–613].

[253] Letter from Abraham S. Hyman, Exec. Secy. of the WJC, to Sen. Everett M. Dirksen, May 9, 1956, AJA, WJC Papers, Box H342, U.S. 1954–57 [341874].

[254] "Survey of OAP Vesting Orders to Obtain Estimate of Heirless Jewish Accounts," Mar. 6., 1950, Central Archives for the History of the Jewish People, Jerusalem, TWEA-916a [336611–613].

[255] Ibid. [336611–613].

[256] Ibid., 2 [336612].

[257] Ibid., 3 [336613]. A subsequent memorandum recalculated the figures, concluding that the total amount of Jewish heirless assets held at OAP neared $2 million. See letter from David L. Glickman to Dr. Eugene Hevesi, May 5, 1950, Central Archives for the History of the Jewish People, Jerusalem, TWEA-916a [336614–619].

[258] Memo from Am. Jewish Committee, "Heirless Property Legislation in the United States," Jan. 24, 1950, YIVO, 347.17, Am. Jewish Committee (Gen-10), Box 296, File 7 [345287]; P.L. 826, The War Claims Act of 1948, July 3, 1948, 62 Stat. 1246–1247.

[259] Letter from Seymour J. Rubin to Dr. Eugene Hevesi, Am. Jewish Committee, Feb. 1, 1950, YIVO, 347.17, Am. Jewish Committee (Gen-10), Box 296, File 3 [345266].

[260] Amendments to War Claims Act of 1948, Hearings before a Sub-Committee of the Interstate and Foreign Commerce Committee, U.S. House of Representatives 81st Congress, 2nd Session, 168–69.

[261] Letter from Seymour J. Rubin to Judge Robert P. Patterson, Mar. 22, 1950, YIVO, 347.17, Am. Jwsh. Cmtee. (Gen-10), Box 296, File 3 [345264–265].

[262] Amending Section 32 of the TWEA, as Amended, with Reference to the Designation of Organizations as Successors in Interest to Deceased Persons, Rpt. (no. 600) to accompany S. 1748, Comm. on the Judiciary, U.S. Senate, 82nd Congress, 1st Session, July 30, 1954 [332732–733].

[263] Heirless Prop. (S. 2420), Hearing before a Subcomm. on the Judiciary, Apr. 14, 1954, U.S. Senate, 83rd Congress, 2nd Session [332715].

264 Seymour Rubin, typescript of "Statement Before the Subcomm. on the Trading with the Enemy Act of the Senate Committee on the Judiciary," no date [fall 1955], YIVO 347.17, Am. Jewish Committee (Gen-10), Box 295, File 12 [345197].

265 P.L. 626, An Act to Amend Section 32 of the TWEA, as Amended, Aug. 23, 1954, 68 Stat. 767–768 [332703–704].

266 3 CFR, 235–236 (1954–1958 Compilation), Exec. Order 10587, Administration of Section 32 (h) of the TWEA, Jan. 13, 1955 [332706–707].

267 Seymour Rubin, Washington Counsel of the JRSO, "Report to the Executive Committee of the JRSO Re: Heirless Assets in the United States," Sept. 1955, Central Archives for the History of the Jewish People, Jerusalem [332763].

268 Saul Kagan & Ernest Weismann, *Report on the Operations of The Jewish Restitution Successor Organization* (New York: The JRSO, circa 1972), 33.

269 Seymour Rubin, "Report to Executive Committee of Jewish Restitution Successor Organization Re: Heirless Assets in the United States," Sept. 1955, attached to a memo from Saul Kagan, Oct. 5, 1955, YIVO, RG 347.17, Am. Jew. Committee (Gen 10), Box 295, File 6 [345080].

270 JRSO, *Annual Report*, Nov. 1, 1955-Oct. 31, 1956, Stanford Univ., Special Collections, Papers of Salo W. Baron, Box 44, File 2 [326562].

271 Letter from Paul V. Myron, Deputy Director, OAP, to Sen. Everett M. Dirksen, Mar. 27, 1956, appearing in Return of Confiscated Prop., Hearings before a Subcommittee of the Comm. on the Judiciary, U.S. Senate, 84th Congress, 1st and 2nd Sessions, Apr. 20, 1956 [332787].

272 Letter from Lawrence E. Walsh, Deputy Attorney Gen., to Rep. Oren Harris, Aug. 26, 1959, appearing in Settlement of Claims of Successor Organizations for Return of Vested Heirless Prop., Rpt. (no. 1233) to Accompany H. R. 6462, House of Representatives, 86th Congress, 2nd Session, Feb. 1, 1960 [332748].

273 Settlement of Claims of Successor Organizations for Return of Vested Heirless Prop., Rpt. (no. 1233) to Accompany H. R. 6462, House of Representatives, 86th Congress, 2nd Session, Feb. 1, 1960 [332747].

274 Statement of Seymour J. Rubin, appearing in Return of Confiscated Prop., Hearings before a Subcommittee of the Comm. on the Judiciary, U.S. Senate, 84th Congress, 1st and 2nd Sessions, Apr. 20, 1956 [332787].

275 Letter from Paul V. Myron, Deputy Dir., OAP, to Sen. Everett M. Dirksen, Mar. 27, 1956, appearing in Return of Confiscated Prop., Hearings before a Subcomm. of the Comm. on the Judiciary, U.S. Senate, 84th Congress, 1st & 2nd Sessions, Apr. 20, 1956 [332787].

276 Settlement of Claims of Successor Organizations for Return of Vested Heirless Property, *Congressional Record*, Mar. 1, 1960, 4043 [332723–731].

277 Ibid., 4045 [332723–731].

278 Ibid., 4045 [332723–731].

279 Statement of Seymour J. Rubin, July 25, 1959, AJA, WJC Papers, Box H 343, TWEA-1958–59 [341648–649].

280 PCHA Interview with Saul Kagan, New York City, Aug. 15, 2000.

281 P.L. 87–846, An Act to Amend the War Claims Act of 1948, to Provide Compensation for Certain World War II Losses, Oct. 22, 1962, 76 Stat. 1114–1115 [332794–795].

282 3 CFR, 721–722 (1959–1963 Compilation), Exec. Order 11086, Amendment of Exec. Order 10587, Relating to the Administration of Sec. 32 (h) of TWEA, Feb. 26, 1963 [332801–802].

283 Kagan & Weismann, *Report on the Operations of The Jewish Restitution Successor Organization,* 33–34.

284 JRSO, *Annual Report*, Nov. 1, 1955–Oct. 31, 1956, Stanford Univ., Special Collections, Papers of Salo W. Baron, Box 44, Folder 2 [326562].

[285] Estimates of the value of heirless assets held by the OAP differed widely. In 1950, Seymour Rubin thought that the War Claims Commission could be prevailed upon to accept a $5 million ceiling. Former Secretary of War Robert Patterson suggested that the ceiling be $3 million and legislation authorizing that ceiling was passed in 1954. However, adjudication of JRSO claims was never finalized. In 1956, Paul Myron, Deputy Director of the OAP, wrote to Senator Everett Dirksen that he thought the value was likely to be half of the $865,000 heirless assets returnable to the JRSO, about $435,000. In April 1956, Seymour Rubin proposed that Congress authorize $865,000 as a lump sum settlement to resolve all JRSO claims. In July 1956, Congressman Arthur Klein suggested $750,000 be given to the successor organization. It appears that the longer the legislative effort dragged on, the more likely the JRSO was willing to reduce the size of its estimate of the value of heirless assets. See Letter from Seymour J. Rubin to Dr. Eugene Hevesi, Feb. 1, 1950, YIVO, RG 347.17, Am. Jewish Committee, (Gen-10), Box 296, File 3 [345266]; Amendments to the War Claim Act of 1948 and the Trading with the Enemy Act (S.603), Hearings before a Subcomm. of the Committee on Interstate and Foreign Commerce, U.S. House of Representatives, 81st Congress, 2nd Session, May 5, 1950, 168–69; Return of Confiscated Prop. (S2227), Hearings before a Subcommittee of the Comm. on the Judiciary, U.S. Senate, 84th Congress, 1st and 2nd Sessions, Apr. 20, 1956 [332786–787]; Letter from Paul V. Myron, Deputy Director, OAP to Congressman Arthur G. Klein, Aug.10, 1956, YIVO, RG 347.17, Am. Jew. Committee (Gen-10), Box 295, File 11 [345164]; Letter from Congressman Arthur G. Klein to Dallas S. Townsend, Dir., OAP, no date [July 11, 1956], YIVO, RG 347.17, Am. Jewish Committee (Gen-10), Box 295, File 11 [345169]; Memo from Seymour J. Rubin to Nathaniel Goldstein, "Proposed Bulk Settlement Legislation," Mar. 28, 1956, YIVO, RG 347.17, Am. Jew. Committee (Gen-10), Box 295, File 11 [345172–174].

Chapter VI

Heirless Assets and the Role of Jewish Cultural Reconstruction, Inc.

Jewish Cultural Reconstruction, Inc.: Origins and Purposes

The Jewish Cultural Reconstruction, Inc. (JCR) grew out of the Commission on European Jewish Cultural Reconstruction which had been established in 1945 as the central research and coordinating body for all American activities in Europe relating to the identification, salvage and restitution of Jewish cultural property. Headed by Professor Salo Baron of Columbia University, the Commission's first and most important publication was entitled, "Tentative List of Jewish Cultural Treasures in Axis-Occupied Countries," which listed cultural treasures known to have existed before the Nazi occupation.[1] This publication, which included only movable assets such as books, documents and museum pieces, was the first of its kind and helped various organizations in Europe to locate Jewish cultural property. Later, the JCR would publish several additional, more specific guides.[2]

The Commission recognized by 1946 that only a joint effort by Jewish organizations could effectively salvage heirless cultural objects. Moreover, it believed that unity among the Jewish organizations was a precondition to State Department agreement to transfer looted Jewish cultural objects to the custody of a Jewish organization. In August 1946, therefore, the Commission announced the creation of a membership corporation representing major Jewish organizations that would act as the trustee for heirless Jewish cultural objects.[3] Such a corporation, argued the Commission, would enable all interested Jewish organizations to participate in the final decisions on the distribution of property. Thus, the Jewish Cultural Reconstruction, Inc., was established in April 1947.[4]

The World Jewish Congress, the American Jewish Committee, the American Jewish Conference, the Commission on European Jewish Cultural Reconstruction, the Council for the Protection of the Rights and Interests of Jews from Germany, Hebrew University and the Synagogue Council of America founded the JCR.[5] The American Joint Distribution Committee and the Jewish Agency for Palestine, which also became members of the corporation, provided its operating funds.[6] At the JCR's first meeting on May 5, 1947, Professor Baron became President, and

Professor Jerome Michael, formerly the Acting Chairman of the Commission on European Jewish Cultural Reconstruction, became Chairman of the Board.[7] Also active among the JCR officers were Joshua Starr, who served as Executive Secretary until his death in 1949, and Hannah Arendt who replaced him.[8] Other distinguished members of the JCR leadership included Rabbi Leo Baeck and Professor Gershon Scholem, both of whom served as Vice Presidents.

Whereas the JRSO served as a trustee for recovering property of economic value, the JCR set its sights on recovering property of cultural value.[9] Given the nature of heirless property, however, a clear distinction between economics and culture was not always easy to define. The boundary between the JRSO and the JCR remained fluid: the two organizations shared similar origins and overlapping memberships.[10] The relationship between these organizations was reflected in an agreement signed in August 1947, in which the JCR agreed to act as an agent of the JRSO in tracing, restituting and allocating Jewish books, Jewish ceremonial objects, and other Jewish cultural property found in the U.S. Zone in Germany.[11] In spite of the fact that many of the same individuals and organizations figured prominently in both the JCR and the JRSO, they functioned largely independent of each other.

The recognition of the JCR as trustee to heirless cultural property came only after lengthy debates within the Jewish world as well as between Jewish groups, the United States government, and occupation authorities. Discussions between the U.S. State, War, and Navy Departments and OMGUS "concerning Jewish material" began as early as December 1945, at a time when it was reported that "even the Jewish peoples are far from unanimous in their ideas with respect to the disposition of such religious and cultural objects."[12] There was the fear that even if Jewish unanimity were achievable, "difficulties inherent in permitting any private organization to abrogate the powers of governments" would still remain and, at least as of May 1947, the Military Government was the sole organization "recognized as a proper trustee for this material."[13] Nevertheless, there was a sense of urgency within the Military Government to release the property under its control: General Lucius Clay noted that he "was awaiting the formation of a representative Jewish organization to take over the custody" of Jewish cultural property at the Offenbach Archival Depot (OAD).[14]

Although the State Department had been willing to recognize the JRSO as a successor organization in November 1947, differences of opinion with the War Department delayed the recognition of the JRSO until June 23, 1948. Under Military Law 59 the JRSO was given the right to claim identifiable heirless and unclaimed Jewish property in the U.S. Zone in Germany and to act as a successor to the interests of Jewish persons and communities.[15] In contrast, OMGUS officially recognized the JCR as the trustee for all unidentifiable heirless Jewish cultural objects that could not be claimed under Law 59.

OMGUS defined such unidentifiable Jewish property as property for which "no claims have been received… and no identification of prior ownership can be reasonably established," while the JCR in turn agreed to exercise reasonable diligence in trying to locate owners for two years.[16] When accepting the heirless property, the JCR certified "that individual ownership of subject items cannot be determined and [it] undertakes to act as trustee for the Jewish people in the distribution of said property to such public or quasi-public religious, cultural or educational institutions as it sees fit, to be used in the interest of perpetuating Jewish art and culture, or to utilize them for the maintenance of the cultural heritage of the Jewish people."[17]

The JCR Board recognized that its task was daunting. The JCR was obligated to keep properties intact and to return them to the military government if an heir was located.[18] However, deciding what should be done with the thousands of ceremonial or ritual objects, many of them damaged, was far more difficult. Complete and identifiable library collections of books and manuscripts could readily be returned, but the basis on which the thousands of unidentified books should be distributed remained to be determined. It was unclear if owners or heirs could be found for some of the materials that had been judged unidentifiable.

After considerable discussion and consistent with its agreement with OMGUS to use property to "benefit the Jewish people," the JCR decided to distribute property to existing and viable Jewish communities and to institutions that could best use and care for them. Particular Jewish institutions, such as the Bezalel Museum and Hebrew University in Israel, were given first selection rights in the process.[19] The disposition of the heirless property of Jewish communities, particularly that associated with religious observance, held immense symbolic importance. Practical questions of what was to be sent where, however, were not easily resolved and it would take many months for a global distribution formula to be approved. Heirless books and manuscripts were testimonials to the Jewish intellectual heritage, and while their distribution to libraries might have seemed more straightforward, in practice, U.S. policies and Jewish interests conflicted, as did the parties' political considerations.

Communal Property

Torah Scrolls

As part of its agreement with OMGUS, in 1949 the JCR received custody of what were estimated to be 1,000 unclaimed Torah scrolls, and as no claims had been received and no identification of prior ownership could be established for them, they and other religious objects "were to be utilized for the maintenance of the cultural heritage of the Jewish people."[20] The U.S. Army seemed well aware of the significance of the materials it was holding, as it had set aside a "Torah Room" at the OAD that held "about 1,000 torah scrolls or parts thereof which present a special problem in disposition."[21]

Torah scrolls had to be handled in a manner different from all other ritual objects because according to Jewish practice the sacred nature of the Torah dictated burial of torn or mutilated scrolls that could not be repaired. This meant that before the JCR could distribute the scrolls, all of them (including fragments) had to be carefully examined and then sorted. Scroll repair was eventually carried out in Israel, but the examination and sorting was first undertaken by the American Joint Distribution Committee (AJDC) office in Paris, in a disposition that had taken some time to agree upon.[22] Of the 1,151 Torah scrolls distributed by 1952, the vast majority went to Israel (931), with the remainder sent to the United States (110), Western Europe (98) and Great Britain (12). While it is unknown how many of the scrolls sent to the United States were torn or mutilated, 127 Torah scrolls sent to Israel were buried.[23]

Ceremonial Objects

In 1948, the OAD estimated it held about 17,000 items other than Torah scrolls in its "Torah Room," "the great majority of which are metal cult objects, largely silver." According to a memorandum of agreement between the JCR, the JRSO and OMGUS, such "Jewish ritual objects of precious metals are to be utilized as such and not converted to monetary metal."[24] These ceremonial objects had been looted from synagogues and homes throughout Europe, and many were damaged or bore "visible marks of willful destruction."[25]

Faced with such a large quantity, the JCR Advisory Committee decided in early February 1949 that ceremonial objects should first be divided into the categories of "art objects suitable for museums; and other ceremonial objects, which should be available for presentation to synagogues in various countries," a formulation that was adopted verbatim in a resolution adopted by the JCR Board of Directors the following month.[26] A field report from early April, 1949, assessing the property collected together at Wiesbaden, found it "consists primarily of synagogue appurtenances, together with other objects of religious significance, some household silver and a few hundred pounds of material damaged beyond repair." Of the approximately 9,000 objects counted, nearly 60 percent consisted of silver in scrap condition, ribbons with mounted silver plates, spice boxes and menorahs.[27]

Between July 1949 and January 31, 1952, the JCR distributed 7,867 ceremonial objects around the world, the vast majority of which were sent to Israel and the United States.[28] Appropriate global distribution of these objects was discussed at length by the JCR. In early February 1949, the JCR's Advisory Committee had suggested distributing one-third of the ceremonial objects to synagogues in Israel, one-third to the United States, and one-third to other countries.[29] In March, the JCR Board of Directors decided instead that approximately 40 percent were to go to Israel, "while the remainder is to be allocated to synagogues in other countries."[30] Some of those present at this March meeting reported having heard that the allocations would be 40 percent to Israel, 40 percent to other countries, and 20 percent to the United States, numbers that had been arrived at "after a lengthy discussion."[31] In June, Dr. Bernard Heller, the Field Director at Wiesbaden and a distinguished rabbi, educator, and author, was instructed to allocate the ceremonial objects according to yet another formula (Israel, 40 percent; Western Europe, 25 percent; Western Hemisphere, 25 percent; Great Britain, 5 percent; South Africa and other countries, 5 percent).[32] But by October 1949, agreement finally seems to have been reached that 40 percent of all items should go to Israel, 40 percent to the Western Hemisphere (including the United States), and 20 percent to other countries. This 40:40:20 ratio was adhered to in practice.[33]

The JCR decided that the Bezalel Museum in Jerusalem would receive "first priority in the distribution of art objects which represent styles now lacking in the Bezalel collection." To sort through the thousands of heirless ceremonial objects and select those that the museum lacked, Dr. Mordechai Narkiss, then director of the Bezalel Museum, traveled to Germany in 1949.[34] Narkiss found this an extremely difficult task, as many of the objects appeared to be of only average quality, and among the museum objects he selected, "it happens that the damaged items are probably the oldest and most interesting."[35] Nevertheless, of the 187 cases that were packed by July 8, Narkiss was able to ship 61 cases worth of museum material to Jerusalem (along with 26 cases of synagogue material). He commented that "the objects left for the other museums are only of average quality and often inferior to that."

Narkiss noted that in total, 133 museum material cases and 54 synagogue material cases had been shipped (of which 72 and 11, respectively, were sent to New York), and a JCR account prepared in New York soon afterwards indicated about five times as many museum objects as synagogue objects had been sent.[36] In contrast to the museum pieces, the materials selected for synagogues had to be able to withstand regular use, and yet many of the objects were "damaged beyond repair."[37] Unlike Torah scrolls, however, ceremonial objects are not sacred, and if damaged could be discarded or converted for other uses, including through smelting. Narkiss noted that 25 cases "containing silver fragments which are to be smelted" had been packed up, and a JCR letter states that "4,208 metal objects, of which 3,713 were silverware, have been sent to a British firm in Sheffield for melting."[38] The smelting of silver fragments could have violated the OMGUS memorandum of agreement that precluded conversion of ceremonial objects into monetary metal, if the goal had been to raise funds.[39] No clear evidence exists that this was the intention. In any case, there is evidence that the action was undertaken without the consent of the JCR Board of Directors.[40]

The JCR asked recipient institutions to agree in writing to take good care of the objects, indicate their origins on a label, and furnish itemized receipts. Recipients also agreed to return any item at the request of the JCR, and to pay handling charges of sixty cents per item to cover the cost of transportation from Germany.[41]

In the United States, the Jewish Museums in New York and Cincinnati were given first priority for museum objects, followed by Yeshiva University, though by mid-August 1950 other colleges and institutions were also the recipients of the 1,698 objects distributed. The largest categories of ceremonial objects were (in descending order) spice boxes, Torah shields, Hanukah lamps, and pointers.[42] In terms of priority, synagogue objects were first to go to "congregations of recent arrivals from Central Europe," and at least in the eyes of a World Jewish Congress (WJC) representative who participated in the JCR meetings, "it is understood that the objects to be allocated to American museums and synagogues are mainly of sentimental value."[43]

Because the JCR allocation policy favored the distribution of cultural assets to communities outside of Europe, it provoked resentment and criticism from the remaining European Jewish communities. In one case in 1950, the JRSO filed a claim for 18 cases containing approximately 450 ceremonial objects that had formerly belonged to the Frankfurt Jewish Museum.[44] The Frankfurt Jewish community claimed that it was entitled to the objects, and in late 1950 some of its members gained access to the boxes of ceremonial silver, took some items for themselves and returned others to the Frankfurt municipality.[45]

As long as the Frankfurt Jewish community claimed the property, the JRSO could not successfully claim heirless Jewish objects that had been in the museum. To resolve this conflict, the JCR Board of Directors decided to employ Dr. Guido Schoenberger, a member of the JCR Advisory Committee, to examine markings on the objects to try to identify those that belonged to the Jewish community and the Frankfurt municipality.[46]

The JCR Board of Directors thought if some objects were sent to Israel, the Frankfurt Jewish Community might drop its claim. On the other hand, some members of the Board also objected to sending still more objects to the Bezalel Museum which already had a chance to get the best of the ceremonial objects. By returning to the Frankfurt Jewish community the objects it had requested, the

JCR Executive Board hoped that it could distribute the rest of the collection to museums around the world.[47]

JCR eventually made a gift of some objects to the Frankfurt Museum, which satisfied the demands of the Frankfurt Jewish community. The JCR members voted to divide the remainder of the museum collection according to a 40:40:20 allocation (United States: Israel: other countries). All synagogue pieces other than those claimed by the Frankfurt Jewish community were sent to Israel.[48] American museums, for the first time in the JCR allocations, received first priority for museum-quality ceremonial objects, and the JCR Board of Directors approved because the Frankfurt Museum objects would greatly enhance the value of American museum collections.[49]

Paintings

There was one instance when the JRSO came into possession of approximately 1,000 paintings and other art objects that had remained at the collecting points because they had been deemed unidentifiable.[50] The collection included 35 old masters paintings that the JRSO sent to Israel.[51] It decided to sell the rest at private auction in New York.[52] The valuations of the paintings varied widely and eventually the JRSO hoped only to recover the expenses it incurred for shipping the art from Europe to the United States.[53] At sales between May 1950 and May 1951, the JRSO netted approximately $3,200.[54] Paintings that found no buyers were sent to the Jewish Museum or the Bezalel Museum in Israel.[55] In the years following, a number of claims were submitted to the JRSO for the return of various paintings.[56] It appears that the JRSO settled at least some of the claims.[57]

Books

The books that were transferred to the JCR fell into several categories: unidentifiable books of Jewish content in the German language, identifiable books and other archival materials belonging to private owners and Jewish institutions in Germany, unidentifiable and partially identifiable books in languages other than German, and identifiable books from the Baltic states.[58] Before books could be distributed they had to be sorted, identified and returned to their original owners, if possible. Then decisions on allocation and distribution could be made for the unidentifiable material. Cataloguing the rare books and manuscripts was a special, additional task.[59]

Identification and Return

The process of sorting and identifying books and other material in the Collecting Points was extremely important and difficult.[60] Book identification had two aspects: establishing what a book was and to whom it belonged. The OAD did not have a staff large enough to sort and catalogue several hundred thousand books by title and author. This task was made even more difficult because much of the material was in Hebrew and Yiddish, and U.S. officials had difficulty finding qualified experts who could help in identification.[61]

As early as March 1946, Jewish organizations realized that the lack of qualified personnel to sort through the books could have serious effects on the prospect of restitution. In a letter to the World Jewish Congress, Mr. A. Aaroni, who was assigned by the U.S. Army to the Rothschild Library in Frankfurt, Germany, recommended that a Hebrew scholar be sent to the library immediately. "This recommendation is to take precedence over all others," he wrote, because at the time, there was not a single person with knowledge of Hebrew to help with the sorting of the books.[62] Two years later, in 1948, OAD still employed only a rabbinical student and a German rabbi who were qualified to sort the Hebrew and Yiddish materials.[63] Joseph Horne, the Director of OAD at the time, explained that their work "is of highest importance in solving one of the most difficult problems of the Offenbach Archival Depot."[64]

Soon it became clear that the lack of qualified experts impeded restitution of identifiable books from OAD. In an example that says more about the problems of restitution under the military government than it does about the JCR, on June 7, 1949 Rabbi Dr. O. Lehmann of Oxford University protested the OAD's lack of cooperation in his attempt, under Law 59, to reclaim 78 of his books and 56 books that belonged to his late brother. To claim the books, Rabbi Lehmann was required to submit the books' titles, even though all of the books had his name and that of his brother inscribed in them. Although he had written to the OAD on several occasions requesting the books, he did not receive a reply. This incident created "a most unfortunate impression in Jewish and academic circles in this country as to the attitude of some of the officials of Military Government to the position of victims of Nazi dispossession."[65]

In response to Rabbi Lehmann's letter, Lieutenant Colonel Milton L. Ogden explained that OMGUS was in possession of several hundred thousand books, but "due to their number and the inability to allocate sufficient personnel for the purpose, it has not been possible to sort and catalogue them by title and author."[66] Colonel Ogden expected that, at a later date, the books that were inscribed with the name of an owner would be separated "and be available for delivery to the person entitled to receive them."[67]

To help solve this problem the JCR needed to work with military officials to separate identifiable from unidentifiable Jewish books, its first step toward becoming trustee of the heirless unidentifiable books. Recognizing the importance of this task, the JCR appointed Dr. Bernard Heller as Field Director to coordinate the efforts of numerous experts working at the OAD.[68] Accordingly, Dr. Shunami of Hebrew University, author of "Bibliography of Jewish Bibliographies", and the Director of the Bezalel Museum were appointed as supervisors on the cultural aspect of the collections.[69] With their help, the JCR sorted through the thousands of books in U.S. military custody in a relatively short time period.

In addition to sorting the books, the experts who worked at the OAD also identified rare Jewish books and manuscripts. As a result of the efforts of scholars such as Dr. Gershom Scholem of Hebrew University, a list of all the rare books transferred to the JCR was produced and circulated among the recipient libraries and institutions.[70]

Allocation and Distribution

Once the books were sorted and identified, the JCR had to decide where to send them. After careful consideration, the Board of the JCR adopted the same 40:40:20 allocation formula for books as it used for ceremonial objects. Within this allocation, Hebrew University in Jerusalem was given the first choice of books.[73]

By 1952 the JCR had distributed 426, 921 books around the world.[75] Israel received the largest number with 191,423 books, while the United States was the second largest recipient with 160,886.[76] The distribution of books elsewhere was administered either directly from Germany or through the JCR's depot in New York, which served as the center for distribution to the United States, Canada, Latin American, Africa, and Australia.[77] Recipient countries paid freight expenses from the German border. The JCR paid freight expenses to the United States, but these expenses were later recovered by a charge of 30 cents for each book, payable by the recipient institution.[78]

Under a special agreement with the JCR, the Education and Culture Department of the World Jewish Congress (WJC) handled distribution to Latin America.[79] Affiliates of the WJC in Latin America assessed the needs of the local Jewish communities. Books were then sent to the central Jewish organization of each recipient country. A report of the activities of the Department of Culture and Education of the WJC noted the gratefulness of the Latin Jewish communities:

> The response of our affiliates and the central organizations thus far has been very favorable, and even enthusiastic. They are very eager to have the books and cultural objects to enlarge their existing libraries or to open new libraries in places where there are none at present. They feel that such libraries will give a great impulse to their cultural life. They are well aware, also, that these books, apart from their cultural importance, have a high sentimental value as they constitute the heritage of the once great Jewish communities of Europe.[80]

By 1952, Jewish communities in Latin American countries had received 11,679 books.[81]

As in Latin America, local Jewish organizations administered distribution within each country. For example, in Israel, unless property was transferred directly to Hebrew University or the Bezalel Museum, the Ministry of Religious Affairs made the final distribution decisions.[82] In Western Europe, the Joint Distribution Committee effected the distribution.[83]

Some agencies took care to identify the origin of these books. For instance, the Canadian Jewish Congress, which distributed Jewish books in Canada, placed a label in every book that read:

> This book was once the property of a Jew, victim of the Great Massacre in Europe. The Nazis who seized this book eventually destroyed the owner. It has been recovered by the Jewish people, and reverently placed in this institution by the Canadian Jewish Congress, as a memorial to those who gave their lives for the Sanctification of the Holy Name.[84]

The JCR made a similar gesture, asking its recipient libraries in the United States to acknowledge the origin of the books by placing a bookplate in the volume.[85]

Distribution in the United States

The JCR undertook distribution in the United States. It made extensive efforts not only to protect the books for future generations, but also to commemorate the former owners who, in most cases, were deceased.

In March 1949, before the distribution began, the JCR sent a questionnaire to all potential recipient libraries. Its accompanying letter stated that, "[I]t would be very helpful to us to have the enclosed questionnaire answered by the librarian in charge of your collection of Judaica and Hebraica. The answers should deal exclusively with this particular department of your library."[86] The questionnaire primarily addressed the subject of the library's major Hebraic collections, number of readers, annual budget, and the Hebrew, Yiddish, and German books that the library was interested in purchasing.[87] When the books were ready for distribution, each recipient was required to sign an agreement with the JCR that stated "each library is asked to adhere to the following procedure, so that all books will be treated as part of the cultural heritage of European Jewry."[88] The terms of the agreement were:

1. No books received may be sold, nor may any be exchanged for other books without the permission of Jewish Cultural Reconstruction obtained prior to the exchange.[89]

2. The recipient will furnish Jewish Cultural Reconstruction with an itemized receipt, listing authors and their titles, within six months after the delivery of each shipment.

3. The recipient places at the disposal of Jewish Cultural Reconstruction all duplicates of publications already in its library unless Jewish Cultural Reconstruction authorizes the recipient in writing to retain them specifically.

4. Any books identified by a claimant as his property to the satisfaction of Jewish Cultural Reconstruction within two years of its delivery to the recipient shall be returned promptly to the claimant or to Jewish Cultural Reconstruction upon the latter's request.

5. Any book which Jewish Cultural Reconstruction may desire to re-allocate to another library within two years of its delivery to the recipient shall likewise be promptly returned to Jewish Cultural Reconstruction upon its request. However, the total number of items requested for re-allocation shall not exceed 10% of the number of items allocated to the recipient.[90]

After signing the agreement, the libraries received bookplates and the following request:

[W]e feel that it will be of great importance to have each volume marked, so that present and future readers may be reminded of those who once cherished them before they became victims of the great Jewish catastrophe.

Without such distinctive mark it will also be impossible for present and future scholars to retrace the history and the whereabouts of the great cultural treasures of European Jewry which once were the pride of scholars, institutions and private collections.

We therefore are sending you today bookplates which should be pasted into each of the volumes which you received from us. We trust that you will understand the historic significance of this request and will gladly comply with it.[91]

Although this request was not a prerequisite for receiving books, the JCR expected participating libraries to comply.

After each library or institution signed the agreement, the JCR began distribution from its warehouse in Brooklyn, New York. In a letter to Professor Harry

A. Wolfson of Harvard University, Hannah Arendt, Executive Secretary of the JCR, described the distribution process:

> Either the interested librarian makes an appointment with our depot manager to come down to our depot and select the titles from the shelves, or we send a specified number of books in each category [sic] to the librarian who returns to us those books which turn out to be duplicates in the library's collection. As for periodicals, we ask the librarians to draw up lists of those issues which they need in order to complete their own sets, as well as lists of periodicals which the library does not possess at all but would like to add to its present collection, even if only broken sets are available.[92]

The distribution of rare books constituted an exception to these procedures. A list of rare books was created and sent to each library. Upon receipt, the librarian was invited to choose a predetermined amount of book titles from the list. For example, Harvard University was invited to choose 100 rare books from the master list.[93] After making a selection, the libraries would send the names and numbers of the selected titles to the JCR, which would grant the request if those books were still available.

At first, only Jewish libraries, institutions and religious schools received these books. However, "[i]n view of the great assistance given by American authorities in the work of the JCR in Germany,"[94] the Judaic departments of non-Jewish institutions and libraries were later added to the receipt list, most notably the Library of Congress, Harvard University, the New York Public Library, Columbia University, and Yale University.[95]

Distribution in the United States ended in 1952, when the JCR terminated its activities. By that time, 160,886 books had been distributed to 48 libraries and institutions. Some 17 libraries were designated as "priority libraries," such as the Jewish Theological Seminary in New York, which received 13,320 books and periodicals; Brandeis University in Massachusetts, which received 11,288 books and periodicals; and the Yiddish Scientific Institute in New York, which received 12,360 books and periodicals.[96]

Identifiable Books in the JCR Shipments

Unavoidably, some books that were received and distributed by the JCR were identifiable. In these cases, the JCR returned the books to their rightful owners or to the Office of the United States High Commissioner for Germany.[97] The JCR agreed to restore to the Office of the United States High Commissioner for Germany for proper disposition "any object which has been delivered to it by mistake".[98] In a letter to the JRSO, Hannah Arendt explained that "among the books which we handled, there were a certain number of stray volumes where former individual owners could be identified. These books were returned by us."[99] In total, the JCR returned 6,176 identifiable books from the United States distribution.

Although the period to file a claim for restitution under Law 59 expired on December 31, 1948, the JCR did not close the door to potential heirs for the books in its custody. In its agreement with each recipient institution in the United States, the JCR incorporated a provision that stated:

> Any books identified by a claimant as his property to the satisfaction of Jewish Cultural Reconstruction within two years of its delivery to the recipient shall be

returned promptly to the claimant or to Jewish Cultural Reconstruction upon the latter's request.[100]

In order to locate the owners of identifiable books and manuscripts transferred from OAD to Hebrew University, the JCR took the following steps:

> In all cases in which one owner possesses six or more books, we shall make every effort to locate the former owner or his heirs. We shall type out the list of all these persons, photo-stat them, deposit them in the major Jewish organizations and institutions all over the world and then give this list vast publicity through newspaper advertising all over the world.[101]

By 1952, the JCR had restituted 19,400 identifiable books and archival materials to institutions and individuals worldwide.[102]

Difficulties with Distribution

The distribution of books classified as "unidentifiable" and "heirless" was not without problems. Some books loaned to the AJDC for distribution in Displaced Persons camps turned out to be identifiable, and record keeping was such that valuable books may have been distributed, and subsequently lost.

Books for the DP Camps

Unfortunately, one episode involving the loss of a number of books marred the restitution efforts of the JCR. The American Joint Distribution Committee (AJDC) played a crucial role in providing humanitarian relief to Jews in camps for displaced persons (DPs) throughout Europe. As part of its humanitarian effort, the AJDC distributed more than 20,000 books from the OAD to various DP camps immediately after the war.

The AJDC had asked OMGUS for a loan of 25,000 books to distribute to DP camps in late November 1945, but because the book identification process was not complete, the request was denied in mid-December.[103] It took a personal approach to General Lucius Clay the following month by Judge Simon Rifkind, advisor to the Theater Commander on Jewish Affairs, on behalf of the AJDC for this loan to be approved. Judge Rifkind described the efforts by AJDC and other organizations to create educational and cultural programs in the camps, arguing that the need was acute, that those living in the camps were "starved for reading and study materials," and that some in the camps had not seen a Hebrew text in more than six years.[104]

Judge Rifkind suggested books come from OAD and other repositories where thousands of ordinary Jewish books of "no historical or artistic merit" could be found, and

> that no book be borrowed that is in any way unusual, irreplaceable, very valuable, or very difficult to procure [and] that no book be withdrawn that has been established as the property of any known institution or individual.[105]

Three experts would ensure that no valuable items would be included in the loan; men who were "eminently qualified to make a selection which would in no way prejudice the preservation of the historical, rare and valuable character of the collection nor interfere with its restoration to rightful owners."[106]

By June 1946 more than 19,100 books claimed to be of unknown ownership or origin were transferred to the AJDC and then distributed in DP camps by the United Nations Refugee and Relief Agency.[107] Some 5,000 more books were subsequently transferred. Though the books were sent to the camps as a loan, the JCR staff thought that "the possibility of their being returned is quite remote."[108] In the chaotic conditions of the camps, with large and transient populations, the possibility that books would be lost or misdirected was a real one.

One such incident involved a United Nations Refugee and Relief officer. Mordechai Breuer, who was in charge of education at the Belsen camp, discovered that identifiable books were arriving at the camp:

> To my great astonishment I found among the books several of which were clearly inscribed with the name "FANNY BREUER." I also found several other books by well-known German-Jewish orthodox writers such as S.R. Hirsch, parts of the title pages of which, where obviously the owner's name had been inscribed, had been cut away. All these books carried the stamp "AJDC LIBRARY—NOT TO BE REMOVED FROM PREMISES."

> The discovery of the name mentioned above, the bearer of which, incidentally a cousin of mine, lives at Tel-Aviv, 4 Weisel Street, as well as other names of well-known Frankfurt families, must lead to the obvious conclusion that AJDC incorporated in their library many books the rightful owners of which are still alive in many parts of the world including Palestine and the U.S.A.[109]

Though the AJDC explained the books were being loaned, and Mr. Breuer's relatives were advised to file a claim for the return of their books, this discovery meant that at least some identifiable books were included among those lent to the residents of the camps.

A subsequent MFA&A investigation in February 1947 found further cause for alarm: some of the DP camps that had received books had since been dismantled, and several, including Belsen, were not even in the U.S. Zone. No lists of books that had been sent to the DP camps existed at the AJDC offices. On July 15, 1947, OMGUS terminated its agreement with the AJDC to distribute books to DP camps, explaining to the AJDC that, "it apparently was not possible to discover the whereabouts of approximately 4,300 out of the total of more than 19,000."[110]

The Hebrew University

The Hebrew University, recognizing the importance of preserving important Jewish collections, played an important role in the fate of heirless Jewish books captured by the U.S. Military Government in Germany. In 1945, the Hebrew University became involved in the long political process that eventually led the JCR to allocate a large portion of heirless Jewish cultural property to the university. Furthermore, officials from the Hebrew University helped to identify, sort and catalogue books stored in various U.S. collecting points in the U.S. Zone of Occupation of Germany and then provide a home for a large portion of these books. However, at least on one occasion, efforts by university officials resulted in the involvement of the university in the unauthorized removal of valuable books and manuscripts from OAD.

As early as May 16, 1945, Dr. Judah L. Magnes, President of the Hebrew University, expressed interest in receiving Jewish books, manuscripts and other historical objects looted by the Nazis and held by the U.S. Army. In a meeting with

L.C. Pinkerton, the American Consul General in Jerusalem, Palestine, Dr. Magnes explained that these Jewish cultural objects belonged to Jews, should be sent to Palestine, and held at the Hebrew University because it was the sole university for the Jewish people, it had the greatest Jewish collection in existence, and it employed a large number of Jewish scholars that had the expertise to study the material.[111] Dr. Magnes wanted to ensure that the assets would be quickly moved to a location where they could be of use to the Jewish people as a collective. In his letter to the State Department, the American Consul General recommended that Dr. Magnes's request receive "every proper sympathetic consideration" given the university's high regard in the Jewish world and in the United States.[112]

Another Hebrew University official who supported Dr. Magnes's efforts was Professor Gershom Scholem, the pre-eminent scholar of Jewish mysticism. In 1946, Professor Scholem traveled to Europe on a mission for the Hebrew University in search of books of Jewish interest.[113] During the summer of that year, he worked as an expert advisor at Offenbach, helping to organize and evaluate Jewish books and manuscripts.[114] After sorting the items, Dr. Scholem packed a number of valuable items into five boxes marked "Scholem" which were then stored in the "Torah Room."[115]

On January 20, 1947, the Director of OAD, Joseph A. Horne, discovered the absence of the five boxes.[116] After investigation, the Army Inspector General learned that the boxes had been sent to the Hebrew University without OAD authorization. On April 25, 1947, OMGUS directed the American Consulate in Jerusalem to open and inventory the five boxes and leave them at the Hebrew University until General Clay had the opportunity to appoint a trustee to represent world Jewry and assist in determining the final disposition of the five boxes.[117] An inventory of the five boxes counted 366 books and manuscripts.[118] The inventory revealed that almost one-third of the books and manuscripts were identifiable and therefore subject to restitution under Law 59.[119]

These items remained at the Hebrew University in the care of the head librarian until 1949. A solution emerged in 1949, when the JCR signed an agreement with OMGUS to act as trustee to unidentifiable Jewish cultural property, including the five boxes removed to Hebrew University.[120] The JCR agreed to give appropriate notices to owners of identifiable works and to have the identifiable works delivered to their rightful owners.[121] By contrast, the unidentifiable materials in the five boxes were to be transferred to the JCR "with the sole provisio[n] that the properties are to be utilized for the maintenance of the cultural heritage of the Jewish people."[122]

Although the five boxes were transferred to the JCR's custody under this agreement, it is unlikely that they ever left Hebrew University, which was never blamed for the unauthorized removal of the five boxes from Offenbach.

Books from the Baltic states

Certain library and archival collections that the Nazis looted from the Baltic states were recovered by U.S. forces and stored at collecting points such as the OAD. This property was not restituted to these countries for several reasons. The United States did not recognize the status of the Baltic states as Soviet Republics. In addition, very few Jews remained in the area; the Nazis had wiped out practically the entire community. As of September, 1948, the OAD held about 20,000 books from Jewish, and about 8,000 books from non-Jewish, institutions in the

Baltic states.[123] Among other things, the OAD housed the papers of the Yiddish Scientific Institute (YIVO), formerly of Vilnius, Lithuania, a collection whose size was estimated to be over 50,000 "items," including documents, sheet music, brochures, and newspapers. By mid-1947 these had already been shipped to YIVO, which had re-established itself in the United States.

The disposition of the remaining "items" from the Baltic states remained in doubt. The matter was discussed in May 1946, not only in the State-War-Navy Coordinating Committee, which was considering transfer of the property to "representative international Jewish groups," but also by the Joint Chiefs of Staff.[124] By July 22, 1949, the JCR was given access to the Baltic material even though the owners of most of the materials could be identified. By September, the JCR had shipped 214 cases with about 29,000 books, 78 of them (12,418 books) to Israel. The 136 remaining cases (16,346 books), which contained mostly identifiable volumes, were shipped to the warehouses of the AJDC in Paris, for a two-year trusteeship during which identifiable books could be claimed.[125] As part of its obligation, the JCR attempted to locate the owners of these books by "advertising in the centers of the Jewish world the names (16,000) of the owners," though not if they owned less than five books.[126] In 1951, after the two years' trusteeship ended, the JCR proposed to send all remaining Baltic books to Israel, since they contained "chiefly rabbinical and other Hebrew literature of a rather high quality." However, "innumerable requests from libraries in the United States" for this type of material, as well as from Western Europe, prompted the Board to vote instead to distribute the remaining Baltic collection according to the 40:40:20 ratio to Israel, the Western Hemisphere, and all other countries.[127]

Summary

Though the JCR suspended its activities by early 1952, the organization performed one more service for Jewish cultural institutions after 1954 by making Hebrew and Yiddish documents in European libraries widely available on microfilm. In so doing, the JCR continued to act as "a trustee for the Jewish people," a role that key figures like General Clay and John J. McCloy had been happy to see it play.

During the war, the Nazis succeeded in destroying not only millions of individual Jews, but also many centers of European Jewish culture. In many cases, the cultural objects handled by the JCR were the only identifiable remnants of what had one been thriving Jewish communities. The Board of the JCR grappled with difficult issues and reached conclusions about its allocation policies that were often unpopular, particularly among the surviving Jewish communities in Europe. Nevertheless, the work of the JCR and related organizations that distributed heirless Jewish cultural objects helped preserve a vital link between those lost communities and the rest of the Jewish people.

Throughout its ten-year trusteeship, the JCR reflected a collective Jewish attempt to salvage what objects remained of an intellectual and cultural patrimony. Owners and even direct heirs to these objects could in most cases no longer be found, and even the communities that had once used or possessed these objects no longer existed. The JCR leadership that carefully considered these circumstances decided that the preservation of Jewish cultural heritage meant distribution of these assets to new and thriving Jewish communities in other parts of the world. It decided to allocate what had been collective—Torahs, ceremonial objects, books—to institutions whose purpose was also collective: synagogues, museums, and libraries. The transmission was not perfect: valuable books may have been diverted, or ceremonial objects perhaps melted in error. But this also was not restitution in the sense of restoration of once-owned goods, or compensation for loss, or even replacement. It was instead reconstruction, the physical transmission of pieces from a vanished world to a world of vibrant and growing communities, in a form that was both material and symbolic.

Endnotes for Chapter VI

[1] Supplement, Commission of European Jewish Cultural Reconstruction, "Tentative List of Jewish Cultural Treasures in Axis-Occupied Countries," Vol. VIII, No.1, 1946, AJA, WJC Papers, Box E10 [116139–240].

[2] JCR, "Summary of Three Reports by M. Bernstein Library Investigator, April 17, May 25, and June 1949," no date, Central Archives for the History of the Jewish People, JRSO, NY, file 923b [115535–538].

[3] Letter from Jerome Michael, Commission of European Jewish Cultural Reconstruction, to Gen. J. H. Hillbring, Asst. Secy. of State, Aug. 26, 1946, LC, European Mission Papers, Box 34, Rest. of "Unrestituted Materials" [120194–199].

[4] Saul Kagan & Ernst H. Weismann, "Report on the Operations of The JRSO, 1947–1972," no date, pp. 30–31 [120174–193].

[5] Memo from Dr. Simon Federbusch , to the Office Comm., "Re: Jewish Cultural Reconstruction, Inc.," May 6, 1947, AJA, WJC Papers, Box E10 [116261]. At the suspension of the JCR's activities in Dec. 1951, the member organizations also included Agudath Israel World Organization, Alliance Israelite Universelle, Anglo-Jewish Association, Board of Deputies of British Jews, Committee on Restoration of Continental Jewish Museum, Libraries and Archives, Counsil Representatif des Juifs de France, and Interessenvertretung der Judischen Gemeinden und Kultusvereinigungen in der US Zone. Memo from Hannah Arendt, Secy. JCR, "Notice of Annual Meeting to be Followed by Meeting of the Board of Directors," Mar. 10 1954, AJA, WJC Papers, Box E10 [116029–030].

[6] Memo, "Recovery and Distribution of Jewish Cultural Treasures Through the JCR," Sept. 25, 1950, AJA, WJC Papers, Box E10 [116010–012].

[7] Other Officers selected included Dr. Federbusch, Dr. Leo Baeck, Mr. Allen, and Ms. Strook, Vice-Presidents; Rabbi Ahron Offer, Secy.; and Mr. David Rosentein, Treasurer. Memo from Dr. Federbusch , to the Office Comm., "Re: Jewish Cultural Reconstruction, Inc.," May 6, 1947, AJA, WJC Papers, Box E10 [116261].

[8] Appendix to Minutes of the Meeting of the Bd. of Dirs., "Minutes for Joshua Starr," Dec. 19, 1949, CAHJP, JRSO NY, file 923b [116958].

[9] This is how Salo Baron, a key actor in both organizations, drew the distinction shortly before both organizations were founded. Letter from Salo Baron, Commission on Eur. JCR, to Rabbi [Philip S.] Bernstein, Adv. on Jewish Affairs to the Cdr. in Chf., EUCOM, Mar. 25, 1947, NACP, RG 260, Ardelia Hall Collection, Box 129 [101113–114].

[10] Both the Jewish Restitution Commission (the JRSO predecessor) and the Commission on European Jewish Reconstruction (the JCR predecessor) were founded in 1945 and both JRSO and JCR incorporated in mid-1947. The World Jewish Congress, the American Jewish Conference, and the American Jewish Committee were initial member organizations of both JRSO and JCR, and later expansion in the membership in both organizations sometimes involved the same organizations, such as Agudath Israel. The Jewish Restitution Commission was supported by grants from the American Joint Distribution Committee, the American Jewish Committee, the American Association for Jewish Education, and the Conference on Jewish Relations, and when the JCR was founded, it was funded by the American Joint Distribution Committee and the Jewish Agency for Palestine. Letter from Salo W. Baron,Chairman, Commission Eur. JCR, to Dr. A. Leon Kubowitzki, WJC, Apr. 29,Apr. 29, 1946, AJA, WJC Papers, Box E10 [116248–249]; "Recovery and Distribution of Jewish Cultural Treasures Through the JCR," Sept. 25, 1950, AJA, WJC Papers, Box E10 [116010–012]. Other early JCR members included the Council for the Protection of the Rights and Interests of Jews from Germany, Hebrew University, and the Synagogue Council of America. Memo re: Jewish from Cultural Reconstruction, Inc., Dr. Federbusch to the Office Committee,Office Comm., "Jewish May 6, 1947, AJA, WJC Papers, Box E10 [116261].

[11] JCR, Inc., Minutes of a Special Meeting of the Board of Directors, Oct. 7, 1947, AJA, WJC Papers, Box E10 [116273–277].

[12] Memo from Col. L. Wilkinson, OMGUS, Econ. Div., to Chf. of Staff, "Material Wrongfully Sent from Offenbach Archival Depot and Presently at Jerusalem," May 27,

1947, NACP, RG 260, Ardelia Hall Collection, Box 283 [101117–118]. For the 1946 discussions among the State Department, WJC, the Committee for Recovery of Jewish Cultural Property (CRJCP), and an advisor to General Clay in Germany, see Memo from WJC and CRJCP to John H. Hilldring, Asst. Secy. of State, "Restitution of Looted Jewish Cultural Property in Europe," June 18, 1946 [116126–129]; memo from Dr. S. Federbusch to Members of the Office Comm., (forwarding letter to John H. Hilldring, Aug. 30, 1946), Sept. 6, 1946, AJA, WJC Papers, Box E10 [116131–134]; memo from Dr. Federbusch to Members of the Office Comm., "Report on My Conference at the State Department, Washington, on November 5, 1946, on Recovery of Jewish Cultural Property in Europe," AJA, WJC Papers, Box E10 [116102–104].

[13] Memo from Col. L. Wilkinson, OMGUS, Econ. Div., to Chf. of Staff, "Material Wrongfully Sent from Offenbach Archival Depot and Presently at Jerusalem," May 27, 1947, NACP, RG 260, Ardelia Hall Collection, Box 283 [101117–118].

[14] Letter from Rabbi Philip S. Bernstein, Adv. on Jewish Affairs to the Cdr. in Chf., EUCOM, to Dr. Salo W. Baron, Commission on Eur. JCR, Apr. 9, 1947, NACP, RG 260, Ardelia Hall Collection, Box 129 [101115–116].

[15] Not only had American Jewish organizations played a role in drafting this law, but General Lucius Clay and his successor John J. McCloy had been supportive of restitution and compensation efforts. Nana Sagi, *German Reparations: A History of the Negotiations* (New York: St. Martin's Press, 1986), 41; Constantin Goschler, *Wiedergutmachung: Westdeutschland und die Verfolgten des Nationalsozialismus 1945–1954* (Munich: Oldenbourg Verlag, 1992), 111.

[16] Memo of Agreement, Orren McJunkins, OMGUS, Joshua Starr, JCR, & Benjamin Ferencz, JRSO, "Jewish Cultural Property", Feb. 15, 1949, NACP, RG 260, Ardelia Hall Collection, Box 125 [102605–606]; Frederick Draper, OMGUS, Bernard Heller, JCR, & Saul Kagan, JRSO, "Addendum II to Memorandum of Agreement of 15 February 1949, Subject 'Jewish Cultural Property,'" July 22, 1949, NACP, RG 260, Ardelia Hall Collection, Box 66, OAD [311759].

[17] See, for example, HICOG Office of Econ. Affairs, Prop. Div., "Receipt for Jewish Cultural Properties," May 29, 1950, NACP, RG 260, Ardelia Hall Collection, Box 102 [101921–923]. This notion of trusteeship was supported by OMGUS even before the JCR was formed. See Cable WX–81072 from AGWAR to OMGUS and USFA, Sept. 22, 1946, NACP, RG 260, Ardelia Hall Collection, Box 283, Jewish Art [117160–161].

[18] Orren R. McJunkins, Memorandum of Agreement, Jewish Cultural Property, Feb. 15, 1949, Restitution Branch, Reports Pertaining to Restitution, 1945–49, NACP, RG 260. Quoted in Michael J. Kurtz, *Nazi Contraband: American Policy in the Return of European Cultural Treasures, 1945–1955* (New York: Garland, 1985), 211.

[19] Memo of Agreement, "Jewish Cultural Property," no date, CAHJP, JRSO NY 923a [115488–489].

[20] Ibid.

[21] Memo from Joseph Horne, Dir. OAD, June 24, 1948, NACP, RG 260, Ardelia Hall Collection, Box 144 [101063–064]; Field Rpt. No. 7 from Joshua Starr, JCR, "Ritual Objects and Other Property At Wiesbaden," Apr. 11, 1949, CAHJP, JRSO NY 923a [115539–540]. Horne noted the "careful attention given to this collection by the American authorities."

[22] Thus, in December 1948, the JCR Advisory Committee had suggested sending half the scrolls to New York and half to Israel for examination and repair, then decided to send all of them to the JDC offices in Tel Aviv and Jerusalem. JCR, Mtg. Mins., Adv. Comm., Feb. 6, 1949, CAHJP, JRSO NY 923a [115542–545]. Several months later "it had been found most economical and practical to ship the scrolls to the JDC in Paris," where scribes would be employed "to select those which were fit for use, and to report the result to JCR, which would control their distribution." JCR, Mtg. Mins., Adv. Comm., May 8, 1949, CAHJP, JRSO NY 923a [115499–500]. By September, "35 cases with 484 Torah scrolls plus fragments" had been sent to the AJDC in Paris. Letter from Hannah Arendt, Exec. Secy., JCR, to Eli Rock, AJDC., Sept. 21, 1949, CAHJP, JRSO NY 923b [115531–532].

[23] JCR, "World Distribution of Ceremonial Objects and Torah Scrolls, July 1, 1949–January 31, 1952," no date, Stanford Univ. Lib., Salo Baron Papers, Box 231, File 18 [117125].

[24] Memo from Joseph Horne, Dir. OAD, June 24, 1948, NACP, RG 260, Ardelia Hall Collection, Box 144 [101063–064]; memo of Agreement, Orren McJunkins, OMGUS, Joshua Starr, JCR, & Benjamin Ferencz, JRSO, "Jewish Cultural Property", Feb. 15, 1949, NACP, RG 260, Ardelia Hall Collection, Box 125 [102605–606].

[25] "Recovery and Distribution of Jewish Cultural Treasures through the JCR," Sept. 25, 1950, AJA, WJC Papers, Box E10 [116010–012].

[26] JCR, Mtg. Mins., Adv. Comm., Feb. 6, 1949, CAHJP, JRSO NY 923a [115542–545]; "JCR Resolution (Adopted at Board of Directors Mtg., JCR, March 14th, 1949)," CAHJP, JRSO NY 923a [115548].

[27] Field Rpt. No. 7 from Joshua Starr, JCR, "Ritual Objects and Other Property At Wiesbaden," Apr. 11, 1949, CAHJP, JRSO NY 923a [115539–540].

[28] JCR, "World Distribution of Ceremonial Objects and Torah Scrolls, July 1, 1949–January 31, 1952," no date, Stanford Univ. Lib., Salo Baron Papers, Box 231, File 18 [117125]. 4,162 were museum and 3,369 were synagogue pieces; 336 were mixed. The New York depot of the JCR handled the world distribution of all museum items other than those that went to Israel, while for synagogue objects the Paris AJDC office distributed to Western Europe, the JCR distributed in the United States, and the WJC distributed to Latin America. Memo from Hannah Arendt, JCR, to Bd. of Dirs. & Adv. Comm., July 1952, AJA, WJC Papers, Box E10 [116022–023]; Anon. note, "Ceremonial Objects to Latin America," no date, AJA, WJC Papers, Box H341 [116339].

[29] JCR, Mtg. Mins., Adv. Comm., Feb. 6, 1949, CAHJP, JRSO NY 923a [115542–545].

[30] "JCR Resolution (Adopted at Board of Directors Mtg., JCR, March 14th, 1949)," CAHJP, JRSO NY 923a [115548].

[31] Memo from Dr. Blattberg, WJC, to Dr. Marcus & Dr. Robinson, Mar. 15, 1949, AJA, WJC Papers, Box E10 [116078].

[32] JCR, Mtg. Mins., Spec. Mtg. of the Bd. of Dirs., June 7, 1949, CAHJP, JRSO NY 923a [115549–552]; JCR, Mtg. Mins., Adv. Comm., Sept. 19, 1949, CAHJP, JRSO NY 923b [115553–555]. The latter part of this allocation evidently also affected distribution of what was received in New York: Great Britain "should receive her usual share of 5–7% of the total, that is, 250–350 objects," while South Africa, Canada and Argentina were each to receive five percent (about 150 objects each). Together, these 700 or so objects would thus amount to twenty percent of the 3,200 or so objects sent to the United States, at least according to the 1952 JCR summary of world distribution.

[33] JCR, Mtg. Mins., Ann. Mtg. of Bd. of Dirs., Oct. 17, 1949, CAHJP, JRSO NY 923b [116960–963]; letter from Hannah Arendt, Exec. Secy., JCR, to Eli Rock, JRSO, Sept. 1, 1950, CAHJP, JRSO NY 923c [116939–943]; JCR, "World Distribution of Ceremonial Objects and Torah Scrolls, July 1, 1949–January 31, 1952," no date, Stanford Univ. Lib., Salo Baron Papers, Box 231, File 18 [117125]; "Recovery and Distribution of Jewish Cultural Treasures Through the JCR," Sept. 25, 1950, AJA, WJC Papers, Box E10 [116010–012]. "All" items thus also included books, and just as the Bezalel Museum had priority in selecting museum objects, so too Hebrew University had priority in selecting books.

[34] "JCR Resolution (Adopted at Board of Directors Mtg., JCR, March 14th, 1949)," CAHJP, JRSO NY 923a [115548]. Joshua Starr also noted that Narkiss was not only to separate museum from synagogue pieces, but "in his capacity as agent for the Israeli Ministry of Religious Affairs," would also indicate which objects were needed by synagogues in Israel. See Field Rpt. No. 7 from Joshua Starr, JCR, "Ritual Objects and Other Property At Wiesbaden," Apr. 11, 1949, CAHJP, JRSO NY 923a [115539–540].

[35] M. Narkiss, Dir. of Bezalel Museum, "Two Reports on Ceremonial Objects . . . June 19, 1949 and July 10, 1949," no date, summarized from Hebrew, CAHJP, JRSO NY 923b [115533–534].

[36] The JCR statement that "museum pieces outnumber the synagogue pieces almost in the proportion of 9 to 1" did not take into account that 4,200 of the approximately 10,600 pieces shipped from Wiesbaden were damaged beyond repair, 5,000 were museum objects, and 1,400 were suitable for synagogue use. JCR, Mtg. Mins., Adv. Comm., Sept. 19, 1949, CAHJP, JRSO NY 923b [115553–555].

[37] Letter from Hannah Arendt, Exec. Secy., JCR, to Eli Rock, AJDC., Sept. 21, 1949, CAHJP, JRSO NY 923b [115531–532].

[38] M. Narkiss, Dir. of Bezalel Museum, "Two Reports on Ceremonial Objects...June 19, 1949 and July 10, 1949," no date, summarized from Hebrew, CAHJP, JRSO NY 923b [115533–534]; letter from Hannah Arendt, Exec. Secy., JCR, to Eli Rock, AJDC., Sept. 21, 1949, CAHJP, JRSO NY 923b [115531–532].

[39] Documentary evidence is lacking here but Starr's report states that "The scrap metal and household silver will be turned over to the JRSO, which has undertaken the responsibility of exploiting this material to the best advantage." Joshua Starr, "Field Report No. 7, Ritual Objects and other Property at Wiesbaden," Apr. 11, 1949, CAHJP, JRSO NY, File 923a [115539–540].

[40] JCR, Mtg. Mins., Ann. Mtg. of Bd. of Dirs., Oct. 17, 1949, CAHJP, JRSO NY 923b [116960–963]. It also suggests the smelting was undertaken based on the JCR Advisory Committee recommendations rather than with the approval of the Board of Directors.

[41] JCR, Mtg. Mins., Adv. Comm., Sept. 19, 1949, CAHJP, JRSO NY 923b [115553–555]; JCR, Mtg. Mins., Adv. Comm., Feb. 6, 1949, CAHJP, JRSO NY 923a [115542–545]. Repair was the responsibility of recipient institutions, though the Jewish Museum in New York offered restoration services.

[42] Some of the recipients included, in mid-1950, the Museum of Hebrew Union College, Hebrew Theological College, and B'nai Brith Hillel Foundation, as well as the Brooklyn Museum and New York University's Library of Judaica and Hebraica. A total of 1,698 museum pieces are listed. Memo from Hannah Arendt, Exec. Secy., JCR, to Bd. of Dirs. & Adv. Comm., "Distribution of Ceremonial Objects, New York Depot," Aug. 18, 1950, AJA, WJC Papers, Box E10 [116004]. A different summary claims 3,250 ceremonial objects were distributed to the U.S. by 1952, 1,326 of which were museum pieces, but this is at odds with the figure Arendt cites. JCR, "World Distribution of Ceremonial Objects and Torah Scrolls, July 1, 1949–January 31, 1952," no date, Stanford Univ. Lib., Salo Baron Papers, Box 231, File 18 [117125]. It is also not consistent with the 1,028 ceremonial objects going to Jewish museums, the 55 objects going to non-Jewish museum, and the 1,746 objects going to synagogues listed on still another list. JCR, "Distribution of Ceremonial Objects from New York Depot, 1950, According to Institutions," no date, Stanford Univ. Lib., Salo Baron Papers, Box 231, Folder 18 [117126].

[43] JCR, Mtg. Mins., Adv. Comm., Sept. 19, 1949, CAHJP, JRSO NY 923b [115553–555]; memo from Dr. Blattberg, WJC, to Dr. Marcus & Dr. Robinson, Mar. 15, 1949, AJA, WJC Papers, Box E10 [116078].

[44] Memo from Hannah Arendt to Bd. of Dirs., JCR, "Disposition of 18 Cases Containing about 450 Ceremonial Objects from Frankfort/M," June 12, 1951, AJA, WJC Papers, Box E10 [116016–017].

[45] JCR, Mtg. Mins., Spec. Mtg. of Bd. of Dirs., Dec. 21, 1950, CAHJP, JRSO NY 923c [115765–772].

[46] Ibid.

[47] Ibid.

[48] Ibid.; letter from Samuel Dallob to Hannah Arendt, JCR, Oct. 26, 1951, CAHJP, JRSO NY 296b [115556]; memo from Hannah Arendt to Bd. of Dirs. & Adv. Comm., JCR, "Mail Vote on the Baltic Collection and the Frankfort Ceremonial Objects," July 11, 1951, AJA, WJC Papers, Box E10 [116018].

[49] Memo from Hannah Arendt to Bd. of Dirs., JCR, "Disposition of 18 Cases Containing about 450 Ceremonial Objects from Frankfort/M," June 12, 1951, AJA, WJC Papers, Box E10 [116016–017]; memo from Hannah Arendt to Bd. of Dirs. & Adv. Comm., JCR, "Mail Vote on the Baltic Collection and the Frankfort Ceremonial Objects," July 11, 1951, AJA, WJC Papers, Box E10 [116018].

[50] The transfer was made through the JCR, Inc., the cultural agent of the JRSO. "Schedule A: List of Objects transferred from the Munich CCP to JCR Nuernberg," May 29, 1949, CAHJP, JRSO NY, File 301 [115805–840]; letter from Saul Kagan to Alexander Roseman, "Hq. JRSO New York Letter #139," June 29, 1949, CAHJP, JRSO NY, File 296a [115593–603].

[51] JRSO Exec. Comm. Mtg., Mar. 29, 1950, CAHJP, JRSO NY, File 296a [115684–688].

[52] Letter from Edward M.M. Warburg to Dr. Stephen S. Kayser, Nov. 1, 1949, CAHJP, JRSO NY, File 296a [115785–786]. JRSO Exec. Comm. Mtg., Mar. 29, 1950, CAHJP, JRSO NY, File 296a [115684–688].

[53] For a complete list of the items in the two 1949 shipments to New York please see "Jewish Unidentifiable Property," May 29, 1949, CAHJP, JRSO NY, File 296 [115787–805]; letter from Saul Kagan to Mr. Alexander Roseman, "Hq. New York letter # 139," June 29, 1949, CAHJP, JRSO NY, File 296a [115593–603]. Letter from Benjamin B. Ferencz to Eli Rock, "Hq. JRSO NY letter #126" June 10, 1949, CAHJP, JRSO NY, File 296a [115641–642]; memo, "RE: Paintings and other art objects turned over to the JRSO by Military Government," Mar. 14, 1950, CAHJP, JRSO NY, File 296a [115679–680]; letter from Edward M. M. Warburg to Dr. Stephen S. Kayser, Nov. 1, 1949, CAHJP, JRSO NY, File 296a [115785–786].

[54] The following is a breakdown of proceeds by month: May 1950, $1,922.60; June 1950, $926.70; August 1950, $345.65; October 1950, $58.10; May 1951, $166.60. These numbers are not amount received but rather the sums received from purchasers by Mr. Odell less his commission of $22^1/_2$ %, and less a minor sum expended for repairs and transportation of the pictures involved. Memorandum, from Antonie Neiger to Saul Kagan, "Art objects shipped by JRSO Nuremberg to New York in 1949," Sept. 11, 1952, CAHJP, JRSO NY, file 296a [115695–698].

[55] Letter from Saul Kagan to Mr. Kottlieb Hammer, Dec. 12, 1951, CAHJP, JRSO NY, File 296b [115692]. The shipping cost was $100. Memo from Saul Kagan to Maurice M. Boukstein and Moses A. Leavitt, "Disposal of remaining JRSO paintings," Nov. 23, 1951, CAHJP, JRSO NY, File 296b [115691].

[56] Letter from Benjamin B. Ferencz to Eli Rock, "Hq. JRSO New York Letter # 193," Sept. 14, 1949, CAHJP, JRSO NY, File 296a [115675–676]; letter from Eli Rock to Benjamin B. Ferencz, "Re: Narkiss- ' Folly," Aug. 22, 1950, CAHJP, JRSO NY, File 296a [115610–613]; For Example, see letter from Toni to Saul Kagan, "Re: Paintings: a) Portrait of a Man by Mierevelt- #21837/Kogl 370/3, b) Landscape with Flock of Sheep by Zuccareli- #21839/Kogl 372/5," Sept. 26, 1957, CAHJP, JRSO NY, File 296c [121932–932]; letter from Saul Kagan to Mr. Mark Uveeler, Aug. 14 1959, CAHJP, JRSO NY, File 296c [121879–880]; letter from Dr. E. Katzenstein to Bezalel National Museum, Aug. 3 1959, CAHJP, JRSO NY, File 296c [121884–885].

[57] Letter from Eli Rock to Benjamin B. Ferencz, "Re: ' Folly," Aug. 23, 1950, CAHJP, JRSO NY, File 296a [115606–608]; "Proceeds from Sale of Paintings in New York," CAHJP, JRSO NY, File 296b [115698].

[58] Memo from Dr. W. Blattberg to Members of the Exec. Comm., "Report on Recent Activities of the Department of Culture and Education," Jan. 13, 1949, AJA, WJC Papers, Box E9 [116316–319]; memo from Orren R. McJunkins, Chf., R&R Br., "Jewish Cultural Properties," Jan. 19, 1949, NACP, RG 260, Control Office Recs., Box 469 [320107]; Frederick Draper, OMGUS, Bernard Heller, JCR, & Saul Kagan, JRSO, "Addendum II to Memorandum of Agreement of 15 February 1949, Subject 'Jewish Cultural Property,'" July 22, 1949, NACP, RG 260, Ardelia Hall Collection, Box 66, OAD [311759].

[59] Letter from Hannah Arendt, Exec. Secy., JCR, to Eli Rock, JRSO, Sept. 1, 1950, CAHJP, JRSO NY 923c [116939–943].

[60] Robert G. Waite, "The Handling of Looted Books in the American Zone of Occupation, 1944–1951," (U.S. Dept. of Justice, OSI, Washington, DC, photocopy); Michael J. Kurtz, *Nazi Contraband: American Policy on the Return of European Cultural Treasures, 1945–1955* (New York: Garland, 1985).

[61] Memo from [Ardelia] Hall to Mr. Kiefer, "Disposition of Jewish Cultural Property," Oct. 6, 1948, NACP, RG 59, Cent. Eur. Div., Entry 381ABC, Box 2, Claims Rest. [114560–561]; Draft letter from Lt. Col. Milton L. Ogden to E. J. Cohn, no date [ca. June 1949], NACP, RG 260, Prop. Div., Gen. Recs. 1944–50, Box 2 [120204–205].

[62] Memo from A. Aaroni to Dr. Federbusch, "Looted Jewish Books, Archives and Religious Articles," Mar. 4, 1946, AJA, WJC Papers, Box E10 [116084–086].

[63] Memo from [Ardelia] Hall to Mr. Kiefer, "Disposition of Jewish Cultural Property," Oct. 6, 1948, NACP, RG 59, Cent. Eur. Div., Entry 381ABC, Box 2, Claims Rest. [114560–561].

[64] Ibid. [114560–561].

65 Letter from E.J. Cohn to Private Secy. to the Military Governor, June 7, 1949, NACP RG 260, Prop. Div., Secretariat Section, Gen. Recs. 1944–50, Box 2 [120202–203]

66 Letter from Milton L. Ogden to E.J. Cohn, no date, NACP, RG 260, Prop. Div., Secretariat Section, Gen. Recs. 1944–50, Box 2 [120204–205].

67 Ibid.

68 Minutes, JCR, "Special Meeting of the Board of Directors," May 5, 1949, CAHJP, JRSO NY, File 923a [115495–498].

69 Memo from W. Blattberg to Dr. Marcus, "Report on Meeting of Jewish Cultural Reconstruction, Inc., which took place on January 11, 1949," Jan. 12, 1949, AJA, WJC Papers, Box E9 [116315]; letter from Hannah Arendt, Exec. Secy., JCR, to Eli Rock, JRSO, Sept. 1, 1950, CAHJP, File JRSO NY 923C [116939–943].

70 For a complete list of rare books distributed by JCR, see Dept. of Special Collections and Univ. Archives, Stanford Univ. Libraries, Salo Baron Papers, Box 232 Folder 12 [122358–525].

71 Letter from Hannah Arendt to Ernest H. Weismann, JRSO, Sept. 27, 1961, CAHJP, JRSO NY 923d [115530]; JCR, "World Distribution of Books, July 1, 1949–January 31, 1952," Stanford Univ. Lib., Salo Baron Papers, Box 231, Folder 18 [120227–228]; HICOG Office of Econ. Affairs, Prop. Div., "Receipt for Jewish Cultural Properties," May 29, 1950, NACP, RG 260, Ardelia Hall Collection, Box 102 [101921–923].

72 Form, "Agreement Between Jewish Cultural Reconstruction, Inc., and Recipient Libraries," no date [ca. 1950], NACP, RG 260, Ardelia Hall Collection, Box 66, JRSO [311758].

73 Letter from Hannah Arendt, Exec. Secy., JCR, to Eli Rock, JRSO, Sept. 1, 1950, CAHJP, JRSO NY 923c [116939–943].

74 JCR, "World Distribution of Books, July 1, 1949–January 31, 1952," Stanford Univ. Lib., Salo Baron Papers, Box 231, Folder 18 [120227–228]. In the U.S., 6,176 books were returned.

75 Chart, JCR, "World Distribution of Books, July 1, 1949—January 31, 1952," Stanford Univ. Libraries, Salo Baron Papers, Box 231, Folder 18[120227–228].

76 Ibid.

77 Letter from Hannah Arendt, Exec. Secy., JCR, to Eli Rock, JRSO, Sept. 1, 1950, CAHJP, JRSO NY, File 923C [116939–943].

78 Ibid.

79 Memo from Dr. Blattberg to Dr. Goldman, Dr. Steinberg & Dr. Marcus, "Present Activities of the Department of Culture and Education," Nov. 14, 1949, AJA, WJC Papers, Box E9 [116324–328]. According to Military Regulation 16–260g, the cost of packing and shipping to the German border or to JCR's depot within Germany was paid by the German Government of the Land from which the property was shipped. See Memo of Agreement, Orren McJunkins, OMGUS, Joshua Starr, JCR & Benjamin Ferencz, JRSO, "Jewish Cultural Property," Feb. 15, 1949, NACP, RG 260, Ardelia Hall Collection, Box 125 [102605–606].

80 Memo from Dr. Blattberg to Dr. Goldman, Dr. Steinberg & Dr. Marcus, "Present Activities of the Department of Culture and Education," Nov. 14, 1949, AJA, WJC Papers, Box E9 [116324–328].

81 Memo from Dr. Wolf Blattberg to Dr. Marcus, "Activities of the New York Office of the Cultural Department," Sept. 22, 1950, AJA, WJC Papers, Box E9 [116297–299]. For complete list of world distribution, see chart, JCR, "World Distribution of Books, July 1, 1949—January 31, 1952," Stanford Univ. Libs., Salo Baron Papers, Box 231, Folder 18 [120227–228].

82 Memo from the JCR, "Minutes of Meeting of the Advisory Committee," Feb. 6, 1949, CAHJP, JRSO NY, File 923a [115542–545].

83 Ibid. [115542–545]; letter from Hannah Arendt, Exec. Secy., JCR, to Eli Rock, JRSO, Sept. 1, 1950, CAHJP, File JRSO NY 923C [116939–943].

84 Memo, "Canadian Jewish Congress Puts Labels in Books Recovered from Germany," Oct. 23, 1952, AJA, WJC Papers, Box E10 [116024].

85 Letter from Hannah Arendt, Exec. Secy., JCR to "Dear Friends," Sept. 1949, Harvard Univ. Lib., Correspondence between the Harvard Lib. & JCR Org. [123235].

86 Letter from Joshua Starr, Exe. Secy., JCR, to Librarian, Harvard Univ., Mar. 7, 1949, Harvard Univ. Lib., Correspondence between the Harvard Lib. & the JCR Org. [122322].

87 Questionnaire, JCR, Harvard Univ. Lib., Correspondence between the Harvard Lib. & the JCR Organization [122323–324].

88 JCR, Inc., "Memorandum to Libraries Co-operating with JCR," June 20, 1949, Dept. of Special Collections and Univ. Archives, Stanford Univ. Libs., Salo Baron Papers, Box 232, Folder 10 [123234].

89 However, after the termination of the activities of the JCR, the Board of Directors decided that, "a free exchange among recipient libraries be permitted, without prior approval on our part. JCR should, however, be informed of the transaction." Letter from Hannah Arendt, Exe. Secy., JCR, to "Dear Friend", Feb. 4, 1952, Harvard Univ. Lib., Correspondence between the Harvard Lib. & the JCR Org. [122356].

90 "Agreement Between Jewish Cultural Reconstruction, Inc., and Recipient Libraries," NACP, RG 260, Ardelia Hall Collection, Box 66, JRSO [311758]. See also, memo from JCR, "Memorandum to Libraries Co-operating with JCR," June 20, 1949, Dept. of Special Collections & Univ. Archives, Stanford Univ. Libs., Salo Baron Papers, Box 32, Folder 10 [123234].

91 Letter from Hannah Arendt, Exe. Secy., JCR, to "Dear Friends", Sept. 1949, Harvard Univ. Lib., Correspondence between the Harvard Lib. & the JCR Org. [122325].

92 Letter from Hannah Arendt, Exec. Secy., JCR, to Prof. Harry A. Wolfson, Widener Lib., Harvard Univ., May 25, 1950, Harvard Univ. Lib., Correspondence between the Harvard Lib. & the JCR Org. [122326–327].

93 Letter from Hannah Arendt, Exe. Secy., JCR, to Dr. Wm. A. Jackson, Harvard Univ. Lib., Mar. 1, 1951, Harvard Univ. Lib., Correspondence between the Harvard Lib. & the JCR Org. [122328].

94 Memo "Recovery and Distribution of Jewish Cultural Treasures Through the JCR," Sept. 25, 1950, AJA, WJC Papers, Box E10 [116010–012].

95 Ibid.

96 See JCR, "Distribution of Books in the U.S. From July 1, 1949 to Jan. 31, 1952 [117123–124] for a list of books distributed in the United States.

97 Letter from Hannah Arendt to Mr. Ernst H. Weismann, Sept. 27, 1961, CAHJP, File 923d [115530]; Chart, JCR, "World Distribution of Books, July 1, 1949–January 31, 1952," Stanford Univ. Libraries, Salo Baron Papers, Box 231, Folder 18 [120227–228].

98 Office of HICOG for Germany, "Receipt for Jewish Cultural Properties," May 29, 1950, NACP, RG 260, Ardelia Hall Collection, Box 102, [101921–923].

99 Letter from Hannah Arendt to Mr. Ernest H. Weismann, Sept. 27, 1961, CAHJP, JRSO NY, File 923d, [115530].

100 Jewish Cultural Reconstruction, Inc., "Agreement between Jewish Cultural Reconstruction, Inc., and Recipient Libraries," July 1950.

101 Letter from Hannah Arendt to Theodore A. Heinrich, Jan. 21, 1950, NACP, RG 260, Ardelia Hall Collection, Box 66 [120225–226].

102 See Chart, JCR, "World Distribution of Books, July 1, 1949—January 31, 1952", Stanford Univ. Libs., Salo Baron Papers, Box 231, Folder 18 [120227–228] for world distribution list.

103 Memo from Richard F. Howard, Chf., MFA&A, to Office of the Inspector Gen., OMGUS, "Report and Request for Investigation," Feb. 20, 1947, NACP, RG 260, Ardelia Hall Collection, Box 66, Wiesbaden [117138–140].

104 Ibid. [117138–140]; memo from Simon H. Rifkind to Lt. Gen. Lucius Clay, "Jewish Books," Jan. 7, 1946, NACP, RG 260, Ardelia Hall Collection, Box 66 [120229–230].

[105] Memo from Richard F. Howard, Chf., MFA&A, to Office of the Inspector Gen., OMGUS, "Report and Request for Investigation," Feb. 20, 1947, NACP, RG 260, Ardelia Hall Collection, Box 66, Wiesbaden [117138–140].

[106] These experts were Dr. Koppel S. Pinson, Professor of History at Queens College, editor of *Jewish Social Studies,* Secretary of the Commission for European Cultural Reconstruction, and Vice-chairman of Academic Council of Jewish Relations; Rabbi Alexander Rosenberg, member of the Executive Committee of Union of Orthodox Rabbis, founder and ex-president of the Rabbinical Council of America and an authority in Rabbinical scholarship; and Professor Samual Sar, Dean of Yeshiva University and vice-president of Mizrachi. Memo from Simon H. Rifkind to Lt. Gen. Lucius Clay, "Jewish Books," Jan. 7, 1946, NACP, RG 260, Ardelia Hall Collection, Box 66 [120229–230].

[107] Koppel S. Pinson, "Jewish Life in Liberated Germany: A Study of the Jewish DP's," *Jewish Social Studies* 9 (Apr. 1947), 121. [120232–256]; memo from Maj. L. B. LaFarge to Mr. Cronin, Rest. Br., "Jewish Cultural Material," June 3, 1946, NACP, RG 260, Ardelia Hall Collection, Box 66 [305581–582].

[108] JCR, "Excerpts from Dr. Joshua Starr's Report dated Frankfurt, June 2, 1948," no date, AJA, WJC Papers, Box E10 [116063–066].

[109] Letter from Mordechai M. Breuer to the Eur. Head Office, AJDC, Jan. 12, 1946, CAHJP, JRSO NY 875 [115485].

[110] Letter from Lt. Col. G. H. Garde to AJDC, "Loan of Books," July 15, 1947, NACP, RG 260, Ardelia Hall Collection, Box 66 [100551–552].

[111] Letter from L. C. Pinkerton, Am. Consulate Gen., to The Honorable Secy. of State, "Jewish Cultural Material Saved from Nazi hands," May 16, 1945, NACP, RG 260, Ardelia Hall Collection, Box 66 [101020–021].

[112] Ibid.

[113] Letter from Prof. C.G. Scholem to Gen. Lucius D. Clay, Aug. 7, 1946, NACP, RG 260, Econ. Div., Box 46 [101065].

[114] Memo from Joseph A. Horne to Office of MG for Hesse, "Valuable materials missing from the Offenbach Archival Depot," Feb. 4, 1947, NACP, RG 260, Ardelia Hall Collection, Box 253 [100731–732].

[115] Ibid.

[116] Memo from Richard F. Howard to Office of the Inspector Gen., "Report and Request for Investigation," Feb. 20, 1947, NACP, RG 260, Ardelia Hall Collection, Box 66 [117138–140].

[117] Note from Gen. Clay to Colonel Wilkinson, "27 May- Wilkinson-Material from Offenbach Archival Depot at Jerusalem," June 7, 1947, NACP, RG 260, Ardelia Hall Collection, Box 66 [117176].

[118] Memo from Office of Political Affairs to Richard Howard, Nov. 6, 1947, NACP, RG 260, Ardelia Hall Collection, Box 66 [305576–578].

[119] Letter from Property Div. to R&R Br., "Disposition of MSS," Mar. 25, 1947, NACP, RG 260 Box 253 [101095–106].

[120] The JRSO was also a signatory on the agreement since the JCR acted as the JRSO's agent. Addendum I to Agreement of Feb. 15, 1949, Orren McJunkins, OMGUS, Joshua Starr, JCR & Benjamin Ferencz, JRSO, "Jewish Cultural Property," Apr. 5, 1949, NACP, RG 260, Ardelia Hall Collection, Box 66, JCR [120200–201].

[121] Addendum I to Agreement of Feb. 15, 1949, Orren McJunkins, OMGUS, Joshua Starr, JCR & Benjamin Ferencz, JRSO, "Jewish Cultural Property," Apr. 5, 1949, NACP, RG 260, Ardelia Hall Collection, Box 66, JCR [120200–201].

[122] Ibid.

[123] Of these, most were from Lithuania (13,000 Jewish-origin, 3,500 non-Jewish origin, and 48 "boxes"), Latvia (6,500 Jewish-origin, 4,200 non-Jewish origin, and 12 "boxes"), and Estonia (100 Jewish-origin, 300 non-Jewish origin, and 2 "boxes"). Cable from OMGUS to Dept. of Army for CSCAD, Ref. No. CC–5899, Sept. 11, 1948, NACP, RG84, Entry 2531B, Box 211, File 400B [114584].

[124] Memo from Donald R. Heath, Dir., Office of Pol. Affairs, to Col. J. H. Allen, Chf., Rest. Br., Econ. Div., "Restitution of Property Which Was Removed from the Baltic states," May 1, 1946, NACP, RG 84, Entry 2531B, Box 55, File 400B [114590].

[125] Field Rpt. No. 9 from Bernard Heller, JCR, Sept. 1949, CAHJP, JRSO NY 923b [115507–508]. Of the 78, 33 cases with the remnants of the Mapu library were given to the Hebrew University library in trusteeship for two years, and the remainder, with the libraries of Kohel, Kovno, and the Slobodka Yeshiva, were restituted to their former owners now living in Israel.

[126] JCR, Mtg. Mins., Spec. Mtg. of Bd. of Dirs., Dec. 19, 1949, CAHJP, JRSO NY 923b [115518–519].

[127] Memo from Hannah Arendt, Exec. Secy., JCR, to Bd. of Dirs., "Disposition of the Baltic Collection," June 12, 1951, AJA, WJC Papers, Box E10 [116015]; memo from Hannah Arendt to Bd. of Dirs. & Adv. Comm., JCR, "Mail Vote on the Baltic Collection and the Frankfort Ceremonial Objects," July 11, 1951, AJA, WJC Papers, Box E10 [116018].

Chapter VII

Conclusion

Every generation writes its own history. When writing the history of the policies and procedures that governed the U.S. treatment of Holocaust victims' assets, however, the Commission staff benefited from the contributions of several generations of scholars. As a result of this undertaking, this project has identified several significant themes that emerge from this exceedingly complex story:

- First, government officials did not initially distinguish between assets belonging to victims of Nazi persecution and those that did not. The evolution of American thinking later led to explicit legal and policy recognition in 1945 and 1946 that "persecutees" and "stateless persons" deserved special status as well as special measures to facilitate recovery of their assets.

- Second, the onset of the war led to aggressive strategic efforts to prevent assets owned by foreign nationals and held in the United States being used by the Nazis to fuel their war effort.

- Third, issues the Allies considered more pressing—in particular the imperative to do the maximum economically and politically to win the war, to rebuild the German and European economies after the war, and to wage the Cold War—continually overshadowed concern for restitution.

These themes, in turn, suggest that there are today certain appropriate responses by the United States that would recognize the work left undone by our government's policies in the years leading up to, during, and immediately after the Second World War.

In addition to identifying these themes, the Commission staff also decided in several instances that time and resource constraints could not justify further research on particular topics addressed in its report, even though such research was relevant to the Commission's mandate. Despite efforts that included the examination of hundreds of thousands of documents and interviewing some of the key participants in the events it was investigating, several factors limited the ability of the Commission staff to write the entire history of this topic.

In the United States, the National Archives holds more than 50 million documents related in one way or another to the Second World War and the Holocaust, more paper than any one team of researchers could read and analyze in the limited time frame available to the Commission. In addition, as a result of the efforts of the Inter-Agency Working Group on the Declassification of Nazi Era Documents (IWG), still more documents are being declassified and added to this total every day. While the Commission was able to see classified documents from the archives of the Federal Bureau of Investigation, there are many other potential document sources scattered throughout government agencies that only the patient work of the IWG can be expected to discover over the next several years.[1]

Still another part of the story is to be found in foreign archives, some of which are more difficult to access and exploit than their U.S. counterparts. In many cases, researchers in other countries that have addressed the issue of Holocaust-era assets have used these archives; other archives are only now being opened to scholars of any nationality; and still others remain inaccessible. Again, the time and resources available to the Commission staff did not permit it to conduct extensive research in foreign archives or to consult thoroughly and systematically with researchers abroad.

The Commission's primary mandate called for comprehensive original research into the Federal government's handling of Holocaust victims' assets. A secondary mandate directed the Commission to review the research conducted by others into the handling of these assets by non-federal entities, including state governments and the private sector. In addition to areas of inquiry that could not be pursued for reasons of time and resources, a research effort of this scope inevitably identifies new avenues of inquiry that must be left for others to pursue because they are insufficiently central to the research plan being implemented.

In these categories, the staff has identified a number of areas that merit further research, the most important of which are:

Seizures of assets from Sinti and Roma, homosexual and disabled victims of the Holocaust

The staff made a number of efforts to investigate the fate of material assets belonging to non-Jewish victims of Nazism. Acts of genocide against the Sinti and Roma peoples, and the policies of persecution and murder of disabled and homosexual German citizens, have now been well documented. Unfortunately, virtually no work has been done on the fate of the property of these victims.

The Roma and Sinti populations were generally poor and itinerant. As a result, their material possessions are virtually impossible to quantify. Nevertheless, it is impossible to imagine that these groups did not lose articles of immense cultural significance, and further investigation into these cultural and material losses is certainly warranted.

In the case of disabled and homosexual victims, the persecution was less systematic and its documentation less complete. It may be that tracing the confiscated assets of these victims can only be done on an individual basis, but more work into the history of these aspects of Nazi persecution is certainly needed.

The impact of the Cold War and the creation of the State of Israel on the formulation and implementation of American restitution policy

These two significant and complex historical events interacted with the United States' policy in ways that impinged on the handling of victims' assets. The influence of the Cold War may be seen, for instance, in the restitution of certain assets to the non-communist Hungarian government and in the transfer of other Hungarian assets to Austria after the communist takeover of Hungary. Other instances of such interaction between Cold War considerations and the restitution of assets emerge in the incidents involving the restitution of various libraries to the Baltic states.

The effect of the creation of the State of Israel during the period in which restitution was being implemented, and its effect on decisions regarding the disposition of unidentifiable victims' assets, is less clear. It seems likely that the struggles in Palestine between 1945 and 1948 helped to shape the attitudes and positions of the Jewish community in the United States and affected its ongoing dialogue with the United States government about restitution issues. The birth of the State of Israel also affected the distribution decisions of the Jewish Cultural Reconstruction, Inc., which allocated 40 percent of various assets to the new state.

Third country avenues for the importation of looted assets into the United States

Several hints emerge from the records of the Federal Bureau of Investigation and other files about the possible role of Latin American countries in the traffic of looted art from Europe to the United States during and after the war. Such avenues could readily have escaped the scrutiny of the U.S. Customs Service if the provenance of the art were obfuscated or if it was imported through ports of entry where officials were ill-equipped to value it. The Argentine Commission of Enquiry into the Activities of Nazism in Argentina (CEANA) has done important work in this area, but the topic would benefit from a multi-national approach. Other evidence suggests that Switzerland became a postwar haven for looted art that eventually found its way into American collections.

The quantification of Holocaust victims' assets

Because of the paucity and uneven quality of documentation at its disposal, the Commission staff was able to provide only a very rough estimate of the value of the victims' assets that came into the possession or control of the U.S. government. Because the United States did not distinguish victims' from other assets, and because the raw data that might have permitted the creation of a reasonable estimate have been destroyed, it is exceedingly difficult to quantify the value of those assets.

For example, with regard to Foreign Funds Control and the share of victims' assets caught up in the processes of freezing and defrosting, the 1941 census of foreign-held assets asked financial institutions throughout the United States to return to the Treasury detailed descriptions of the assets on deposit. Those forms have been destroyed, and the staff's investigations have uncovered no duplicates. As a result, it is not possible to estimate the amount of victims' assets in the United States in 1941. It might be possible to fill in some of the gaps by examining the defrosting data in the archives of countries to which defrosted assets were returned.

The relationship between Jewish organizations and U.S. Government agencies

It is clear from the research conducted by the Commission staff that the full story of the work done by the Jewish successor organizations and their relationship to the various agencies of the U.S. government is yet to be written. One example of a significant gap in our knowledge is the case of the "Becher ransom," in which it appears that identifiable assets belonging to survivors of the Holocaust were turned over to the Jewish Agency for Palestine, which later shared the proceeds with the Jewish Restitution Successor Organization. Although the Commission staff conducted research on this and other topics at a few of the most important Jewish archives, without more systematic and extensive research it is reluctant to reach conclusions in this complex area.

The presence of victim gold circulating in the international market

It is possible that gold bars and coins purchased by the Department of Treasury through the Federal Reserve Bank of New York before, during and after the war contained trace amounts of recast gold items looted from victims of Nazism. The Department of Treasury purchased gold for the Exchange Stabilization Fund, resmelted it into U.S. Assay Office bars, and incorporated it into the monetary reserves of the United States. Because of a lack of documentation, the amount of victim gold the Nazis seized and monetized by intermixing it with other gold in the German gold reserves has never been established. It is certain, however, that some of this gold was later used to acquire hard currency and material from neutral countries that deposited gold on earmark at the Federal Reserve. The entire story of the circulation of gold on the international market and the efforts to maintain gold as the international basis of exchange has yet to be written and merits further attention.

The role of state governments in handling dormant assets

The Commission staff's research has demonstrated the likelihood that Holocaust victims' assets, originally deposited in U.S. banks by individuals and subsequently frozen by the Federal government, escheated to the states in which the banks were chartered. The Commission has made recommendations regarding appropriate ongoing efforts by the banking industry and state governments to identify such escheated assets. However, evidence encountered by the staff indicates that the role of state and local governments in handling dormant assets may have been more complex.[2]

Another element of this research involves the amount of victims' assets in the omnibus or bundled accounts—pooled accounts held in the names of banks in which the names of the individual depositors were not known—maintained by Swiss, Dutch, French, German and other European banks in the United States that may also have escheated to the states. About 40 percent of the approximately 300 omnibus accounts listed in the OAP Annual Reports for 1951 and 1952 were not returned, presumably because there were no claimants or because the claims were disallowed. Without access to the actual bank records, however, it is impossible to determine how much of the remaining unclaimed property may have belonged to victims.

There is also evidence of the involvement of both the county government and the state tax commission in the post-war inventorying of a previously frozen safe deposit box in New York. It appears that under the law in effect at the time other agencies of state government may have had jurisdiction over corporations' treatment of their shareholder rolls, including purging from those rolls the names of shareholders who did not cash dividend checks or respond to other notices and whose whereabouts were unknown. The role of these entities is only poorly understood, and additional research into this topic is warranted.

Comprehensive integration of findings from other national commissions

The single most important research task remains to be undertaken—and one that the Commission firmly believes must be completed—is the integration of this Commission's research findings with those of all the other historical Commissions that have been at work on related issues. It would indeed be a loss if the work of these commissions was not synthesized to tell the most comprehensive and detailed history of the Holocaust that has ever been assembled. Such an effort, complex and expensive though it may be, must be made in order to get the full benefit of the extraordinary scope of Holocaust research that has been completed around the world in recent years.

The existence of these important areas of exploration demonstrates that continued support of research into the area of Holocaust assets is appropriate. This is another area that the staff has drawn the attention of the Commission for its consideration in making recommendations to the President.

The Commission staff is acutely aware that history is no more than a window onto the past. It can never entirely re-create the human experience of the past. If the work and the suggestions for additional work presented here lead to a better understanding of what the victims of the Holocaust experienced and—in the strictly material sense—what they lost and only partially regained, then the Commission's historical work will have fulfilled its purpose, and the "higher ground" mentioned by President Clinton and cited by the Commission in its Findings and Recommendations will be realized.

Endnotes for Chapter VII

[1] The records of the Federal Bureau of Investigation (FBI) offer insights into the activities of the Office of Alien Property (OAP). Starting in 1947, the OAP called on FBI agents for assistance. The Bureau "conducted investigations of various types involving the ownership and control of unvested and vested property subject to claims and litigation, "at the request of OAP. Savings and recoveries from these investigations amounted to several million dollars. The FBI did general investigative work, in the United States and abroad, on many different types of cases including, of course, investigative work to counter espionage and sabotage. It examined the veracity of claims of Nazi persecution including whether claimants were Jewish and checked the validity of passports and visas. The FBI also focused on the provenance of looted securities, paintings, and diamonds and tracked the movement of German funds in to the United States and that of Swiss funds from the United States.

[2] See Rpt. of James A. Matthews, FBI Office, New York, "Alien Property Custodian Matter—Estate of Sophie Schiele, Deceased," May 11, 1956, FBI Files [124736–743].

Abbreviations and Glossary

ACA (Allied Control Authority). The supreme governing authority in postwar Germany.

ACC (Allied Control Council). On June 5, 1945, the Allies created the quadripartite Allied Control Council, the executive component of the Allied Control Authority (ACA), to function as the chief Allied agency to govern occupied Germany. The council members, the commanders of the four Allied armies, first met on July 30 in Berlin. The final session was held on March 20, 1948, when the Soviet participants walked out just prior to the Berlin blockade.

AGWAR (Adjutant General, Department of War).

AHC (Allied High Commission).

AJC (American Jewish Congress). *See* WJC.

AJDC (American Jewish Joint Distribution Committee). Founded in 1914 by Henry Morgenthau Sr., to aid Jews in Europe and Palestine.

ALIU (Art Looting Investigation Unit), created in the Office of Strategic Services in 1945.

APC (Alien Property Custodian). On March 11, 1942, by executive order, the APC was established within the Office for Emergency Management. APC was responsible to seize certain types of enemy property not already frozen or regulated by the Treasury Department. While Treasury continued to manage blocked assets such as currencies, bullion, and securities, the APC was authorized to seize (and manage or liquidate) enemy-owned businesses, patents, and copyrights in the U.S. The APC was abolished on October 14, 1946, and its functions transferred to the Office of Alien Property in the Department of Justice.

Ardelia Hall, Monuments and Fine Arts Advisor in the U.S. Department of State; also head of the Office of International Information and Cultural Affairs of the State Department between 1944 and 1964.

Aryanization, the forced transfer of Jewish-owned businesses or property to German or "Aryan" ownership. It had two stages, the "voluntary," in which Jews were excluded from German economic life, and the compulsory stage that began immediately after Kristallnacht (Night of the Broken Glass) on November 9, 1938. Jewish businesses were liquidated or transferred to Aryans and often Jews who emigrated had to "donate" their remaining property to the state.

ASA (American Security Agency).

BEW (Board of Economic Warfare). On December 17, 1941, the Economic Defense Board became, by a change of name, the Board of Economic Warfare. Until 1942, the Board's powers were limited chiefly to the control of exports, but an Executive Order on April 13, 1942, increased its authority by giving the Board a large measure of control over imports. The Board was also directed to "represent the United States Government in dealing with economic warfare agencies of the United Nations for the purpose of relating the Government's economic warfare program and facilities regarding the importation of strategic and critical materials." On July 15, 1943, an Executive Order terminated the Board of Economic Warfare, and its functions, personnel, and records were transferred to the Office of Economic Warfare (OEW).

BIS (Bank for International Settlements). Established as an international financial institution, enjoying special immunities, pursuant to the Hague Agreements of January 20, 1930. Its main objectives were to act as trustee or agent in regard to international financial settlements, particularly in regard to German reparations, to promote central bank cooperation, and to provide additional facilities for international financial operations.

CCP (Central Collecting Points). The U.S. military established CCPs to house cultural objects found in the United States Zone of Germany in need of preservation or suspected of having been looted by the Nazis. U.S. authorities established temporary facilities at Munich, Wiesbaden, Marburg, and Offenbach in 1946. On June 15, 1946, the Marburg Central Collecting Point was closed, and the three remaining CCPs became specialized. The Wiesbaden CCP held mostly German-owned material and closed in August 1951. The Munich CCP specialized in materials subject to restitution and material of the Bavarian State Museums and also closed in August 1951. The Offenbach Archival Depot was devoted primarily to Jewish materials, books, and archives and closed in June 1949. Upon the closure of the CCPs, the remaining objects continued to be stored, and authority over these objects was exercised by HICOG.

CIA (Central Intelligence Agency).

CIC (Counter Intelligence Corps). Evolved from the Military Intelligence Service's Counter Intelligence Branch. CIC detachments were quite active in postwar activities in Germany and Austria in an effort to locate war criminals, Nazi records, and looted property.

CID (Criminal Investigative Division of the U.S. Army).

CIG (Central Intelligence Group).

CINCEUR (Commander in Chief, European Command). *See* EUCOM.

COSSAC (Chief of Staff, Supreme Allied Commander). COSSAC was created as an Anglo-American organization in the spring of 1943 to plan for the Allied invasion of France and Germany, while also planning for eventual civil affairs and military government responsibilities.

Defrosting, the unblocking of "frozen" assets by the Treasury Department.

DP (Displaced Persons). A wide array of individuals, such as those imprisoned in Nazi concentration and death camps, forced laborers, prisoners of war (POWs), and evacuees who were uprooted from their homes during and after World War II.

ECEFP (Executive Committee of Economic Foreign Policy of the U.S. State Department).

Einsatzgrüppen, mobile killing units that accompanied German troops on the eastern front.

ERP (European Recovery Program). *See* Marshall Plan.

ERR (*Einsatzstab Reichsleiter Rosenberg*). A special Nazi task force under Alfred Rosenberg. A looting agency that seized archives and artwork, particularly of Jews, in German-occupied western and eastern territories from 1940 to 1945.

ETO (European Theater of Operations). Designated the area of operation in Europe of the United States air, ground, naval, and supply forces that joined the British forces after December 7, 1941. The theater area stretched from the British Isles to eastern Germany, from Scandinavia to the Pyrenees and the northern border of Italy and the Balkans.

ETOUSA (European Theater of Operations, U.S. Army). On June 8, 1942, the European Theater of Operations, United States Army (ETOUSA) was created as the commanding headquarters for U.S. troops in Europe. On January 17, 1944, ETOUSA became a subordinate element of SHAEF, the combined British-American headquarters. On July 1, 1945, ETOUSA was redesignated United States Forces, European Theater (USFET) in preparation for the dissolution of SHAEF.

EUCOM (European Command). On August 1, 1952, EUCOM is redesignated the U.S. Army, Europe (USAREUR) at the same time the office of Headquarters, U.S. European Command is established.

FBI (Federal Bureau of Investigation).

FEA (Foreign Economic Administration).

FED (Foreign Exchange Depository). Opened in April 1945, in Frankfurt, Germany, as the successor organization to the Currency Branch, SHAEF. In addition to its currency operations, in the early part of 1945, the FED began to receive foreign exchange assets from various sources in Germany. FED also supervised the shipments of valuables from the Merkers mine. The FED received, stored, inventoried, and disbursed over $500 million worth of loot and valuables. On September 21, 1949, FED responsibilities were turned over to the office of the U.S. High Commission for Germany.

FFC (Foreign Funds Control). In 1940, the Foreign Funds Control was created within the U.S. Treasury Department in accordance with the Trading With The Enemy Act.

FRB-NY (Federal Reserve Bank – New York).

GEPC (German External Property Commission).

Gestapo Geheime Staatspolizei (State Secret Police). Instituted by Göring in 1933 and operating under the control of Himmler by 1936, the Gestapo was instrumental in the Nazis pursuit of repression and terror.

Gold pool. Monetary gold looted by Germany and accumulated in neutral nations.

HICOG (U.S. High Commissioner for Germany). Established in the Department of State on June 6, 1949. On September 21, 1949, HICOG, a civilian agency, replaced OMGUS, a military agency, as the U.S. occupation government for Germany.

IARA (Inter-Allied Reparations Agency). Located in Brussels, Belgium, the IARA allocated German reparations among member governments of the agency, provided information on items available for reparation, and dealt with restitution of property. The agency's members included representatives from Albania, Australia, Belgium, Canada, Czechoslovakia, Denmark, Egypt, France, Greece, India, Luxembourg, the Netherlands, New Zealand, Norway, South Africa, the United Kingdom, the U.S., and Yugoslavia.

IGCR (Intergovernmental Committee on Refugees). Organized in London in August 1938 to assist in the resettlement of refugees from Europe in countries allowing permanent immigration. The organization disbanded in 1947, and its functions and records were transferred to the International Refugee Organization (IRO) of the United Nations.

IRO (International Refugee Organization). In July 1947, the International Refugee Organization (IRO) superseded the United Nations Relief and Rehabilitation Administration (UNRRA) and the Intergovernmental Committee on Refugees (IGCR) and continued to arrange for the care and repatriation or resettlement of displaced persons. In 1952, the IRO concluded its work and was replaced by the Office of the United Nations High Commissioner for Refugees.

JA (Jewish Agency for Palestine). The governing body of the world movement to promote the development of Palestine and, after 1948, of Israel by supporting the immigration of Jews to Palestine and to Israel.

JAG (U.S. Army Judge Advocate General).

JCR (Jewish Cultural Reconstruction). The JCR, Inc. was established in April 1947 as a membership corporation made up of several major Jewish organizations. The JCR became the trustee and distributor of unidentifiable heirless Jewish cultural property discovered in the U.S. Zone of Germany that could not be claimed under military government laws.

JCS (Joint Chiefs of Staff). The JCS was created as a result of the decision made during the Anglo-American military staff conference in Washington in 1941-1942 to establish Combined Chiefs of Staff. The Joint Chiefs of Staff served as the United States representative on the Combined Chiefs of Staff. The JCS became the principal agency for coordination between the army and navy. It gained legislative recognition as a permanent agency, the U.S. Joint Chiefs of Staff, by the National Security Act of 1947.

JRC (Jewish Rescue Committee).

JRSO (Jewish Restitution Successor Organization). On May 15, 1947, the Jewish Restitution Commission (later renamed the Jewish Restitution Successor Organization) was incorporated as a charitable organization in New York to "acquire, receive, hold, maintain and distribute for purposes of Jewish relief, rehabilitation, reconstruction, resettlement, and immigration, the property of Jews, Jewish organizations, cultural and charitable funds and foundations, and communities which were victims of Nazi or Fascist persecution or discrimination." The JRSO, first recognized by General Clay in Germany, was appointed by President Eisenhower on June 23, 1948, as the official successor organization allowed to claim identifiable heirless assets and to obtain title to Jewish property in the U.S. Zone of Germany unclaimed as of December 31, 1948.

JTC (Jewish Trust Corporation).

London Declaration. The U.S. and 16 other countries declared on January 5, 1943, that the Allies reserved the right to invalidate transfers or dealings with property, rights, and interests that had been situated in the territories that were under direct or indirect Nazi control. This warning applied to both looted material and transactions that were legal in form.

Macmillan Commission (The British Committee for the Preservation and Restitution of Works and Art, Archives, and Other Material in Enemy Hands), generally known as the Macmillan Commission after its chairman, Lord Macmillan; founded in May 1944 as a counterpart to the American Roberts Commission. The Macmillan Commission limited its interest primarily to problems of restitution and reparations, leaving protection of assets to the military authorities.

Marshall Plan, created to help reverse the economic, social, and political deterioration of Western Europe after World War II. Western European governments set up reconstruction plans and the U.S. offered $12.5 billion in aid from April 13, 1948, through June 30, 1951.

MCCP (Munich Central Collecting Point). *See* CCP.

Merkers Mine. In April 1945, U.S. troops with the 3rd Army discovered the contents of the Reichsbank in the Wintershal AG Kaiseroda potassium mine near the town of Merkers, Germany. The army required thirty ten-ton trucks to transport the treasure to Frankfurt, and the gold found was worth $238.5 million. The Merkers cache was the most astonishing discovery of looted materials by the U.S. military.

MEW (Ministry of Economic Warfare, United Kingdom).

MFA&A (Monuments, Fine Arts, and Archives). The MFA&A Branch provided the army with specialist officers and guidelines shaped with the intent to protect and salvage cultural treasures and monuments in Europe—those on the battlefield and those uncovered by U.S. forces. MFA&A worked in the restitution program and operated CCPs throughout Germany and many art depots throughout Austria.

MG (Military Government).

MTO (Mediterranean Theater of Operations).

NATO (North Atlantic Treaty Organization).

NSC (National Security Council, United States).

NSDAP (Nationalsozialistische Deutsche Arbeiterpartei). The word "Nazi" is derived from the German name for the Nationalist Socialist German Worker's Party.

OAD (Offenbach Archival Depository). The Offenbach Archival Depository (OAD) was one of the central collecting points in Germany, holding mostly Jewish materials, books, and archives. *See also* CCP.

OAP (Office of Alien Property). On October 14, 1946, the Alien Property Custodian (APC) was abolished and its functions, funds, and personnel transferred to the Office of Alien Property within the Department of Justice. *See also* APC.

OCCWC (Office of the Chief of Counsel for War Crimes).

OE (Division of Economic Security Controls, U.S. Department of State).

OFD (Office of Financial and Development Policy, U.S. Department of State).

OIC (Office of International Information and Cultural Affairs, U.S. Department of State).

OMG (Office of Military Government).

OMGUS (Office of Military Government for Germany, United States). OMGUS was established on October 1, 1945, to administer the U.S. Zone of occupation in Germany and the U.S. Sector of occupied Berlin. OMGUS succeeded the USGCC (May 8 to October 1, 1945) and was abolished December 5, 1949, when its functions were transferred to HICOG.

OMGUSZ (Office of Military Government, United States Zone).

OSS (Office of Strategic Services). The OSS was established by a military order of June 13, 1942. Its two basic functions were gathering, evaluating, and analyzing intelligence in support of the war against Axis Powers and planning and executing intelligence operations.

Paris Agreement on Reparations, the result of an 18-power conference held in Paris between November 9 and December 21, 1945. The Paris Agreement established polices and procedures for the division of German assets among the 18 governments.

PCIRO (Preparatory Commission, International Refugee Organization). *See* IRO.

PCO (Property Control Office of U.S. Military Government).

POLAD (Political Advisor in USFET and EUCOM).

RD&R (Reparations, Deliveries, and Restitution Division).

Reichsbank The Central Bank of the German Government.

RM (Reichsmark), the currency of Nazi Germany. It was replaced by the Deutschmark in the three western zones of Germany as a result of currency reform in 1948.

Roberts Commission (The American Commission for the Protection and Salvage of Artistic and Historic Monuments in War Areas). An advisory commission created on August 20, 1943 under the chairmanship of Owen J. Roberts, Justice of the U.S. Supreme Court, and composed of government and civilian representatives. The Roberts Commission was instrumental in the creation of the MFA&A.

Safehaven Program. The Safehaven Program, formally launched in July 1944, aimed to prevent Germany from transferring assets to neutral European nations, to ensure that German wealth would be available for the reconstruction of Europe and for the payment of reparations to the Allies, to return properties looted by the Nazis, to prevent the escape of German personnel to neutral havens, and to deny Germany the capability to start another war.

SCAEF (Supreme Commander, Allied Expeditionary Forces).

SCAP (Supreme Commander for the Allied Powers).

SHAEF (Supreme Headquarters, Allied Expeditionary Forces). On January 17, 1944, the Supreme Headquarters, Allied Expeditionary Force (SHAEF) was created as a joint British-American command for military operations in Europe. On February 13, 1944, SHAEF absorbed the Chief of Staff Supreme Allied Command (COSSAC). SHAEF was dissolved on July 11, 1945.

SS (Schutzstaffel). The SS was an elite military and police organization within the Nazi Party controlled by Heinrich Himmler, with wide-ranging responsibilities including internal security, protection, intelligence, and the persecution of enemies of the Reich.

SSU (Strategic Services Unit).

STEG (Staatliche Erfassungsgesellschaft). German semipublic corporation to handle surplus war materials.

SWNCC (State-War-Navy Coordinating Committee).

TD (Treasury Decision).

TFR (Textual Financial Records). Forms used by the U.S. Treasury Department to gather information on assets in the U.S., such as assets in the U.S. belonging to blocked countries or their nationals (Form TFR–100), and later for a more general census of foreign-owned assets in the U.S. (Form TFR–300).

TGC (Tripartite Gold Commission). Established by the United States, France, and the United Kingdom for the restitution of monetary gold. See also Tripartite Brussels Conference.

Tripartite Brussels Conference. The outcome of the conference included the redistribution of gold from a "gold pool," accumulated in neutral nations obtaining looted monetary gold from Germany, to nations whose gold reserves had been looted by Germany.

Tripartite Gold Agreement of September 27, 1946, was to implement Part III of the reparation agreement signed in Paris on January 14, 1946. The governments of the

U.S., the UK, and France established the Tripartite Gold Commission for the restitution of monetary gold. *See* Tripartite Brussels Conference *and* TGC.

TWEA (Trading With the Enemy Act).The legal instrument used by the U.S. Treasury Department for controlling foreign assets before and during the war.

U.K. (United Kingdom).

UN (United Nations).

UNIRO (United Nations International Refugee Organization). *See* IRO.

UNRRA (United Nations Relief and Rehabilitation Administration). Established in 1943 to give aid to uprooted persons in areas liberated from the Axis powers, including the distribution of food and medicine, reinstatement of public services, and restoration of agriculture and industry. In March 1949, UNRRA disbanded and its responsibilities were distributed to other UN agencies, primarily the International Refugee Organization (IRO).

USACA (U.S. Allied Commission for Austria). Responsible for civil affairs and military government administration in the U.S. Zone of Austria and the U.S. sector of Vienna. It was organized concurrently with the establishment of Headquarters, United States Forces Austria (USFA), July 5, 1945, as a component of U.S. Forces European Theater. USACA was abolished following the transfer of U.S. occupation government from military to civilian authority in September 20, 1950.

U.S. Bureau of Customs. Beginning in 1940, the Foreign Funds Control (FFC) in the U.S. Treasury Department relied on customs inspectors to question and determine whether incoming travelers were carrying securities. The U.S. Customs agents monitored the currency that was entering the U.S. during 1940 and 1941, when the U.S. was still a neutral nation. Customs agents began seizing currency in March 1942 as a result of General Ruling 6A which dealt with "securities or evidences thereof." The U.S. Customs Bureau was responsible for ensuring that assets did not enter the United States illegally during and after World War II.

USFA (United States Forces Austria). On July 5, 1945, the United States Forces Austria, under General Mark Clark, was created out of the U.S. element of the 15th Army Group. USFA remained subordinate to USFET and EUCOM until May 23, 1949, when it became an independent command under the Joint Chiefs of Staff. [On June 28, 1946, military government ended in Austria.]

USFET (U.S. Forces, European Theater). On July 1, 1945, the U.S. Forces, European Theater replaced ETOUSA as an independent American command and, on July 15, assumed command of all American forces in Europe. On March 15, 1947, USFET became the European Command (EUCOM) under General Clay as commander in chief and military governor.

USGCC (U.S. Group, Control Council). On August 9, 1944, the United States Group, Control Council (Germany) was established as a planning group under ETOUSA to prepare for the military government of Germany; on March 5, 1945 it became a command under ETOUSA. On October 1, 1945, the USGCC was redesignated the Office of Military Government for Germany, United States (OMGUS). (On January 27, 1945, a U.S. Group, Control Council (Austria) is created under the Mediterranean Theater of Operations.)

WDCSA (War Department, Chief of Staff Army).

WJC (World Jewish Congress). Established in 1932 with the purpose of defending Jews against Nazism and anti-Semitism with its affiliate, the American Jewish Congress (AJC).

WRB (War Refugee Board). Created by an executive order from President Franklin Roosevelt in January 1944 for the purpose of rescuing Jews from occupied Europe.

X-2 (Counter Intelligence Branch of the Office of Strategic Services).

YIVO (Yiddish Scientific Institute). A Jewish historical research institution founded in 1925 in Vilnius, Poland. YIVO was considered to have the largest collection on eastern European Jewish history and culture and the Yiddish language and literature. After the German occupation of Vilnius in 1941, the Nazis closed YIVO and murdered most of its students and scholars.

Chronology of Key Events

1/30/33	Germany	Adolf Hitler becomes Chancellor of Germany.
3/33	Germany	Nazis establish a concentration camp at Dachau to intern communists, Social Democrats, and trade unionists.
4/1/33	Germany	Nazis launch boycott of Jewish businesses with demonstrations in streets of Berlin.
4/7/33	Germany	Law for the Restoration of the Professional Civil Service and a series of laws exclude "non-Aryans" from employment as instructors in all public educational institutions; as officials of public works, public banks, and insurance companies; as employees of other public or semi-public agencies; and as police officers and civil employees of the army.
5/6/33	Germany	Licenses of non-Aryan tax consultants, judges, professors, instructors, and lecturers in universities or colleges are revoked. Jews are subsequently barred from professions, trades, and educational institutions.
7/26/33	Germany	German citizenship of Jewish immigrants from eastern Europe is revoked, except World War I veterans on the German side or those who rendered special service.
1/34	Germany	Citizenship laws divide the population into four categories. Jews are placed in category 4 as "aliens."
5/34	Germany	Decree permits only "Aryans" to serve in army.
8/31/35	USA	President Roosevelt signs the first of several Neutrality Acts.
9/15/35	Germany	Nuremberg Laws officially recognize two categories in Germany's population, Aryans and non-Aryans. Jews denied German citizenship and reduced to status of "subjects." Concept of "race defilement" introduced in criminal law.
7/2/37	Germany	Jews are forbidden to teach Aryans, whether in schools or privately.
3/12/38	Austria	Austria is annexed to Germany in the Anschluss. Anti-Jewish laws apply henceforth, though some laws and regulations are specially promulgated.
3/28/38	Germany	Jewish communities are deprived of legal status. Status of "church organizations" is denied to Jewish congregations, compelling them to pay full taxes.
4/26/38	Germany	Jews required to declare property valued over RM 5,000.
5/20/38	Austria	Nuremberg Laws introduced.
8/17/38	Germany	Jews are required to adopt Jewish middle names, Israel for men and Sarah for women.
10/1/38	Germany	Czechoslovakia surrenders control of the Sudetenland to Germany.
10/28/38	Germany	12,000 Polish Jews expelled to Poland.

11/9–10/38	Germany	Kristallnacht (The Night of Broken Glass). Following the assassination of Ernst vom Rath, Nazi supporters throughout the Reich attack Jewish synagogues and businesses.
11/12/38	Germany	Jewish community is required to pay atonement fine (20% levy on Jewish property) for Kristallnacht destruction. Should the total be less than RM 1 billion, the levy would be raised.
11/12/38	Germany	Decree prohibits Jews from owning retail businesses or mail order houses, from owning export businesses or handcraft concerns. Jews are forbidden to display wares at markets or fairs or to act as business managers for Aryans.
11/17/38	Italy	Mussolini's decree, "Measures for the Defense of the Italian Race," is modeled on German laws and bans Jews from public service and universities, and prohibits a significant amount of Jewish economic activity.
11/19/38	Germany	Jews are denied public relief.
12/3/38	Germany	Jews are compelled to sell all agricultural property and real estate within a given period.
12/5/38	Germany	Ghetto is set up in Berlin. Jews are banned from certain sections of the city, particularly amusement and recreation areas.
12/13/38	Germany	Aryanization decree transfers Jewish property to Aryans.
2/16/39	Germany	Jewish patents and industrial copyrights are expropriated by Aryans.
3/15/39	Germany	Czechoslovakia ceases to exist as Germany occupies Bohemia and Moravia and establishes the puppet state of Slovakia.
4/19/39	Slovakia	First of series of laws modeled on anti-Jewish laws of Germany are promulgated.
4/30/39	Germany	Jews are deprived of protection from summary notice by landlords.
8/11/39	Bohemia-Moravia	Jews are ordered to leave provinces and concentrate in Prague; ghettos are established in other towns.
8/39	Slovakia	Nazi Pogroms occur throughout the country.
9/1/39	Germany	Germany invades Poland and WWII begins.
9/2/39	Germany	Jews aged 16–55 are drafted for forced labor.
10/12/39	Austria	Deportation of 8,000 Jews to Lublin, Poland begins.
10/12/39	Bohemia-Moravia	Deportation of about 45,000 Czech Jews to Lublin, Poland begins.
11/15/39	Poland	Decree blocks all Jewish bank accounts and credits, ordering Jews to deposit funds in a single bank by December 31, 1939.
1940–42	Slovakia	Tens of thousands of Jews are arrested and sent to concentration camps.
1940–41	Poland	Tens of thousands of Jews are expelled from smaller towns and sent to larger cities, especially Warsaw.
1/24/40	Poland	Registration of all Jewish property is required.
1/40	Bohemia-Moravia	Jews are forbidden to maintain any business enterprises.
2/8/40	Poland	Ghetto is set up in Lodz; over 150,000 Jews are concentrated there.
4/9/40	Germany	Germany invades Denmark and Norway.

4/10/40	USA	The U.S. begins issuing "freezing" orders to protect assets in the U.S. belonging to nationals of occupied countries in order to prevent their use by Axis powers. Executive Order 8389 establishes Foreign Funds Control (FFC) in the Treasury Department.
5/10/40	Germany	Germany invades the Netherlands, Belgium, Luxembourg, and France.
5/10/40	USA	The FFC extends freezing controls to cover assets of foreign nationals from the Netherlands, Belgium, and Luxembourg.
5/15/40	Poland	Decree forbids Jews to withdraw more than 500 zlotys from post office accounts.
5/40–6/40	Bohemia-Moravia	Prague ghetto laws are strengthened.
6/3/40	USA	Treasury Department issues General Ruling 3, extending freezing control to prohibit acquisition, transfer, disposition, transportation, importation, exportation, or withdrawal of securities registered by a national of blocked countries.
6/6/40	USA	Treasury's General Ruling 5, Control of Imported Securities, prohibits sending, mailing, or importing securities into the U.S.
6/17/40	USA	The FFC freezes accounts of nationals of France and Monaco.
7/10/40	USA	The FFC freezes assets of nationals of Estonia, Latvia, and Lithuania.
7/25/40	Slovakia	Jews aged 18–50 are drafted for forced labor.
8/8/40	USA	General Ruling 6 allows impounded securities to be moved from the Federal Reserve Bank into special blocked accounts in U.S. banks.
8/10/40	Romania	Anti-Jewish laws are enacted.
9/7/40	Luxembourg	Jews are barred from professions. Registration of Jewish property required. Jewish businesses are expropriated by Aryans. Nuremberg Laws introduced.
9/16/40	Slovakia	Registration of all Jewish property required.
9/40	Poland	Jews in Warsaw are forced into ghettos surrounded by ten-foot wall and prohibited from entering German and Polish districts.
10/3/40	Vichy France	Anti-Jewish laws are enacted.
10/3/40	Norway	Jews are barred from all professions and from state employment. Jewish shops are required to bear distinctive signs.
10/17/40	Poland	Official order forces Jews into Warsaw Ghetto, which is sealed on November 15. 450,000–500,000 Jews compelled to live within 100 city blocks.
10/21/40	Netherlands	Registration of all Jewish property is required.
11/17/40	Occupied France	Jewish artists are barred from exhibiting works.
12/24/40	Belgium	40,000 Jews from Antwerp and Flanders are interned in concentration camp at Hesselt.
12/40	Bohemia-Moravia	Jewish bank accounts above 3,000 crowns blocked.
1941–42	Belgium	Jews concentrated in four cities—Brussels, Antwerp, Liege, and Charleroi.

1941–42	Hungary	Hundreds of Jews are sentenced to long prison terms for alleged sabotage. 50,000 Jews are sent to concentration camps.
1941	Poland	Ghettos are set up in Lublin, Cracow, Kielce, Bialystok, Lvov, and smaller towns.
1/1/41	Occupied France	Liquidation of all Jewish businesses valued at over 25,000 Ff.
1/21/41	Romania	Anti-Jewish riots—vandalism, looting, murder.
2/41	Austria	10,000 Jews interned; 1,100 sent to Poland.
2/41	Netherlands	12,000 Amsterdam Jews sent to concentration camps in Austria.
2/41	Slovakia	Liquidation of 3,000 Jewish firms.
2/41–5/41	Netherlands	Waterloo Square in Amsterdam is closed off as a ghetto. Ghetto set up in Rotterdam.
3/3/41	Netherlands	Fine of fl 15 million imposed on City of Amsterdam. Jews required to pay 1/3 of the fine by May 1; rest of population given six months in which to pay.
3/41	Slovakia	Jews are ordered into ghettos.
3/41	USA	The U.S. passes the Lend-Lease bill, allowing the U.S. to lend Great Britain food, weapons, and other goods.
4/6/41	Germany	Germany invades Greece and Yugoslavia.
4/41	Greece	Wholesale arrest of Jews in Salonika.
5/15/41	Romania	Jews drafted for forced labor.
5/20/41	Occupied France	Jews completely eliminated from economic life, barred from all trades and professions.
5/28/41	Norway	Nuremberg Laws introduced.
6/14/41	USA	Executive Order 8785 extends the "freezing" control for foreign national assets to cover all nationals of continental Europe, including aggressor nations, annexed or invaded territories, and neutrals.
6/14/41	USA	Comprehensive census of foreign-owned assets in the U.S. as of this date reveals foreigners own $12.7 billion of U.S. property, of which $8 billion is blocked.
6/22/41	Germany	Germany invades the Soviet Union.
6/41–8/44	USSR	Nazis kill over one million Jews during invasion and occupation of territory of the Soviet Union.
7/41	Belgium	Declaration of Jewish real estate holdings is required. Nazis demand closing of 7,600 Jewish firms. Jews are forbidden to make bank deposits.
7/41	Hungary	125,000 Jews machine-gunned after having been deported to Galicia.
7/41–2/42	Lithuania	30,000 Jews are massacred in Vilna.
8/8/41	Netherlands	Decree centralizes all financial transactions by Jews and requires deposit of their financial assets in a Nazi-designated bank.
8/21/41	Occupied France	6,000 Paris Jews are seized and taken to Drancy.
9/1/41	Germany	Jews throughout Reich are required to wear yellow Star of David.

9/41	Belgium	Curfew imposed on Jews of Brussels. Jews forbidden to travel outside specific areas in Brussels, Antwerp, Liege, and Charleroi.
10/41	Austria	5,000 Jews are sent to Polish ghettos.
11/41	Germany/ Poland	The Nazi regime starts building the first extermination centers in Chelmno and Belzec.
12/7/41	USA	Japanese attack Pearl Harbor; the U.S. and Britain declare war on Japan on December 8, 1941.
12/11/41	Germany	Germany declares war on the U.S.
12/18/41	USA	The First War Powers Act gives the President the power to vest or take over the title to the property, including businesses, of any foreign country or national.
12/41	USA	President Roosevelt issues three proclamations placing restraints on aliens of German, Italian, and Japanese nationality.
1/20/42	Germany	Nazi leaders meet outside Berlin to coordinate "A Final Solution to the Jewish Question."
2/23/42	USA	Treasury's General License 42 declares that any individual residing in the U.S. as of February 23, 1942 (including stateless refugees) is a generally licensed national.
3/1/42	Poland	Extermination begins at Sobibor, two weeks later at Belzec.
3/11/42	USA	Roosevelt establishes the Alien Property Custodian to vest enemy assets in the U.S.
3/42	Netherlands	All Dutch Jews are forced into the Amsterdam ghetto.
4/30/42	Germany	The Nazis instruct camp officials to exploit prisoners as slave labor without regard to health and life in policy of "extermination through work."
5/42	Belgium	Liquidation of Jewish enterprises and real estate.
6/42	Norway	Registration of Jewish businesses is required; businesses are subsequently confiscated.
6/42–8/42	France	35,000 Jewish-owned businesses are expropriated. Value of total property taken from Jews of France Ff 10 billion.
7/14/42	Netherlands	Beginning of deportation of over 100,000 Jews to Auschwitz.
7/22/42– 9/12/42	Poland	Over 300,000 Jews are deported from the Warsaw Ghetto to the extermination camp at Treblinka.
8/42	Belgium	Jews with special skills are sent to Germany for forced labor. 35,000 foreign Jews are sent to Belgium for labor.
9/24/42	France	4,000 Romanian Jews are arrested and sent to Drancy.
9/42	Netherlands	Five-sixths of Jewish-owned property in German hands.
10/1/42	France	145,000 Jews are arrested. Orphaned children seized as hostages.
10/42	Germany	All Reich Jews concentrated in Berlin in preparation for deportation.
10/42	Norway	Quisling orders all Jewish property in Norway confiscated.
12/7/42	USA	The President directs the Alien Property Custodian to seize all patents controlled by the enemy, regardless of nominal ownership, allowing patents to be freely available to U.S. industry.
12/9/42	Vichy France	All Jews aged 18–55 are arrested in Clermont-Ferrand and sent to labor camps.

12/20/42	Vichy France	10,000 Jews are deported.
1942	Greece	Ghettos are established; all Jews aged 18–45 drafted for forced labor; 8,000 Jews from Salonika deported to unknown destination in Macedonian mountains.
1942	Italy	5,600 foreign and Italian Jews are confined in Italian concentration camps.
1942	Latvia	24,000 Jews are machine-gunned in Riga.
1942	Lithuania	60,000 Jews are executed in Vilna province; most Jews are concentrated in ghetto of Slobodka.
1942	Poland	By the end of year Jews are concentrated in 55 towns and cities, of which 13 have ghettos; 500,000 Jews are deported to concentration camps and labor camps; 1,000,000 Jews are massacred.
1/5/43	Great Britain	Inter-Allied Declaration Against Acts of Dispossession Committed in the Territories Under Enemy Occupation or Control (London Declaration), in which the Allies reserve the right to declare invalid transfers of property in occupied countries, even if they appeared to be legal.
2/3/43	Yugoslavia	Most Croatian Jews exterminated; government-in-exile announces that 1,000 remaining Jews were interned.
2/43	Slovakia	Value of confiscated Jewish property is said to amount to 17 million crowns. Total of 19,771 hectares of Jewish-owned land is expropriated by Aryans. All insurance policies held by Jews are confiscated.
4/19/43–5/16/43	Poland	Destruction of the Warsaw Ghetto follows a month-long uprising by its Jewish inhabitants, most of whom are deported.
7/25/43	Italy	Mussolini is arrested and his fascist government falls.
7/43	Germany	Remaining Jews in Cologne and Munich are sent to Terezin. Last 400 Jews in Hamburg are sent to Poland.
9/3/43	Italy	The new Italian government signs an armistice; the surrender is announced on September 8 as the Allies invade the mainland. Germany controls central and northern Italy.
10/2/43	Denmark	Danish population smuggles 7,200 Jews to safety in Sweden. Five hundred Jews are deported to Theresienstadt, of whom 450 survive the war.
10/16/43	Italy	Persecution of Jews in Nazi-occupied northern Italy begins, including deportations to Auschwitz.
10/43	Italy	Rome's Jewish community is forced to pay ransom of 50 kg of gold and 2.5 million lire in currency. Thirty-five percent of Jewish property in northern Italy confiscated.
11/1/43	USSR	Allies sign Moscow Declaration stating their intention to regard Austria as the "first country to fall victim to Hitlerite aggression," and to see "re-established a free and independent Austria." They declared, however, that Austria still had a "responsibility, which she cannot evade, for participation in the war" at the side of Nazi Germany.
11/30/43	Italy	Nazis order Italian Jews sent to concentration camps.
2/22/44	USA	The U.S. declares it will not recognize the transfer of looted gold from the Axis and will not buy gold from any country that has not broken relations with the Axis.
3/44	Vichy France	More than are 1,000 Jews arrested and deported in Dordogne region.

4/10/44	USA	The memorandum "Recommendations on Restitution" suggests that "no attempt should be made to make restitution to the original owners individually."
4/44	Hungary	After Nazi occupation of Hungary in March, entire Jewish population of Carpatho-Ruthenia (60,000–80,000) is deported to extermination camps.
5/26/44	USA	General Eisenhower demands preservation of centers and objects of historical and cultural significance in Europe.
5/44	Poland	Liquidation of Lodz ghetto begins with deportation to extermination camps; completed by August.
5/44	France	Special tax on Jewish property rises to 20 percent.
5/44–7/44	Hungary	Nearly 450,000 Hungarian Jews are deported to Auschwitz.
6/5/44	Italy	Allies capture Rome.
6/6/44	France	D-Day. Allied forces land in Normandy.
7/24/44	Poland	Soviet troops liberate the extermination camp at Majdanek.
8/1/44	Poland	Warsaw uprising against Nazi occupation begins; resistance ends on October 2.
8/4/44	USA	The Executive Committee on Economic Foreign Policy approves a revised "Report on Reparation, Restitution, and Property Rights—Germany."
8/9/44	USA	The U.S. Group Council, Germany (USGCC) is established.
8/25/44	France	Paris is liberated.
10/9/44	USA	FFC Director proposes to defrost foreign funds.
1/26/45	Poland	Soviet troops liberate Auschwitz.
2/45	Germany	25,000 Jews are transferred from Terezin to slave labor camps in Germany.
4/8/45	Germany	U.S. troops discover the Merkers mine in Kaiseroda. The contents are moved (April 15, 1945) to the future U.S. Zone of occupation.
4/12/45	Germany	Allied troops liberate Buchenwald, Bergen-Belsen, and later, Dachau.
4/29/45	Germany	Major H. M. McBee finds suitcases of looted assets near the Buchenwald concentration camp.
5/7/45	Germany	Germany surrenders unconditionally. Allies ban the Nazi Party, confiscate assets, and supplant authority over Germany and Austria.
5/16/45	Germany	Seven truckloads of assets found at Buchenwald are moved to Frankfurt.
5/30/45	USA	State Department, Treasury, and the Office of Alien Property Custodian (APC) recommend to President Truman the complete elimination of German ownership of property in America.
5/31/45	Germany	MG Law 53 requires persons in Germany to deposit foreign currency in the Reichbank.
6/8/45	USA	Executive Order 9567 provides that liquid assets of Germany and Japan can be vested.
6/30/45	USA	The U.S. controls 46,442 patents, patent applications, and inventions from nationals of enemy and enemy-occupied countries.
6/45	Germany	322 UNRRA teams help Allied forces administer displaced persons camps.

9/2/45	Japan	Japan unconditionally surrenders; WWII ends.
11/9/45–12/21/45	USA	Paris Reparation Agreement is negotiated.
12/7/45	USA	General License (GL) 94 unblocks all current transactions and all new dollar assets all blocked countries (except Germany, Liechtenstein, Japan, Tangier, and the four European neutral countries).
12/29/45	USA	Treasury's General License 95 stipulates that once foreign countries certify that blocked property of their nationals contains no enemy ownership, the property is no longer blocked. GL 95 agreements with France, Belgium, Norway, and Finland.
2/13/46	USA	GL 95 agreement with the Netherlands.
3/8/46	USA	Congress amends the Trading With The Enemy Act (TWEA) by Section 32 to permit claims from friendly nationals for the administrative return of property vested by the APC.
4/26/46	USA	GL 95 agreements with Czechoslovakia and Luxembourg.
6/14/46		Five-Power Conference on Reparation of Non-Repatriables leads to agreement signed by the U.S., Great Britain, France, Czechoslovakia, and Yugoslavia to provide reparations from certain assets found in Germany and neutral countries to "non-repatriable victims" for Jewish resettlement and rehabilitation.
6/14/46	USA	GL 95 agreement with Denmark.
6/28/46	USA	The four powers recognize an autonomous Austrian National Government.
7/25/46	USA	OMGUS introduces a draft law proposing the establishment of indemnification agencies.
8/8/46	USA	Congress amends Section 32 (a) of TWEA so that "technical enemies" deprived of life or liberty because of laws discriminating against political, racial, or religious groups can regain their property.
9/27/46	Belgium	The Tripartite Gold Commission (TGC) meets in Brussels to discuss the distribution of monetary gold among claimant nations and to open gold accounts in New York, England, and France.
10/14/46	USA	The APC is terminated. Functions are transferred to Attorney General.
11/20/46	USA	GL 95 agreement with Switzerland and Liechtenstein.
1/16/47	USA	GL 95 agreement with Austria.
5/15/47	USA	The Jewish Cultural Reconstruction, Inc. (JCR) is created as a charitable organization in New York.
8/5/47	USA	Congress passes a law permitting return of all vested Italian property to Italy under procedures of Section 32 of TWEA.
8/12/47	USA	OMGUS approves the return of envelopes filled with personal belongings of Holocaust victims to national governments. On July 2, 1948 it begins to release the envelopes to Belgium, Poland, Italy, the Netherlands, Norway, Yugoslavia, and Czechoslovakia.
9/15/47	USA	Vesting program for Bulgaria, Hungary, Romania, and Italy ends with signing of peace treaties with each former enemy.
9/15/47	Hungary Romania	Peace treaties with Hungary and Romania specifically provide for heirless assets.

11/10/47	USA	General Clay promulgates Military Law 59.
2/2/48	USA	Treasury Secretary Snyder-Senator Vandenberg Letter announces that information on dollar holdings of nationals of Marshall Plan countries will be shared with those countries and that the U.S. might vest remaining blocked assets.
2/27/48	USA	General License 97 removes freezing controls from blocked accounts whose total value on February 1st was not more than $5,000 and were not held for persons in the five enemy countries.
5/15/48	USA	OMGUS deadline for individuals who suspect that their possessions had been looted to report them.
6/23/48	USA	Recognition of the Jewish Restitution Successor Organization.
7/3/48	USA	War Claims Fund is created. It provides that vested German property is not to be returned and proceeds of liquidated German property is to go into Fund.
9/15/48	USA	OMGUS deadline for submitting claims for restitution of cultural items.
9/30/48	USA	Treasury Secretary Snyder announces Treasury will cease to have jurisdiction over blocked foreign funds. Foreign Funds Control in Treasury ends; remaining functions are transferred to OAP in Justice Department.
12/31/48	USA	OMGUS deadline for filing claims for restitution; as well as the deadline for submitting claims for securities to be restituted.
1/19/49	USA	OMGUS deadline for claims to be accepted by U.S. officials.
2/15/49	USA	The JCR agrees to act as trustee of unidentifiable Jewish property.
6/21/49	USA	$25 million is the amount of first deposit into War Claims Fund, beginning series of deposits provided for in War Claims Act of 1948.
7/22/49	USA	The JCR is given the right of access to material from the Baltic States. It ships 214 cases with 29,000 books from the Offenbach Archival Depot (OAD) to the U.S.
9/21/49	USA	The Office of the U.S. High Commission for Germany (HICOG) replaces OMGUS, signaling a final shift of responsibility from military to civilian authorities.
3/10/50	USA	International Claims Settlement Act of 1949 is passed. It provides for lump sum payments to settle wartime claims of Americans for loss and damage to property in Europe.
3/15/50	USA	Additional $15 million is deposited in War Claims Fund.
8/30/50	USA	Justice Department announces intention to vest remaining uncertified blocked assets under the Snyder-Vandenberg program.
10/2/50	USA	Census on Form OAP–700 of remaining blocked assets reveals $140 million is still blocked. Of this, $15.8 million belongs to nationals of the Marshall Plan Countries, $2.2 million to Switzerland; and the rest to nationals of Eastern European countries.
2/51	USA	OAP begins to vest blocked accounts maintained by Swiss banks in the U.S. for persons whose names are unknown.
10/19/51	USA	Joint Resolution of Congress formally ends state of war between U.S. and Germany but authorizes continued vesting of all German property in U.S. that was blocked before January 1, 1947.

1/22/52	USA	Justice Department announces completion of the vesting of Swiss accounts of indirectly held, uncertified assets under the Synder-Vandenberg program. It also announces intention to unblock remaining assets of Marshall Plan countries, Liechtenstein, and Switzerland.
7/52–4/53	USA	Senate Judiciary Committee investigates OAP. Hearings study handling of procedures governing claims for return of vested assets.
4/17/53	USA	Vesting of German property in the United States ends. Net equity of all vested property at dates of vesting totals almost $392 million.
6/1/53	USA	Treasury's General License 102 unblocks accounts not exceeding $100 in value.
6/27/53	USA	Treasury's General License 101 removes remaining controls on blocked property in the U.S. held by governments or nationals of the Marshall Plan countries, Sweden, Switzerland, Liechtenstein, Japan, and West Germany. Only Eastern European countries remain subject to blocking controls.
7/1/54	USA	Congress creates the Foreign Claims Settlement Commission; transfers functions of abolished War Claims Commission to it.
8/54	USA	Total in War Claims Fund Reaches $225,000,000.
8/23/54	USA	Congress amends Section 32 of the Trading with the Enemy Act to allow the President to designate a successor organization to receive heirless assets.
1/13/55	USA	President Eisenhower appoints the JRSO as the successor organization to receive heirless assets (E.O. 10587).
9/2/58	USA	Congress passes P.L.85–884 authorizing the payment of $3,750,000 into the War Claims Fund; bringing the total to $228.8 million.
3/30/60	USA	Settlement of Claims Agreement with Romania provides for lump sum payment to compensate Americans for war damage as specified in 1947 Peace Treaty and for nationalization of property. Blocking of all Romanian property in U.S ends.
7/16/60	USA	Settlement of Claims Agreement with Poland provides for lump sum payment to compensate Americans for nationalization of property. Blocking of all Polish property in U.S ends.
10/22/62	USA	Congress passes a law to allow the President to pay $500,000 out of the War Claims Fund to a successor organization.
2/26/63	USA	President Kennedy designates the Foreign Claims Settlement Commission to pay the JRSO $500,000 authorized by Congress.
6/23/63	USA	The JRSO receives the $500,000 lump settlement, used in the U.S. for rehabilitation of Nazi persecutees.
6/30/66	USA	Office of Alien Property ceases to exist. Residual vested assets program transferred to the Civil Division, Department of Justice.
6/30/83	USA	Census of all remaining blocked WWII foreign assets in the United States by Treasury's Office of Foreign Assets Control reveals an amount over $71 million, most of it gold bullion belonging to the governments of Latvia and Estonia. Private assets in the names of individuals in Czechoslovakia, East Germany, Lithuania, Latvia, and Estonia total $1.2 billion with $885,598 being in state abandoned property accounts.

5/13/92	USA	Settlement of Claims Agreement with Germany provides for lump sum payment to compensate Americans for war damage and for nationalization of property.
6/29/95	USA	Treasury ends all residual Foreign Funds Control regulations of World War II.
9/19/95	USA	Agreement between United States and Germany to settle claims of U.S. citizens interned in concentration camps, or who suffered loss of liberty or damage to health due to Nazi persecution.
9/9/98	Belgium	The TGC is closed.
11/30/98–12/3/98	USA	44 governments and 13 non-governmental organizations attend the Washington Conference on Holocaust-Era Assets.

Sources:

Independent Committee of Eminent Persons, *Report on Dormant Accounts of Victims of Nazi Persecution in Swiss Banks*. Bern: Stampfly, 1999.

Staff Report of the President's Commission

U.S. National Archives, OSS files

U.S. Holocaust Memorial Museum website at http://ushmm.org

Bibliography

Archives and Libraries Consulted

Archives of American Art, Washington, DC

Archives of the Dutch Ministry of Foreign Affairs, The Hague, Netherlands

Archives of the New York Federal Reserve Bank, New York, NY

American Jewish Historical Archives, New York, NY

American Jewish Committee, New York, NY

American Joint Distribution Committee Archives, New York, NY (AJDC)

Central Archives for the History of the Jewish People, Jerusalem, Israel (CAHJP)

Columbia University Law Library, New York, NY

Federal Bureau of Investigation, Washington, DC

The Getty Research Institute, Los Angeles, CA

Harvard University Library, Cambridge, MA

Hoover Institution Library and Archives, Stanford University, Palo Alto, CA

Hungarian National Archives, Budapest, Hungary

The Jacob Rader Marcus Center of the American Jewish Archives, Cincinnati, OH (AJA)

Library of Congress, Washington, DC (LC)

National Archives and Records Administration, College Park, MD (NACP)

National Archives and Records Administration, Washington, DC

National Gallery of Art, Washington, DC

Seely Mudd Manuscript Library, Princeton University, Princeton, NJ

U.S. Army Center of Military History, Washington, DC (CMH)

U.S. Customs Service, Historian's Office, Washington, DC

U.S. Department of State, Washington, DC

U.S. Department of Treasury, Washington, DC

United Nations Archives, New York, NY

Washington National Records Center, Suitland, MD

YIVO Institute for Jewish Research, New York, NY (YIVO)

Record Groups Consulted at the National Archives

RG 28   Post Office Department

RG 36   Office of U.S. Customs

RG 38   Office of the Chief of Naval Operations

RG 39   Bureau of Accounts (Treasury)

RG 43   International Conferences, Commissions, and Expositions

RG 46   U.S. Senate

RG 49   Bureau of Land Management

RG 56   Department of Treasury

RG 59   Department of State & Foreign Affairs

RG 60   Department of Justice

RG 64   National Archives and Records Administration

RG 65   Federal Bureau of Investigation

RG 82   Federal Reserve System

RG 84   Foreign Service Posts of the Department of State

RG 104 U.S. Bureau of the Mint

RG 107 Office of the Secretary of War

RG 131 Office of Alien Property

RG 151 Bureau of Foreign & Domestic Commerce

RG 153 Judge Advocate General

RG 159 Office of the Inspector General (Army)

RG 165 War Department General & Special Staff

RG 200 Gift Record Collection

RG 216 Office of Censorship

RG 218 U.S. Joint Chiefs of Staff

RG 226 Office of Strategic Services

RG 238 War Crimes Records

RG 239 American Commission for the Protection & Salvage
        of Artistic & Historic Monuments in War Areas

RG 260 U.S. Occupation Headquarters, WWII

RG 263 Central Intelligence Agency

RG 265 Foreign Assets Control

RG 299 Foreign Claims Settlement Commission of the United States

RG 319 Army Staff

RG 331 Allied Operational & Occupation Headquarters, WWII

RG 338 United States Army Commands, 1942–

RG 353 Interdepartmental and Intradepartmental Committees (State Department)

RG 389 Provost Marshal General 1917–

RG 407 Adjutant General's Office

RG 466 High Commissioner for Germany

Books

Ableitinger, Alfred, Siegfried Beer, and Eduard Staudinger, eds. *Österreich unter alliierter Besatzung 1945–1955*. Vienna: Böhlau Verlag, 1998.

Abzug, Robert H. *Inside the Vicious Heart: Americans and the Liberation of Nazi Concentration Camps*. New York: Oxford University Press, 1985.

Acheson, Dean. *Present at the Creation*. New York: Norton, 1969.

Adam, Uwe. *Judenpolitik im Dritten Reich*. Düsseldorf: Droste Verlag, 1972.

Alford, Kenneth D. *The Spoils of World War II: the American Miltary's Role in Stealing Europe's Treasures*. New York: Birch Lane Press, 1994.

Ambrose, Stephen E. *Rise to Globalism. American Foreign Policy Since 1938*. 8th rev. ed. New York: Penguin, 1997.

Arendt, Hannah. *Eichmann in Jerusalem*. New York: Penguin, 1982.

Baradet, Leon. *Political Ideologies*. 5th ed. Englewood Cliffs: Prentice Hall, 1994.

Barkai, Avraham. *From Boycott to Annihilation: The Economic Struggle of German Jews, 1933–1943*. Translated by William Templer. Hanover: University Press of New England, 1989.

Bauer, Yehuda. *Out of the Ashes*. Oxford: Pergamon Press, 1989.

Benz, Wolfgang. *Die Geschichte der Bundesrepublik Deutschland*. Frankfurt am Main: Fischer Verlag, 1989.

Berenbaum, Michael, ed. *A Mosaic of Victims: Non-Jews Persecuted and Murdered by the Nazis*. New York: New York University Press, 1990.

Berenbaum, Michael, ed. *Witness to the Holocaust*. New York: Harper Collins, 1997.

Bird, Kai. *The Chairman. John McCloy: The Making of the American Establishment*. New York: Simon & Schuster, 1992.

Biss, André. *A Million Jews to Save*. New York: A. S. Barnes & Co., 1975.

Black, Edwin. *The Transfer Agreement: The Untold Story of the Secret Agreement Between the Third Reich and Jewish Palestine*. New York: Macmillan Publishing Co., 1984.

Boehling, Rebecca. *A Question of Priorities: Democratic Reform and Economic Recovery in Postwar Germany*. Providence: Berghahn Books, 1996.

Bower, Tom. *Nazi Gold*. New York: Harper Collins, 1997.

Braun, Hans-Joachim. *The German Economy in the Twentieth Century*. New York: Routledge, 1990.

Breitman, Richard. *The Architect of Genocide: Himmler and the Final Solution*. Hanover: University Press of New England, 1991.

Breitman, Richard. *Official Secrets: What the Nazis Planned, What the British and Americans Knew*. New York: Hill & Wang, 1998.

Browning, Christopher. *Nazi Policy, Jewish Workers, German Killers*. Cambridge: Cambridge University Press, 2000.

Browning, Christopher. *Ordinary Men: Reserve Police Battalion 101 and the Final Solution in Poland*. New York: Harper Collins, 1992.

Bullock, Alan. *Hitler: A Study in Tyranny*. New York: Harper, 1964.

Burleigh, Michael, and Wolfgang Wippermann. *The Racial State: Germany, 1933–1945*. New York: Cambridge University Press, 1991.

Calvocoressi, Peter, and Guy Wint. *Total War: Causes and Courses of the Second World War*. New York: Penguin, 1979.

Clay, Lucius D. *Decision in Germany*. Garden City: Doubleday & Co., 1950.

Coles, Harry L., and Albert K. Weinberg. *Civil Affairs: Soldiers Become Governors*. Washington: Office of the Chief of Military History, Department of the Army, 1964.

Dawidowicz, Lucy S. *The War against the Jews, 1933–1945*. New York: Holt, Rinehart & Winston, 1975.

Dinnerstein, Leonard. *America and the Survivors of the Holocaust*. New York: Columbia University Press, 1982.

Dinnerstein, Leonard. "The U.S. Army and the Jews: Policies Toward The Displaced Persons After World War II." In *The End of the Holocaust*, edited by Michael R. Marrus. Vol. 9 of *The Nazi Holocaust: Historical Articles on the Destruction of European Jews*. London: Meckler, 1989.

Domke, Martin. *The Control of Alien Property*. New York: Central Book Co., 1947.

Domke, Martin. *Trading with the Enemy in World War II*. New York: Central Book Co., 1943.

Dressen, Wolfgang. *Betrifft: "Aktion 3"—Deutsche verwerten jüdische Nachbarn*. Berlin: Aufbau-Verlag, 1998.

Duignan, Peter, and L. H. Gann. *The Rebirth of the West: The Americanization of the Democratic World, 1945–1958*. Cambridge: Blackledge, 1992.

Eichengreen, Barry. *Elusive Stability*. New York: Cambridge University Press, 1990.

Eichengreen, Barry. *Golden Fetters: The Gold Standard and the Great Depression, 1919–1939*. New York: Oxford University Press, 1992.

Eichholtz, Dietrich. *Geschichte der deutschen Kriegswirtschaft*. Berlin: Akademie Verlag, 1996.

Eisenhower, Dwight D. *Crusade in Europe*. Garden City: Doubleday, 1948.

Encylopaedia Judaica. Jerusalem: Keter Publishing House, 1972.

Feliciano, Hector. *The Lost Museum*. New York: Basic Books, 1997.

Fischer, Klaus P. *Nazi Germany*. New York: Continuum, 1995.

Foster, H. Schuyler. *Activism Replaces Isolationism: U.S. Public Attitudes 1940–1975*. Washington: Foxhall Press, 1983.

Frederiksen, Oliver J. *The American Military Occupation of Germany 1945–1953*. Darmstadt: Historical Division, HQ, U.S. Army, Europe, 1953.

Friedländer, Saul. *Nazi Germany and the Jews*. New York: Harper Collins, 1997.

Friedman, Milton, and Anna Schwartz. *A Monetary History of the United States 1867–1960*. Princeton: Princeton University Press, 1963.

Friedrich, Carl J., et al. *American Experiences in Military Government in World War II*. New York: Rinehart & Co., 1948.

Frohn, Axel, ed. *Holocaust and "Shilumim:" The Policy of "Wiedergutmachung" in the Early 1950s*. Occasional Paper no. 2. Washington: German Historical Institute, 1991.

Gilbert, Martin. *Atlas of the Holocaust*. New York: William Morrow & Co., 1993.

Gimbel, John. *The American Occupation of Germany: Politics and Military, 1945–1949*. Stanford: Stanford University Press, 1968.

Goschler, Constantin. *Wiedergutmachung: Westdeutschland und die Verfolgten der Nationalsozialismus 1945–1954*. Munich: Oldenbourg, 1992.

Grosser, Alfred. *Germany in Our Time: A Political History of the Postwar Years*. New York: Praeger Publishers, 1971.

Guinsburg, Thomas. *The Pursuit of Isolationism in the United States Senate from Versailles to Pearl Harbor*. New York: Garland Publishing, 1982.

Harclerode, Peter and Brendan Pittaway. *The Lost Masters: The Looting of Europe's Treasurehouses*. London: Gollancz, 1999.

Henke, Klaus-Dietmar. *Die amerikanische Besetzung Deutschlands*. Munich: Oldenbourg, 1996.

Hilberg, Raul. *The Destruction of the European Jews*. New York: Holmes & Meier, 1985.

Hilberg, Raul. *Perpetrators, Victims, Bystanders: The Jewish Catastrophe 1933–1945*. New York: Harper Collins, 1992.

Hilliard, Robert. *Surviving the Americans: The Continued Struggle of the Jews After Liberation*. New York: Seven Stories Press, 1997.

Holbo, Paul. *Isolation and Interventionism, 1932–1941*. Chicago: Rand McNally & Co., 1967.

Holborn, Hajo. *American Military Government: Its Organization and Policies*. Washington: Infantry Journal Press, 1947.

Hosking, Geoffrey. *The First Socialist Society*. Cambridge: Harvard University Press, 1990.

Jewish Restitution Successor Organization. *After Five Years: A Report of the Jewish Restitution Successor Organization on the Restitution of Identifiable Property in the U.S. Zone of Germany*. Nuremberg: JRSO, 1953.

Johnson, Griffeth. *The Treasury and Monetary Policy 1933–1938*. Cambridge: Harvard University Press, 1939.

Jonas, Manfred. *Isolationism in America 1935–1941*. Ithaca: Cornell University Press, 1966.

Junz, Helen. "How the Economics of the Holocaust Add," Appendix S. *Report of the Independent Committee of Eminent Persons*. Volcker Commission, 1999.

Kagan, Saul, and Ernest H. Weismann. *Report on the Operations of the Jewish Restitution Successor Organization, 1947–1972*. New York: JRSO, [1972?].

Keegan, John. *The Second World War*. London: Hutchinson, 1989.

Kimball, Warren F. *The Most Unsordid Act: Lend-Lease 1939–1941*. Baltimore: Johns Hopkins University Press, 1969.

Klewitz, Bernd. *Die Arbeitssklaven der Dynamit Nobel*. Schalksmühle: Verlag Engelbrecht, 1986.

Klopstock, Fred. *The International Status of the Dollar*. Essays in International Finance, no. 28. Princeton: Department of Economics and Sociology, Princeton University, 1957.

Königseder, Angelika, and Juliane Wetzel. *Lebensmut im Wartesaal. Die jüdischen DPs (Displaced Persons) im Nachkriegsdeutschland*. Frankfurt am Main: Fischer, 1994.

Kopper, Christopher. *Zwischen Marktwirtschaft und Dirigismus. Bankenpolitik im "Dritten Reich" 1933–1939*. Bonn: Bouvier Verlag, 1995.

Kurtz, Michael J. *Nazi Contraband: American Policy on the Return of European Cultural Treasures, 1945–1955*. New York: Garland, 1985.

Laqueur, Walter. *Europe Since Hitler: The Rebirth of Europe*. New York: Penguin, 1982.

Latour, Conrad, and Thilo Vogelsang. *Okkupation und Wiederaufbau. Die Tätigkeit der Militärregierung in der amerikanischen Besatzungszone Deutschlands 1944–1947*. Stuttgart: Deutsche Verlags-Anstalt, 1973.

LeBor, Adam. *Hitler's Secret Bankers*. Secaucus: Birch Lane Press, 1997.

Lewy, Guenter. *The Nazi Persecution of the Gypsies*. New York: Oxford University Press, 2000.

Lipstadt, Deborah E. *Beyond Belief: The American Press and the Coming of the Holocaust, 1933–1945*. New York: The Free Press, 1986.

Loth, Wilfried and Bernd A. Rusinek, eds. *Verwandlungspolitik: NS-Eliten in der westdeutschland Nachkriegsgesellschaft*. New York: Campus, 1998.

MacDonald, Charles B. *The Last Offensive*. Washington: Office of the Chief of Military History, Department of the Army, 1973.

Moeller, Robert, ed. *West Germany under Construction*. Ann Arbor: University of Michigan, 1997.

Nicholas, Lynn. *The Rape of Europa: The Fate of Europe's Treasures in the Third Reich and the Second World War*. New York: Alfred A. Knopf, 1994.

Paucker, Arnold, et al. *Die Juden im nationalsozialistischen Deutschland*. Tübingen: J. C. B. Mohr, 1986.

Peterson, Edward N. *The American Occupation of Germany: Retreat to Victory*. Detroit: Wayne State University Press, 1977.

Petropoulos, Jonathan. *Art and Politics in the Third Reich*. Chapel Hill: University of North Carolina Press, 1996.

Pingel, Falk. *Häftlinge unter SS-Herrschaft*. Hamburg: Hoffman und Campe, 1978.

Pinson, Koppel S. *Modern Germany. Its History and Civilization*. 2nd ed. New York: MacMillan Publishing, 1989.

Pötzsch, Horst. *Deutsche Geschichte nach 1945 im Spiegel der Karikatur*. Munich: Olzog, 1997.

Powaski, Ronald. *Toward an Entangling Alliance. American Isolationism, Internationalism and Europe, 1901–1950*. New York: Greenwood Press, 1991.

Proudfoot, Malcolm J. *European Refugees: 1939–52*. Evanston: Northwestern University Press, 1956.

Quigley, Carroll. *The World Since 1939: A History*. New York: Macmillan Co., 1968.

Read, Anthony, and David Fisher. *Kristallnacht: The Nazi Night of Terror*. New York: Random House, 1989.

Reichsbürgergesetz vom 15. September 1935; Gesetz zum Schutze des deutschen Blutes und der deutschen Ehre vom 15. September 1935; Gesetz zum Schutze der Erbgesundheit des deutschen Volkes vom 18. Oktober 1935. Munich: C. H. Beck'sche Verlagsbuchhandlung, 1936.

Reimann, Guenther. *Patents for Hitler*. London: Victor Gollancz, 1945.

Rethmeier, Andreas. *"Nürnberger Rassegesetze" und Entrechtung der Juden im Zivilrecht*. Frankfurt am Main: Peter Lang Verlag, 1995.

Ristelhueber, Rene. *The International Refugee Organization*. International Conciliation, no. 470. New York: Carnegie Endowment for International Peace, 1951.

Robinson, Nehemiah. *Indemnification and Reparations, Jewish Aspects*. New York: Institute of Jewish Affairs of the American Jewish Congress and World Jewish Congress, 1944.

Ryder, A. J. *Twentieth-Century Germany: From Bismarck to Brandt*. New York: Columbia University Press, 1973.

Sagi, Nana. *German Reparations: A History of the Negotiations*. New York: St. Martin's Press, 1986.

Schleunes, Karl. *The Twisted Road to Auschwitz: Nazi Policy Toward German Jews 1933–1939*. Urbana: University of Illinois Press, 1990.

Schwartz, Gudrun. *Die nationalsozialistischen Lager*. Frankfurt am Main: Campus, 1990.

Schwartz, Thomas Alan. *America's Germany: John J. McCloy and the Federal Republic of Germany*. Cambridge: Harvard University Press, 1991.

Schwarz, Walter. *Rückerstattung nach den Gesetzen der Allierten Mächte*. Munich: Verlag C. H. Beck, 1974.

Simpson, Elizabeth, ed. *The Spoils of War—World War II and its Aftermath: The Loss, Reappearance, and Recovery of Cultural Property*. New York: Harry N. Abrams, 1997.

Steinlauf, Michael C. *Bondage to the Dead: Poland and the Memory of the Holocaust*. Syracuse: Syracuse University Press, 1997.

Vincent, Isabel. *Hitler's Silent Partners*. New York: Morrow, 1997.

Wagenführ, Rolf. *Die deutsche Industrie im Kriege 1939–1945*. Berlin: Duncker & Humblot, 1954.

Weinberg, Gerhard L. *A World At Arms: A Global History of World War II*. New York: Cambridge University Press, 1994.

Weiss, Stuart. *The President's Man: Leo Crowley and Franklin Roosevelt in Peace and War*. Carbondale: Southern Illinois University Press, 1996.

Weisz, Christoph. *OMGUS-Handbuch. Die amerikanische Militärregierung in Deutschland, 1945–1949.* Munich: Oldenbourg, 1994.

Wilkins, Mira. *The Maturing of Multinational Enterprise: American Business Abroad from 1914 to 1970.* Cambridge: Harvard University Press, 1974.

Wistrich, Robert. *Austrians and Jews in the 20th Century.* New York: St. Martin's Press, 1992.

Wolfe, Robert, ed. *Americans as Proconsuls: United States Military Government in Germany and Japan, 1944–1952.* Carbondale: Southern Illinois University Press, 1984.

Woodbridge, George. *UNRRA: The History of the United Nations Relief and Rehabilitation Agency.* New York: Columbia University Press, 1950.

Wyman, David S. *The Abandonment of the Jews: America and the Holocaust, 1941–1945.* New York: Pantheon Books, 1984.

Wyman, David S. *Paper Walls: America and the Refugee Crisis, 1938–1941.* New York: Pantheon Books, 1985.

Wyman, Mark. *DPs: Europe's Displaced Persons, 1945–1951.* Ithaca: Cornell University Press, 1989.

Ziemke, Earl F. *The U.S. Army in the Occupation of Germany, 1944–1946.* Washington: Center of Military History, 1975.

Zink, Harold. *American Military Government in Germany.* New York: Macmillan, 1947.

Articles and Manuscripts

"Alien Enemies and Japanese-Americans: A Problem of Wartime Controls." *Yale Law Journal* 51 (1942): 1317–38.

Alk, Isadore, and Irving Moskovitz. "Removal of United States Controls Over Foreign-Owned Property." *Federal Bar Journal* 10 (1948): 3–31.

Banta, Doris. "Alien Enemies: Right to Acquire, Hold, and Transmit Real Property: Recent Change in New York Real Property Law abolishing All Disabilities." *Cornell Law Quarterly* 30 (1944): 238–42.

Bloch, Arthur, and Werner Rosenberg. "Current Problems of Freezing Control." *Fordham Law Review* 11 (1942): 71–87.

Borchard, Edwin. "Nationalization of Enemy Patents." *American Journal of International Law* 37 (1943): 92–97.

Bradsher, Greg. "Nazi Gold: The Merkers Mine Treasure." *Prologue: Quarterly of the National Archives and Records Administration* 31 (Spring 1999) 7–21.

Brandon, Michael. "Legal Control over Resident Enemy Aliens in Time of War in the United States and in the United Kingdom." *American Journal of International Law* 44 (1950): 382–87.

Breitman, Richard, and Shlomo Aronson. "The End of the 'Final Solution'?: Nazi Attempts to Ransom Jews in 1944." *Central European History* 25 (1992): 177–203.

Butler, William. "Proving Foreign Documents in New York." *Fordham Law Review* 18 (1949): 49–71.

Carey, Jane Perry Clark. "Some Aspects of Statelessness since World War I." *American Political Science Review* 40 (1946): 113–23.

Carlston, Kenneth. "Foreign Funds Control and the Alien Property Custodian." *Cornell Law Quarterly* 31 (1945): 1–30.

Carroll, Mitchell. "Legislation on Treatment of Enemy Property." *American Journal of International Law* 37 (1943): 611–30.

"Civil Rights of Enemy Aliens During World War II," *Temple University Law Quarterly* 17 (1942): 87–93.

Davie, Maurice. "Immigrants from Axis-Conquered Countries." *The Annals* 223 (September 1942): 114–122.

Dickinson, John. "Enemy-Owned Property: Restitution or Confiscation?" *Foreign Affairs* 21 (1943): 126–42.

Dulles, John Foster. "The Vesting Powers of the Alien Property Custodian." *Cornell Law Quarterly* 28 (1943): 245–60.

Eagleton, Clyde. "Friendly Aliens." *American Journal of International Law* 36 (1942): 661–63.

Edelheit, Abraham J. "The Holocaust and the Rise of the State of Israel: A Reassessment Reassed." *Jewish Political Studies Review* 12 (2000): 97–112.

Eisner, Frederick. "Administrative Machinery and Steps for the Lawyer." *Law and Contemporary Problems* 11 (1945): 61–75.

Fallon, Francis. "Enemy Business Enterprises and the Alien Property Custodian, I." *Fordham Law Review* 15 (1946): 222–47.

Fallon, Francis. "Enemy Business Enterprises and the Alien Property Custodian, II." *Fordham Law Review* 16 (1947): 55–85.

Fierst, Herbert A. "A View of the Jewish Problem from the Pentagon and State Department, 1945–1948." Unpublished transcript of taped memoirs, ca. 1972.

Ford, Alan. "Protection of Nonenemy Interests in Enemy Corporations." *California Law Review* 40 (1952): 558–70.

"Former Enemies May Sue in Court of Claims to Recover Value of Property Unlawfully Vested by Alien Property Custodian." *University of Pennsylvania Law Review* 106 (1958): 1056–60.

Freutel, Edward. "Exchange Control, Freezing Orders and the Conflict of Laws." *Harvard Law Review* 56 (1942): 30–71.

Friedmann, Tuviah. "Das Vermögen der ermorderten Juden Europas." Haifa: Institute of Documentation, 1997.

"Friendly Alien's Right to Sue for Return of Property Seized by Alien Property Custodian." *Yale Law Journal* 56 (1947): 1068–76.

Gordon, Charles. "Status of Enemy Nationals in the United States." *Lawyers Guild Review* 2 (1942): 9–20.

Hofmannsthal, E. von. "Austro-Hungarians." *American Journal of International Law* 36 (1942): 292–94.

Holland, Carolsue, and Thomas Rothbart. "The Merkers and Buchenwald Treasure Troves." *After the Battle* 93 (1996) 1–25.

Jessup, Philip. "Enemy Property." *American Journal of International Law* 49 (1955): 57–62.

Karasik, Monroe. "Problems of Compensation and Restitution in Germany and Austria." *Law and Contemporary Problems* 16 (1951): 448–68.

Lewy, Guenter. "The Travail of the Gypsies." *The National Interest* (Fall, 1999): 78–86.

Littauer, Rudolf. "Confiscation of the Property of Technical Enemies." *Yale Law Journal* 52 (1943): 739–70.

Littauer, Rudolf. "The Unfreezing of Foreign Funds." *Columbia Law Review* 45 (1945): 132–74.

Machlup, Fritz. "Patents." *International Encyclopedia of the Social Sciences*. Vol. 11. New York: Macmillan, 1968.

Marcus, Philip. "The Taking and Destruction of Property Under a Defense and War Program." *Cornell Law Quarterly* 27 (1942): 317–46.

Mason, Malcolm. "Relationship of Vested Assets to War Claims." *Law and Contemporary Problems* 16 (1951): 395–406.

Maurer, Ely. "Protection of Non-Enemy Interests in Enemy External Assets." *Law and Contemporary Problems* 16 (1951): 407–34.

McClure, Wallace. "Copyright in War and Peace." *American Journal of International Law* 36 (1942): 383–99.

Myron, Paul. "The Work of the Alien Property Custodian." *Law and Contemporary Problems* 11 (1945): 76–91.

"New Administrative Definitions of 'Enemy' to Supersede the Trading with the Enemy Act." *Yale Law Journal* 51 (1942): 1388–98.

Perry, Donald. "Aliens in the United States." *The Annals* 223 (September 1942): 1–9.

Pinson, Koppel S. "Jewish Life in Liberated Germany: A Study of the Jewish DP's." *Jewish Social Studies* 9 (April 1947): 101–26.

Polk, Judd. "Freezing Dollars Against the Axis." *Foreign Affairs* 20 (1) (Oct 1941).

Pratt, Lawrence. "Present Alienage Disabilities under New York State Law in Real Property." *Brooklyn Law Review* 12 (1942): 1–21.

Reeves, William. "The Control of Foreign Funds by the United States Treasury." *Law and Contemporary Problems* 11 (1945): 17–60.

Reeves, William. "Is Confiscation of Enemy Assets in the National Interest of the United States?" *Virginia Law Review* 40 (1954): 1029–60.

"Remedy Available to Alien Friend whose Property has been 'Vested' by Alien Property Custodian." *Columbia Law Review* 47 (1947): 1052–61.

"Return of Property Seized during World War II: Judicial and Administrative Proceedings under the Trading with the Enemy Act." *Yale Law Journal* 62 (1953): 1210–35.

Ristelhueber, Rene. "The International Refugee Organization." *International Conciliation* 470 (April 1951).

Rubin, Seymour. "Inviolability' of Enemy Private Property." *Law and Contemporary Problems* 11 (1945): 166–82.

Sargeant, Howland, and Henrietta Creamer. "Enemy Patents." *Law and Contemporary Problems* 11 (1945): 92–108.

Sommerich, Otto. "Recent Innovations in Legal and Regulatory Concepts as to the Alien and his Property." *American Journal of International Law* 37 (1943): 58–73.

Staring, Merlin. "The Alien Property Custodian and Conclusive Determinations of Survivorship." *Georgetown Law Journal* 35 (1947): 262–71.

Sterck, Frank, and Carl Schuck. "The Right of Resident Alien Enemies to Sue." *Georgetown Law Journal* 30 (1942): 421–37.

Waite, Robert G. "The Handling of Looted Books in the American Zone of Occupation, 1944–1951." U.S. Department of Justice, OSI, Washington, DC, 1998, unpublished.

Warren, George. "The Refugee and the War." *The Annals* 223 (September 1942): 92–99.

Werner, A. M. "The Alien Property Custodian." *Wisconsin State Bar Association Bulletin* 16 (1943): 12–18.

Wilson, Robert. "Treatment of Civilian Alien Enemies." *American Journal of International Law* 37 (1943): 30–45.

Woodward, Kenneth. "Meaning of 'Enemy' Under the Trading with the Enemy Act." *Texas Law Review* 20 (1942): 746–54.

Yudkin, Leon, and Richard Caro. "New Concepts of 'Enemy' in the Trading with the Enemy Act." *St. John's Law Review* 18 (1943): 56–61.

Government Publications

A Decade of American Foreign Policy: Basic Documents, 1941–1949. Washington, DC: Government Printing Office, 1950.

Bradsher, Greg. *Holocaust–Era Assets: A Finding Aid to Records at the National Archives at College Park, Maryland*. Washington, DC: NARA, 1999.

Memo to America: Final Report of the United States Displaced Persons Commission. Washington, DC: Government Printing Office, 1952.

Nazi Gold: Transcript of The London Conference. London: Her Majesty's Stationery Office, 1997.

Report of The American Commission for the Protection and Salvage of Artistic and Historic Monuments in War Areas. Washington, DC: Government Printing Office, 1946.

U.S. Alien Property Custodian. *Annual Report: Office of Alien Property Custodian*. Washington, DC: Government Printing Office, for fiscal years ending June 30, annually from 1943 through 1945.

U.S. Army, European Command, Historical Division. *The First Year of the Occupation*. Frankfurt-am-Main, Germany: Office of the Chief Historian, European Command, 1953.

U.S. Justice Department. *Annual Report: Office of Alien Property Custodian*. Washington, DC: Government Printing Office, fiscal year ending June 30, 1946.

U.S. Justice Department. *Annual Report: Office of Alien Property*. Washington, DC: Government Printing Office, for fiscal years ending June 30, annually from 1947 through 1971.

U.S. Justice Department. *Annual Report of the Attorney General of the United States*. Washington, DC: Government Printing Office, for fiscal years ending June 30, annually from 1940 through 1979.

U.S. Senate Committee on the Judiciary. *Hearings on Administration the Trading with the Enemy Act*. 83rd Cong., 1st Sess., February 20, 1953.

U.S. Senate Committee on Military Affairs, Subcommittee on War Mobilization. *Hearings on Scientific and Technical Mobilization*. 78th Cong., 1st Sess., 1943.

U.S. Senate. *Return of Vested Property to Persons not Hostile to the United States: Hearings on H.R. 3750*. 79th Cong., 2nd Sess., September 12, 1945, S. Rept. 920.

U.S. State Department. *Germany 1947–1949: The Story in Documents*. Washington, DC: Government Printing Office, 1950.

U.S. State Department. *Preliminary Study on U.S. and Allied Efforts To Recover and Restore Gold and Other Assets Stolen or Hidden by Germany During World War II*. Coordinated by Stuart E. Eizenstat and prepared by William Z. Slany. Washington, DC: Government Printing Office, May 1997.

U.S. State Department. *U.S. and Allied Wartime and Postwar Relations and Negotiations with Argentina, Portugal, Spain, Sweden, and Turkey of Looted Gold and German External Assets and U.S. Concerns About the Fate of the Wartime Ustasha Treasury*. Coordinated by Stuart E. Eizenstat and prepared by William Z. Slany. Washington, DC: Government Printing Office, June 1998.

U.S. State Department and U.S. Holocaust Memorial Museum. *Proceedings of the Washington Conference on Holocaust-Era Assets, November 30–December 3, 1998*. Coordinated by Stuart E. Eizenstat, Miles Lerman, and Abner J. Mikva; edited by J. D. Bindenagel. Washington, DC: Government Printing Office, April 1999.

U.S. State Department and Senate Committee on Foreign Relations. *A Decade of American Foreign Policy: Basic Documents, 1941–1949*. Washington, DC: Government Printing Office, 1950.

U.S. Treasury Department, Foreign Funds Control. *Administration of the Wartime Financial and Property Controls of the United States Government*. Washington, DC: Government Printing Office, 1942.

U.S. Treasury Department, Office of Foreign Assets Control. *Blocked Foreign Assets in the United States: Summary Report of 1983–84 Census of Blocked Property*. Washington, DC: Government Printing Office, May 1985.

U.S. Treasury Department. *Annual Report of the Secretary of the Treasury on the State of the Finances*. Washington, DC: Government Printing Office, for fiscal years ending June 30, annually from 1942 through 1949.

U.S. Treasury Department. *Census of American-Owned Assets in Foreign Countries*. Washington, DC: Government Printing Office, 1947.

U.S. Treasury Department. *Census of Foreign-Owned Assets in the United States*. Washington, DC: Government Printing Office, 1945.

U.S. Treasury Department. *Customs Bulletin: Treasury Decisions Under Customs and Other Laws, July 1938–June 1939*. Washington, DC: Government Printing Office, 1940.

U.S. Treasury Department. *Customs Bulletin: Treasury Decisions Under Customs and Other Laws, July 1943–December 1944*. Washington, DC: Government Printing Office, 1945.

U.S. Treasury Department. *Documents Pertaining to Foreign Funds Control*. Washington, DC: U.S. Treasury Department, annually from October 1, 1940 through September 15, 1946.